Single

for Men

It's Not You.
It's Your Technique!

Enjoy more DATES, CHEMISTRY,
and mutual INVESTMENT.

Alisa Goodwin Snell, M.A.

Published by the Lasting Love Academy, Plain City, Utah.

Third Edition

ISBN numbers: 979-8-9991623-2-8

Printed in the United States of America

10 9 8 7 6 5 4 3 2 1

Cover design and layout by Think Tank Creative

Editors: Angela Eschler, Kat Gille, Brooke Hemsley, Todd Goodwin, and Madison Eckman

Important information

Disclaimer

In this book the author gives general principles derived from her education, experience, training, and life observances. These resources are intended to help the reader evaluate the suitability of personal relationships but are not intended to instruct the reader in regards to any specific relationship. The interaction of personalities in all human relationships is complex; while the principles discussed in these resources should be helpful to all, the decision to enter, maintain, or leave a relationship, with the risks that follow, is the sole responsibility of the reader as a result of considering his/her circumstances.

Alisa Goodwin Snell makes no promises that the advice given will result in an individual's safety, confidence, success, love, or marriage. Rather, the *Lasting Love Academy* program is intended to guide individuals to learn things they need to know and do to increase their odds for greater safety, confidence, and success in dating. Results will vary depending upon the many factors of relationships and an individual's choices. Thus, each individual should follow the advice herein at his/her own risk and in accordance with his/her personal goals and feelings.

Please note

All references made in this book to the stories and experiences of individuals have been changed to protect the individuals' privacy.

Acknowledgments

First and foremost, I would like to thank my husband, Eric. Without his encouragement and support of my work with singles, his patience relative to the demands of writing, and his advice about the male psychology, these books would never have been possible. Years before I wrote my first book, he encouraged my dreams to become an author, and it's fun to see his excitement about my success now. I love that he is proud of me.

I'm equally grateful to my son, Todd, and daughter, Leia, for their patience and support. It's been wonderful being the mother of a young man who is still willing to share details about his dating and relationship life with me. He used to flatter me by saying I was his dating coach when, in reality, I was never able to act like anything but his mom. Fortunately, his love of what I do has evolved into a years-long dedication to working beside me as we release a new version of the Lasting Love Academy books and content into an updated app with community and group coaching features. This has been a huge undertaking, and I couldn't have achieved it without his help. Madison Eckman, has also been instrumental in our work. Through Todd's and Maddi's painstaking edits of this book and audio transcriptions, you now have content in a new and improved form that has been updated for a younger generation. I love them both and am thoroughly enjoying their participation and ongoing investment in the next stage of the Lasting Love Academy. You can learn more from Todd through our ongoing Lasting Love Podcast. And his contributions through group and individual coaching will ensure that the Lasting Love Academy reaches hundreds of thousands of new people.

Leia is now a vibrant, beautiful teenager who faces all the challenges that come with being in junior high. She has taught me things I never could have understood any other way. I have learned so much from her, and I strive to be better and more than I am because of my deep love for her. I look forward to the many challenges and successes we will be able to witness as she continues to mature and create the life she desires. She is a driven, ambitious, and unstoppable force that will accomplish many great things in life.

Relative to the first edition of this book, I want those who contributed to its existence to be remembered for their integral role in supporting and encouraging me. These people include: Alice Faulkner, Kimberly Daich, Kelleigh Cole, Anne Marie Saint Felix, Amy N. Stevens, Kristen Snyder, Dr. Garth K. Daniels, Jerry C. Perez, Aubreona Richardson, Danielle Batson, Patricia Baker, Monica Dixon, Sharon Davis, Dona Hancock, Lisa Pilkington, Janalyn Kennard, Melanie Comerio, Eric Litster, Christopher Krause, Angela Eschler, Josh Hall, and Kat Gille. For the second edition of this book, Brooke Hemsley's final edits were immensely helpful.

I learned a long time ago that as hard as it can be to accept advice, critiques, and suggestions, it's the only way to grow, improve, and excel. Not only am I grateful that each of these individuals was willing to share his or her time and insights, but I am grateful that they also did it in a way that truly added to my personal and professional success. Thus, although saying thank you simply never feels like it is enough, thanks!

When you don't get what you want

Much in life seems to follow a pattern of creation (in which everything seems perfect or ideal), fall (in which challenges, loss, or disappointment occur), and redemption (in which healing or atonement brings meaning and purpose to one's suffering).

Creation: my Garden of Eden

For me (a tall, lanky, four-eyed girl with braces and unruly hair), my story began in a fruit orchard with my cousins up the road, my grandparents down the road, and three siblings with whom I was the fortunate middle child. Much of my childhood was spent with my siblings and cousins, romping and stomping on adventures along the bench of a mountain, picking fruit off trees in my grandparents' orchard, and damming up irrigation canals (much to my grandfather's frustration). Thus, my young childhood was full of fun, carefree pleasures, and family connections. Unfortunately, this all changed during my teen years.

The fall

My parents' marriage was rocky. After five miscarriages, they decided to adopt two special needs babies (at separate times). These boys became the light and joy of our family during a tumultuous period in our lives. They made us laugh and brought us together.

Unfortunately, each family member faced significant turmoil and had to survive in their own way. For me, anxiety drove me to withdraw into myself and seek perfection. Two of my siblings were sexually abused (by those in our neighborhood) and bore this burden and its consequences for years to come. My father suffered several severe mental breakdowns, and my mother (who felt easily overwhelmed and regularly unhappy) sought control by busying herself outside of the home. All this culminated in my parents' divorcing before the end of my senior year. Additionally, their resulting remarriages caused us older kids to drift farther apart, as there was simply little to no room left in their lives for us.

Alisa Goodwin Snell, M.A.

Redemption

A year later, during my family studies class in college, my heart found hope in the idea that if I knew all the right things to do in marriage, I could avoid the same painful outcome. Emboldened by my already existing tendency toward perfectionism, I sought healing and empowerment through education and enlightenment. I also discovered that my teenage awkward inability to get the attention of boys (while my voluptuous younger sister drew them in like honey) was miraculously replaced by ready attention from college men.

Creation and fall

My college years were fun and full of confidence, and by the age of 24, I graduated with my master's and entered my career as a marriage and family therapist. I got married at 25 and had my son, Todd, at 27. I was set for success and a happy ending. I had achieved everything for which I dreamed.

Unfortunately, shortly after I turned 28, despite my well-planned and executed goals, my world fell apart. I went through a devastating divorce and was forced to face the trauma, fears, betrayal, and financial reality of providing for my son, with no physical comforts to show from my three-year marriage.

Facing the reality of the verbal abuse, control, and manipulation which I had been denying for years, moving in with a friend (to sleep on the floor), and filing for divorce did not end my ex's abuse. Since my former spouse saw me as a possession, walking away with nothing was not enough of a concession to end his threats and retaliation. Eventually, a protective order stopped his harassment, and for the first time, I was able to relax, rebuild my sense of self, and dream of a new future.

The one thing I knew for certain was that it was infinitely better to be happily single than miserably married, and I would stay this way until I was certain I was moving into a better and happier situation. I felt blessed to have my son and my hard-fought freedom. Yes, I lost everything else, but that was the price I paid for my new beginning.

Over the next three years, I studied, pondered, and prayed for wisdom to avoid repeating the mistakes of my past. It made no sense to stay with my ex and tell my son that the way his dad treats women is not right, when my very presence in the marriage would say it was good enough for me. Similarly, it seemed equally tragic to divorce his dad and then marry someone as bad or worse. Instead, I needed to learn a better way to date and how to fix my core problem: discerning toxic men before I get attached (and start making excuses for the red flags I see).

During this time, I continued to perform marital therapy with those who suffered from drug, alcohol, and sexual addictions, infidelity, financial dishonesty, and abusive behavior. Some demonstrated real promise and growth while they healed their marriages. Many others did not. The core differences I discerned between these individuals were an underlying pattern of empathy, self-control, and personal responsibility (which I coined as E.S.P.). By contrast, those with narcissistic or borderline personality disorder, repeat infidelities, and chronic abusive behaviors or addictions showed a profound lack of E.S.P.

Single? It's Not You. It's Your Technique!

Thus, my personal goal was to identify these attributes (or a lack thereof) in men as early as the first three dates.

However, one glaring reality remained: I could not hope to date and marry such a responsible and loving individual if I did not resolve my man-hating tendencies and general distrust. It wasn't enough to escape my situation; I had to learn how to attract the right kinds of men.

Additionally, it became apparent that I couldn't help single women who wanted relationships with men and secretly hate men. I couldn't raise my son to be a man and hate men. And I couldn't remain single, leaving my son with only one significant male role model from whom to model his life and attitudes.

Thus, the best option for me and everyone else was to believe in the goodness of men, date differently, and succeed in marrying a man with the skills of empathy, self-control, and personal responsibility. I wasn't exactly sure how to accomplish this task, but I had to believe it was abundantly possible.

To achieve this goal, I created a therapeutic model for dating (and recognizing the attributes of good men) and followed it diligently. Not surprisingly, this resulted in a bland, cautious, and emotionless dating experience. Yes, I acted kind, warm, thoughtful, and friendly, but my actions had the natural effect of establishing myself as a pal, not a gal. I had forgotten the fun and flirtatious skills from my college years and was, instead, interacting with men with all the warmth and lack of femininity that a colleague, neighbor, counselor, or sister brings.

Consequently, even when I was interested, my dates wouldn't have known it. With all my well-intended strategizing, I simply didn't relax, and so my dates couldn't either. I wasn't having bad experiences, but I wasn't having fun and playful ones either.

Redemption

Then, three years after my divorce, I met Eric! From the first phone call, he put me at ease. He made me laugh and enjoy the moment. When we met for our first date, something felt different. It seemed as if the calculated therapist and mother were somehow sedated by the heavy narcotic of chemistry, and my old flirty college self took over. I touched him easily and playfully. I smiled and laughed at his stories, with an utter inability to think of anything to say. He saw this as endearing and handled my obvious speechlessness, while I slowly tore my straw paper to pieces over dinner, by pushing his paper across the table (when I came to the end of my own) and saying, "In case you need this." He was so charmingly fun and sweet that I picked it up, smiled, nodded, and tore some more.

Eric was intoxicating enough to be around that it wasn't until 10:30 at night, while we were driving up a mountain (with blankets and pillows in the back seat of his truck to stargaze) that my brain woke up and I blurted out, "Just so you know, I am a slow mover when it comes to kissing and commitment. I can't afford to make the same mistakes from my past, so it will probably take me months before I will consider being exclusive, and the idea of sexual contact literally makes me feel nauseous." He simply nodded his head and said, "Good to know." And somehow, I didn't doubt that he would not kiss me or push any of my limits. This pacified my analytical brain as my flirty friend pushed herself back in control.

Fortunately, every time I felt overwhelmed or anxious, Eric responded with confidence and respect. He didn't push limits. He validated my feelings, and he asserted his own. I felt confident, capable, and empowered. I didn't fear losing him, nor the possibility that things would end. Either option would be okay. I had been addicted to my ex's validation (after each episode of his abuse), but with Eric, he just added to my life. He didn't make me dependent, but more free and confident. I would be okay either way, which is what made me enjoy him even more. He only made my life better.

I had taken chemistry off my list of expectations in a partner and relationship, but fortunately, I discovered that relationships with empathy, self-control, and personal responsibility can have chemistry, too.

After a reasonable dating period, Eric and I married, bought a home, and began our lives together. I always knew I wanted to share my theory about empathy, self-control, and personal responsibility, but I refused to do so until I had proof that I, in fact, married differently.

Creation, fall, and redirection (while longing for redemption)

Two years into our marriage, Eric asked me when I was going to write that book I wanted to write. I trusted our marriage and felt confident in my theory, but what I really wanted to create was not my book, but my family. In truth, I didn't become a marriage and family therapist with the idea of working full-time. It was always a side hobby and a way to prevent failure, not a life plan. So, after careful consideration, I decided not to write my book and instead focus on getting pregnant and raising my children.

What I didn't know was that I was already premenopausal at the age of 33. After a year of not getting pregnant, I believed it was just not the right time (or God's will yet).

Perhaps writing a book would be a good distraction. I was working with so many singles who struggled to find and create relationships, and the pattern of avoidant attachment issues in both men and women seemed ever more prevalent. I researched other books to find that professional ones focused primarily on relationships or healing from trauma after abuse. The wonderful theories and science behind relationships didn't offer behaviorally specific dating skills. For that, I had to rely on popular, entertaining books written by authors who were often uneducated or unmarried.

The lack of common-sense books that applied sound relationship theories into practical dating skills was startling. And so I wrote my first book, *Want to Marry a Good Man? Here's How.*[1] It was a fun and passionate experience that distracted me from another year of failed pregnancy tests.

---

1   Snell, A.G. (2007) *Want to Marry a Good Man? Here's How!* Springville, UT: Bonneville Books.

     Single? It's Not You. It's Your Technique!

Finding a publisher was reasonably easy, but I had no idea that most authors didn't really make any money. A dollar in royalties per $14.95 book (in spite of my many TV and radio appearances) didn't provide much incentive to write more.

Accomplishing this goal was rewarding, but when every year ended the same, with more failed infertility treatments and lost adoption opportunities, the only thing that kept me from slipping into a deep depression was my work.

As my boy grew older and I neared the age of 40, I'd written six more books. This time, these books would be offered as a high-end box set with video demonstrations of the many behaviorally specific techniques that I had developed. This was a two-year, $40,000 investment.

To recover my costs and respect the willing sacrifices of my family, the Lasting Love Academy Dating System could only be sold as a high-value product. I regretted not making it publicly available, but I didn't see another option. The dating system could at least provide a curriculum for my growing dating and relationship clientele.

While writing these books for singles, working with clients, and enjoying my marriage and family, I continued to struggle to accept the reality of my infertility. After six years of hoping and my final infertility option failing, I responded to my pain and powerlessness by angrily concluding that I would no longer try. I got rid of every reminder of my hopes and dreams for more children, put our adoption application on hold, and angrily concluded that my plan was beautiful, and God's plan for me sucked!

Nothing about my life had evolved the way I dreamed it would!

I never wanted my parents to have mental health issues and marital problems that burdened their young kids with inappropriate pressure to meet their emotional needs. I didn't want or need their second and third marriages to spouses who were difficult or unloving. What I needed was an intact family I could depend on for love, safety, and belonging (not just as a kid but also during the challenges of adulthood).

I did not seek an educational degree and career because I valued it. I sought those because I had mistakenly believed that perfection was a path to lasting love and a happy family.

When marriage and family had finally come, I never thought it would include emotional abuse, control, infidelity, and divorce. I didn't plan on single parenthood and sharing my son part-time with someone who had vastly different values and attitudes (and would cycle through many other marriages, all of which would impact my son).

My neighborhood was full of pregnant women who sent baby shower announcements, pushed strollers past my door, had more children, and sent their kids to school, all while I remained unable to achieve a pregnancy.

I loved and adored Eric and my new life. Todd was thriving. I loved watching him grow. We had a fun and joyful family, but I longed for more children, and it seemed unfair that so many were born to families that abused them when I was open-armed and ready to receive them.

There were abundant blessings all around me, and as an optimist, I never failed to recognize and appreciate them, but after six years of faith and hope that I would have more children, I felt betrayed and angry. Hope was simply too painful. I refused to believe that anything I did would make a difference, and so I submitted to my feelings of victimization, powerlessness, and hopelessness.

Choice, courage, and redemption

After a few months of anger and deep depression, I began to accept my fate. I decided to dream of new possible adventures for my life. Perhaps Eric and I could travel or move to new places (once our son is raised). I considered different goals and accomplishments, as well as ways I might find meaning and purpose. Others struggled with infertility and resolved their grief. They found fulfillment. Certainly, I could find peace, too. So, I put the victimization behind me, squared my shoulders, and accepted that life was not fair, but I still had choices and options that I could pursue.

With each possibility that I explored, I found some measure of excitement about the experience Eric and I could share. However, when it came to what felt most meaningful, nothing seemed as satisfying as my desire to love another child. I loved watching my son and his friends grow. I loved being a part of their lives. I cherished my memories with him and simply didn't want this to be the only experience I could enjoy.

Yes, I had the freedom to choose a new life. The option of pregnancy was a closed door, and adoption appeared to be one as well, but there were other doors through which I could explore, including foster care. As much as I angrily refused to have hope, once my grief had lessened and I explored other possibilities, I simply knew pursuing foster care was the right choice for me. I was scared of the trauma and unpredictable challenges that each child might have, but I bravely chose to believe that we could have the power and skills we needed to succeed with the child that came into our home. I wanted to choose love, and there were so many children in foster care who needed exactly that.

Surprisingly, as we were in the final weeks of the foster care process (and as we began preparing a baby's room), a birth mother chose us to adopt her unborn child. It seemed unreal that I was truly at the end of my long and painful journey.

Like so many others who finally achieve their heart's desire, my prolonged suffering was immediately forgotten while holding my baby girl, Leia. The joy that replaced my sorrow and the events that felt so miraculously suited to both our needs and those of the birth family helped me to find meaning and purpose in my trials.

A better plan than mine

At the end of our trials, it can be easy to forget the pain and discomfort of those who are walking the same (or similar) paths alone.

There is no doubt in my mind that if my parents' marriage had been stable and secure, I would not have been drawn to become a marriage and family therapist. Similarly, if my first marriage had been happy, I wouldn't have become so personally aware of singles' issues and the need to identify early signs of toxic relationships.

Single? It's Not You. It's Your Technique!

However, above all these, I am absolutely confident that if I had not struggled with infertility, my work with singles would have never evolved. The gap created by my prolonged delay of what I wanted most (marriage and family) is the only reason I kept doing something worthwhile, nonetheless.

If I had gotten what I wanted when I wanted it, I wouldn't have had the time, energy, or desire to serve singles so passionately. I would have been too content and busy to invest so much of myself in my career or the needs of singles. As it was, however, by the time I was blessed with my daughter, I was so fully invested in my passion for singles that I simply couldn't walk away.

When Leia was young, my time was limited, but once she entered school, I had time to introduce the new strategies and techniques I developed to address the growing challenges of singles, with updated versions of the books and videos.

The Lasting Love Academy dating system was originally published in 2011[2] (after which my daughter, Leia, was born a few months later). I completed the revised editions of the books in 2018.[3]

Then, in 2024, after my son, Todd, graduated with a degree in psychology and family studies, his passion for singles led us to collaborate on our latest update to the Lasting Love Academy, including app versions of our courses. Fortunately, this time, the 2026 release of *Single? It's Not You. It's Your Technique!* would be publicly available, so that Todd and I could reach a national audience and bring my concepts to a whole new generation.

At 55, I have enjoyed a 32-year career serving singles and couples as they pursue lasting love. I've individually helped thousands of singles get married. My greatest desire for the final decade of my career is for my life's passion for happy marriages and families to reach a worldwide audience.

Your journey of lasting love

Just as my journey has been full of highs and lows, so has yours, but it's not one you have to endure alone. Like me, your story will have a beginning, middle, and end (full of creation, falls, and redemption).

The rest of this book is dedicated to you. Whether you are new to dating (with all the optimism of youth), returning to it after a painful loss (betrayal or divorce), or persevering after decades of trying to find the right companion, you are not alone!

I understand how hard it is to continue choosing hope when your dreams keep being delayed or held just out of reach. However, I also know that with every delay, there is eventual redemption, especially when you remain willing to keep learning, sacrificing, and investing. Your grief and loss may overwhelm you at times, and healing breaks can help, but if you remain committed to the goal of lasting love, in time, those who are seeking the same will recognize and invest in you.

---

2   Snell, A.G. (2011) *Single? Discover the Truth about Successful Dating, Being Irresistible, and Achieving Lasting Love,* Salt Lake City, UT: Lasting Love Academy.

3   Snell, A.G. (2018) Snell, A.G. (2011) *Single? It's Not You. It's Your Technique! to Marry a Good Man? Here's How!* Salt Lake City, UT: Lasting Love Academy.

Lasting love is possible. My clients have created and maintained it, and so can you when you remain willing to do your part.

This book, *Single? It's Not You. It's Your Technique!* focuses extensively on the many challenges singles experience during the first six weeks of dating. More books for identifying the early red flags and other stages of dating or relationships will be released soon (as part of our updated Lasting Love Academy series), but this one is tailored to the most common problem singles face: getting past the first six weeks of dating (and with an emotionally available and empathetic partner).

For many reasons, singles can struggle to attract the people they desire, get first dates, navigate dating challenges, and enjoy ongoing dates. In fact, most dating experiences do not last past the first six weeks. This isn't unique to just you. This world is experiencing an epidemic of loneliness and an inability to make meaningful connections that develop into relationships, but that doesn't mean something is wrong with you!

As you use this book, it will guide you in attracting the people you desire, avoiding common dating traps, managing rejection well, understanding the opposite sex, building stronger connections, feeling more resilient, and creating greater chemistry.

It's extensive because my work with singles has identified hundreds of ways in which singles can better maximize every opportunity, not for the purpose of perfection, but for ongoing growth and connection. No matter your current strengths and weaknesses, you will find empowering strategies in this book to fit your early dating situation and needs.

As you remain willing to dream, hope for, practice, explore, grow, live, and love more fully, you not only feel more personally secure, but you also act more desirable, too. Creating secure attachments isn't simply about understanding your and your partner's anxious or avoidant attachment behaviors. It is found in understanding what secure behaviors look and feel like in your body, thoughts, emotions, and when interacting with others.

Secure attachments are developed when you have a secure foundation and choose secure relationship patterns. This book can't address anxious and avoidant attachment patterns, since they're better explained in the Lasting Love Academy's other books, but all the techniques taught here are based on secure attachment behaviors and attitudes (and how to demonstrate them during the early stages of dating). Thus, you don't need to know what it looks like when things are going wrong, but how to act on and build upon secure behaviors instead.

For now, please know that you are not alone. It's not you. It's your technique. Anyone can get a different result when they know what to do. Achieving lasting love is worth your investment. And now, you have an expert guide to help you navigate the dating world and achieve lasting love.

You CAN do this!

Sincerely,

Alisa Goodwin Snell

Contents

　　　　　　　　Single? It's Not You. It's Your Technique!

             Single? It's Not You. It's Your Technique!

        Single? It's Not You. It's Your Technique!

Develop a secure foundation

Real life. Real people. Real love!

Being someone who comes from a diverse family background that includes a gay brother, an atheist father, family members with various religious affiliations, two adopted siblings, five step-siblings, and an adopted daughter, I know that one size does not fit all—life, individuals, marriages, and families can be wonderfully complex.

I've spent three decades as a marriage and family therapist and dating coach. My clients' lives are no less diverse than mine. They come to me with fears, pain, issues, and challenges, and they need real solutions to match their real lives.

However, most singles only want to date exceptional people who live exceptional lives. They want to be with the best, most attractive, and desirable singles in spite of their current circumstances. This, of course, is a tall order, especially since I am too intimately aware of the realities of life. Even if I could help clients find their ideal match, it wouldn't take long before they discovered how human their partner really is. For this reason, I try to steer singles away from the thinking errors that permeate our modern society with its glamorized entertainment and social media practices.

Instead of looking for perfection in others (and themselves), I encourage singles to focus on connection.

This goal of connection can be a difficult transition for many singles. The fear of missing out on something better (FOMO) usually has strong and deep roots that are hard to remove; however, once singles feel the heavy burden of perfection lifted from their shoulders, the resulting peace they experience can be exhilarating. Accepting themselves and others, with an appreciation for each person's strengths and weaknesses, helps them to love themselves and others more fully.

Likewise, if you are to learn to love and be loved, you need to rid yourself of the barriers that hold you back. These barriers include fears, thinking errors, distractions, and self-centeredness. Confronting and changing your deep-seated patterns and limiting, albeit cherished, beliefs can be painful and almost impossible unless you are holding on to something you value more: love, faith, hope, peace, joy, companionship, acceptance, family, and growth.

A person's ability to find meaning amidst their challenges can dramatically alter their view of their life, problems, and relationships. The inability to do this can leave them feeling victimized, angry, or entitled.

The sacrifices you will make for a loving relationship need to be based on your values; otherwise, they will not have sufficient meaning and purpose to sustain you during the challenges that will inevitably come. Furthermore, the more deeply you sacrifice, the more deeply you love—but only if you do so willingly.

You really do buy love

Whether you know it or not, you're buying the experiences that you're having, both good and bad. You're buying them with your time, money, emotional investment, energy, words, thoughts, fears (or faith), and beliefs. All these things are your universal currency.

So, are you living the life that you want? Do you like the experiences you're buying? Or do you wish that you had more, and if so, what are you willing to pay to get it?

Having worked exclusively with singles for three decades, I know that everyone who comes to me wants something, but there is a difference between those who get it and those who don't, and I call it the window shopper, the browser, and the buyer phenomenon.

The window shopper

The window shopper walks down the streets of life, passively looking in the store windows to see if anything (or anyone) wows them. They haven't made up their mind what they want or what they are willing to pay for it. Unless something really grabs them or compels them to action, they view what's available from a safe distance. They often fear "buyer's remorse" later, so they also act skeptical and critical of what they see. All this ensures that they buy nothing from life, which is exactly what they end up getting from life—nothing. In the end, they discover that their lack of action is currency, too, and whether they knew it or not, they were buying the passionless life they lived.

The browser

The browser is more invested than the window shopper. They have money (or energy) they're willing to spend, but they have only a vague idea of what (or who) they would like to spend it on. So they go into shop after shop looking for a shirt, watch, job, and vacation (or dating partner) that grabs their attention. Sometimes they buy. However, more often than not, they wonder what they might find in the next shop.

The buyer

The buyer knows what they want to buy. They've researched the pros and cons and are ready to put their time and energy into finding and, more importantly, buying it. Thus, when they find what they want at one shop for a price they're willing to pay, they buy it. They don't perpetually shop around or waste time on their anxieties. They take action and enjoy what they have by not looking back.

I know that relationships take investment; sometimes, those investments don't pay off how you might hope. However, from my experience, only those who are willing to be buyers end up with something worth buying. They are the ones who feel passionate about their lives and relationships. They are the ones who get passionate investment and affection from others.

Are you ready to buy love?

When considering the patterns of a window shopper, browser, or buyer, which fits you? Which would your ex say fits you? What would you need to change in order to become a browser or a buyer in your dating and relationships?

Buying love requires the use of **life's universal currency** (rather than just money). This currency is made up of your time, energy, emotions, money, beliefs, conscious thoughts, humility, vulnerability, and willing faith in yourself, others, and relationships. Buying love means accepting that people are not new cars: no one is free of scratches, dents, or flaws. Everyone has issues, fears, and imperfections, and so do you, but their value as a whole is greater than their individual parts. Thus, buying love necessitates a commitment to accepting real life and real people while learning to offer, create, and maintain real love.

You can be right, or you can be effective

Amber was a reasonably attractive 29-year-old college graduate. She was religious and concerned about being a good person. She was actively involved in her church's singles group and attended every meeting. She tried hard to do what she felt was right, prayed often, and frequently served others. However, she rarely dated. She had not had a boyfriend since high school. The dates she did have involved her asking men out or nursing them into asking her out. Most of the time, she didn't go on more than three dates with the same man. Even her attempts at dating apps proved to be a disaster. She believed she was doing everything there was to do, yet it was getting her nowhere, which is why she met with me for dating-coach services.

She said (as so many singles do), "It's not fair. It shouldn't be this way. I do all the right things, but relationships don't work out for me. When is it going to be my turn? Why am I going through this? What's wrong with me?"

To this, I said (as I always do), "You have only two options. You can be right, or you can be effective." Then, I drew a large rectangle across a piece of paper and a dividing line down the middle. On the left-hand side, I wrote "the Be Right Box," and on the right-hand side, I wrote "the Be Effective Box."

I explained, "What I mean is you can remain stuck by insisting that you're right in your view of how life, dating, and relationships should be, how you want them to be, or even how you need them to be. You can focus on what is good and bad about social situations, how men are right and wrong, or what is fair and unfair about dating. You can believe you need to be better, smarter, thinner, prettier, and richer—or, in other words, perfect—before you will be deserving of love or entitled to a relationship. However, all such thoughts, no matter how right you think they are, will only lead you to feel anger, frustration, depression, anxiety, powerlessness, hopelessness, victimization, fear, shame, and other negative emotions."

To this, Amber responded, "That's exactly how I feel."

"And it makes total sense that you do," I said. "Such feelings, thoughts, and beliefs are typical and normal, especially for singles. I will never tell you your feelings are wrong. If anything, the more I understand your past and situation, the more I will agree with your feelings. However, no matter how right you are from your perspective, I cannot help you from within the Be Right Box. I know that life and dating aren't fair, but knowing all this does not change the fact that *it is what it is*. Life plays by its own rules. I can hold your hand and cry with you, which may be needed and appreciated, but in the end, I can only help you if I move you out of the Be Right Box and into the Be Effective Box."

The Be Right Box	The Be Effective Box
Should, ought, must, need, want	*IT IS WHAT IT IS*
Right/wrong, good/bad, fair/unfair	What works?
What's wrong with me?	Who did what and when?
Why?	How did others react?
Perfect/flawed	Experiment and observe
All or nothing, successful/failure	Look for cause and effect/results
Justice, deserving, entitled	
= Leads to increased feelings of anger, frustration, depression, anxiety, powerlessness, hopelessness, victimization, fear, shame, etc.	= Leads to personal responsibility, understanding, awareness, neutral or positive emotions, acceptance

Amber nodded, so I continued, "The Be Effective Box is based on my observations of over three decades spent as a marriage and family therapist and dating coach. This box focuses exclusively on what works. It asks *Who did what? When? How did others react?* and more, all for the purposes of evaluating the world as it is and of learning to be more effective in it. It is built on the attitude of observation and experimentation, and it focuses on cause and effect.

"With the strategies I have learned about how to be effective, I can help you change the way you think and act when you're dating. I can help you attract—and maintain the attraction of—the kind of person you are looking for. I can help you take rejection less personally and act with more confidence. I can help you have more faith in yourself, the opposite sex, your future, and God. I can help you be more successful from flirting to the first date and beyond—and in a way that fits your value system—but only if you commit yourself to being effective instead of being right."

From there, I explained the eight Be-Effective Facts that create the foundation for all the techniques and strategies I teach in my dating-coach practice and workshops. These Be-Effective Facts are also essential to your progress.

Be-Effective Fact #1—Your situation does not define your value

Many singles fear that they are not enough—that they have to establish their value through some external criteria to be loved, to prove their worth in order for others to see it. If you look at your situation, your past, your education, your employment, your financial status, your height, or your weight as being critical to your success, you will likely never feel you are worthy of love, especially if you constantly compare yourself to others that have more of all the above. The truth is, your situation does not define you, your value, or your worth. You are good enough to be loved.

You may feel tempted to minimize the significance of this point. You may feel it has little power to change your situation. You may belittle your value. You may have a dozen different reasons for why you believe these negative self-assessments—and you may be right from a limited point of view—but you won't be effective. You have value, and refusing to recognize it will only put and keep you in the Be Right Box, which mindset, as I explained earlier, fosters depression, anxiety, shame, fear, anger, etc. Do you really want to be there? If not, you need to accept that you have value and move on.

Be-Effective Fact #2—Confidence matters: fake it 'til you make it

Confidence matters. You do not have to feel confident to act confident. Everyone struggles with fears and self-doubts. Everyone feels inadequate from time to time. Everyone, men included, has mood swings. However, you look more attractive when you invest in all aspects of your appearance. You seem more confident when you square your shoulders, make eye contact, and smile. You appear more interesting and worth knowing when you accept compliments. Just *act* confident, and in time, you will *feel* more confident.

Be-Effective Fact #3—You are not failing at dating and relationships; your technique is failing you

If you experience early rejection, it has more to do with your technique than it has to do with you, your personality, your issues, etc. All people see in the first six weeks of dating is behavior (or, in other words, technique). You can learn a new technique and get better results. This book provides the goals, behaviors, and strategies you need for success, but if you are to be truly effective in applying them, you must accept that *It's not you—it's your technique.*

Be-Effective Fact #4—The more you practice, the better you get

Practice is essential for success in mastering any skill, from sports to music, and the dating game is no different. When you go to singles activities, interact with the opposite sex, talk on the phone, or go on dates, these events are opportunities to practice new behaviors (i.e., techniques) and observe the reactions you get. Don't take others' reactions too personally. Most new relationships won't last six weeks, even when your techniques are flawless (the other person may be in a bad place in life, may have just gotten out of a relationship, or may already be developing a relationship with someone else). Even if you are afraid of rejection or others don't react the way you hope, continue practicing anyway. The person with whom you're flirting is not the only one who will notice you. The time is coming when these specific skills will come in handy for attracting—and keeping the interest of—someone you're compatible with who will recognize and appreciate your value.

Be-Effective Fact #5—Faith works

Believing is seeing, not the other way around. Your confidence will be greatly enhanced if you choose to have faith in yourself, your future, and the goodness of the opposite sex and that your growth and happiness are part of the spiritual world's (or God's) plan. If all you see around you are jerks, nags, weirdos, money diggers, and creeps, those are all you will attract because they are the only ones who get your attention. If you talk negatively about your experiences, you will create a negative future because you won't see the value or growth that comes from your challenges. But if you act with faith that the kind of qualities and people you desire are all around you—you need only recognize them and remain committed to that truth—then you will thrive and succeed. The more positive attention you give to those who have the qualities you desire, the more positive attention you will get back from them. The more hope you express in your future, the more attractive, interesting, and worth knowing you will be.

Be-Effective Fact #6—To be successful, you must recognize and invest in what you want

Most people don't plan to fail; they fail to plan. What do you want in a relationship? What qualities do you need in a partner? What are you looking for? If you can't answer these questions, then you will wander aimlessly in the dating process, will experience repeated loss, will not attract the kind of people you really want to be with, or, worse yet, will not appreciate the kind of people you're looking for even if you do meet them. Thus, to be successful, you need to recognize what you want, which means you need to create a Top-Ten List of what you're looking for. It needs to be a prioritized list, with the top five items being non-negotiable. If you're dating someone who doesn't have these top five qualities, you will know that you're settling. The last five qualities are important and will be things that you'll need to know the other person values and is working on, but they are not as essential as the top five. Once you create this list and start looking for those who have these qualities, you'll begin to find them because you'll be watching for those traits rather than just for attractive faces. Doing this increases your focus on, attention to, appreciation for, and faith in the kind of person you're looking for, which also increases the attention you receive from these types of people because that focus and openness change your demeanor.

Be-Effective Fact #7—The more deeply you sacrifice, the more deeply you love

You will never feel passionate about another person or a relationship if you do not sacrifice deeply for that individual or relationship. If you're being passive about dating (or are waiting for others to do their part before you do yours), you won't feel excited about the relationship. Love is deeply connected to sacrifice. It always has been and always will be. What you put into relationships is what you experience in return. If you don't give great love, no matter how much someone loves you, you cannot and will not fully feel their love. You have not opened your heart for it. You are the only one who is holding you back from the love you want.

On the flip side, no one will love you passionately if you do not allow them to sacrifice deeply for you in return. Do not fall into the trap of doing everything in a relationship. You will find great disappointment if you do. The fact is people who act overly responsible attract people who are irresponsible, which is why *you cannot afford to give the best of you to those who don't invest in you, too.* Irresponsible people simply will not value you in the end, no matter how much you sacrifice and invest. They do not have the emotional maturity to appreciate all you're doing or have done. Furthermore, the more you sacrifice, the more likely you are to stay in an unhealthy situation simply because you have invested too much to walk away. Like so many others before you, you'll keep investing in the hope that your investment will trigger the other person's love and your efforts will pay off, but they won't. Without your dating partner's mutual investment in you and the relationship, they can lie, cheat, act selfishly, ignore your needs, and walk away on a whim. Such people simply do not have the empathy, self-control, and personal responsibility (E.S.P.) necessary to think of you first, and they have not invested enough of themselves to care about the outcome of their relationships.

So do your part: be invested in the process, but expect the same in return. Those you date need the benefits of doing their part, too. The techniques described in the chapters that follow will help guide you in how to invest and match others' efforts while not exceeding them.

Be-Effective Fact #8—If they don't respond, someone else will

If you play your role and actively participate in the dating process, you need to have faith that

- If they don't respond, someone else will.

- They are not your only chance for happiness.

- The kind of person you're looking for is looking for someone like you. They will see you for what you have to offer and will respond to you.

Unless you accept and believe in these simple truths, dating will be more difficult than it has to be, and you will act more desperate and insecure. So repeat these statements to yourself every time you meet someone new. You will look more confident and worth pursuing if you do.

These eight Be-Effective Facts are essential to everything I teach in my coaching practice and encompass all the techniques you will learn in this book. If you accept these Be-Effective Facts as true (or at least effective), they will keep you from burning out, taking rejection too personally, or worrying about the outcome of one relationship.

Applying these Be-Effective Facts and setting goals is essential to success

Drew was a thirty-four-year-old insurance agent who struggled to believe he could maintain the attraction of women—at least at that point in his life. He felt he wasn't established enough. He didn't make enough money, and his career as an insurance agent was too uncertain. These facts contributed to his worry that women would think he didn't have much to offer. Thus, for Drew, the first Be-Effective Fact, *Your situation does not define your value,* was liberating.

The second Be-Effective Fact, *Confidence matters: fake it 'til you make it,* was equally helpful, largely because Drew unknowingly demonstrated a lack of confidence. Although good-looking, he sat in my office with his back slouched, his arms close to his body, and his hands in his lap. He leaned forward as we talked with his knees close together and his legs and feet at a 90-degree angle from the knees—in other words, his posture looked square, tight, and awkward and dramatically reduced others' perceptions of his attractiveness.

I explained to Drew, "Confident behavior matters. As a woman, I can't tell a man how to be a man, but I can tell a man what it *looks* like and *feels* like to me when I see strength and confidence in him. Everything women find attractive in men can be broken down into what men do and say, which means it is all behavior. Behavior you can learn and use. Behavior that will make you look confident—whether you feel confident at the time or not—and that can be used to increase a woman's interest in you."

We then set three specific goals to help him apply the first, second, and sixth Be-Effective Facts:

- Goal #1—Several times a day, especially whenever I feel doubt in myself or my future, I will repeat, *My situation does not define my value.*

- Goal #2—Three times a day, I will pause, square my shoulders, lean back in my seat, put my right leg on my left knee, make eye contact with others, express my opinions, and make others feel great.

- Goal #3—I will create a Top-Ten List and begin looking for these qualities in the women around me.

Before he left, Drew committed to paying twenty dollars to a charity of his choice if he didn't complete these goals.

I wasn't sure if Drew would return. He seemed hopeful, but it had also taken him a great deal of courage to ask for help. Often clients feel embarrassed at facing the need for new skills, or their motivation quickly slackens when they have to change their behavior, but Drew did return two weeks later, and his posture was greatly improved. Others seemed to be noticing him more, he reported, and he appeared to have developed more comfort with his new skills.

The first question he asked was, "How can I be sure when a woman is flirting with me?" I smiled. The process was working.

Set goals and be accountable to others

All my clients set three goals during each visit, as you saw from Drew's example. This greatly increases their motivation, commitment, and progress. I recommend that you do the same.

Your goals may be very challenging at times, and without accountability, you may abandon them rather than push yourself to follow through. To avoid this and give yourself some accountability, commit to paying twenty dollars to a charity of your choice at the end of any week in which you don't complete your goals. This will help redeem you from a bad week while increasing your motivation for the next week— and it will also bless the lives of others. This process works, and my clients swear it is critical to their progress and success.

Do you choose fear or faith?

Fear exaggerates the intensity of human experiences until lies, misunderstandings, and insignificant details appear to be factual, unavoidable, and unchanging realities. Thus, something does not need to be true or real to be perceived that way.

"What I fear must be true"

Cali was thirty-three years old. She was successful in her career, felt confident in most areas of her life, was happy overall, and had many friends. However, her first words to me when she appeared for counseling were, "I have never been in a significant relationship. I feel like I am miles away from getting married. I hate being alone, and it makes me miserable to think that I won't have a family. Everyone says I just need to move on with my life and be happy. I am here so that I can accept that I may never get married and let it go." She said this in a matter-of-fact way, as though resigned to her fate.

I looked at her and shook my head. "That is a terrible goal. I don't want to help you with that. This is not a fate that you need to accept or a reality that you have no control over. Your problem is that you don't know how to flirt. You don't put yourself where other singles are. And you are listening to your fears rather than acting with faith."

Cali's fears were many. She had fears of being alone, of losing control, and of making mistakes, and she feared that she was somehow different from others and thus not entitled to what others had. I wrote her fears on the dry-erase board in my office. I then drew a circular arrow and explained that when she acted on her fears, she gave her fears power and by doing so created a self-fulfilling prophecy (i.e., she feared men weren't interested in her, so she didn't interact in a meaningful and playful way with them, which in turn made men not interested in her; thus, she made herself less interesting in her and their eyes—just as she feared).

Cali's Fears

<table>
<tr><td>

- Being alone
- Being different
- "I can't have what others have"
- Losing control
- Not being good enough
- Not being attractive enough
- Making mistakes

</td><td>

Acting on fears creates them over and over again.

</td></tr>
</table>

"What I fear keeps happening, over and over again"

Zac's first wife was drug and alcohol dependent as well as unfaithful. After divorcing her, he quickly fell in love with Debbie, a woman who was dating several other people. When Debbie resisted commitment, he continued being her friend, hoping that with time she would fall in love with him. He felt optimistic and confident because she often relied on him, shared her feelings with him, called him, and even kissed him. He asked very little of her, was happy to please, and was readily available to help her with her kids, car, and more. He was patient due to the depth of his devotion and his positive regard for her many wonderful qualities, but she never fell in love with him. After two years, Debbie became serious with someone else.

Zac felt devastated, lonely, and depressed. He was tired of hearing that he was such a nice guy and that a woman would be lucky to have him when the woman who said such things was single and available but chose to pass him by. He feared her rejection, and so he did everything he could to avoid her rejection without realizing that being excessively available and accommodating her every need only made it easier for her to take him for granted, value him less, and keep him around while she looked for something better. Thus, Zac's actions, motivated by fear that he couldn't expect others to invest in him or that they might reject him, led others to undervalue him and then reject him.

After experiencing Debbie's rejection, Zac feared it was yet another sign that something was wrong with him, that he was unlovable or undesirable, and that he was a failure at relationships. Of course, the truth was that it was not him—it was his technique (or pattern of behaviors in relationships), and he could change that.

Cali's and Zac's fears are common and reflected in nearly every story I hear. These fears make sense, and they are intense, personal, and backed by many stories and experiences. They convince the believer to give up trying and to accept his/her fate, which seems less painful than grasping at hope only to fail once more. It can be terrifying to try again after so much pain. It is much easier to give in and accept

Zac's Fears

- Being alone
- Rejection
- Failure
- Not being loved and appreciated
- Not being good enough
- "Something's wrong with me"
- "I am unlovable or undesirable"

Acting on fears creates them over and over again.

loneliness. But no matter how great their anxiety, singles long to experience lasting relationships. They just need the knowledge, beliefs, tools, and techniques to succeed.

The antidote to fear is faith. My dating-coach program is a faith-based program for one simple reason: faith works. Faith is a principle that has been proven time and time again to lead to more positive attitudes and outcomes when people act on it and wait patiently to see its fruits. This is why faith is the focus of the fifth Be-Effective Fact for success in dating and relationships.

Let me explain what I mean by faith. I am not simply talking about the idea that those who believe in something can create it, even though that often happens. I have personal experiences with a loving God who cares about the individual lives of people and has a vested interest in their happiness. Thus, when I refer to the power of faith, I mean the power of faith in *true* principles. God has stated that "the truth shall make you free" (King James Bible, John 8:32), and I believe it.

No matter how much you understand your fears, this understanding and insight cannot set you free. What matters is that you discover the truth relative to your situation. The truth is the only source through which new light can be shed on an old problem or issue.

If you are to succeed in dating and increase your chances for new and better outcomes in relationships, you need to know the truth, especially as it relates to your fears. If you do not choose to believe in something greater than your fears, you will be left to the mercilessness of your fears. Now is the time to let go of the hold your fears have on you (and you have on them) and grab on to something more—something truly real, powerful, and freeing. You cannot easily make your fears disappear, but you can choose to redirect your attention from them each time they come up. You can choose to focus your attention on the truth.

Provided on the pages that follow is a list of the many fears that plague singles. Grab two sheets of paper and title one My Fears and the other My Truths. Review the list of fears that follows the sample box below, then write your fears on your My Fears sheet. It is important that you write them down, not just think about them; to change the pattern of self-fulfilling prophecies, you must first make your fears as physical and real as possible so you can transform them as described later in this chapter.

My Fears

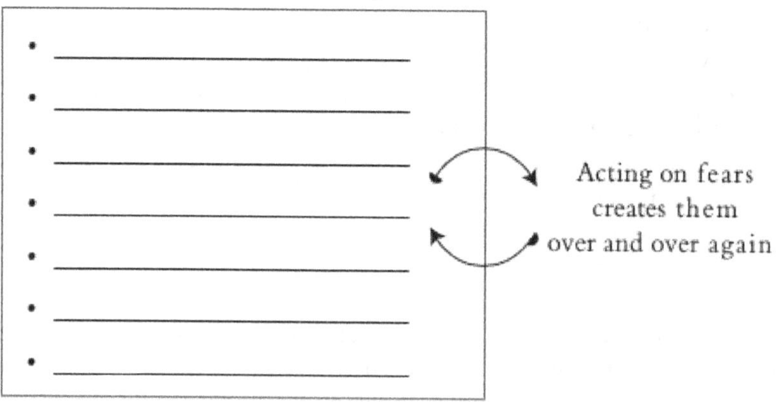

I fear

losing control	looking foolish	showing anger, hurt, sadness
appearing desperate	having a bad relationship	not being good enough
settling	losing someone I love	not having enough status
needing others	failing	not doing what others want
offending others	rocking the boat	not being able to commit
making mistakes	causing problems	not getting approval
admitting weakness	looking weak	not getting what I want
appearing arrogant	wasting my time	making others uncomfortable
rejecting others	disappointing others	missing out on something better
hurting others' feelings	getting my hopes up	repeating mistakes
experiencing rejection from my friends or family	experiencing rejection from my date's friends or family	trying hard but quitting before I succeed

I fear being

abandoned	undesirable	loved
rejected	controlled	happy
criticized	deceived	successful

Single? It's Not You. It's Your Technique!

vulnerable	manipulated	unworthy
alone	abused	ignored or forgotten
embarrassed	neglected	the center of attention
imperfect/flawed	used	too educated/uneducated
not enough	pitied	too opinionated
unlovable	too plain	too high maintenance
powerless	too overweight	exploited

I fear that

Something is wrong with me	I can't change
No matter how hard I try, I'll fail	I don't have much to offer
To feel okay, I need others to like me	I am a failure
I need others' validation to make decisions	I can't do it—I don't have what it takes
I am not okay when I'm alone	I can't ask for what I want
Something bad will happen if I say no	It's never good enough
My feelings and needs are not okay	I am not attractive enough
I will appear foolish if I do something new	I will not be able to have kids
I am not enough	I am not in the same league as others
I am unlovable	Love is not meant to last
I am destined to be alone	I am the only one who feels this way
If I get close to someone, he/she will hurt me	I always mess things up
If they learn the truth, he/she will leave me	I don't have the skills—I'll fail
I can't have what I want	I am different
Others will view my children as baggage	I will fall in love with someone who is too different from me

Now that you have discovered your fears, it is time to discover the truths that will set you free from them. Grab your paper titled My Truths. Review the list of truths provided over the next several pages, and then write down the ones that reduce your fears, give you hope, or feel spiritually empowering relative to your situation. Alter them as needed so they are meaningful to you. It will be easier to discover and embrace the truths you need if you pray or meditate first. Be courageous. Some people may say these ideas are merely positive affirmations or rational beliefs (which is accurate), but when you choose to see them as truths, you will act with greater trust in their power.

My Truths

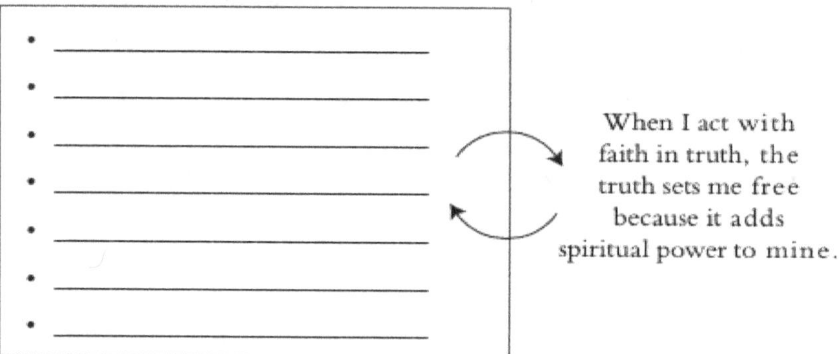

The truth about me and my future The truth about me and my future

- I am not meant to be alone. I can have lasting relationships.

- If I do my part, I will have the opportunity to marry the kind of person I desire.

- The kind of person I am looking for is looking for someone like me. They will see me for what I have to offer and pursue, respond to, and invest in me.

- I am meant to be powerful in my life.

- I have what it takes to get the things I desire when I pursue a path that leads to it.

- I am lovable.

The truth about my relationships with others

- When I am with someone who is emotionally mature, I can be vulnerable, imperfect, and make mistakes while still being accepted, valued, and loved.

- My mistakes, past, or situation do not define my worth. Others will see value and appreciate ______________ about me.

- I show others I trust and need them when I ask for help. Most people like feeling trusted, needed, and helpful. They feel closer to me when I let them into my life.

- Being divorced, unemployed, financially strapped, overweight, etc., does not define my worth. I have value that transcends my situation.

- My weaknesses, vulnerabilities, and imperfections make me more likable and lovable.

- The person I want to be with now may not be the person I end up with—but that's okay. The person I end up with will be the right person for me.

- Some amount of rejection, criticism, and loss is a part of life. I can cope with and learn from such experiences.

    Single? It's Not You. It's Your Technique!

- I am powerless over some things, but not all things. I can share power with others, accept what I can't control, discover wisdom, trust others, and find balance in life.

- I will never have complete control or no control, but I will have enough control.

- If I know what to look for, I can avoid most abuse and manipulation. I will be able to get away from the abuse and manipulation that I can't avoid.

- I can say no, and others will be okay.

- I have the right to set boundaries, say no, and end relationships that aren't meeting my needs.

- When others are angry, sad, hurt, afraid, or in need, I can trust that they will find a way to work out their situation. I can support them without having to fix their problems.

- I have the right to be the final judge of my feelings and needs; they are valid and important.

- My value, feelings, rights, and needs are not dependent upon the validation and approval of others. I know what is right and best for me.

- I do not need to act small or inadequate for others to feel good about themselves. Expressing the truth (about the things I am doing, my accomplishments, and my strengths) is not arrogance. It is the truth about me. I can trust others to see my value while seeing their value as well. I need others, and they need me. That is the way things are supposed to be.

- I am attractive, lovable, and desirable.

- I can stand up for the truth even if it makes others feel uncomfortable. Others will be okay and resolve their emotions or problems.

- I can feel okay even when I don't have the approval of others.

- Sometimes, I will feel and appear foolish, but most people won't notice or care. They are too busy thinking about themselves and their lives or worrying about what others are thinking about them.

- If I get close to someone, at some point, they may move on or leave me. I will be okay. I will love again. I will be loved again.

- Love is meant to last, especially when I choose emotionally mature people to have relationships with. Relationships may change over the years, but they can last and bring continual fulfillment.

- I can be honest with others so they will truly know me. Most of the time, they will not leave me; they will trust and love me more. Being vulnerable and honest helps others to do the same and fosters deep attachment.

- People want to know me.

- When I act as though I am good enough, strong enough, or attractive enough, I feel better, and others see my value as well.

The truth about my trials

- My struggles often become my greatest lessons, teachers, and blessings.

- I can do hard things even when I think I can't. I can endure and progress even during my trials.

- Pain and disappointment are unavoidable. I can grieve while still choosing to have hope for a better future.

- I feel better when I accept imperfection, focus on my strengths, smile, and laugh.

- Even while life is imperfect, I can choose to be happy, see myself as successful, and feel loved.

- I feel self-respect when I exercise self-control.

- I can ask for help; it does not push others away or make me appear weak.

- My feelings of sadness, anger, or hurt don't make me bad or wrong. They make me aware so that I can be wise and cautious.

- I am not a failure. I have experienced success in many areas of my life and will continue to do so.

- I am not perfect, I do have issues, and I do things that are not effective—but I have value. I am lovable. And others will like me in spite of my imperfections.

- Anxiety, depression, fear, and anger are emotions I can accept, especially when I take action and show faith in the truth.

- My problems don't define who I am, but my progress does.

- When I try hard, accept feedback, and persist, I succeed.

- Taking action feels better than overthinking decisions and being inactive.

- Bad things will happen from time to time, but I can deal with them. I will be okay.

- I can find happiness and blessings in all phases of my life, even when I am alone.

- I can benefit from the advice of others, but I am capable of knowing what is best for me.

- All decisions are imperfect and have both positive and negative consequences and unforeseen complications. The more I look for the perfect choice before taking action, the longer I suffer from anxiety and doubt. I can make a decision and trust that I will be able to work out whatever challenges may follow. I won't be alone during the process.

The truth about my spiritual nature

- My inner voice recognizes what is true, right, and wise for me. I sense it by the light, peace, confidence, hope, joy, and love it builds in me. I can discern truth from the religious or spiritual sources I seek.

- I feel better about myself when I act congruent with good values (including those that increase empathy, self-control, and personal responsibility). Living a life based on good values has the power to attract positive things and people to me.

- Life has meaning and purpose. I am not alone. I am meant to love and be loved. I have the power to rise above my challenges because I am more than my experiences.

- I can cope with my situation by focusing on what I can do today. I believe that there will be an end to this trial. I will learn and grow while I wait.

- Believing is seeing. The more faith I have, the more evidence I see. The more I appreciate what I have been given, the more I am blessed.

- I can choose fear or faith, despair or hope, and disbelief or trust. I know where these will take me. Faith, hope, and trust may be harder for a time, but ultimately they will take me to a better place.

- Exercising faith and hope may bring disappointment, but if I'm willing to learn from my mistakes, I will progress. My efforts will turn for my greater good.

- Engaging in my spirituality and personal growth makes me more attractive, lovable, and desirable to others because I feel whole, forgiving, accepting, loving, and worthy of love in return.

- I can forgive, be forgiven, feel peace, and be whole again. Forgiving others is a healing gift I give myself.

- When I take action, I will have the power and skills I need to succeed. There is logic and order in the world, science, relationships, healing, and love. I can learn from and trust the successful patterns I see around me. I will succeed, too.

- Having hope in what is not seen but is true leads to faith, more action, and eventual miracles. Faith unlocks unseen power that is added to my efforts and opens doors on my behalf.

- *"For God hath not given us the spirit of fear; but of power, and of love, and of a sound mind."* 2 Timothy 1:7 KJV of the Bible

After you finish your truths, put your My Fears and My Truths in front of you, as shown by Cali and Zac's examples below.

Cali's Fears

- Being alone
- Being different
- "I can't have what others have"
- Losing control
- Not being good enough
- Not being attractive enough
- Making mistakes

Cali's truths

- I am not meant to be alone.
- Others will see what I have to offer and will love me.
- I can have the happiness I desire if I pursue it.
- I will never have complete control or no control, but I will have enough control.
- I am good enough, lovable, likable, and appreciated by many people in my life.
- I make lots of mistakes, but they do not define my value or my future; they add to my progress and growth.

Zac's Fears

- Being alone
- Rejection
- Failure
- Not being loved and appreciated
- Not being good enough
- "Something's wrong with me"
- "I am unlovable or undesirable"

Zac's truths

- I am not meant to be alone.
- Others will see what I have to offer and will love me.
- I succeed when I am determined, wise, and teachable.
- There are many women out there who will love and appreciate me.
- I am good enough.
- I work hard in relationships. I just need to be with people who give as much to me as I give to them.
- I am attractive, lovable, and desirable.

Cali is now married and has a two-year-old son, and Zac has a girlfriend who invests in him and the relationship.

You can learn to diminish and even eliminate your fears by redirecting your attention to your truths, just as Cali and Zac did. To do this, post your truths in a place where you will see and read them often. Write several of them on sticky notes. Make them into daily reminders on your phone. Or write your favorite truths on the bathroom mirror so you will see them every morning. Most importantly, repeat them every time you feel fear or doubt.

Once you have done this, tear each of your fears from your My Fears into small pieces. Either throw the pieces away or burn them in a fireplace or a metal can outside. Enjoy weakening and transforming your fears. Then state, "I choose to have faith and believe _______________ [insert one of the truths from your truth box]." When your fears attempt to haunt you again, repeat your truths. Choose to act with courage on these truths. Meditate on them. Meditation can be a great way to get these ideas into your subconscious.

As you act with faith in these truths, you will quickly look and feel more confident. Your appearance, your weight, your hair (or lack thereof) will mean much less to others and yourself. And you will find it easier to believe and accept the Eight Be-Effective Facts from Chapter 1.

Make them feel great

Often, what singles focus on in attracting the opposite sex is misguided and utterly ineffective because they don't understand what men and women need.

It's not just about you—it's about them, too!

Tabatha readily admitted that she was shy, but she didn't realize that her shyness was so extreme as to be diagnosed as social anxiety. Most people were unaware of the painful emotional turmoil she felt when in social situations. They couldn't see how much she worried about what others were thinking of her or how afraid she was of saying something stupid. All they saw was a pretty girl who was quiet. Sometimes, they tried to initiate conversations with her, but Tabatha usually answered their questions with one-word responses, which discouraged further dialogue. Some people even felt uncomfortable around her since they couldn't tell why she was quiet; was it because she disapproved of what they were saying, or because she was disinterested and bored by them? They didn't know that she was actually afraid of *their* disapproval. She just appeared to be acting cool, distant, and aloof, which left a lot of room for doubt and misunderstanding.

Tabatha was only comfortable, funny, and open when with close friends and family. Many of her friends tried to set her up on blind dates with men who also struggled with shyness, hoping this would make it easier for both of them to communicate. It didn't. Tabatha and her dates just suffered in silence throughout the evening. She didn't want to be with someone who struggled as she did. She wanted to be with someone who was more social, fun, and outgoing. She felt she needed these types of people to draw her out and to balance her personality.

I told her that, unfortunately, her shy, aloof-appearing behaviors would prevent this kind of man from knowing that she was, in fact, interested in him. At first, she felt it wasn't fair that she would need to change in order to attract the kind of men she was looking for. She had hoped that these types of men would see her for what she had to offer and would pursue her. But what she had to offer wasn't in question—how she conveyed it was. To be effective, she needed to look at the situation from a man's perspective and accept that *dating is what it is.* A man is not going to walk across a room to meet a woman who doesn't meet his eyes, smile at him, or act interested in him. Again, her value was not in question, but her technique was. She needed to accept that her behaviors needed to be friendly to the male psychology and that flirting was critical to her success because dating wasn't just about her—it was about them, too.

Create a healthy foundation for all techniques

Carter's cool and aloof behaviors were based on reasons entirely different from shyness. Carter contacted me by email after I spoke at a conference he attended. The focus of my lecture was on common mistakes singles make and how to change those techniques; thus, I was not surprised that Carter spent most of the email outlining the various techniques he used when approaching women. He described how often he called, how many days he waited after a date before he called again, the things he said in his emails and on dates, and more. I was both amazed and disturbed by these elaborate and calculated strategies.

Carter was truly good at the game of getting attention. He was cool, charming, and assertive, which he felt prevented him from appearing needy or aggressive. However, it was very apparent to me that all these techniques lacked a healthy foundation and instead were meant to maintain control and keep the upper hand in his relationships. He seemed afraid of showing vulnerability, and so he focused on doing the things that would make him intriguing. However, he failed to realize that his approach was not friendly to the female psychology or to maintaining long-term relationships.

The number-one need of a woman is to feel safe and secure, and Carter's behaviors definitely did not help women feel either. He had learned many of these techniques from a male dating coach. Although these techniques typically help men appear mysterious, intriguing, confident, and desirable, they are also prone to causing women doubt and insecurity, which the male coach must not have realized. At first, women find this exciting and thrilling because, unfortunately, most women are attracted to arrogance, forbidden love, the bad boy, and men who are unobtainable (believing that gaining the love, approval, and commitment of such a man is more valuable, thrilling, and rewarding than gaining the love of an ordinary man). However, most emotionally mature women eventually become turned off and disinterested in the drama and emotional highs and lows of playing the game to keep the interest of such an emotionally unavailable man. They are looking for safety and security, and he won't give it to them, especially when he is so focused on maintaining control. This was Carter's primary problem—he couldn't keep the interest of the women he really liked and with whom he wanted to develop long-term relationships.

I explained that if his goal was to be a player, to score, or to have highly intense relationships, he should keep doing what he was doing. However, if he ever ended up in a relationship, he would still have to face his fears of losing control, being vulnerable, or exposing his feelings and needs.

If his tactics, unfortunately, attracted a woman who was emotionally immature (as these types of techniques do), he would have additional reasons for concern. Emotionally immature people, or in other words, those who lack *empathy, self-control,* and *personal responsibility,* need the drama and intensity, the highs and lows, and the back-and-forth chase to feel connected to others, and they quickly become bored without intense interactions.

Thus, if he developed a relationship with someone who was emotionally immature, when he felt vulnerable and needy she would likely become irritated, distant, and critical; when times were good, she would become increasingly anxious, lose interest and passion for him, or stir up problems; when she felt angry about how much control he had in the relationship, she would be prone to infidelity or secretive behaviors.

Carter then admitted that this described *his* past behavior in relationships, which was not surprising given the lack of empathy he demonstrated for others' feelings. As he elaborated on his past, it also became evident that he typically withheld his feelings in relationships and then acted passively and withdrawn rather than taking personal responsibility for communicating his needs. When he felt angry or bored, he would act with less self-control by picking fights, contacting other women, secretly drinking, or cheating. He enjoyed the pursuit when a woman was ready to leave the relationship, but he quickly lost interest and felt annoyed again when the relationship was back on track.

Carter was ill-prepared for stable relationships and needed to change this pattern if he was to find lasting success. His problem was that he kept focusing on the desired results while failing to understand the psychological foundations that should support his techniques.

Technique matters and can open doors, but for people to develop healthy relationships, their techniques need to have a basis in empathy. Thus, consistent with the idea that *it's not you—it's your technique,* I encouraged Carter to do the following:

1. Increase his skills for recognizing, valuing, and respecting others' feelings (i.e., develop empathy)

2. Admit when he is in need and when he is wrong (i.e., express more personal responsibility)

3. Exercise more restraint and control over his impulses and behaviors (i.e., maintain self-control)

4. Recognize emotionally immature people early on so he can avoid them

5. Take steps to appreciate emotionally mature people and invest deeply in them and their needs

Unfortunately, Carter struggled to understand the significance of these steps. Empathy was a difficult concept for him to grasp, largely due to his experiences as a child. He didn't understand how his behaviors prevented women from feeling safe and secure. He wasn't physically abusive, so he felt his behaviors were safe enough. Thus, he doubted my techniques, fearing they would be less effective than the techniques he had learned from the other dating coach.

For instance, when I encouraged him to replace his sarcasm and vague responses to questions with directness and personal opinions, he argued this would cause less intrigue and interest in women. I explained that this was only partly true. Women like a little mystery, but they value strength and confidence more. Furthermore, his sarcasm would increase a woman's doubt and discomfort, which is nerve-racking for a woman. Humor, playfulness, non-personal jokes, and confidence are more effective. These techniques still bring in attention and dates, but their foundation in empathy also results in long-term and happier relationships, which would be best for all involved.

In spite of my efforts each month, however, it seemed Carter never really understood where I was coming from, as I am sure his current girlfriend or wife might say as well. I hope he has found love, but I can't imagine that his relationships will last without empathy, self-control, and personal responsibility.

Empathy is essential to making each other feel great

If you use the techniques described throughout this book, you will be more successful in getting attention and starting relationships, just as Carter was temporarily successful using his techniques. However, to achieve a secure, long-lasting relationship, you need to ensure that you are good for the other person and that he or she is good for you in return. To do this, you both will need to give and receive empathy, too (which is covered in greater detail in the Lasting Love Academy's other books and courses).

Empathy should begin at your first contact and then continue as a lifelong investment throughout the relationship. To ensure this, you need to cultivate your empathy by accepting that another person's feelings, rights, and needs are valid and important, and then you need to act in a way that is friendly to their male or female psychology. Likewise, if you are to enjoy the full benefits of empathy, you need to expect the same treatment in return.

The best way to approach this process and to ensure an attitude in tune with the needs of the opposite gender is to set a singular goal—*to make them feel great*. Making each other feel great may include doing things that you wouldn't expect the other person to do or that you wouldn't value in return, but until you see it from the other person's perspective, you will not understand what these behaviors mean to them.

Empathy versus red-flags

Creating a meaningful connection with the opposite sex must start with empathy. It is too easy for both genders to misunderstand and judge the other, especially when one's friends share the same negative opinions as oneself. The opposite sexes' feelings and needs may be different from yours, but that doesn't make them wrong. As you understand and empathize with the Male and Female Psychology and their unique needs, motivations, or reactions to stress, you will begin to trust that win/win solutions are possible and that the sacrifices involved in creating them are meaningful.

The deepest human desire is to be truly understood. We all want to feel that our perspective is important and that we individually have value. We want to be connected and to belong. We may not always make the right choice, but we want to know that our feelings and needs matter.

Often, the best way to achieve win-win solutions is to take the mutually respectful position that we are both right and neither of us is wrong, especially as it relates to our feelings and perspectives. We can be understood and validated while also seeing the need to change. Instead of hearing "yes but," we all need to hear "yes and" more often.

Empathy is at the heart of respect. It helps us understand another person's experiences and the triggers that can follow. Solutions exist to help us connect more meaningfully, but these only occur in an environment that allows both men and women to be right rather than denigrating the needs or perspectives of the other.

In spite of men's and women's best efforts to understand each other (which typically occurs in conversations with equally oblivious same-sex friends), we often get it wrong. Instead, we need to listen more intently to men as they describe men and vice versa. Unfortunately, when we are emotionally triggered by our differences or misunderstandings, we often reject another's perspective outright or make conclusions that minimize or villanize the opposite sex. Fortunately, when a third party is able to hear and relate to both perspectives, bridges of understanding are often built.

Some singles may argue that not all individuals have the benevolent attributes that are described in the 17 Secrets to the Male and Female Psychology, which is true. It is essential that you never justify the warning signs of a lack of Empathy, Self-control, and Personal responsibility (or E.S.P.) in those you date. Those with drug, alcohol, or sexual addictions, personality disorders, or abusive and unfaithful behaviors can't help but reveal their E.S.P. issues, especially when you know what to look for.

Although your ability to recognize toxic individuals will protect you, it won't liberate you. You also need to become skilled at understanding and attracting emotionally mature men and women who have Empathy, Self-control, and Personal responsibility (and offer it to) if you are to succeed in creating a Secure Attachment and lasting love.

Both men and women are good--flawed but good. Calling someone a good man or woman is like saying their gender is innately bad, and this one individual is the exception. Instead, it is better to say that those who deviate from the normal standards of men and women are Jerks or toxic individuals. Good people are in the majority, not the minority. You just haven't learned how to appreciate, recognize, and attract them as effectively yet.

Succeeding at recognizing and appreciating men and women more fully will require more personal responsibility and empathy on your part. You will need to confront those behaviors and attitudes that are getting in your way if you are to get a different result and outcome. Too many singles have negative and destructive attitudes and faulty beliefs about the opposite gender. Their biases and male or female-hating attitudes can be too easy to accept as normal or socially acceptable. When you take the time to understand each other, you will see how common and wrong these attitudes really are.

The strategies and techniques you will learn in the next few chapters will help you find your match through everyday experiences, social media, and dating apps. However, understanding the deeper concepts about the opposite sex will help you do more than this. They will help you to also be good for the people you find, just as you will want them to be good for you. This can only be created through mutual understanding and respect.

The appeal of seductive women

Women may criticize men for not pursuing obviously good and healthy women and being so easily drawn to toxic, seductive, and manipulative women. However, many women fail to recognize why this is and how they participate in the problem.

A man desires to feel strong emotions. When a woman acts aloof, mysterious, indifferent, or confusing (no matter how beautiful), a man will conclude that she is not interested. The more he experiences such dispassionate exchanges with women, the more vulnerable he will become to the enticing emotions that manipulative, playful, and seductive women offer. These gestures can be very appealing (at least initially) because they make men feel great, wanted, needed, or important. A manipulator's true motivations may prove destructive later, but her initial passion for him is intensely compelling and difficult to ignore. It simply makes him feel great. The other women he meets are kind, fun, or outgoing, but also less affectionate, confident, flattering, vulnerable, or exciting. If these healthy women could stir his emotions (which doesn't refer to sexual desire alone) while leaving him wanting more (rather than being too eager and anxious for commitment), he may find them more compelling, too.

Most men know that decisions based primarily on emotions are often problematic, but they'll choose that over the boredom and confusion of dating good girls who never touch them in playful and affectionate ways. Men are visual, so when women don't invest in their appearance and engage in feminine behaviors, they do not stir the needed feelings to see them as more than friends. A man hopes that an unstable but beautiful and passionate woman will become more so over time. Finding out if this is the case is often worth the risk. As he invests in her or her situation (which deepens his attachment), he feels like a hero because he's needed and appreciated. All of these emotions can be compelling and even addictive.

Of course, less respectable men are willing to exploit women if she'll let them. However, without meaningful sacrifice, it will mean nothing more to them than a good time or fun sexual opportunity, especially once they get bored or a woman becomes needy and demanding. However, like all men, if they sacrifice their time, money, and emotional investment, they will often become attached. It is this investment that makes it hard for a man to walk away, even when a woman becomes nagging, manipulative, unfaithful, or exploitative. It's not her beauty that makes it hard for them to walk away, but the sacrifices they make. Even though the seemingly high highs and the ever-descending lows of relationships with women who are toxic can be incapacitating, men prefer to feel something over nothing and will soldier on rather than walk away, especially if they see any sign that the good times could return. Most men struggle to accept that a relationship is a lost cause. Break-ups can feel like a personal failure, which adds to their pain and can prevent them from easily walking away (unless they never invested deeply in the relationship). In time, however, the pain and the illogical nature of the relationship will help them cut off contact.

After a manipulative relationship ends, men may be willing to reconsider their healthy female friends. Ultimately, most men want to date women with whom they can feel respect and even settle down, as long as this doesn't include a passionless future. They don't like to invest in things that disappear. It makes them feel that their experiences are pointless. Nevertheless, if a man doesn't feel chemistry in a relationship that seems healthy, this also makes him feel terrible. Men don't want to feel regret or question if they are settling. They want a relationship that resonates with both their mind and heart. And they don't want to lead a woman on if they can't see their feelings and sexual chemistry growing.

Thus, when stable, responsible, and healthy women fail to recognize the importance of sharing touch, passion, validation, appreciation, playfulness, and hobbies together, they alienate the men they desire

Just like women say they want a good man, men want a loving woman who makes them feel like a success. Consequently, if men are to pursue high-caliber individuals, they need these women to be more feminine, vulnerable, flirtatious, and encouragingly affectionate in both their words and simple touch.

Unfortunately, if a woman is too easy, available, and all in before a man is, the pressure and guilt he feels may also push him away. Thus, it is important that she feels confident on her own and can step back, so he has to step forward in his efforts. He knows she will take action or end the relationship if he doesn't treat her right. These behaviors and attitudes help him to remember that he does want and need her and is afraid of losing her (versus knowing he has her, so he questions if he wants her). These steps are not about playing games but about understanding the effect that such things have on men and why it is important for them to work and sacrifice for a relationship (which they are usually willing to do if she communicates her needs in a warm and confident way).

The appeal of toxic men

Just as men can be drawn to seductive women, women can find jerks to be irresistible. It is exasperating for men to hear women complain that there are no good men, all while they are listening to, investing in, and offering to date her. They can't understand what is so compelling about jerks that women will repeatedly go back to them despite their cheating, lying, selfish, irresponsible, or abusive behaviors.

What these men don't see is how Jerks make a woman feel wanted, needed, important, desirable, and special while simultaneously making her do all the work. Jerks excel at using their body language, tone, words, and touch to make a woman feel amazing. The love-bombing effect of their affection, attention, and fast devotion dispels the anxiety, confusion, and emptiness that dating a good or normal man can create (since they are less likely to lie or manipulate to get what they want). Women want to feel excited about the men they date, and they feel special when a confident and attractive man pursues them. It bolsters their confidence, and they want to believe his words are sincere.

Many men fail to see the art behind how Jerks pursue women, and so they don't utilize the respectful techniques that can instill more chemistry in the women they desire. Where a Jerk loves the thrill of pursuit and the power or advantage that his ability to exploit a woman's emotions offers, men don't think or care about such games. They are too busy or preoccupied with their everyday interests or responsibilities and find romanticism to be too phony or unrealistic to participate in. They are willing to pursue a woman's attention but are not interested in exploiting or manipulating her emotions with insincere intentions (since this could hurt her and make him feel bad).

What men need to know is that women find strength and confidence to be essential to attraction. By contrast, jerks use arrogance and selfishness as exciting counterfeits. Their masculine bravado and unabashed adoration can seem confident when, in fact, it is merely a smoke screen to cover their deeper insecurities and fears of vulnerability. When jerks relentlessly pursue a woman, it's not about her as much as it is about the conquest and self-importance that gaining her affection offers.

Men don't act this way. They respect women and don't seek unnecessary rejection because they also respect themselves. When a woman shows discomfort, hesitation, or disinterest in time together, they will usually back off rather than impose themselves on her. This is not the case for intelligent and social-skilled Jerks. They enjoy the challenge of overcoming her objections. They seem unshaken by her rejection, not because of confidence but because it is the chase that they enjoy, and she isn't anything special. Once they catch a woman (even if they are initially obsessed), everything will change when another attractive option appears.

A Jerk will often tease women with their playful affection while evading unnecessary commitment so they can continue to play the field. However, if they question a woman's wavering interest in them, it doesn't take more than a few playful hints with confusing inaction to spike her affection and hopeful mind-reading enthusiasm, which reassures him he can have her anytime he chooses. On other occasions, a Jerk will wear a woman down with his enduring flattery or confident persistence. As long as it doesn't feel needy, creepy, or obviously manipulative, this can make a woman curious about what he sees in her that is so desirable while also being curious about what she is missing in him that makes him so confident, driven, and resilient.

Of course, a jerk's body language, proximity, smile, and touch are essential to his success. Since stirring the needed excitement can't be done by text, messaging, or on the phone, at least not initially, his in-person skills must excel at stimulating chemistry.

It is these types of pursuit skills that nice men, just-friends, and good-for-now guys are often missing and would be wise to learn, but not for the purpose of manipulation. When men and women learn to maximize the skills that toxic people exploit, they can level the playing field. These emotionally stirring masculine or feminine gestures, words, and simple forms of affection are not inherently bad. It is the manipulator who is wrong for exploiting them for personal gain. These techniques are simply effective, and when men and women learn to understand and use them appropriately, they can have an incredible impact on the connection, chemistry, and passion that is needed to stimulate a deeper interest and excitement in the other.

Level the playing field

Understanding how toxic men and seductive women manipulate potential partners is rarely attractive to men and women, since they do not enjoy exploiting each other. For them, one-night stands, selfish expectations, and insecure attachments are unsatisfying and empty. Real connections are what they enjoy.

However, recognizing how the compelling emotions that these toxic individuals invoke in others through their use of masculine and feminine gestures can be enlightening. Learning to use these same techniques to stimulate chemistry but with sincere intent feels empowering. If there is anyone who can be entrusted with the ability to influence the emotions and excitement of others, it is the nice guys and sweet girls who normally get overlooked. They are the ones who can handle such power and achieve mutually beneficial outcomes.

When singles learn to improve their effectiveness through greater expressions of confidence and masculine or feminine energy on a date (along with skills for connection, fun, and playfulness), greater excitement and chemistry will follow. This helps others to bring out the best in themselves, too. Everyone wins when the goal is to make others feel great without demands or expectations beyond mutual respect. A warm smile, simple touch, confident look, teasing gesture, and soft response can make a powerful impression on a date. And if the time is right, a short and passionate kiss goodnight can leave the other person curious and wanting more time together.

Thus, it is essential that you seriously consider the mutually positive benefits that unlocking your innate masculine or feminine nature can have on others and how it helps to create the passionate relationship you desire.

Attraction, confidence, and chemistry matter

Getting the attention of the most desirable singles is the greatest frustration that men and women experience in dating and on apps. This is due to a variety of factors, including your and others' relative attractiveness and the techniques, behaviors, or anxious and avoidant attachment patterns of singles. However, you can skew the odds in your favor and get better results. To do this, you need to understand the role of chemistry in attracting the opposite sex (and this does not require the misuse of sexual power).

This knowledge about what motivates and attracts the opposite sex must come before you select your pictures, create your profile, or send the first messages. Without it, you may get a few dates but nothing more. If you are to get the results you desire, you need more than the concepts you learn here for meeting singles through dating apps and social media. Your goal needs to be more than experiencing an endless stream of first dates with no lasting results. If you can't convert the people you desire into relationships, you will become convinced that the problem is you, not your technique.

Thus, you need more than dating techniques. You need foundational concepts that will make the opposite sex feel great at first contact, on the first date, three weeks into a relationship, throughout a relationship, and 30 years into marriage. And you will want a partner who can do the same. Making each other feel great needs to be a lifelong skill and shared experience.

As a Marriage and Family Therapist and Dating and Relationship Strategist with nearly 30 years of experience, I've helped thousands of singles and couples understand the differences between the Male and Female Psychology and what motivates or brings them together. These concepts have had predictable and lasting results, and they can help you, too!

First, you need to know that attraction and confidence matter, and both men and women care about them. They will notice a person's clothing, hair, posture, and attention to good hygiene. These say a lot about their social skills and self-respect. A woman's curves, hair, smile, touch, and efforts to look attractive play an important role in driving chemistry. This is very true for men as they are, by nature, more visually stimulated than women. For women, a man's height, jawline, shoulders, muscles, and raw, masculine features can have a great effect on them, but only if they also have other desirable traits. Women, by nature, are more protective and inclined to dismiss attraction if they don't feel comfortable.

Nevertheless, those with less striking physiques need not despair. They can also grab attention with their confident attitude and desirable personality traits. This must also include the skills for making others feel great because the one thing everyone remembers is how you make them feel. This explains why men and women with average features can marry someone who is out of their league, while others can't keep relationships despite their stereotypical good looks.

Although it is true that on dating apps, 90% of people will swipe up on the same 10% of women and 20% of men, surprisingly, these highly desirable individuals aren't having as much success as it might seem. They can feel overwhelmed and frustrated by their inability to get the attention and commitment of those they desire, too.

The good news is that your success in love is not dependent on a perfect body or resume. People of all shapes, sizes, and incomes get married every day and enjoy a good sex life. So, how does this happen when the gateway to dating always begins with attraction, and when most people are average-looking rather than exceptional? Love is found through connection, not perfection, and chemistry is not dependent on attraction alone, which is why those of average appearance and achievement get married every day and enjoy passionate sex lives.

Chemistry and love are not the sole province of a select few. As a matter of fact, attraction, as important as it is, is not the binding force that ensures a lifetime of love. The endorphins, vasopressin, estrogen, testosterone, and norepinephrine that a loving, committed couple share during intimacy have an incredible impact on their chemistry with each other. These chemicals keep their bond and sexual responsiveness vibrant throughout a lifetime, in spite of the aging and bodily changes they both experience.

Thus, you need to invest in your appearance and market yourself more effectively because it will make a difference and is essential to getting more attention and better results. However, these steps are also needed to ensure you feel the added confidence and self-respect that come from your efforts to look good. With the right pictures and posture, you will stand out and make others curious to learn more. When you also succeed in making them feel great, they will come back for more.

Descriptions of how to select the right pictures for social media and dating apps will be discussed later in this book. You will also learn how to communicate with confidence in your profile, messages, and texts as you demonstrate your personality. But for now, you need to understand how making the opposite sex feel great motivates them in the early stages of dating and secures their ongoing investment in the later stages. This is not about flattery, being suave, or false pretenses that are actually about your desire to make others admire you.

Instead, it's about providing your partner the ability to relax, have fun, and feel a mutual connection or excitement that stimulates the desired chemistry that you both need.

The power of masculinity and femininity

Your appearance and confidence (or great hair and clothes) are not enough to make others feel great in your presence. If they are to want more contact with you, you need to understand how your masculine or feminine posture, gestures, words, and touch can impact them.

Masculinity and femininity matter because both sexes experience powerful feelings and chemistry when they experience a spontaneous moment of warmth, touch, or verbal affection. They react to the playful changes in another's smile, posture, proximity, or a shared kiss. Such courageous moments open a space for both of them to feel accepted, wanted, and curious about what might come next. It makes them feel alive in the presence of the other, especially when these gestures are returned.

It is exciting when a woman makes a man feel like a man and a man makes a woman feel like a woman. They are not colleagues, friends, neighbors, parents, divorcees, or widows. When they share gestures that are playful, gentle, flirty, teasing, and sensual, they make the other feel wanted and important. Such interactions leave the other curious and excited. The power released in these exchanges is not that of sexual conquest (which is a false and temporary substitute for real connection) but of shared passionate and meaningful experiences that have the potential to bring out the best in both of them, with a desire for it to last.

Because chemistry can be incredibly influential, you can take heart in knowing that you do not need to change your bone structure, get hair plugs, or invest in expensive surgeries that alter your appearance. Chemistry is not limited to sleek bodies and perfect faces. The rejection of your past is not because you are inherently unattractive. You can get a different result if you know what to do. Thus, it's not you. It's your technique! Your untapped masculine or feminine nature can have a powerful influence on how desirable you appear to others.

Many singles are unaware of how to tap into their masculine and feminine natures. Others fear using such gestures because they don't want to appear vulnerable or be rejected. Some have experienced painful exploitation from the worst men and women. Thus, many singles hide their fear of vulnerability and rejection behind neutral or safe words, actions, and body language. They do not want to appear weak, needy, or undeserving of love. Their detached expressions are mostly unconscious but easily readable to others. They appear stand-offish and disinterested even when they are inwardly excited and hopeful for connection.

Unfortunately, such dispassionate exchanges create the very thing they fear: disinterest and rejection from the opposite sex. In time, they even convince themselves they do not care or want a relationship, especially when faced with another person's issues. It's easier to be indifferent than vulnerable or hopeful.

Regardless of your reason for walling away your innate and passionate nature (behind frumpy clothes, bland hair or beards, poor posture, a just-friend vibe, or indifferent attitude), you can not hope to reveal it again (or for the first time) if you don't know how.

The specific techniques you need for success with dating apps and social media will be described in great detail in this book. But before you learn them, you need to understand what they mean to the opposite sex and how they can help you achieve the deep connections you desire.

Women need safety and security—men need faith and trust

As a female dating coach, I do not tell men how to be men (which, unfortunately, so many women try to do). It would be disrespectful and ineffective primarily because the number-one need of a man in a relationship is to feel that a woman has faith and trust in him and his competence. To assume that I can tell him how to be a man is to say that I do not trust that he is a man. This is counterproductive and simply not true. I trust men and their goodness and know that when an emotionally mature man cares about a woman, he'll find a way to reach her in spite of the many differences between them. So, instead of critiquing and changing a man, I coach him on how to better understand women, which is all a man usually wants to know. I tell him what it says to a woman when he engages in certain behaviors: what looks attractive, strong, and confident in him, what makes her feel great, and what meets her needs. In other words, I build on his empathic abilities and try to help him develop a female-friendly psychology.

It is a man's need for a woman's faith and trust that explains why a woman's behaviors of nagging, criticizing, whining, and chronic complaining are toxic to a man. Such behaviors communicate in a dozen ways that she does not trust or respect him. Unfortunately, when I try to explain this to some women, they will not see my point. They argue that a man shouldn't feel this way, he should accept a woman's need to express herself, or that he shouldn't take it personally. But *it is what it is*. Men and women are different. Women need to feel emotionally safe and secure (as explained before), and men need to feel trusted and respected. Empathy for each other's needs is the only tool that will bridge their differences and help them find mutual respect, love, and acceptance.

To make someone feel great, you must be willing to accept and give them what they need in the way they need it (as long as it does not contradict your feelings, needs, or rights). This may be difficult because it may not be the way you feel you should or want to give it, but like it, or not, *it is what it is,* and in relationships, *it's not just about you—it's about them, too.*

Changing your thoughts and behaviors to accommodate the needs of the opposite sex may be hard and may force you to step out of your comfort zone, but if you want to love deeply, you will need to sacrifice deeply. Being passive in dating and in your interactions with the opposite sex will never make them, or you, feel great. You need to give them what they need.

Whether you like it or not, a man needs a woman to flirt with in order for him to feel interested in pursuing her, and a woman needs a man to pursue her in order for her to feel safe and secure in his interest in her. Understanding the needs of the opposite sex in this regard is necessary to be successful in the early stages of dating.

Additionally, the goal of making others feel great will have more meaning and give you greater purpose than the goal of just getting dates. Such empathy can help you relax and enjoy the process more and can provide a useful distraction from the many emotions that may plague you otherwise. Making others feel great can also become a powerful antidote to your anxiety. Whereas in the past, you may have worried about what others thought of you, now you will be focused on making others feel great about themselves (of course, your efforts need to be carefully balanced to avoid the too-nice trap or abuse, but techniques to prevent that will be covered later in this book).

For now, you need to understand the 17 Secrets to Male and Female Psychology in dating and relationships, and why they matter to the opposite sex.

Please note that the following secrets evolved from decades of listening to men and women describe their thoughts, feelings, and motivations. Although they are useful guidelines, there will be several that do not resonate with specific individuals. Nonetheless, empowering and validating conversations can grow from discussing them with a partner. Both genders will identify with the other gender's needs since, as humans, we are more alike than dissimilar. However, there are important ways in which men and women experience the world differently and, as such, have unique needs that should be explored.

The 17 Secrets to the Male Psychology

1. Men seek out relationships that make them feel trusted and respected.

2. Men develop love through sacrifice.

3. Men are largely logical about their relationships and commitments; thus, they do not commit easily to things in which they have not invested over a period of time.

4. Men are driven to succeed, face challenges, and compete.

5. Men like women who like themselves.

6. Men love to be heroes.

7. Men like being appreciated.

8. Men like femininity.

9. Men like women who have opinions and assert their needs.

10. Men pursue women who are approachable and appear to be available.

11. Men who have empathy want sex with a woman who feels good about having sex with them and will wait until commitment or marriage (especially if they both share similar values).

12. Men need to be needed.

13. Men are repelled by criticism, nagging, and whining.

14. A man experiences anxiety in every conversation a woman initiates until she tells him what she wants him to do.

15. Men bond *more* through *talking about things* and *doing activities* than they do through talking about people, problems, feelings, or ideas.

16. Men adore women who give them love, attention, and affection.

17. Men are often willing to talk openly and honestly when they feel it will help them or another person to do so.

The 17 Secrets to the Female Psychology

1. Women thrive when they feel safe and secure.

2. Women develop love through sacrifice, but need men to communicate their needs if that sacrifice is to be helpful rather than hurtful or over-responsible.

3. Women often take a man's words very seriously, get excited, assume commitment, and then get hurt when he pulls away due to the added pressure.

4. Women are insecure about their bodies and fear competition from other women.

5. Women are attracted to strength and confidence.

6. Women are turned off by men who are too nice.

7. Women often fall in love with friends.

8. Women like to be pursued and to feel wanted.

9. Women enjoy touch, kissing, and affection, but feel vulnerable and prone to shame after sexual contact (especially when a man withdraws afterward).

10. Women want men who hold off sexually—it makes them feel respected and wanted rather than like an object.

11. Women want immediate relationships, but trust and value slowly, progressing relationships.

12. Women long to feel adored.

13. Women are repelled by moping, brooding, and the silent treatment.

14. Women worry—they need to know they are not alone in dealing with the problems of the relationship.

15. Women who don't trust and respect their men fall out of love, especially if there is no communication.

16. Women like gifts, surprises, reasonable spontaneity, and excitement—the extra effort makes them feel special.

17. Women would rather have open and honest communication about misdeeds than be protected from the truth.

Men seek out relationships that make them feel trusted and respected

Because a woman's core need is to feel safe and secure, women thrive best in relationships with partners who are actively invested in them and their happiness. To ensure your present and future confidence in your relationship, you need to establish a pattern in which men pursue you rather than you handing out your number, calling them frequently, setting up a date or time to hang out, or trying to drive the relationship in any other way. These behaviors will typically turn a man off.

The need to feel trust and respect from a partner is not the first thing a man will express. Instead, he will say that he wants a woman's affection, warmth, playfulness, compliments, attention, and responsiveness. He wants to feel wanted and needs to feel needed (in appropriate ways over time). A man likes being a (reasonable) hero and to know that his sacrifices make a difference. He's willing to invest in those he cares about, but hopes his efforts will be appreciated. Although he fears being exploited by a partner, a man is often willing to take the risk because he desires to be with a loving woman. He just needs to know that a relationship with her has a good chance of being successful and making them both happy. This is why critical, cold, rejecting, or unhappy women repel men. It makes them believe that they are not enough and are failing.

Women frequently criticize a man's behavior because they do not understand how men think. This misunderstanding leads them to believe that men are wrong and should do things differently. For example, women can be hurt or offended by a man's lack of pursuit in dating. They can criticize him for pursuing some women and rejecting others due to superficial reasons. His desire for fun can seem shallow. His sudden loss of interest or lack of follow-through can seem rude and thoughtless. His avoidance of difficult conversations can seem neglectful or rejecting. His hobbies and habits can seem immature. His tendency to withdraw when relationships get hard can seem untrustworthy. Women can resent the implication that they need to lose weight or work on their appearance. Women want to be accepted as they are and believe that men should be more willing to commit and engage fully. These statements are common expressions among women, and they are not wrong for feeling this way, but being right rarely leads to the mutually beneficial goal of being effective.

Additionally, men aren't wrong. There are reasons they do these things, and criticizing them will only repel them further. Entitlement and expectations (which increase anger and resentment in both parties) rarely motivate or inspire men. Such negative emotions shut men down and make them more passive as a means of avoiding failure. This is why faith and trust with positive encouragement are far more enticing and meaningful to men. When a woman offers patience, shows confidence that he cares, and trusts that he wants to please her, she will usually discover that his empathy and effort increase over time.

What faith and trust from a partner means to a man

When a woman acts as if she believes in the general goodness of men and their intentions, it shows in her words, body language, touch, femininity, warmth, happy demeanor, and direct communication. These things make her seem open, engaging, and confident enough to take small risks. In turn, a man feels encouraged to participate, invest, and communicate. He feels less anxious about making mistakes because he trusts she may give him the benefit of the doubt. He believes that she will anticipate his success rather than hyper-focus on small details to predict his inevitable failure.

Not only does her warm and positive behavior encourage his confidence, but it also makes her more desirable. Men like women who like themselves. They respect a woman who expresses her feelings and needs (because they can't read her mind). They are willing to do hard things for someone they care about (if they know what it means to her). And they want to be with someone who makes them a better man (as long as her requests are reasonable and he sees a good possibility for success). Thus, a woman who is happy and confident is simply more challenging and rewarding to invest in.

The willingness of a man to sacrifice for a woman's happiness is what helps him to eventually commit. A man loves through sacrifice: his, not hers. This is why a woman who lacks the confidence to ask for a man to invest (and leave if he won't) rarely gets the best of him (or his commitment). The more a man sacrifices, the more he loves the person in whom he invests. It's hard for him to walk away from something he's devoted himself to (whether it's a relationship, career, hobby, or possession). His efforts strengthen the depth of his commitment. When he receives the appreciation, love, affection, and adoration of those he sacrifices for, he feels like a success and believes that his sacrifices make a difference (especially when her requests are reasonable and not excessive or lacking in empathy on her part). He hates failing, and he doesn't want to lose the people (and things) he values.

A man is willing to do what is right and will keep doing so unless he feels it is never enough (which makes him feel that he is not enough). This also explains why he resists pursuing highly demanding, unrewarding, and dispassionate women who don't make him feel great at first contact, when texting, or during dates. Such women make him feel bad rather than excited, competent, and wanted.

Although many people encourage women to take the lead, it rarely works for men in the early stages of dating because it feels like nagging and immediately causes a woman to act less feminine. Men like femininity and can be highly motivated by it, so anything that decreases her tendency to show femininity further disables her efforts.

When a woman pursues a man (rather than warmly inviting more contact and confidently walking away), it unconsciously sends the message that she doesn't believe he would see or value her enough to do it on his own. In other words, when she pursues, she seems desperate, and men like women who like themselves and avoid people who don't trust that they can or will play their role. By contrast, men seek out relationships that make them feel trusted and respected and that allow them to enjoy reasonable and fun challenges. They feel their best when they face challenges and compete. They want to feel like a success, and they are willing to sacrifice for what they value. When something comes easily, it makes it difficult for a man to feel passionate or excited about the accomplishment, the woman, or the relationship.

Thus, if you start a relationship as the aggressor and pursuer, you will feel less secure and confident about your investment and commitment. In time, you will become less feminine, confident, and happy in the relationship. As you express yourself, you will be more likely to criticize, nag, whine, or complain (rather than appear loving, confident, and self-respecting) to get him to invest more. This will repel him further, and for all the reasons above. In return, he will become more passive, pursue you less, and increase his desire to avoid you, which is the opposite of what you want.

To prevent these problems and increase your effectiveness with men, you need to learn to rely on your femininity and its power to motivate men. Many of the essentials of flirting are built on the power of your femininity, so let me first explain what I mean by the term.

What men recognize as feminine behaviors (a soft touch, a warm tone, a gentle word, a loving smile) is just an outward manifestation of the deeper feminine emotions that men find attractive and desirable (gentleness, nurturing, and vulnerability). A man needs to feel physically attracted to you, but from there, what he psychologically desires is an emotional connection. In this regard, he does not need or desire for you to over-focus on your appearance—there are many beautiful women out there who fail to make a man feel great. He needs and desires your softness, warmth, gentleness, confidence, self-respect, and trust. These are the things he craves, and they make him feel like he is a man.

It is when you risk these softer emotions, show a little vulnerability, ask for his help (men need to be needed), or express your opinions in a way that makes him feel your trust and respect (because men like women who have opinions and assert their needs), that you immediately become more feminine and attractive to him. It is your willingness to show your tender emotions that compels him to give the best of himself to you in return. Additionally, when you express your opinions, maintain your values, say no when needed, and accept his sacrifices and investment with gratitude, you make yourself and the relationship appear even more attractive and desirable.

Thus, it is your feminine tones, reactions, and expressions that become the tools by which a man feels protective and desires to nurture and sacrifice for you. In other words, this is how he learns to look beyond himself and love it (and you for it). As you learn to express these deeper emotions through behaviors he recognizes and values, you will increase his ability to feel great when he's with you.

Some women may argue that acting more feminine will only make a woman more vulnerable to abusive and manipulative men. However, this is not necessarily the case. Feminine behavior alone usually does not motivate manipulative men. They often require immediate gratification of their needs (sexual and otherwise) in order to stick around. They are also not tolerant of a woman's needs or opinions and will not sacrifice much to spend time with her. Therefore, a woman who relies on her femininity to attract men—with a healthy dose of boundaries—effectively weeds out the jerks from the gems.

Accessing the gentle, playful, and soft elements of your personality (with the youthful posture, curves, and banter of a woman interacting with the man she adores) may feel foreign to you at first. However, when a man acts strong and confident with you, it is often easier to react in more carefree and affectionate ways. Just as a man's masculinity can solicit your femininity, the reverse is true. Your femininity can draw out his masculinity. Consequently, you have the potential to bring as much power and chemistry to your interactions as he does when you are willing to recognize and access your feminine nature. These tokens of good faith and trust make him feel great, but they make you look great, too. Thus, you both win. Whether something develops or not, making others feel great during a brief exchange is a worthy goal that blesses you both. You can always pull these gestures back if you recognize that something is off. It merely shows that you are an open and warm person.

A man's desire to feel that a partner has **faith and trust in him** and his goodness also relates to how she sees him **emotionally, physically, sexually, spiritually, and financially**. He wants to be invited in, to make a difference, and to be recognized and appreciated. Those who understand this and are willing to treat him in these ways are the ones he will pursue and work even harder to please.

When a woman believes that most men mean no harm to anyone, it shows in the little things she does and says to men and about men. When a woman trusts that men want to be helpful and to make a difference (at least with the people they love), she engages differently. This attitude shows and draws more men to her.

Men are visual, and so a woman who invests in herself and cares about being attractive has more appeal to them. It can also indicate that she could be more open to attention. However, men will look to her soft words, touch, laughter, encouragement, and feminine posture and gestures to determine if she is comfortable with them and wants more contact. These help him to take a risk and pursue her number or a date.

However, if a man enjoys an exchange but doesn't feel a romantic attraction, he will rarely pursue more contact or physical affection. Some women may get discouraged when they have been friend-zoned, but ramping up their appearance, confidence, and femininity may break the curse. Being soft, playful, and a little mysterious (so a man has to invest to get more time with her) also helps. If these things don't change how one man feels, they will definitely affect other men. The fact that men are so visual isn't fair, but a woman's decision to invest in her appearance, confidence, and happiness isn't going to hurt her either.

Men don't enjoy disappointing a woman whom they are less attracted to. They want her to be happy and confident, not angry and offended. Men know they can be shallow and selfish in this way, but when a woman takes it personally, this only makes them both feel worse. When a woman responds to a man's rejection by investing in herself, her happiness, and her confidence, it makes them both feel more empowered and excited about the other. A man wants a woman to like herself and others. He wants her to be resilient and strong.

When a man pursues a woman, he may be curious and open to physical affection or sex, but he only wants it if it is mutually desirable. Physical affection triggers powerful emotions and desires that he enjoys, but he dreads feeling trapped later, hurting her, or discovering secret expectations or resentment. Some men are more timid with their touch, and others are more assertive, but both want to feel desired and are looking for reassurance that they should continue with more contact. Thus, if a woman expresses her boundaries, men will respect her for clearly stating her limits.

Men don't need immediate sexual gratification, especially if they know she doesn't want it. The men who push sexual contact are jerks, not men. Men wish women knew this. However, they also want a woman to be clearer, more direct, and more consistent because they can't read her mind. And if they briefly misread her signals, they want her to speak up about her boundaries and trust their goodness. When given a chance (and if they are sincerely interested in her instead of a hookup), they will do their part to help a woman feel sexually safe while continuing to pursue her.

Men like seeing confidence in their partners. It makes a woman more desirable, and her healthy boundaries and requests help a man know that his sacrifices are meaningful. Men want to make others happy and feel needed, wanted, and appreciated. They care about succeeding in their relationships. If a man enjoys being with you without feeling premature pressure to make decisions about the future, he will be more likely to want more time with you. From there, he will become more invested and willing to deepen the connection and build a relationship. As he continues to feel like a success in the relationship, he will take on more reasonable challenges.

A man may need time before he is ready for commitment or exclusivity, but the positive and reasonable challenges of the relationship make him feel good about himself. As a woman shares what his sacrifices or efforts mean to her, it helps him to feel more connected and less controlled by her. He wants to connect and become attached, but he needs to feel she has faith and trust in him, too. When he has both, he thrives in the relationship.

Women thrive when they feel safe and secure

In this age of dating confusion, both men and women often struggle to know their role, how to play it, and its importance in being successful. They don't know who should pursue the other or in what way. Since both sexes experience an abundance of rejection, they often choose to play it safe rather than risk exposing their intentions. This confusion leads men and women to fail at making a lasting impression by making the other feel great.

To begin, you need to understand that *women are attracted to strength and confidence*. It is a woman's desire for these attributes that makes her vulnerable to "jerks" and "bad boys." Women do not like being treated poorly, but unfortunately, many women can't tell the difference between strength and confidence and arrogance and selfishness, which are the deceptive counterfeits that jerks use to attract women. Fortunately, you do not need to become a jerk to get attention—quite the opposite, actually—but you do need to understand what makes you look confident and what does not.

There are many ways that you can demonstrate your strength and confidence, from the way you stand to the way you express your needs, but none of these techniques will have as lasting an impact on a woman as when you boldly pursue her time and attention. It is only when you pursue her number, ask for a date, invest time and money, and seek her affection that she feels safe and secure (in your interest and investment in her) and wanted or adored. Thus, unless you pursue her, she will never feel great, and you will never look strong, capable, and confident in her eyes.

Learning to act confidently can make a tremendous difference, as women will overlook a man's physical flaws simply because they are impressed by his attitude, drive, and ambition. Fortunately, every behavior, word, or attitude that a woman finds confident and attractive about men can be broken down into specific techniques you can apply. However, you can not afford to forget that a woman's number one need is to feel safe and secure.

It is this need that drives much of a woman's decision-making and eventual beliefs about a man or her relationship. Men do not intuitively understand this because they don't feel the same level of vulnerability and powerlessness that women do. This explains why women look for and scrutinize a man's behaviors, words, stories, and life experiences to judge whether they can trust, respect, and be safe with him.

A woman may initially find a jerk to be hot and tolerate bad behavior for a time, but if she doesn't respect a man's actions, she will fall out of love with him. She can't endure threats to her emotional, financial, or physical safety and security for very long; thus, she will eventually leave (provided that she has sufficient self-respect and options). A man doesn't need to be a true jerk to be falsely perceived as one.

When an average man fails to understand a woman's needs, he will suffer the same loss of respect because she can't tell if his inattentiveness to her emotional welfare is due to a lack of awareness, indifference, or wilful neglect. Similarly, the too-nice guy, who over-provides for her desires, won't create sufficient attraction and excitement because if he doesn't respect his needs enough to expect her respect in return, she will struggle to trust him. And, finally, the man who misreads social cues, makes uncomfortable or sexual comments, or applies too much pressure for her number will also be rejected because he seems creepy and insincere. He may have been genuinely trying, but his unwise use of a bad technique will make her feel unsafe, nonetheless.

Thus, when you view your dating behaviors (while pursuing a woman's number, time, attention, or affection) through the lens of her desire to feel wanted and her need to feel safe and secure, the resulting empathy you demonstrate will communicate your sincere intent and obvious emotional maturity. Not only does this make you more desirable, but it also helps her relax and enjoy your company.

There are many dos and don'ts for achieving this through dating apps and social media. These will come later in this book series, but first, you need to understand the intricacies of what feeling safe and secure means to a woman.

What feeling safe and secure means to a woman

Feeling safe and secure includes all elements of a woman's relationship and life experiences, including emotionally, physically, sexually, spiritually, and financially. Men want this for women, too; however, most men know they are not a threat to women, so they dismiss the significance of this topic. However, when you accept that safety and security are a concern for a woman and you show her that you can anticipate her needs in this way, she will feel more supported and validated by you. This helps you stand out from others and be viewed more favorably. Greater still, it makes it easier for a woman to relax, have fun, and want more contact later.

Relative to a woman's **physical and sexual safety**, she needs to know that you will respect her space, personal information, and verbal and non-verbal sexual limits. Until a woman knows a man well enough to feel comfortable being alone with him, she will feel vulnerable sharing her full name and address. She may also resist providing her phone number. Most cell numbers can't be traced to a person or address these days, but she may be concerned that a man could use her information for this purpose. Men don't fear being attacked or assaulted by women, but all women do fear this from men. Thus, offering to meet her in a public space shows that you understand and respect her need for safety.

When you give appropriate compliments that focus on her personality traits or general attractiveness (rather than saying she is sexy or asking for explicit pictures), you show her that you're interested in getting to know her and are not pressuring her for sex. When you offer to give her your full name or suggest that she can learn more about you on Facebook or Instagram (without expecting the same from her), you help her see that you have nothing to hide and aren't a con man or criminal.

To show a woman that she can be **emotionally safe** with you, make sure your messages, texts, phone calls, and in-person interactions include active listening skills. Say things like, "That must have been exhausting (frustrating, exciting, fascinating, or scary)," "That sounds hard. I'm sorry you had to go through that," or "Wow! Tell me more. What happened next?" Such statements help a woman to feel heard or validated while making you seem emotionally mature.

To prove that you are listening to her, be sure to respond to her questions or comments. Neglecting a person's questions is a common complaint that both genders share. If you don't have the same experiences and opinions, redirect to something you may have in common or show curiosity and interest in what she talks about. Then, be sure to reveal something about yourself, too. She can't keep a conversation going if you don't share a brief experience, opinion, belief, or interest. You can do this by saying, "That makes me think of an experience I had and would enjoy sharing when you are done." As long as your experience is loosely related, it will feel conversational and make the exchange more enjoyable and mutually engaging.

It is uncomfortable to be the only one who is vulnerable, so if she shares something personal, respond to her experiences by reciprocating with a small personal story, flaw, or difficult experience of your own. If you do this with self-respect and confidence, she will feel that it is safe to be human with you, which makes you more likable. For example, "I bet that was so challenging. I've had experiences that have made me feel that way, too. How did you rise above the situation?"

When a man helps a woman to feel understood and supported, she feels less alone, vulnerable, and scared. This is what she really wants. You don't need to go deep into each other's trauma in the first few dates (since this isn't safe for you or her and will overwhelm a new relationship), but handling small issues with compassion shows you can handle bigger vulnerabilities when the time is right. You can also set an appropriate boundary to keep your discussions on track by saying, "I can share more details about this when we know each other better, but here is a short version for now."

And finally, a woman also wants to **feel safe and secure financially**. This is important for men to understand because it affects a woman's ability to feel feminine with them. This doesn't mean that she expects him to be the sole provider (although some might). A modern woman may hope that a man can provide a comfortable lifestyle, and she may desire to be a stay-at-home mom, but most women have adjusted their expectations and realize that a two-income family is frequently necessary. Some women will also be unwilling to stop working.

However, a man who wants to live off a woman's efforts has little to no appeal to women since a lazy or exploitive attitude will cost him her respect. If he is dishonest or secretive about his financial choices or makes outright poor decisions (such as racking up credit card debt, gambling, or buying things he can't afford and neglecting his family's legitimate needs), she will have a hard time trusting him or forgiving this threat to her security.

It's not the possibility that a woman will make more money than a man (which is becoming more common than in the past) that will drive her loss of respect for a partner, but his poor work ethic or lack of responsibility. Whether inaccurate or not, she will interpret a man's consistent disregard for their financial situation as a sign that he is not invested in her and the family's happiness.

If she respects his efforts and decisions, she can partner with him in adjusting the family income (provided she has the needed empathy to recognize his needs and investment). When they are cooperative partners at work and home, she can relax and be vulnerable and feminine with him. When this isn't the case, she feels forced to exude more masculine energy, which in turn impacts his perception of her and himself. In time, she may become more aggressive in her words and actions, which in turn will trigger a man's defensiveness, anger, disconnection, or avoidance. This negative cycle is destructive for both their confidence and chemistry. Just as she needs to feel safe and secure to thrive, he needs to feel she has faith and confidence in him, too.

When men and women understand the important connection between these needs, their empathy for their partner can grow and, with it, a willingness to change their techniques to reach the other person better. Men and women alike hate to fail at their relationships, and when given an option, they will try new strategies if they have a reasonable hope that the other will recognize their efforts and match them.

The tips provided in this book and the video examples provided within the Lasting Love Academy App are essential because your ability to appear strong and confident in the early stages of dating is primarily illustrated in pursuit behaviors. You are about to learn the strategies for messaging, texting, calling, planning dates, communicating details, using appropriate and simple touch, and following through with consistency during the first few months of dating. It is these behaviors that make men seem more driven, ambitious, masculine, trustworthy, and capable of ensuring a woman's safety and security while ensuring her respect.

Understanding these techniques throughout the dating stages will help you to maintain the confident attitude that is essential to the success and chemistry you both need. Confident men act differently from those who are less secure. They know how to handle rejection well without it defining the way they feel about themselves. They aren't afraid to pursue what they want in the face of real-life challenges, complications, or rejection. Their ability to sustain pursuit behaviors in a relationship (with ongoing self-respect) makes a woman respect them more. His strength and confidence also help her to feel more secure, confident, and feminine when with him.

The techniques for confidence and consistent pursuit behaviors that you learn here will keep a woman feeling intrigued and flattered enough to take a chance to meet you in person. When you know how to take the lead by arranging the details, she won't have to worry, which makes it easier for her to relax and enjoy the date. This allows her to feel more feminine, too.

When you are relaxed and skilled at taking the pressure off by reminding her that you only hope for mutual respect and a good time, she will spend less time overanalyzing your interactions. When you listen to her concerns and address her time restraints or needs in creative ways, you seem resilient and capable of creating win/win solutions. When you touch her in brief and socially appropriate ways, you show you aren't afraid of simple affection or being misunderstood.

All these things make her feel safe and secure. They also help you to stand out from the other, less socially and emotionally skilled men she meets. Such driven and competent men leave a woman intrigued and wanting more contact, especially when you end the evening without pressuring her for another date.

Focus on developing flirting and pursuing skills, not immediate results

When you play your role of flirting or pursuing, others may not respond exactly the way you want. However, you need to believe they are not your only chance for happiness—if they don't respond, someone else will. You are flirting with or pursuing them to practice making others feel great. If nothing else comes from the encounter, the experience is still invaluable. You can't have the skills you need for success in dating and relationships if you never practice. Viewing your experiences in this way will not only help you be more effective in dating, but it will also help you feel less fear and take rejection less personally.

The 17 Secrets to the Male and Female Psychology have been included in Appendices A and B of this book. These 17 Secrets will help you develop a better understanding of the needs of the opposite sex and the differences between the two genders. Review them frequently until you have them memorized or until you have developed a habit of thinking about and acting in a way that is friendly to the male or female perspective.

Your skills for understanding the opposite sex and making others feel great matter from first contact to two weeks into a relationship and forty years into marriage. Thus, they need to become relationship habits, not just dating skills.

Single? It's Not You. It's Your Technique!

Find and attract your match

Singles often dislike the idea of marketing themselves to others. This seems impersonal, superficial, or fake, but it makes them more strategic, practical, and effective when they do it right. Whether singles recognize it or not, when in live interactions, their body language, hygiene, confidence, and tone of voice send positive or negative messages that either attract or repel the opposite sex. Similarly, their dating and social media profiles, pictures, posts, and comments communicate things they may not intend, which can repel the people they want to attract.

Identifying your priorities, goals, and target audience is important to avoid sending the wrong messages. This will give you a greater sense of control over the image you portray and the experience you hope others will have when they engage with you.

Clarify who you are so you can market your *personal brand* effectively

Consider who you are, what you value, the people you love and enjoy, and the qualities you hope others will appreciate about you. Do you see yourself as kind, funny, outgoing, athletic, hardworking, or a sports enthusiast? Are you family-centered, fitness-oriented, spiritual, outgoing, artistic, creative, or serious-minded? Are you intelligent, generous, responsible, forgiving, or accepting? Which accomplishments or values best define you? Write your answers on a piece of paper.

Prioritize these qualities down to your top five. These **Top Five Attributes** will be used to guide your strategy for live interactions, social media, and dating apps. In essence, they become your **Personal Brand**. Like any business or marketing strategy, it is important to represent yourself in a congruent way that also appeals to your desired match (or target audience). Refer to these Top Five Attributes when posting on Facebook and Instagram or creating your dating app profiles and messages. Doing so will help you to stay focused on attracting and succeeding with your desired population of singles.

Alisa Goodwin Snell, M.A.   51

If you question whether you have effectively identified yourself in an appealing and positive way, ask close friends or family for feedback. They may help you to identify your strengths and positive attributes in ways that you are reluctant or too modest to acknowledge.

Define the *compelling emotions* you want to create

Whether you do so intentionally or accidentally, you create emotions in others that make you desirable, memorable, unremarkable, dull, or repulsive. Don't leave this unavoidable reality up to chance. Instead, be intentional and empowered about creating deeper connections and mutually fulfilling experiences. You both win when your goal is to make others feel great while also looking great to them.

When you are honest about your strengths and intentions to get to know others who are looking for someone like you, this isn't misleading, manipulative, or disingenuous. Instead, it is effective and pragmatic. Emotion is a critical primary motivator when initiating first contact, but your deeper substance, connection, and compatibility will keep them coming back for more.

Thus, ask yourself what emotions you would like others to experience when they meet you or read your profile. Do you want them to laugh, be curious, or feel compelled to learn more? Do you want others to feel warmth, safety, excitement, positivity, or connection with you? Do you hope they will be entertained, inspired by your intelligence and creativity, or fascinated by your experiences? Do you want them to feel important, understood, respected, and appreciated? What can you do in your words, messages, texts, actions, and body language to help them feel this way?

It is not as effective to tell others who you are as it is to reflect your core values or (personal brand) in your stories about your life, work, family history, vacations, or friendships. With a little effort, you can prepare interesting versions of your experiences that communicate much, show warmth, provide a little vulnerability, and leave them curious and wanting more.

A good storyteller includes emotional words, body language, or vocal tones while including details that illuminate or provide hints about your education, successes, relationships, personality, or values. For instance, if you value your family and work and want others to recognize your motivation and stable relationships, include a picture of you and your parents, who took you to dinner to celebrate a recent promotion.

Identify your match (Create Your Top-Ten List)

What do you want in a relationship? What qualities do you need in a partner? What would create a compatible match for you?

If you can't answer these questions, you will wander aimlessly in the dating process, experience repeated loss, not attract the people you want to date, or, worse yet, not appreciate them even if you meet them.

Thus, to succeed, you need to recognize what you want, which means creating a Top-Ten List. It should be a prioritized list, with the top five items being non-negotiable. If you're dating someone who doesn't have these top five qualities, you will know you're settling. The last five qualities are essential and need to be things that the other values, although they may struggle with them. In other words, these qualities are a work in progress. Once you create this list, you'll recognize others with these qualities because you are looking for them rather than just attractive faces. Your focus and openness to these people will change your demeanor and draw them to you. After all, birds of a feather flock together.

Think big picture

In addition to considering the need for attraction or chemistry (which is essential), consider big-picture issues, such as the compatibility of your career or lifestyle choices, religion, cultural differences, or similarities in the desire for children. As the saying goes, "A bird and a fish can love each other, but where would they live?" Initial feelings of love are not enough to make a marriage last. Incompatibility in important areas can cause significant issues, lost love, or divorce later. So be realistic about the things you need to feel fulfilled.

Look for the more rooted emotional tendencies and personal characteristics that form the foundation for the behaviors you observe. For example, if you want to be with someone who is a member of your religion, you'll need to make sure that they value, understand, and live their religion and are spiritually oriented rather than just going through the motions. When trials of faith come or their religion becomes inconvenient, those who aren't converted often walk away.

Likewise, scrutinizing foundational values over surface presentation is essential. For instance, someone who is thin but doesn't care about being fit or following healthy living practices won't be thin—or healthy—for long. Someone who is a wealthy doctor but acts unethically will not remain a doctor for long. Someone who says he/she values family but harbors resentment and cuts off family relationships over small offenses will probably do the same with you and your loved ones. Situations and circumstances change during a lifetime, but core character and personality traits will generally remain the same.

Look for patterns

When discerning foundational traits from momentary weaknesses, consider the person's pattern of character and integrity, or lack thereof. You need to see that they have the emotional maturity to adapt to challenges and sustain long-term relationships. For example, do they justify lying to their mother by saying she is a worrywart, cheats on their taxes, and manipulates the system to get out of a speeding ticket? You may think these incidents are insignificant, but when examined as a whole, they may indicate a pattern of dishonesty. If this is the case, the person will lie to you, too. If their personality lacks empathy, self-control, and personal responsibility, such that they are compulsive, abusive, manipulative, and dishonest, life will get hard quickly. You can't afford to look for only what you want to see because you will live with the truth later.

Identify what's non-negotiable or a work-in-progress

Specify the top five that are "non-negotiable" and then classify the last five as "work-in-progress," meaning that the person needs to value these qualities and actively work on them. For example, if you have "financial responsibility" on your list as a #7, and the person you're dating has thousands of dollars of consumer debt, then you would be watching to see how they address this issue. Suppose they have been working a second job to pay an additional two hundred dollars each month. In that case, this will demonstrate how much they value being financially responsible. Continue to see them if you are okay with their efforts and feel that the problem is being addressed and will be resolved over time.

Top-Ten List
(Non-negotiable)

	Category	Description and details
1		
2		
3		
4		
5		

Organize and categorize what you want

Use a pencil to create your Top-Ten List since it will likely change with time. Review the following list and circle the ones you value most. Then, organize your thoughts into simple categories and start filling them in as non-negotiable or a work-in-progress. For instance, rather than listing "Someone who has good credit" as one of your top-ten qualities, use the category of "financially responsible," followed by details such as "has good credit, pays their bills on time, spends less than they make, as one of your top-ten qualities, use the category of "financially responsible," followed by details such as "has good credit, pays their bills on time, spends less than they make, and values savings."

Top-Ten List
(work-in-progress)

	Category	Description and details
6		
7		
8		
9		
10		

attractive	physically fit	nice body	feminine or masculine
great chemistry	great face	fashionable	socially skilled
popular	athletic	loves exercise	charismatic
nerdy	simple	Christ-like	loves God, Christ
successful	accomplished	intelligent	spiritual (not religious)
educated	has degrees	successful	same values or lifestyle
frugal	wealthy	hardworking	financially stable
driven	fun or playful	witty	communicates well
empathetic	laid back	sensitive	treats me as a priority
thoughtful	respectful	loving	adoring
honest	virtuous	committed	kind
vulnerable	open	extrovert	introvert
loyal	generous	adventurous	service-oriented

homemaker	provider	flexible	good cook
patient	loves to travel	family man	homemaker
handyman	good neighbor	wants family	prioritizes family
values marriage	close to family	wants children	family values
grateful	humble	teachable	tender-hearted
sincere	gracious	musical	loves art and culture
talented	refined	classy	sophisticated
liberal	political	conservative	passionate
supportive	similar beliefs	career-oriented	private and quiet
exciting	spontaneous	funny	optimist
strong	confident	generous	realist
self-aware	similar values	similar hobbies	mutual goals
social	responsible	humble	admits when wrong
good friend	positive	outgoing	loves outdoors
cultured	high self-control	loves sports	emotionally stable
available	responsive	same culture	emotionally engaged
practical	street smart	predictable	respected by others
needs me	makes time for me	strong	same status
well respected	similar interests	values my family	makes me better
similar friends	steady	consistent	likes self-improvement
makes me feel loved	engages in service		

Outline the issues you're willing to accept

After completing your Top-Ten List, you need to identify those issues that are not deal-breakers. As you know, no one is perfect. You may find someone with the qualities you seek from your Top-Ten List. Still, they may also have thinning hair, a gummy smile, a chronic illness, depression, anxiety, child abuse issues, a slight weight problem, or children from a previous marriage. Continuing to date such imperfect people is not settling; settling is compromising on your Top-Ten List.

Too many singles have long lists of what they want, but—since they haven't prioritized them by what is most important to what is tolerable—they walk away from good opportunities that would add to their growth and happiness. Marriage isn't something that people should go into expecting perfection first. Marriage is what perfects individuals. Only through working with another person's needs and feelings will you see the need for your growth, improvement, and development. As a single person, it can be easy to see yourself as pretty awesome. However, once you are in a meaningful relationship, your issues, problems, and weaknesses will be exposed, allowing you to see yourself more clearly and strive for better relationship skills.

Nothing can feel better than being with a partner who has the empathy necessary to see your value beyond your weaknesses and has the commitment and investment required to work with you as you strive to improve yourself and your relationship. In such partnerships, you will feel safe and secure and free to become one with each other.

In this way, marriage is the tool that God (or the spiritual world) uses to make men and women more than they can be on their own. It takes work, commitment, and patience, as does everything that offers real and lasting value. Thus, it would be best if you start now. By recognizing and viewing some issues as acceptable (while keeping your eyes open for unacceptable ones), you will be more realistic, wise, and mature during the dating process. After all, you're not perfect, either.

Identify potential deal-breakers

Lastly, you need to recognize those issues that are deal-breakers. Sometimes people need to learn to be more flexible, whereas others need to become more realistic. If you think you can love and accept anyone in any situation, you will find yourself in a world of pain and chaos later. You need to have the boundaries and self-respect necessary to say no to situations and circumstances that will cause you (and, more importantly, your present or future children) pain. You have the right to walk away from people who do not meet the specific values, beliefs, or minimal standards you expect.

Unless you can respect how someone has dealt with their past problems (due to their use of empathy, self-control, and personal responsibility), do not date anyone with a history of domestic violence (including abuse of children, teens, or animals), addictions, secretive behaviors, theft, fraud, or drug distribution. Empathy won't change much later if it doesn't develop by the early adult years.

Use the following lists to help you identify the deal-breakers and issues you're willing to manage. You may feel all these issues are undesirable, but which ones could you accept if the person were solid in the ways you needed from your Top-Ten List? Which of these is unacceptable?

Do your best to create a healthy list of issues you can accept. The inability to find peace and confidence amid life's imperfections will cause you emotional or relationship distress later. You can have the confidence and skills you need to succeed. There are solutions to most of life's challenges, especially when you and your partner face them with empathy, self-control, and personal responsibility. So stretch yourself to include things you would generally dismiss and start looking for solutions to these issues now. You will feel empowered and more capable of long-term, loving relationships if you do.

Top-Ten List

Issues I can learn to live with and accept	Deal breakers

drug use

prescription abuse

acted abusively in past

never married

crooked teeth

balding

big ankles

tall

older

long distance

dislike their religion

different hobbies
or interests

too frugal

spends a lot

alcohol use

been unfaithful

dishonesty

divorced

bad breath

overweight

short hair

short

hair color

withdraws when upset

doesn't want children

has social challenges

has debt

financial issues

addictions or alcoholism

ongoing pornography use

widowed

multiple divorces

gummy smile
or wrinkles

too thin

unattractive face

younger

different ethnicity

workaholic

has children

has a difficult ex

acts violent
or threatening

high maintenance

Find and attract your match

irresponsible	unemployed	under-employed
rigid	anger management	atheist
agnostic	religious	prejudiced
resentful	experienced abuse or trauma as a child	lacks empathy
jealous	easily offended	defensive
angry	doesn't take responsibility when wrong	plays the victim
bisexual	gay or lesbian	transgender
promiscuos	different lifestyle or religion	depresion
has STDs	history of prostitution	eating disorder issues
schizophrenia	placed child for adoption	bipolar disorder
had an abortion	not involved in children's lives	panic attacks
anxiety	estranged from dysfunctional family	attachment issues
acts rejecting	OCD	doesn't like your family or friends
on the autism spectrum	hoarding	travels for work
quiet and shy	dislikes crowds	takes medication
diabetes	disabilities	doesn't believe in vaccinations
on disability	cancer	not healthy or fitness driven
devalues others	overreacts	bad kisser
dislikes touch	unpopular	not fashionable
unkept	awkward	misunderstood
smokes cigarettes	uses pot	has a pet
dislikes pets	doesn't like sex	pressures for sex
has a swinging lifestyle	frigid	unusual sexual preferences
has too many kids	in military	has past criminal charges
stay at home parent	unresponsive	makes more money than you
doesn't communicate	unavailable	closed off unemotional

Recognize what your match (or TARGET AUDIENCE) needs

People do not plan on failing; they fail to plan. If you do not know what you are looking for, you will not find it. Similarly, if a company fails to define its target audience's goals, problems, needs, and behaviors, it will not effectively reach them. It does not matter how amazing a product is. If it is poorly marketed, either no one will know about it or will fail to appreciate and invest in it.

In dating, recognizing effective sales and conversion strategies isn't about exploiting a person's (or target population's) weaknesses for personal gain. It is about aligning your values, needs, goals, and dreams with a compatible person (because both of you are desirable and valuable products that work better together than apart). Applying sales principles helps you to be more effective at appealing to those who are looking for someone like you and vice versa.

Singles hate the concept of marketing themselves because strong sales pitches often repel them and seem manipulative; however, this is another example of what works and what doesn't.

A salesperson who knows the value of their product and is confident in its worth and desirability will not pressure a potential buyer. The fact that they will let the buyer walk away to think about and return for the product is further evidence that the salesperson is not desperate or in doubt about whether the product will sell. High-pressure sales techniques trigger distrust and suspicion because they exploit emotion and fear and make it hard for the buyer to leave (all of which look like potential warning signs, manipulation, or narcissism when on a date).

This doesn't mean that a salesperson (or man and woman) should act passively. They need to confidently and accurately address the buyer's (or individual's) concerns. However, the value, strengths, features, and benefits of the product (or individual) always need to be emphasized as being greater than the problems or weaknesses of the product. More importantly, an effective salesperson knows that they are not just selling one product today but a resourceful and trusting relationship that invests in the needs of the buyer. This makes the salesperson (or partner) an invaluable, trusted, and resourceful asset for the buyer.

When people focus on their or others' weaknesses, shortcomings, failures, and past traumas, they feel broken and disempowered and see the same in others. By contrast, when they acknowledge their strengths and successes, they feel energized, capable, resilient, hopeful, and connected. In this way, they move from a fear-based mindset to a resilient and faith-based one.

Likewise, you can achieve a new and potentially empowering sense of your worth and value by focusing every day on your strengths, successes, and skills and how these things help you be a great partner. Doing this makes you feel more confident and appear more desirable. The same is true when you recognize and emphasize the strengths in others and the value they bring to relationships.

Invite a *yes* mindset in yourself and others

Seeing the positives in yourself and others helps both of you move from the all-too-common "no" mindset (of singles who swipe down at the slightest imperfection) to a "yes" mindset (in which getting to know others is an open-minded, fun, no-pressure adventure).

Of course, you can not afford to see only the positives in others, or you will be vulnerable to the worst individuals (and suffer abuse and exploitation) or feel betrayed and disappointed (by the inevitable humanness of even the best singles) when a partner's weaknesses, mistakes, and problems become evident. However, relationships and attachment aren't about adding up someone's pros and cons to determine their value to the buyer. It's about "seeing each other" as you are and valuing them as a whole.

Thus, the best practice is to study and understand all facets of your target population (or niche). In other words, don't focus on the worst, most fearful, and repulsive singles (who are not the people you are trying to reach) but on the habits and needs of those you respect and want to date. As you learn what motivates them and adapt your techniques and behaviors (or marketing strategy) to match their interests, you will find it easier to focus on the positives, begin a conversation, and secure their attention. When you discover a potential match's reasonable fears, challenges, or goals and identify how your strengths are beneficial and supportive of their desired outcomes, you build greater trust and confidence in the possibility of a good experience, friendship, or romantic relationship.

So, consider what you have learned about your target population's needs, challenges, interests, and hobbies. How can you share mutually enjoyable recreational activities, goals, dreams, or values with them? How might you express confidence in their resilience and resourcefulness when discussing everyday challenges? When you feel turned off by something negative (that might create a no mindset for you or them), how can you redirect the interaction toward something positive (that creates a yes mindset)?

This task may seem daunting, but once you know what you want, you will be surprised by how easy it is to keep going in the right direction. For example, if someone is complaining about a hard week at work, you could say, "Can we change the subject to something positive?" which could feel like rejection or criticism. Whereas saying, "That sounds rough. I'd love to help you escape that for a few hours. Let's plan something fun we can do this weekend to help you feel better," which acknowledges their pain point (another important marketing term) and offers a mutually advantageous invitation for fun (which is a value add).

Like many singles, these concepts may feel empowering; however, you may still question your ability to attract your target population. All singles can feel inadequate when they consider those they desire. However, identifying and recognizing them as real people with strengths, weaknesses, and needs levels the playing field. It shows you have more in common than you may have considered before. This makes creating a connection more reachable, especially when considering the strengths you offer and the value you both can bring to a relationship.

Focusing on your differences and problems will always create a no mindset (within them or you). This attitude is fear-based, limiting, and excluding. So, when in doubt, keep returning to your similarities for a more inclusive and faith-based "yes" mindset. This will build more hope and faith in yourself and your ability to enjoy and create lasting love together.

Offer a positive and inviting *call to action*

Once you identify your target audience, you need to offer a fun and inviting way for them to engage.

In attachment theory, this is referred to as an invitation (versus a push-away or stalemate). In sales strategies, this is a short and appealing call to action that either resolves a problem or provides a desirable benefit. In a job interview, this is achieved by showing how invaluable your skills and strengths are to a potential employer. In dating, this is done when providing a warm invitation for contact, fun, and a meaningful connection.

So, consider how you can leave them with a clear call to action before you say goodbye. For example, do you want them to message you through the dating app or social media before exchanging numbers? Do you prefer to share in a fun texting exchange before talking on the phone or meeting for a date? Do you like short phone calls or dates rather than long ones? Do you prefer dinner dates or activities? Do you have a list of seasonal events or foods you enjoy sharing with others?

Your answers to these questions can be turned into a compelling call to action once you eliminate any negative or confusing statements and create a positive message that provides easy and clear behaviors you would like them to take. For example, "I'd love to keep talking about this. I wish I had more time. It would be wonderful to connect again soon." This is a straightforward message that expresses that you want more time with them. However, it is unclear who is to take this action. To ensure they know what is needed to get more time with you, state, "I'd love you to call or text me," or "Let's do something fun. Text me with what days are good for you next week."

In both cases, the needed action is short, clear, warm, and direct. It can also be repeated a couple of times, especially when saying goodbye, to ensure they know the ball is in their court.

To inspire action, create scarcity

When using a call-to-action phrase, you must be ready to show that you are confident and happy and will be okay with or without their participation. As long as the ball is clearly in their court with a warm and engaging invitation for more contact, you need to walk away, busy yourself, wait for their response, and make other plans with those who are engaging with you. There is no point in villainizing their lack of action or making negative and personal assumptions.

Personalizing other's actions or inactions makes your sense of self too vulnerable and dependent on them for your happiness. There are a dozen reasons why someone will fail to respond that have nothing to do with you. However, your response and confidence in such situations say a lot about you.

A good salesperson who knows the value of a rare watch will not stand at the door and solicit window shoppers to come inside. They are not her target population. Instead, she knows many collectors will appreciate and recognize the watch's value. When someone questions the timepiece's price, she shows confidence in its value by not eagerly engaging in negotiating its price. Instead, she demonstrates its worth by saying, "It is a beautiful piece and looks amazing on you. It definitely makes a statement and catches the respect of those who recognize how rare it is. It's a wise investment." After a brief pause, and while preparing to remove the watch, she should add, "I'd love to tell you more about it. Let me know if you would enjoy trying it on again."

Such a reaction reinforces the benefits the customer would enjoy from the watch. It proves the salesperson's confidence in the price and that others will desire it. Calling the watch an investment reframes the conversation from what it costs to what it's worth. As the salesperson shifts her eye contact to the other customers while warmly inviting the buyer to reach out if they desire additional help, she proves she is not dependent on or anxious about this one sale.

A salesperson must build a relationship, follow up, and do their part. Still, it is their lack of desperation and consistent redirection toward the value and benefits of the piece (while overcoming resistance) that masterfully closes the deal.

When a customer recognizes that without action, they will lose the watch (because a sale will be ending soon or others are showing interest), their fear of missing out will usually propel them to action.

Likewise, when you focus on your techniques and personal worth, do your part, and prepare to walk away confidently, you will discover that they will take action more often than not. You may secretly fear losing their interest, but lingering too long and following up after delivering your warm and clear call to action only shows fear and insecurity. Thus, rather than overdoing your part, take a deep breath, remember your worth, and trust that if they don't engage, someone else will. You are worth their investment and deserve to be with someone who does their part without being pushed and prodded into providing the least effort necessary.

In many ways, you are the one who trains others how to treat you through the early patterns you allow, create, reinforce, and tolerate.

Outline *where* your match would be

Now that you understand your target audience, what habits, patterns, places, people, or activities might your potential match find interesting? Are they homebodies or outdoorsy? Do they enjoy going to dance clubs, bars, or the gym? Would they participate in yoga classes, reading groups, online gaming, or church activities? Are they working professionals who are too busy for anything besides dating apps or social media? Are they single parents who would be at sporting events with children of a similar age to yours? How can you increase your access to these individuals? What Facebook, Instagram, or LinkedIn groups or pages could you join, like, or follow that match their interests and announce upcoming events?

Once you identify opportunities for finding your match, how can you highlight your shared values, goals, hobbies, or needs so that you get their attention and appeal to them? What call to action would be more meaningful to them?

The above questions can be empowering and insightful, but preparing for casual and comfortable conversation is essential everywhere you go. Over 40% of the adult population is never married, divorced, or widowed. This means they are at the grocery store, walking in your neighborhood, at the doctor's, and in your church group. If you are prepared with appropriate conversation starters or questions that match the situation, you can convert conversations to invitations for more contact more easily than you have previously considered.

The trick is to act like a single man or woman when entering a room, store, or everyday event. This is achieved by keeping your eyes up, looking around at other people, and smiling if anyone makes eye contact. Using confident body language that radiates an open and inviting attitude helps others feel you are warm and approachable. If you look back occasionally to see if they are looking at you and you smile again with a nod or wave when you catch their eye, if they smile back, then you may have their curiosity. This could indicate that starting a simple conversation that reflects the situation might be welcome.

Asking for a recommendation at the game's hotdog stand, commenting on a magazine cover at the dentist, or stating that you haven't seen them in the neighborhood before, so you wanted to say hi, won't creep them out. If they are single and interested, they will help keep the conversation going.

Thus, while searching for your target population, don't discount the fact that you can meet them anywhere. By maintaining an attractive appearance and a positive and hopeful daily attitude, you can be prepared to recognize and attract them in your daily activities. After all, it never hurts to spend a few moments making others feel great.

Why Kendra needs to use social media

Now that you have identified your target audience, consider how this information guides Kendra's plan and the steps she takes.

Kendra is a 32-year-old junior high teacher who has never been married. She was very social during her high school and college years and experienced a fun and engaging friendship and dating life until a few years ago. After graduating and becoming a teacher, she began to feel more isolated from her friends as many of them moved away, got married, or started their own families. Her teaching was initially time-consuming and didn't leave much room for her to feel lonely, but after a few years, she discovered, like her other friends, that once her travel, education, and professional goals had been fulfilled, her difficulty in meeting attractive singles was growing. Whereas she once felt indifferent about getting into a relationship and felt no hurry to commit, she now felt regret that her once easy options for meeting quality men were now harder.

Kendra's answers include:

1. **My brand** needs to reflect that I'm a working professional in my early 30s who is attractive, fit, committed to a Catholic lifestyle, and looking to start a family.

2. **The compelling emotions** I hope to create in others are excitement, curiosity, and humor.

3. **My target audience** includes handsome, educated, outgoing, hard-working people who are interested in having a family. A potential partner would need and desire companionship and fun experiences. He would fear being unhappy, settling, or getting bored in a relationship (which I worry about, too). He may feel turned off by conflict or criticism, so he needs support and encouragement to stay engaged. I may consider someone who is divorced with one young child, but I would prefer someone who has never been married.

4. **The calls to action** I will express are: "I enjoy getting to know someone over a few phone calls before first dates," especially if they want longer dates or if we have to travel to meet each other. "I enjoy activities over dinner" since these are more fun and connecting. "I feel the strongest connections when we have consistent calls and dates that are low-pressure and fun," which can help us both to relax rather than overthink things or run away.

5. **I will find them** on social media, at singles events, through date setups, and in my everyday activities rather than in dating apps.

Because Kendra is targeting those men who are the most desirable due to their education and good looks, she needs to update her social media profiles as a tool for attracting them.

In Kendra's experience, dating apps are a waste of time because she quickly gets inundated by men who don't fit her target audience. She hates sorting through men who she would never consider at an event due to their social awkwardness, appearance, or other challenges. It makes her feel like a bad person. She rarely checks her apps because she finds the dozens of messages she receives daily to be overwhelming and repulsive. Those men she does consider and eventually meets for a date either don't look like their picture, seem too needy and eager, or drop the ball.

Many of her friends feel the same way, so she is convinced that high-quality singles rarely use dating apps, making them a waste of her time.

Kendra moved to a new city two years ago for work. Since then, she has found dating difficult because she rarely finds men to whom she is attracted or excited. She recognizes the need to meet others naturally and tries to go to events or clubs with her friends when she can. However, she tends to meet the same people. Although her friends are attractive (and can easily get dates), they have difficulty securing relationships. They often date within their friend circle, but it never goes anywhere. Like her friends, her dating experiences rarely last beyond three months. When she likes them, they lose interest in her, and vice versa.

There are plenty of men who would keep pursuing Kendra, but she can't make herself feel excited about them. She worries about missing out on something better and wasting their time. She doesn't want to get trapped in the wrong relationship.

Through coaching, she recognizes that she and her target population struggle with an avoidant attachment pattern (discussed in other Lasting Love Academy courses). They put too much pressure on themselves, overthink their feelings, and have stopped treating dating as a fun adventure, which makes it hard for them to relax and enjoy each other's interests or activities. Thus, she recognizes that this should be the call to action she could offer to increase her ability to connect more meaningfully during the first few weeks.

Since she recognizes that others may not be marketing themselves effectively on social media, which may quickly trigger her into a no mindset, she committed to keeping a yes mindset if she sees that they fit the qualities she desires in a match. However, a few phone calls before she meets them will help determine if she can relax and have fun on a date. She is busy with work and prefers more quality dates over quantity. The process of seeking and engaging the men she desires will help her to feel more excited about and appreciative of them. Her calls to action will remain feminine and inviting while leaving the men to pursue her if they are interested. Thus, they both will be playing an active role that is focused on low-pressure, fun interactions, especially in the beginning.

The men Kendra meets are appropriate and compatible options overall. However, she is rarely excited about them. Some of these relationships could become more exciting if they have fun. Still, she also needs to pursue those she desires most to discover whether her expectations are unrealistic or if she is just holding back. For this reason, Kendra needs to use social media to find and connect with those she feels are more desirable. This should include Instagram, Facebook, and, to a lesser degree, LinkedIn, where she might find other working professionals.

Create winning social media profiles

Kendra's Instagram and Facebook profiles, posts, and messages must present her well to her target audience and stay on brand with her goals. Once they are updated, she could join groups where other like-minded and attractive singles are. By curating her social media to match her brand, she will attract a potential match's interest and attention more easily.

Consistent with Kendra's objectives of wanting to have fun with attractive, educated men who respect her religious beliefs and want to have a family, she needs to share posts that present her this way. Because engaging in hiking, travel, athletic activities, and pickleball are so common, she should mention these things in a story (rather than telling others she values them). This will make her statements feel less cliche. Her stories can make her appear more warm, personable, and approachable, too.

Kendra's current Instagram and Facebook accounts are full of funny memes, food pictures, and reposted stories. Because many of these do not match her stated goals, she needs to remove them. However, she can keep some of her vacation pictures, especially the ones with her friends, while engaging in fun activities. This makes her seem more desirable and allows others to comment on the locations or images featured in the background.

To present herself as a working professional who values starting a family, being active and fit, and living a Catholic lifestyle, Kendra needs to demonstrate her sense of humor while simultaneously sharing her values. For example, when posting a picture, she could say, "Hiking with my favorite sister. Ten minutes later, I accidentally (on purpose) pushed her into a stream, and she viciously took me down, too. What a punk kid!" This shows her family values, humor, and playfulness while demonstrating the fun, active lifestyle she lives. This one post presents several possibilities that would make it easy for others to engage. They could send a private message stating, "It's cool that you and your sister are close!" or "Did you survive your near-drowning experience, lol?" or "That seems like an incredible view. Which hike did you take?"

When creating her social media profiles or posts, and especially when reading others, Kendra needs to consider how the image or description may help facilitate a natural and low-pressure way to engage. Sending a simple message is often enough for singles to check the person out, decide if they want to encourage more messages, and then share phone numbers or meet for a date.

Other posts or pictures could include church activities, religious topics, or a fun video with children. She can include comments or photos that share something about her job and what she loves about her colleagues or work. To demonstrate a single and available vibe, posting pictures of her friends at a club could state, "We had so much fun dancing and flirting. My friends are the best!" Sharing photos of her family, nieces, or grandparents would make her seem family-oriented.

Kendra doesn't need to post as much as she did before since this doesn't fit with the perception that she is a serious professional. Once she gets her branding right, she can share new posts only once a month. Before sharing something, it would be wise to review her brand to keep her posts, messages, and comments on target. If she wants to share personal or frustrating experiences with close friends and family, she can keep her current social media private and create new Facebook or Instagram profiles for her public and dating purposes. In this way, new people can find her without learning intimate things about her.

Find, engage, flirt, and pursue with social media

Once Kendra's social media is updated to fit her brand, she can send new friend requests, join singles' groups or pages, and follow or like posts of those with whom she wants to connect.

Whether reviewing members of a specific group, searching through friends of her friends, reviewing her Facebook or Instagram suggestions, or going through LinkedIn to look for people in her industry that seem interesting, Kendra should do a brief review of their relationship status on Facebook or a scan of their recent pictures and posts to see if they are in a relationship or not. If she finds someone on LinkedIn (which doesn't show a person's relationship status), to avoid uncomfortable situations, she will need to search for them on social media to learn this vital information before sending them a friend request or personal message.

Although researching each person will be more time-consuming and lead to some dead ends, it is nevertheless easier and faster than looking for new singles through searching for, scheduling, and attending an event that proves to have few people she would be interested in. It is still wise to participate in these events since they may pay off. Still, the cost versus benefit is more measurable when you get access to people from the convenience of her home. Additionally, the turnaround from a personal message to a phone call or date can be as fast as a few days.

When connecting with people, Kendra needs to do more than send a like or friend request. She also needs to include a personal or direct message that highlights how she found them, and, when possible, include a fun or playful tone. "I saw that you and I have some of the same friends. Obviously, we both have great taste, so I had to say hi," or, "I saw that you are going to an event I may also be attending, so I thought I'd say hi," or if she is feeling particularly flirty and carefree, she could say," Your Instagram posts are hilarious. Since you are so cute, too, I couldn't help but follow you. I'm sure if you messaged me back, I'd be equally compelled to respond." Each message could include a winky face emoji to indicate the intended flirty tone. Kissy face emojis should be saved until after a date. If they are interested, they will send a reply. If they are not interested or are in a relationship, they will just ignore the message.

Kendra need not worry about whether a person will remember her negatively. The likelihood of seeing each other is remote unless they are in similar social circles. Her messages are confident and inviting, and her profile pictures are attractive and positive. Her messages are meant to make others feel great. Since she also looks great, there is no reason to feel uncomfortable or embarrassed.

Additionally, Kendra needs to accept that people rarely pay attention to others. They are easily distracted by their lives and priorities. If they do remember others, it is typically only those who make them feel good (or bad) about themselves. If they are in a relationship, going through a hard time, or not on social media often, they may not have seen or read her message. So, if she sees someone from Facebook in public, she needs only to assume a confident and warm attitude, which always makes a great impression. If they remember her, and she seems unfazed by their rejection, this shows that what others think or do does not define or change how she feels about herself.

If Kendra is to find more singles activities to attend, she needs to search for singles' groups on Facebook and request to join them. Once she is a member, she will gain access to the other members and events that are posted. She will not be able to attend every event, but neither will others, so there is no need to wait until an activity to meet them. A simple, flirty message can get a playful conversation rolling.

As Kendra explores the profiles of members on the singles pages, she should send both friend requests and personal messages. The more she adds friends on Facebook or follows people on Instagram, the more she will get recommendations from these platforms of other people or pages she may enjoy. This makes it easier for her to find desirable men and for them to see her, too.

Move *cold*, *warm*, and *hot leads* to dates

Kendra needs to consider each interesting man she finds through social media to be a cold lead. When he responds to her, he becomes a warm lead. When he exchanges numbers (so they can text or call outside of social media), he becomes a hot lead. As with all sales, lead generation, or job searches, timely and consistent follow-up is essential. She doesn't need to apply pressure. She only needs to be inviting and confident, and leave the ball in their court by using her clear call to action. If they are interested, they will do their part. This ensures that she maximizes the benefits of each lead and the time she spends finding them.

To avoid burnout, rejection, or taking this process personally, Kendra needs to have a resilient, practical, and efficient attitude. She also needs to minimize the time she spends researching each individual. A quick review of their profile and an appropriately warm message is enough. If they respond, she can do a deeper dive later. This time-saving approach will keep her engaged at regular intervals, perhaps twice a week, without being too time-consuming. Pacing her efforts in this way will help her feel more hopeful.

When Kendra gets a response, she needs to acknowledge that this is positive feedback. It is not wise to focus on those who don't respond, which wastes energy and contributes to unrealistic shame and embarrassment. There are too many things going on in others' lives to take their lack of response as a statement about her. Many of her messages may never be read because someone doesn't log in often. This doesn't mean that her time is wasted. When they read it, even a few months later, they may reach out.

In sales, potential customers often need to be exposed to an ad or product seven times or more before they take action. Thus, her efforts on social media may take time before they lead to a potential match's action, but when they do, it could be well worth the investment. Her best path to success is to treat her search process as a numbers game that will pay off when she does her part.

However, one time-wasting hazard she needs to avoid is perusing the endless posts, commentaries, and videos available on social media. These can waste her time and lead to painful and unrealistic comparisons. The adverse effects of social media on self-esteem are real and avoidable.

If Kendra limits her time, stays focused, and gets off social media quickly, her efforts will improve her confidence in herself, her future, and the opposite sex. Being passive leads to discouragement, which is why she felt hopeless about dating apps. If she spends too much time on social media, doesn't engage new potential matches, or avoids it altogether, she will feel it isn't working, too. However, if she creates and checks her progress on a bi-weekly to-do list, she will feel productive while keeping her options open.

Measuring the success of Kendra's social media efforts will seem discouraging unless she understands that a typical response rate is five to ten responses per fifty of her friend requests, follows, or messages. If she is doing better than this, she is getting amazing results. Some communication will fade before leading to phone calls or dates, but that is also normal.

If Kendra isn't achieving at least five messages to her 50 requests, then she needs to reconsider her pictures, posts, and target population so she can strike a better first impression. If she's not using professional photos, now would be a good time to reconsider. No responses would indicate that she is pursuing individuals who are out of her league. She could look at the differences between her profile and theirs to see what she is missing, but she should also consider this feedback as a sign that she needs to reassess her criteria.

Although Kendra is attractive, she is older now, and so are the men who are seeking her. She has resisted considering those in their mid to late 30s, but these men are messaging her more than those of her same age. Although she is still beautiful, she isn't as striking and thin as she once was. Kendra needs to pursue the men she desires to discover if she can secure their attention while also accepting the possibility that, in time, she will need to adjust her expectations.

Instead of depending on the love and approval of a limited population to validate her worth, which is never a good idea, Kendra needs to remember and keep her focus on enjoying the passionate, fun, and mutually positive relationships she has with those who recognize and appreciate her.

The more Kendra engages and invests in her experiences with those who participate fully with her, the more passionately she will feel for them, too. She doesn't need to overthink a first contact or date if her goal is to have fun. If she develops a loving relationship that meets her needs step-by-step or stage-by-stage, she will not be settling. Instead, she will have discovered the match she desired.

Why Manuel needs to use dating apps

Manuel is a 42-year-old father of four kids, ranging from 7 to 17. His wife abandoned the family after having an affair and has little involvement with their children. He has spent the last three years getting back on his feet emotionally and financially. The divorce was long and tumultuous, and although he didn't have to pay child support because he had sole custody, he had to pay her out on her portion of the equity in the home. He was also forced to pay for half of her hidden credit card debt. This has left him feeling distrustful of women, lonely, and exhausted by the responsibilities he bears alone.

Manuel wants to date again, but he hasn't been in the dating scene for nearly twenty years and feels overwhelmed by all that it could entail. Thus, outlining his needs and a strategy for ensuring a better outcome feels empowering.

Manuel's answers include:

1. **My brand** needs to reflect that I am a responsible father, hard-working, serious-minded, kind, and have a strong connection with my siblings and parents.

2. **The compelling emotions** I hope to create in others are feelings of safety and security, empathy, and trustworthiness.

3. **My target audience** would include reasonably attractive women who are happy, loyal, honest, show self-control, and are willing to partner together in life's challenges. **A potential partner would need and desire** companionship, fun experiences, parental encouragement, and a slow, patient partner who won't rush trust or contact with her kids or mine. **She would fear** being unhappy, abused, abandoned, or burdened with someone else's kids or problems. She would be looking for someone who is a responsible and good parent.

4. **The call to action** I will offer is (after a few messages), "I'm busy with work and kids, so I enjoy meeting for a fun activity to get a break and enjoy adult conversation. Would you enjoy this, too?"

5. **I will find them** on dating apps like Christian Singles, Hinge, and Bumble.

Many of Manuel's answers reflect the reality of his life experiences and his desire to be appreciated by someone who recognizes his goodness and shares his values. Although he is moderately attractive and would like to date beautiful women, Manuel is open to those with realistic bodies (which increases his chances that dating apps will work well for him).

Manuel wants to be with someone who is down to earth and makes time for a partner and their family. He is turned off by those who are too driven, fitness-focused, or attention-seeking rather than family-oriented, which feels self-centered to him. He wants to be with a woman who is busy and engaged in productive, meaningful activities rather than wasting their energy on social media. Manuel's ex-wife met her lover through Facebook, so he finds the idea of searching for women and singles' groups or activities through it to be repulsive. Consequently, Manuel chose to use dating apps, which also accommodate his busy lifestyle and needs. He believes many women in his target audience would feel the same.

Social media increases trust and accessibility

Although dating apps would best fit Manuel, he can't afford to ignore social media altogether. Some women will need this if they meet him locally and want to find him. Also, women commonly search the internet before they agree to meet men for a date. For safety reasons, seeing them on Facebook can help build trust and confidence since it can verify what she has already learned about him. Thus, a simple Facebook page has a lot of value.

Manuel hates Facebook, but a quick search revealed he already has a Facebook page. Since he hadn't updated it in years, it showed pictures of him with his ex-wife, and his status said he was married. His photographs were outdated, and most included bad posture or showed him in hats, which cast shadows on his eyes. This would make him seem dishonest when a woman from a dating app found his Facebook page. He also had old posts with political opinions that could be negative or off-putting to some women. His political preferences are not part of his personal brand, so he should remove them.

Manuel prefers to cancel his Facebook page, but this will not improve his situation. Instead, he needs to update his personal bio to state that he is single and upload a few attractive and current pictures of himself. He can use the same photos for his dating app profiles.

Since Manuel has fewer than twenty friends on Facebook, he may seem like a recluse if he doesn't add ten to thirty more. Sending friend requests to extended family, long-time friends, or current colleagues would balance this out. To stay on brand as a responsible, hard-working family man, he should share a few posts about his house projects, work, and kids' activities. He can do this by sharing something he loves about his job or passively describing his work as part of a story.

After posting a few things for a month or two, Manuel can include a post that states, "I am too busy to check social media very often. Calling or texting would be best if you need to contact me. If you don't have my number, send me a message with your number, and since I get on here occasionally, I will respond when I see your message." In this way, he seems inviting and responsive, and they know not to take it personally if he doesn't respond quickly. Once he has five to ten current posts, he can avoid uploading more pictures or posts for another six months.

An updated style, great pictures, and hobbies increase desirability

Unfortunately, Manuel has very few current images of himself since he is usually the one taking the pictures. Thus, he needs to start getting more, especially when doing activities with others. He can do this by taking selfies or asking others to take or share their group pictures. Getting professional photos of him and his kids would also be a great place to start. This must include a few great headshots for his dating apps. His recent selfie attempts were not flattering enough to be used as a profile photo. A photographer would do a better job capturing his smile and confidence.

Manuel also needs to include pictures that increase his likability. These include photos of him with pets, friends, or his extended family. He should use only one or two images or posts about his kids, since a woman wants to build a relationship with him rather than worry that he's looking for a caretaker or maid. Their children will bless each other's lives only after they create a fulfilling relationship.

The idea of professional photos was uncomfortable for Manuel, but updating his wardrobe made him feel guilty since he rarely invests in himself. New clothes and an updated hair and beard style would make a better impression on a date since it would make him seem socially aware, attractive, and self-respecting, but it was equally important for Manuel to feel the confidence and youthfulness that an updated style would provide. He needed to remember that he was more than just an employee, father, and big brother. He was an attractive and desirable man, too, which he hadn't felt for years.

These changes would restore his playful and flirtatious confidence and instill more chemistry and passion in his relationship. He worried that this would make him feel selfish as a parent, but not taking care of himself isn't a good example to set for his kids, either. When he is happy and has a full life with mature relationships, he demonstrates skills that will help them do the same.

With healthy boundaries to ensure balance and moderation, he can create a space to prioritize himself and his relationships without neglecting his children. After consideration, he admitted that he would be more likely to click on a woman's profile who presented herself in similar ways. His identity as a dad is an integral part of him, but it is not all of him. He can't neglect himself or his relationships if he hopes to be happier.

Manuel should also consider what hobbies and interests he could enjoy or pursue with a date, which makes him more interesting. A woman doesn't want to marry a father. She needs to connect with him as a man, adult, friend, and partner, which means sharing experiences together. This can also include their children, but they shouldn't be dependent on them for a relationship, or they won't have anything in common when the children leave.

Once Manuel has new pictures, he can use them for his Facebook page and dating apps. He doesn't need more than five to ten photos. As long as he has a few good headshots that show his bright eyes and fun smile, he can have a few active pictures that are less flattering.

Be consistent, experiment, and pace your efforts

To determine if Manuel's pictures, profile, and personal messages are achieving the desired results, he will need to engage in many likes, swipes, and messages. Ideally, he should do this twice a week or more.

If Manuel likes twenty profiles per week, he could receive two to four responses. This may seem like a low number, but it is a reasonable response rate, especially given how little time and investment he spends generating these leads. When he gets a response or a like that shows they are interested in him too, he needs to message them with a comment that shows he read their profile and is enthusiastic about getting to know them. He can also share a short message about his interests.

If he isn't achieving engagement from his first 20 likes, he needs to add simple and inviting personal messages. This may require paying for an upgrade (many apps limit the number of unsolicited messages until both parties show interest), but it can be worth it if it increases his responses. Personal messages can show confidence and humor or create intrigue that inspires a response in ways that just looking at a profile may not.

After several weeks and potentially 50 or more swipes and messages, Manuel should have five to ten matches who actively engage. If not, he needs to get feedback on his profile, pictures, and messages, and make changes to see if he gets better results. Manuel should remember that not everyone on the app currently uses it. So, a low response rate does not mean they are rejecting him.

After a few months, it would be wise to switch to a different app so he is a new face and will have new options to consider. If he continues to experience few matches, it may be because he is pursuing the most desirable singles (which means an increase in the rejection rate). When he considers a greater variety of women and those who like or say yes to him, he will have a better experience.

To avoid burnout, Manuel needs to pace his efforts in a way that maintains a resilient and practical attitude by investing twice a week for 30 minutes (excluding the time required to follow up with messages, calls, or dates). To avoid being needlessly critical, frustrated, or avoidant, he needs to engage the apps during high-energy times of the day (during his lunch break or after work and exercise) and avoid forcing himself to do it when he is tired, depressed, or anxious (which will create a negative association). Engaging the apps while watching TV, listening to good music, or waiting for an appointment also distracts him from overthinking his options.

To date younger women, David needs to update his style, pictures, and interests

David was a 68-year-old retired attorney whose wife of 40 years had passed away the previous year. He felt lonely and longed for companionship. He enjoyed being married and didn't want to live alone during his remaining years.

David's dating efforts were disappointing. He found women his age less attractive and preferred younger women, which wasn't working for him. Although he handled the new technology of dating apps better than many singles his age, he was getting poor results and wanted to know why.

When David met with me for coaching, it was evident that he needed to update his style and pictures. It was not inappropriate to pursue women 10 to 15 years younger since, at their ages, they both had similar experiences and a strong sense of self (as compared to someone in their 30s or 40s who pursued a 20-year-old). However, David had to present himself as more youthful and attractive if he was going to succeed with those in their 50s.

David got hung up on the wrinkles and weight of those his age and felt they looked like his mom, which impeded his feelings of chemistry. However, I knew the women he pursued would probably say the same about him. It is typical for mature singles of both sexes to express interest in younger partners because they have never been older and thought of the elderly as attractive. They haven't come to terms with their age and how others see them.

Nevertheless, David had a lot to offer. With some changes, he could attract younger women if he were willing to do what it took to get their attention and match their needs.

David's answers included:

1. **My brand** must reflect that I am a kind, respectful, and jovial companion, friend, and lover. I am also financially responsible and maintain ongoing contact with my children and grandchildren.

2. **The compelling emotions** I hope others will experience are safety, humor, empathy, and respect.

3. **My target audience** would include attractive women who are happy, confident, committed, and interested in companionship. **A potential partner would need and desire** love, attraction, and family interactions. **She would fear** being unhappy, abused, lonely, or financially unstable.

4. **My call to action** is, "Let's go to dinner for a nice evening of conversation."

5. **I will find them** on dating apps, through date set-ups, and while attending my grandkids' activities (which they may also be doing with their families).

When I reviewed David's answers, I saw several potential problems. He wanted to date women in their 50s, but didn't present himself in a youthful manner. His sedentary attitude, along with his professional (but outdated) suits, made him seem older than his age. His hair was very white, and his hairstyle was bland. His hobbies included reading, woodworking, and occasional family activities. He was lonely and eager to have daily contact, resulting in him messaging and texting women several times daily. This made him look desperate and needy, especially to women who still had jobs and busy lives.

When I pressed David to consider more hobbies or interests, he resisted the idea of travel, pickleball, e-bike adventures, or dancing. When I explained that attractive and fit women in their 50s would not consider him unless he was more active and updated his style (because they care about their own and a partner's appearance), he insisted that he didn't want to change these things about himself. He was also frugal and wasn't interested in traveling, so he didn't want to be with someone who desired this. He was willing to get new pictures but wanted his daughter to take them with her iPhone.

Additionally, David wanted to date financially stable women who wouldn't need him to provide for them, which significantly restricted his options. Women who needed security (and, as such, might consider an older man for the lifestyle benefits he offered) would be turned off by his frugality and lack of generosity. He didn't want to be used, which was understandable, but this attitude wasn't empathetic or realistic. Divorce can have a devastating impact on men and women financially. Additionally, some women may have been stay-at-home moms with traditional values and ideals like those of his former wife. Financially independent and career-focused women often expect an equal partner in housekeeping and cooking. Since they did not need a man, they were less willing to be with someone unless the relationship was fun and fulfilling.

In other words, David wasn't succeeding with his target audience because he wasn't recognizing their needs. Many women in their 50s and 60s enjoy feeling free from the burdens of family life and the independence it offers. They enjoy their children, grandkids, and friends, travel, discovering new hobbies and activities (if they are in good health), and being with a partner who makes them happy.

Single women fear missing out on opportunities (while their health is good) and being burdened by a man's needs or demands, especially if he isn't willing to join them. David's lifestyle was too sedentary to attract such women, and they may fear he will resent them for being gone all the time, which he agreed he would.

David saw the truth in what I shared because several women in his limited social circles had expressed that they didn't want to date because they weren't interested in taking care of a man. He liked dating apps because he knew the women were open to a relationship.

Despite what they say, some mature women will warm up to the idea of a relationship when a friendship proves fun and supportive. However, David was too impatient and lonely to consider women who said they just wanted to be friends. Even though it would make him less lonely, he knew he would get attached and didn't want to risk the possibility they would never commit.

Thus, David needed to update his wardrobe and hair (so he seemed more youthful), get professional pictures (so he made a better impression), and be more invested in his partner's life, relationships, and interests (so they could share fun and fulfilling experiences). If he was unwilling to do this, he needed to pursue older women and those who were sedentary like him (due to their personal preferences or health issues).

In time, David's lack of success with younger women resulted in him messaging a 70-year-old widow. Like him, she was a homebody, wasn't very active beyond lunch with her friends, and wanted abundant time together.

At first, David struggled with attraction, but he loved her warmth, affection, and adoring appreciation. After a long and unfulfilling marriage, she relished his kindness. However, because she was not as financially secure as he was, she was not willing to sign a prenup that excluded her from his assets if they divorced or he died. If she moved in with him, she would have to sell her house and would struggle to finance another one since she is no longer employed and on a limited income. Thus, he agreed to adjust his will to ensure that she would have what she needed during her most physically and financially vulnerable years.

Ultimately, David found the match he desired. He didn't get everything he wanted, which was never realistic. Instead, he achieved what mattered most: a positive, loving, and supportive relationship that satisfied both of their needs.

To gain access to desirable singles, break into social groups

In our modern era of social media, texting, digital dependence, and remote learning or education, singles feel more disconnected from each other than ever. This has created an increased desire and demand for social gatherings, activities, and events. Although they are more difficult to find than in previous generations, they are available for those who seek them. Church groups remain one of the more successful options for finding like-minded singles and are often more popular than bars. College campuses offer social gatherings, especially in locations with a younger student population (versus non-traditional). Likewise, sporting or athletic activities (like hiking, mountain biking, and cricket) will inspire small groups to develop.

Unfortunately, those who attend these events can still feel that they are an isolating and lonely experience that is unproductive because they cannot break into groups or develop deeper friendships.

Jana and Andre sought out social events for meeting others and potential dates because their primary concerns were focused on their feelings of loneliness and isolation. They weren't anxious to identify their potential match or increase their dating opportunities as much as they were concerned about developing long-term friendships and social belonging.

Jana wanted to meet popular, confident, and charismatic people at events and was glad to see such individuals attending; unfortunately, their presence also made her feel insecure and anxious. She didn't want to embarrass herself or do something wrong. Those who impressed her were always in a group, whether standing and talking, eating, laughing, or dancing. Other people would come and go from the conversation or table where they chatted. Still, Jana worried about whether she could do the same. She assumed they all must know each other well, and her presence would be immediately unwanted.

Andre, however, was bolder. He would often walk up to the group to the group, ask questions about what they were discussing, and add opinions. This was usually met with awkward silence, giggles, or people abruptly walking away (with a few continuing the conversation while not acknowledging his comments or questions). In time, the group would thin out or ignore him until he eventually left, with obvious annoyance or anger.

Many singles can feel equally intimidated and uncomfortable when attending an event where a select few singles talk, laugh, and hang out together. The question of how best to break into a group (or gaggle of girls) is common and often littered with painful memories of junior high and high school cliques or gossip. However, social groups provide invaluable benefits. They create a sense of belonging and allow access and connections to some of the most socially skilled and desirable singles (who seem to have no problem being easily accepted).

For those who feel anxious, insecure, and self-conscious at social events, their most frequent question is how to naturally and easily secure others' acceptance, friendship, or potential dates while at the conferences, church events, parties, or activities they attend. It isn't very encouraging to show up, hoping to meet others and walk away empty-handed (while a select few are energetically planning something fun after the event).

Fortunately, when you know what to do, you can make a better impression and develop fulfilling social relationships, too.

Social anxiety, isolation, and rejection

Jana's problems at social events were that she was painfully shy and consumed with anxious thoughts about how others perceived her. When she went to a party or church mingle, she stood silently by and said very little. She compared herself to others and felt inadequate and inept. She assumed that everyone else was more socially skilled, confident, and connected to others than she was. She feared imposing on others, making them uncomfortable, or saying something stupid. Thus, she endured events in silence while smiling and nodding her head.

Fortunately, Jana was often approached by others who started conversations, but they didn't stay for long. She assumed they left because she was boring or said something wrong. However, this was not the case. Jana wasn't a drag, negative, or unpleasant. She was just quiet and didn't participate enough to support and maintain a conversation. This made it hard for others to know how to engage her. Both men and women were willing to try since they saw her as a tall, thin, and beautiful blonde. Unfortunately, they couldn't read her interest in them or the conversation (which made them uncomfortable), so they usually redirected their attention to others nearby. Occasionally, they would invite her to join them for a bite to eat after events (hoping to get to know her better). However, when Jana went, she didn't seem to have a good time and would not say much. Thus, others rarely included her unless she was close by when discussing their plans.

Inwardly, Jana was desperate to leave every event as soon as possible. Still, she endured until the end, knowing she would not eventually develop friendships or dates if she didn't do her part. Her silent torment included thoughtful topics and comments that she eliminated for various reasons, fears that the subject had already shifted, and panic about what she shared and how it was received, so she rarely said or did anything.

What Jana didn't know was that she suffered from a common and paralyzing form of anxiety known as performance anxiety. She was more relaxed at home and even witty and sarcastic with her sisters, but that's because she didn't care about what they thought. Her internal dialogue inhibits her personality everywhere else. In the past, she developed two close friends who saw her come out of her shell, but one moved years ago, and the other got a boyfriend and doesn't stay in touch very often. These friends had been her wingmen at events in the past. They made it easier for her to relax and included her in conversations. She recognizes that other singles turn to alcohol in social situations to help them relax. She has thought of doing the same, but she fears losing control and doing something dumb, and her religion frowns on alcohol use.

Andre attends events, too, but he acts very differently when there. He approaches many people, asks them questions, and makes comments. They often don't engage, seem annoyed, or don't stay for long before they leave. He can hear them talking about activities he isn't invited to and will ask if he can come or comment on the fact that they didn't include him. Sometimes, he complains to teachers in his college classes or event leaders on campus. He suggests ways to make their activities more inclusive and pressures them to tell others to include him more. His teachers typically say that he needs to work things out on his own when working on group projects. They also recommend that he sign up for a few college counseling sessions to address his social skills. This offends him, too.

Andre's complaints to event organizers also get him nowhere. They often dismiss his suggestions and emails without any follow-up, which he finds unprofessional. When he reports them to the student life department, this results in recommendations for counseling. He continues to go to events and school-sponsored activities, but he usually sits alone. He believes that many of the students are just too cliquy and stuck in a high school mentality. However, he regularly sees newcomers being treated favorably and feels angered by the unfairness of his treatment.

Andre has often felt left out and confused about why, but his defensiveness (and belief that they should adapt to him) prevents him from learning how he can change. He sought my services because, as a dating coach, he felt my advice would be more helpful than counseling. In addition to not being accepted at events, he struggled to find friends, and he often had terrible dating experiences when meeting women from dating apps.

When reviewing his history and observing his body language, tone of voice, eye contact, grooming, and style of dress, it seemed probable that he could be struggling with high-functioning autism. He would need a proper assessment and testing to know for sure, but suggesting this would most likely insult him. I didn't want him to walk away without valuable tools to help his situation, so I offered a metaphor matching one of his favorite topics: baseball. The same metaphor was also helpful for Jana.

Understand social dynamics

The best way to illustrate how social and group dynamics work is to understand the natural structure that instinctively develops. A newcomer can confidently join a group by relating their social experiences to an informal baseball game. To do this, you need to understand the **role of the captain, manager, and other supporting characters** and what it takes to get their acceptance.

Every group has a central person (or unspoken captain) who draws a consistent crowd of willing participants (because of a common need, purpose, or interest). In baseball, the game is the focus, but in social situations, it is to belong, have fun, be entertained, or get access to desirable people. Usually, this captain (in baseball or social situations) has a close friend (or manager) who helps to keep the conversation going, adds value, and supports the captain.

Although **the captain** is often outgoing, entertaining, engaging, attractive, or popular, with a cool or funny demeanor, they also have anxieties and insecurities that drive their behaviors. Their ability to make others feel great (due to their social skills) or their exceptional wit or physical and intellectual talents may get a crowd, but sustaining that position creates additional pressure. Their desire to feel important, belong, or gain attention depends on the validation and acceptance of the group. It is the energy and support of the members that sustain their confidence and ego. Thus, the larger the crowd, the more likable and valuable they feel. This knowledge about the captain can help a newcomer know how best to support the captain (as a group member) or build an individual connection with them through understanding their insecurities and needs (when or if the opportunity for such a connection occurs). Rather than idealizing the captain (as Jana does) or villainizing them (as Andre does), you can relax and anticipate their acceptance since, like you, they are very human. Understanding this open-door dynamic in social circles (larger than four people) allows you to confidently walk up, listen in, participate slightly, laugh, and meet others in a group. Doing this reinforces the importance of the captain and sustains their status unless you draw attention away from them or drag the group's energy down.

Jana can easily step into the group since she has been included in the group in the past. Still, she needs to see each member and their perspective and recognize the purposeful role she can play rather than staying stuck in her head. This will also help her to add to the group rather than burden it (which is one of her fears).

By contrast, when Andre understood that he had been playing a combative role from the sidelines of the field while demanding inclusion, he was able to let go of his anger. By intellectually relating to each team member's role and needs, he could now conceptualize a more effective way to engage.

As long as Jana and Andre choose where to position themselves wisely, they can confidently stand next to others in a group while listening, laughing, nodding, or occasionally commenting. If they do this next to a manager, they will not get as predictable an outcome as when they stand next to other group members. The sign of their group acceptance comes when those next to them unconsciously step back, thus expanding the size of the circle and showing their acceptance of Jana or Andre into the group. This is why Jana, Andre, and you need to understand the role and needs of the manager and other players on the field.

The manager's role in group dynamics is typically focused on building up the captain. Other friends will fill in when needed, but one wingman normally fills this position most of the time. A manager often vibes well with the captain and keeps the flow of a conversation productive and entertaining. They will also help weed out or snub a newcomer who drags the energy down. The manager on their own won't typically draw a crowd unless they are organizing or providing necessary information for the group. A manager will have other side relationships and engage in a few one-on-one activities with individual group members. Still, it is obvious that they love and thrive on the positive energy and status that the captain and group offer. Securing this unique social position adds to their confidence and provides an invaluable sense of belonging and status. The manager also helps take the pressure off the captain (since always having to be exceptional or entertaining is exhausting).

Many singles on the sidelines of a group assume that a group is an elite clique that is tightly knitted together. Since they are unsure how to break into the huddle and fear rejection, they often wait for others to invite them in, which makes them stay aloof and appear indifferent, critical (like Andre), shy (like Jana), or vulnerable and insecure. In baseball, these individuals sit on the fringes of the field. Their behavior seems confusing and rarely draws attention from those enjoying the game. They may hope to be noticed and invited to play, but this seldom happens, especially if they seem to have a passive-aggressive or outright condescending attitude toward the game and players. Every player has human needs and desires, even those on the sidelines who criticize and fear the game (because they don't understand it and are afraid of being rejected, failing, or embarrassing themselves). Those within the game may judge the sideliners, but this, too, is due to their confusion about what the sideliners want. If they notice a sideliner, they may be willing to include them but resist doing so for fear of being rejected, burdened (by the newcomer), or ostracized by the players if the newcomer can't play and brings the team down.

When explaining this to Andre, he was able to understand how those at events would be put off by his behaviors and annoyed by his criticisms (from the sidelines). Because Andre can lock in on what he deems to be fair or unfair, he needs a gentle hand to help him see the bigger picture and create structure or rules for engaging more effectively in the situation. The idea of standing back and observing group dynamics to decide who may be playing each role seemed exciting to him and fit with his logical and scientific mindset. To become more successful, he needed to understand and recognize the other players (who were less central to the action of the game). These people would be the most likely to give him a chance. He tended to yell criticisms at the pitcher and shortstop, but that just provided the team with a common enemy. Instead, he needed to work his way into fellowship within the team by building smaller connections with people already in the game.

In baseball, many supporting characters keep the game going but may get very little action on the field. This includes the right and center fielders, as well as those on the bench. In group dynamics, those on the field represent supporting characters, and the ones on the bench are transitional characters. If Andre wants to fit in, these are the best people for him to align with and the best positions for him to play once allowed on the team.

In group dynamics, **supporting and transitional characters** add (by volume) to the positive vibe of the group. Their investment is often superficial but includes less pressure, responsibility, and risk (making it more desirable for Jana). The captain and manager accept their participation because they add to the group's social status and importance. Fortunately, these characters can be easily accessible to others both inside and outside the group. For them, the value of the group is the reduced anxiety and feelings of belonging and fun that it offers. They want to participate in activities and meet other desirable singles.

Understanding and recognizing these group dynamics and each player's emotional needs can help you humanize and connect with them. To do this, you must identify each player's position in the sporting, academic, religious, or social environment you hope to join. The captain is often the center of attention and receives more eye contact, smiles, compliments, and comments. Managers are usually close by and will periodically support the conversation and arrange inclusive or exclusive events and opportunities. However, transitional and supportive characters can be more challenging to identify because many singles are so focused on the star players that they don't take the time to learn the names and strengths (or stats) of the other players.

Supporting characters maintain regular eye contact, make occasional comments, and actively support the playful attitude and vibe of the group without taking over the flow of conversation. Their eyes are regularly on the captain and manager, and they enjoy the game. They add occasional teasing, banter, comments, and support. They provide suggestions for activities and help with execution and planning if the manager is interested in their ideas. They don't take offense when their ideas aren't accepted because they enjoy being on the team and are not trying to be the star player. They know they don't want the pressure and lack the talent that a leader requires. However, they are loyal to the group and can be relied upon to participate when an impromptu opportunity for fun is offered.

By contrast, **transitional characters** are more like those on the bench or free agents. They provide additional support and can be called onto the field anytime. Still, they have plenty of autonomy and like to join other teams, too. Their self-esteem is also not dependent on whether they are invited to every event, as long as they know they might be included and welcome if they want to join. They usually like themselves and can step in and out of a supportive role (with a nod, smile, laugh, or a short, witty remark). You will recognize them by their frequent attention to their phones, short side conversations (with those in or out of the group), and regular efforts to see what is going on (and with whom) in other groups in case they might be missing a game they'd rather join. They do all this while benefiting from the protective influence of being part of a group. They are social floaters and do not need the validation or responsibilities of only one group. Transitional characters are often less extroverted and even fairly introverted. They can be accepted in groups while also enjoying and preferring one-on-one interactions. Since they are not as loyal to a group, they usually don't participate in (or enjoy) the negative backtalking common in cliques. Instead, they prefer positive interactions with a few members from different cliques (while being responsible for none of them).

As you apply these examples to yourself, you may recognize that you lack the confidence that the group members seem to have. Fortunately, the confidence you desire will grow as you learn what to do and how to do it, and then jump into the game. Don't let yourself overthink things too much. You will discover that navigating group dynamics can become natural.

Strategies for easily joining a group

Before you decide how best to break into a group, you must choose the role you would most enjoy playing (i.e., the captain, manager, supporting, or transitional character) to determine the skills you will need to practice.

Jana does not have the natural skills of a captain and doesn't desire the responsibility or attention of a manager. She prefers instead to be a supportive character who will be included and invited to more activities. To achieve this, she needs to only walk confidently on the field, show that she can play, and stay on the field. Fortunately, others regularly attempt to include Jana. In the past, her interactions have confused them due to her behavior of asking few questions, giving short answers, sitting or standing with little to no movement and enthusiasm, and lingering in the background of a group rather than participating. This is similar to a sideline player who finally gets invited on the field, but their eyes wander everywhere rather than focusing on the ball.

To play a supportive role in groups, Jana needs to connect one-on-one with other supportive characters. To do this, she can walk up to them when they are getting a drink or not engaged in active conversation and say, "Cosette, it's good to see you. What have you been up to lately?" She can use simple phrases and questions while including emotional words to show empathy and active listening. "That's fascinating (awesome, smart, funny, kind, or terrible). What happened next?" When asking questions, she should also provide brief answers to these same questions to allow others options for follow-up questions. Many of these phrases and questions can become her go-to techniques so she doesn't overthink each situation. Jana would also be wise to consider anxiety medications since this will reduce her internal distress and compulsive thoughts.

Later, when Jana sees Cosette in a group, she can walk up, say hello, and stand next to Cosette while enjoying the group's energy and conversation. This action is like that of a newcomer who runs up to the field and says, "I can play. Where do you need someone?" This shows confidence that Jana understands group dynamics and isn't afraid to jump in. If Cosette asks if Jana needs something, Jana can whisper, "I just wanted to say hi. You guys are hilarious (fun or smart), so I was checking out what you're talking about. I'd love to meet some of your friends." This helps Cossette to feel like a valued and important person and gives her a role. If Cossette doesn't engage Jana, but those near her take one or more steps back, thus expanding the circle to include Jana, this indicates her non-verbal acceptance into the conversation and group.

Since Cosette, an established group member, knows her, Jana can confidently turn to someone near her (when there is an appropriate gap in the conversation) and say, "Hi, my name is Jana. I love what you said. It was hilarious. It's nice to meet you." Since she is already in the group, Jana simply needs to stay engaged, maintain eye contact, smile, laugh, and continue introducing herself to others (when a natural opportunity presents itself). She doesn't need to entertain or draw attention to herself. She only needs to relax and maintain her position within the circle (like someone who knows their only job is standing by their base until the ball comes near).

When Jana sees an opportunity to be helpful, she should jump in to support the group's needs or activities, such as offering to drive others when the group is going for ice cream. She can recognize others' efforts, jump in when they are cleaning up, and express her appreciation to those who planned the event. She can also offer to help with future activities, coordinate a GroupMe page for communicating as a group, or bring something to share at parties. All these opportunities help her build relationships and develop closer friendships.

To ensure she is making connections and not just being present, she should also remember that each group member is there due to an internal need. Whether they are lonely, want to belong, need to have fun, or hope to be appreciated, she can be part of their solution and make them feel great, seen, and appreciated. Jana doesn't have to be the biggest and the loudest. She is more shy. But if she can stay out of her head and think of others, she will feel connected, wanted, and needed, make friends, and increase her possibilities for future dates.

To convert these socially rich environments to one-on-one activities with friends and dates, she needs only say, "These events are great but terrible for really good conversations. I'd love to be able to talk more about this. It would be awesome to get to know you better. Let's exchange numbers." Not everyone she engages with will immediately respond to future texts. For this, she will need to discover if they share a common interest, hobby, need (for support or companionship), purpose, or proximity (due to being in the same work, housing, or social situations). Fortunately, many at the event and in the group are there for these reasons. If she can identify their interests and offer to engage in these activities or explore other events they both want to attend, then conversations will become easier to encourage and maintain.

Finding the right group for you

Andre's situation requires more time and assessment because he has, unfortunately, contributed to several negative and confusing social experiences. During his college events, Andre unknowingly misread social cues, interjected comments that didn't fit the flow of conversation, took offense when excluded, and criticized others for not adapting to his needs. Instead of becoming a team player, he challenged the captain and manager by shouting commands and insulting them from the sidelines. Doing this turned the group against him, and since this would be hard to change, he needed to start over in a new group setting.

Andre didn't intend to alienate himself. He fought for what he thought was fair and became blind to the bigger picture. Now that he could conceptualize how social dynamics, roles, and rules work, he could see his mistakes more clearly and was committed to preventing them in the future. He would need some help adapting the concepts appropriately to fit a situation, but with a wingman, he would get better at this.

Andre needed to start afresh somewhere new. Once there, his first goal would be to observe the group, look for transitional and supportive characters, and then engage these individuals in one-on-one conversations when they are away from the group. He could do this by introducing himself, asking for their names, offering to help, and looking for them on social media to learn more about them. When he finds similar interests, he could initiate conversations to build a connection.

After a couple of positive encounters, he should then approach a group where the individuals Andre has been interacting with are (this could include tables, study groups, events, or small group discussions). Like Jana, Andre needs to see if the other members will step back or turn toward him as signs that they are including him (versus turning away or tightening the group, so he is clearly on the outside of the circle). Those who are attractive, well-groomed, and appear socially competent and confident often find that groups expand quickly for them. Those who appear more awkward and unkempt, exude body odor, or make abrupt comments that disrupt the flow of the conversation will discover that the group members will turn their backs quickly while they engage in side conversations.

If Andre experiences acceptance, he needs to be cautious about making anything more than short comments or remarks to see how the other group members respond. Those on the spectrum often need feedback and support to understand when their comments trigger sarcasm or giggling instead of the laughter they hoped their witty or clever remarks would elicit. Giggling, eye-rolling, and side glances directed at other members (with a knowing look and a sheepish laugh or smile) are indicators that he misread a situation or said something that seemed off or foolish. However, he can turn this into a positive relationship-building encounter by engaging the transitional characters he befriended. To do this, he needs to approach them later and ask, "Will you help me out? I can sometimes misinterpret jokes and sarcasm. I'd love your feedback on what I missed," followed by, "When you see this happen again, will you let me know?" This helps that person to feel needed and important.

Andre must be careful not to shadow his transitional characters by following them during social situations. This will annoy and burden transitional characters, and it assumes a deeper friendship or a wingman status that doesn't exist. Transitional characters are like comfortable acquaintances or non-intimate friends. They need their space and social freedom to mingle. Still, they will enjoy Andre's occasional company and be willing to periodically hang out or offer support.

Andre will know that he has developed a more intimate friendship or wingman when this person approaches him, keeps the conversation going, invites him to do things together, and follows him into group circles. A wingman provides a social advantage as long as both of you are included in the expanded circle when you join a group. Andre and his friend can then share insights about social observations and build on each other's contributions to group conversations.

Knowing how to fit into a social group is a valuable tool that can be used in any social, religious, or work environment, neighborhood, or gaming world. Although Andre may want to find acceptance on campus, it is more important for him to *find the right group for him* so he can develop a few more intimate friendships and dating opportunities. Building long-term relationships will provide more emotional and psychological benefits than fitting into a group.

By their nature, social groups are almost always transitional. They rarely last for more than a few months or a year. They typically grow, thrive, stagnate, and then decline. They can even turn toxic due to the backtalking, gossip, and manipulations of a few members who mistakenly exploit one member as a common enemy for bringing the others closer (until one of them becomes the next target). Thus, belonging to several groups and knowing how to move in and out of them allows for better social experiences. A group's most significant life-changing benefit is its access to other members and how it can foster good friendships or romantic relationships.

For Andre to develop these critical friendships, he must use the skills taught to exchange numbers and plan other mutually enjoyable activities. Until this occurs, he should keep looking inside and outside the group for other meaningful opportunities.

When struggling to connect with others in a group, it is worth expanding Andre's view to discover those with similar interests or needs. Those who, like him, are not fulfilled (or accepted) by the group will be more motivated to create a connection or develop their own group. This ability to identify and create a small group of acceptance has driven the success and appeal of Dungeons and Dragons, fishing, hunting, cycling, Iron Man, rock climbing, and pickleball enthusiasts worldwide. Andre will notice that every one of these groups will inevitably develop the same group dynamics, with captains, managers, and supporting characters.

Andre could become a dungeon master within a gaming social circle or help others organize a hiking group. And, if he truly loves baseball and wants to join a city league, he could offer to collect fly balls, practice with the team, or ask the manager if there is anything he could do to help (while simultaneously improving his skills and standing within the group).

Using this analogy helped Andre break the destructive cycle he experienced and deepened his empathy for others at events. He no longer saw himself as a victim but as someone who could play an important role in solving his and others' problems and social needs. Many people on the autism spectrum struggle with higher-than-average rates of depression and loneliness compared to other singles their age, but because Andre feels a strong desire for connection and understands where and how to build on his opportunities, he feels empowered and more confident rather than angry and rejected. He also feels more appreciation for those who invest in him rather than focusing on those who reject him.

When needed, Andre should also include a search for Facebook pages and groups to expand his options. There is a growing interest in organizing and attending such events due to our modern culture's disconnected generation of singles who are marrying later in life and suffering from more loneliness. To find others like yourself, search for Facebook pages that support topics and activities you enjoy (from travel to tennis leagues to Comic-Con events).

Get the date

In Chapter 1, you learned about the Be Right and Be Effective boxes and how life, dating, relationships, chemistry, love, and the opposite sex do not match our expectations. It is essential to accept that life is not fair, the way we need or want it to be, and includes loss or trauma. We need to validate this pain. As we grieve and strive to accept these undesirable experiences, we can also embrace our ability to change and cope with them and then find better skills to transform our situation and relationships.

Balancing the need for **acceptance AND change** is foundational to the Dialectical Behavior Therapy (or DBT)[4] program, which has transformed the lives of millions. It teaches life-changing skills for mindfulness and distress tolerance (to increase acceptance) and for emotion regulation and interpersonal effectiveness (which increase one's ability to participate constructively in a situation and relationship).

For many people, dating increases feelings of anxiety, distress, rejection, loss, abandonment, worthlessness, and anger, which perpetuates their fears and unhealthy beliefs and actions. This is why Chapter 2 focused on recognizing your fears and creating alternate, universally healthier, or more true beliefs.

The proven techniques you learn in this chapter apply the concepts you learned in Chapter 3 (on making others feel great) and Chapter 4 (on identifying and attracting your match) and put them into practical application. You will recognize how they correlate with the deeper principles taught thus far. However, you will also face

---

4   McKay, M., Wood, J. C., & Brantley, J. (2019). *The dialectical behavior therapy skills workbook: Practical DBT exercises for learning mindfulness, interpersonal effectiveness, emotion regulation, and distress tolerance* (2nd ed.). New Harbinger Publications.

natural emotions that resist embracing these changes. As you consider the techniques for getting dates, remember that trying them doesn't mean that you are wrong, that you will become someone you're not, and that you must do them perfectly.

The problem never was you. Likewise, every technique you practice IS JUST A TECHNIQUE. It is not right or wrong or good or bad. It's an option, an educated guess, a proven strategy, and an experiment. It doesn't make you more lovable. It simply removes some of the barriers that are in your way. The only thing that matters is whether it helps you and others to create a more meaningful and positive connection.

View each technique as an experiment that takes time to discover if it becomes comfortable and successful enough for you to continue. Focus on whether it provides better results. Look at the underlying principles that support these strategies and explore other variations that apply the concept to better fit them to your situation or personality. If you like the result and it becomes a comfortable or effective skill, add it to your dating and relationship toolbox to use when needed. If it never becomes natural or enjoyable after an uncomfortable period of exploration, move on to a different technique. Don't focus on what isn't working. Instead, focus on what is and keep doing more of that.

Remember that it's just a technique, not a should, demand, rule, or expectation that will result in failure, shame, or rejection if not followed. You are not your technique. Others do see and appreciate your value, not because you are perfect (which is very uncomfortable to be around) but because you care enough about yourself and them to invest in a mutually satisfying relationship.

To assist you in applying these techniques, the Lasting Love Academy app or LastingLoveAcademy.com provides video examples that may significantly enhance your skills and confidence.

Dating can take time before it ends in a relationship. Much of this depends on others and is beyond your control; nevertheless, every action you take has meaning and purpose and gets you closer to your goal. Thus, when you get discouraged or your hope fades, remember the skills you have developed and how far you have come, which will keep you from despairing or slipping into a victim mentality or defeated thinking.

Techniques by gender and for stronger chemistry

Men and women have many feelings and needs in common. Nevertheless, the strategies in this section have been outlined according to gender due to my decades of experience listening to men and women describe their needs, motivations, and desires. Both genders typically request advice that reaches the opposite sex most effectively; thus, I do not choose to generalize these techniques since this would make them more confusing and less behaviorally clear to those who desire them. They were inspired and tested over 30 years of listening to each gender with regular adaptations to fit the changing realities of the dating world and modern relationships. Please know that the following advice is not intended to stereotype the roles and expectations a man or woman should play and should always be adapted (after considering the underlying principles) to fit your needs, personal style, and preferences.

Although some things have changed through the years, what inspires chemistry and meaningful connections between the genders has remained relatively consistent. Thus, each gender's section provides valuable insights into how the other sex might react. From there, you will need to explore conversations about your date's personal preferences and needs.

For your convenience, the chapters in this section highlight each action or behavioral strategy by using a bullet format. Consider each bullet as a potential goal or technique you can apply. No one can work on more than three goals or behaviors at a given time, so choose the most appealing options first and leave the others for another time.

It is not necessary or desirable for a technique to be a paralyzing distraction when interacting in social situations or on a date. Practicing a new behavior for a few minutes over multiple situations (with friends, family, colleagues, and strangers) is often enough to develop a habit. If you challenge yourself to try three techniques and spend no more than five minutes on each, you can trust and relax, knowing that in time, they will spontaneously appear when needed. Many of these strategies will be useful in situations where skills for confidence, communication, and meaningful connections are needed.

Single? It's Not You. It's Your Technique!

Pursue first contact (with apps and social media)

For your convenience, this chapter highlights each technique (i.e., action or behavioral strategy) by using a bullet format. Consider each bullet as a potential goal or technique you can apply. No one can work on more than three goals or behaviors at a given time, so choose the most appealing options first and leave the others for another time. Remember, making a meaningful connection is the goal, not perfection.

Stand out through updating your style

Chad is a 27-year-old resident physician at a local hospital. He had ignored dating for many years and feels the time is right to get back into it. He has not been in a serious relationship so far and took for granted that it would be easy when he was ready. Discovering social situations that provide access to the women he desires has been harder than he anticipated. Worse yet, when at parties and singles events, his charismatic friends often get the attention he craves. He's not shy, but he's also not as outgoing and quick to ask for a number as they are.

Compared to his friends, he feels that women don't notice him. Chad's body language and overall style are average and don't grab attention. He is farther along in his career and education than his friends, and so his style needs to look the part if he is to get noticed.

Chad doesn't have to be the loudest in the room to inspire a woman's curiosity and respect. His clothing, hair, and quiet confidence can leave a woman wanting more time with him. With the right techniques, he can stand out from his friends, but this must include more confidence and assertiveness. He also needs to be more aware of the subtle signs women send to show their interest (which he is prone to missing).

With a new style (and pictures to match his social media and dating apps), Chad will get better results. Hiring a stylist and shopping at high-end stores would help not only his dating life but also his confidence in his career. These changes improve his overall presence and others' first impressions. Applying the image and behavioral techniques in this chapter will make him less likely to appear arrogant (which could be off-putting). Chad has an overall nice-guy image and demeanor, which has traditionally caused him to be undervalued. Thus, these changes help balance the scales and make him more intriguing.

Chad could consider growing a beard to compensate for his baby face and thinning hair. It will shape his face (if done right) and present a polished, intentional style that makes him seem masculine and mature. Being a little scruffy might provide an edginess that could suit him personally and professionally. He could choose a style that makes him appear fun, rugged, or sloppy. Thus, Chad needs to peruse current beard styles to decide on the statement he is trying to make and find a barber to deliver it. Creating an intentional and consistent beard and clothing style can be more rural, metrosexual, or uptown, depending on a person's work, social environment, or preferences. Either way, he needs to own it.

When others ask about Chad's work or other interests, he needs to respond while leaving them intrigued and wanting to know more. He can capitalize on this by responding to a question with, "That's an interesting story best shared over dinner or a fun activity." If he adds a confident wink and nod, it will deliver a playful hint that a woman could follow up on.

Create a memorable style and first impression

Rather than seeking perfection, choose one or two procedures below and then return for more suggestions when you are ready. Remember, your goal is connection and progression, with the mutually beneficial outcome of making a woman feel great while looking great, too.

- **Either hire a stylist or go shopping with someone you trust who has a great sense of style.** For those with adequate financial resources or an impressive career, shopping at a high-end store can help you attract others in the same situation. Some of these stores offer personal shoppers who can assist you when you request them. You can also hire a stylist in your area. If you have a modest budget, shopping with a female friend who fits your target population may give you the feedback and support you need to up your game. Either way, you can't afford to neglect this step in your dating strategy. You are more likely to flirt and engage in eye contact and pursuit behaviors when you look good. Furthermore, when you invest in yourself, others will feel you are worth their investment, too.

- **Make sure your clothes match the current trends for people your age (or ten years younger).** Regardless of your age, looking socially aware of current trends makes you more youthful and desirable, which is why being intentional about your style helps you stand out and be impressive. Whether you prefer a country, new age, professional, or preppy style, own it with confidence. Depending on your social circles or status, you might prefer not to appear high-maintenance, but modifying this can be done by reducing your accessories or buying less high-end clothing.

- **Your clothes should fit well, accentuate your body type, flatter your hair and skin tones, and showcase your muscles, even if they are a little tighter than you prefer.** It's better to go a size down than buy clothes that are too big unless you are going to have them tailored. They need to showcase your masculine physique. Often, men who are self-conscious about their weight prefer loose-fitting and comfortable clothes. This frequently makes them look sloppy. Tighter-fitting clothes that are wrinkle-free will make a more confident impression. Choose clothes that make you look broad, not narrow or round. If you are overweight, consider shirts that extend several inches past your belt (since this lengthens your mid-section), and never tuck your shirts in unless you pull the shirt out a bit so it looks square against your belly (rather than round). Avoid hiding your insecurities with black clothing. You need patterns and colors since these create more excitement and show confidence. Make sure your clothes don't clash with your hair or skin tone. Men are likely to wear clothes that women have expressed enthusiasm about, so seeking others' opinions while shopping will significantly enhance your confidence.

- **Ask for feedback.** Women are often flattered when someone asks for their opinion and can provide valuable insight. Find someone who represents your target audience (whether married or single) and ask if your hairstyle and beard are too flat, square, round, or thin. Would you look more confident if your hair were spiked, shorter, or colored? If you are thinning or balding, would you look better with a hat, or should you shave your head? Would you look better with a goatee, a little scruff, sideburns, or a mustache?

- **Consider cologne, fashionable shoes, socks, belts, ties, jewelry, or watches.** Until you have included accessories, you have not established a workable style (which includes athletic wear). Cologne that provides those within two feet with a subtle hint can positively impact their impression, increase chemistry, and make being close or hugging more enjoyable. Asking women about their cologne preferences can give you a good place to start. And, of course, soaps and deodorants (such as Lume, which offers a 72-hour stink-free guarantee) are a must. Nothing leaves a lasting impression, for good or bad, like pleasant aromas or repulsive odors (which includes your breath). Your shoes need to be modern, clean, and polished when required, but just as importantly, they must encourage good posture and prevent slouching.

- **Make sure the new outfits you choose are appropriate for dates.** Some of your new clothes can include professional or church attire. Still, most should be functional for a date night or activity. Adding a nice jacket or shoes can dress up a pair of jeans, so ask for suggestions on which pieces could be used interchangeably to fit different events, needs, or activities.

- **Update your hair or beard style by visiting a barber or stylist specializing in men's grooming.** This may be more expensive initially, but once you have a style you like (and receive regular compliments), you can share pictures with a local stylist who might deliver similar results. Rather than visiting Great Clips salons, stick with one stylist and schedule your next appointment before you leave. Men usually prefer to schedule as needed, so they look scraggly and unkept because they take too long to return for a haircut. Thus, booking appointments three to four weeks apart is often best.

- **Invest in good skincare and grooming.** Many women will express frustration that they are expected to invest in their appearance, while men will often do little with theirs. Getting a fresh haircut can make a great impression, but paying attention to good skin care and unsightly hair helps prevent unnecessary distractions or repulsion. Not only does a good cleanser and moisturizer prevent wrinkles, but it can also help with whiteheads, blackheads, and acne. If you have chronic acne or dandruff, a dermatologist can provide options for controlling oily or dry skin. Also, trimming the hair in your nose, ears, and around your beard and eyebrows proves you care about the details. These help you to have a polished look. Some men may invest in Botox or fillers to maintain a youthful look or control wrinkles. Do what is right for you, since this will increase your confidence and engagement with others. Additionally, many women enjoy a well-groomed man as long as he doesn't seem high-maintenance or make them feel criticized or inadequate. If you have dry hands, using Aquaphor or other deep moisturizers at night to soften calluses is also a good practice. A warm and gentle touch is difficult to achieve with rough skin.

- **Whiten teeth and consider braces or fillers.** Men with swollen gums, bad breath, or apparent plaque must visit a dentist, as their smile and hygiene are essential to a good impression. Whitening strips can be purchased at local grocery stores. When you have uneven teeth, a dentist can fill in chips or unappealing wear that distracts from your smile (which can be a quick fix before getting pictures). Braces or Invisalign may also be worth considering, especially if you notice strangers looking at your mouth rather than your eyes. You can also purchase a tongue brush or mouthwash and keep gum or mints on hand to ensure fresher breath.

Because those who invest in themselves are perceived more favorably, all these steps could make a positive impression. However, focusing on more than two from the list above may be unwise and cause you to feel resentment. Instead, recognize your effort and successes. Then, in time, add other grooming practices. It's far more effective to choose realistic goals and celebrate your strengths than it is to burden yourself with a never-ending to-do list to make you lovable.

When you remember everything, you are doing well, and then build on those, you will feel more empowered, happy, and lovable. You can't achieve any goal without

Single? It's Not You. It's Your Technique!

taking uncomfortable steps. Likewise, some of the steps above will be anxiety-inducing, but the rewards will be worth it.

The new confidence and attention you develop will make every new technique feel like a valuable addition to an already impressive presentation.

Strategies for amazing headshot photos

Singles often depend on selfies for their dating apps and social media profiles. While selfies are okay as an additional photo, tey will not impress many people as a main profile picture. Selfies are prone to exaggerating a nose, chin, or brow, and can provide unintended hints about your lifestyle by revealing a messy bedroom, kitchen, or bathroom.

Thus, a professional photographer may get you the best results when possible. If you want to try a friend first, you can always get professional pictures if it doesn't work out. Either way, use the following suggestions to help you get a great outcome that doesn't make your images seem staged or too formal.

- **Tell your photographer you want your pictures to be taken in a public place with a social atmosphere** rather than in a studio, building, or open field. This will make your photographs appear more natural and give the impression that a friend could have snapped the picture while you were in town, at dinner, or on the go. Public places are also where you will be meeting for a first date, which subconsciously creates a more natural impression. An outdoor shopping center with interesting architecture or features can provide a lot for a photographer to work with for a warm and interesting vibe. Good lighting is essential, but they know how to set this up for the right effect. You do not want harsh shadows across your face or squinty eyes from the bright sun.

- **Ask and accept suggestions for posing in more confident and masculine ways that prevent weak ankles, awkward hand positions, or poor posture.** Such positions may seem unnatural to you, but will look good on camera. A photographer usually knows how to achieve. If they make it a fun experience, your smile and eyes will appear warm and bright. So trust your photographer, and you will have an easier time relaxing and enjoying the experience.

- **Bring three outfits to the photo shoot.** Be sure to tell your photographer you will do this so they can plan extra time for you to change. Using multiple outfits allows you to use more pictures and maximize your time and investment compared to images of you in the same clothes.

- **Get head and full-body shots of each outfit with different backgrounds.** Since you will want to select at least two images for each outfit, you will need a lot of pictures. This shouldn't be hard, as the photographer will take dozens of photos.

- **Only use one picture in each outfit.** When you select your photos for social media or dating apps, you will only use one from each outfit at a time so that it doesn't seem obvious your pictures came from the same photo shoot. Spanning these pictures out or rotating them allows others to trust the consistency of your appearance because it seems they were taken at different times.

Experiment and compare results

Chad is already using dating apps but is not getting the results he desires. By updating his pictures with a fresh profile description that emphasizes his successes, he can compare the results to his previous profile. In marketing terms, this is called A/B testing.

In his previous profile, Chad had not wanted to brag about being in med school and feared attracting women who would be interested for the wrong reasons. However, he can discern those women's issues with Empathy, Self-control, and Personal responsibility (or E.S.P.) when he uses the techniques taught in the other Lasting Love Academy courses. By updating his current profile to match his brand (of a smart, hardworking, kind, and social doctor), he can compare the results to his old one. For greater accuracy, he could close his old account and open a new one or use both. This will help him measure the contrast between the two approaches and potentially give him a second chance at making a great impression (with those who had already swiped down on his first profile).

If you have tried dating apps and social media to connect with desirable singles in the past and had little success, it is most likely your pictures and, to a lesser degree, your profile introduction or posts that are turning others off. Marketing agencies spend millions of dollars on images and the right branding to create an emotional impact that drives action. Thus, it should not be surprising that fuzzy photos with harsh shadows, a hat that darkens your eyes, bad posture or camera angles that exaggerate your problem areas (like a double chin, belly, or butt), and critical or negative statements won't illicit the attention or action you desire.

Although most singles join dating apps hoping to find a relationship, they typically look for reasons to reject others. If a picture creates a negative or dark vibe, they often swipe down immediately. If someone's posture looks awkward, they may falsely assume that the person lacks confidence or has social challenges. And, if they read a dating profile just in case the person is more exceptional than their pictures suggest (or see someone on social media who seems interesting), they will still look for any negative detail to justify their desire to guiltlessly dismiss the person as a romantic option.

By contrast, when your pictures have good lighting, bright smiles, and warm backgrounds, singles will linger longer and read your profile to look for reasons to say yes. When you express your positive attributes and experiences creatively, they feel more intrigued and open to a few messages or even a date before they decide to write you off. Thus, if you provide a fun, low-pressure, or compelling way for them to comment or engage, they may take action for no other reason than to satisfy their curiosity.

Every few months, switch your attention to new apps and websites or resume your efforts to connect with singles through social media. This will give you access to

Single? It's Not You. It's Your Technique!

people who have yet to see you. If you are up for the extra time and effort, you can test two sets of pictures and bios on separate apps or social media accounts. For instance, one can represent you as more playful and the other as a working professional. A resilient, curious, and fun attitude about what works and doesn't will help you stay engaged until you achieve the desired results.

If you stay with the same app for over six months, you need to close and reopen a new account, this time with a different bio and pictures. Don't hesitate to take a break from an app and return to it after a few months. You will be surprised by how many new faces there are. Canceling an old profile and creating a new one with new pictures will also allow you to be seen by everyone (including those who have previously rejected you). Just keep shaking things up while having fun with the process and doing more of what works.

Techniques for impressive and engaging profile photos

Because singles will be looking for ways to connect with you, your social media and dating app profiles must present you as likable and inviting.

- **View all your social media as if it were a dating profile.** Since many singles do not like dating apps and are discouraged by the quality of singles they find there, they commonly search social media (i.e., Facebook, Instagram, LinkedIn, Twitter, etc.) for new and better faces. This means that random strangers, friends of friends, and recent acquaintances (who are searching for a way to connect with you) will be reading your posts, viewing your pictures, and sizing you up. Many people treat social media as a journal of their experiences, posting both positive and negative comments, as well as off-color jokes or videos. If this describes you, you need to have a private and public social media page. The private one should be limited to close friends and family, with restrictions on others, including friends of friends, viewing your page. On the public page, make sure you post less, your pictures look great, and your messages are positive. Perhaps you worry that this will represent a false image of who you are, but remember, it is not wise to give the best (or most vulnerable part) of you to those who don't invest in you. Your public image is your advertising tool. Who you are in your intimate life is your privilege to reveal to only those you know and trust.

- **Search for current pictures or start taking them with others.** Singles often say they don't have many photos of themselves, and asking others to find or take pictures of them would be awkward. However, you may discover that friends or family have pinned you in their photos on social media. Thus, a quick search on Facebook or Instagram may give you fast results. You can download or screenshot these images. From here forward, however, be sure to get a selfie while with friends or family or when doing a fun activity. This is more normal than you may think. And don't hesitate to request that they retake a photo if your eyes are closed or you don't like your smile. Others do this all the time, so they won't think it is weird unless you seem sheepish about it. Don't worry about asking others in a picture for permission to use an image on social media or a dating site. If they posed for the camera, it's probably fine. You can crop or blur an image to protect others (like your children) if you feel it is necessary for an occasional photo. If you do this on most of your photos, it will seem that you have excessive concerns or trust issues.

- **Your main profile picture should include a good headshot with a full body picture in your profile.** Your additional photos should also include one full-body image. This will help you feel confident that others are reaching out because they generally accept your body type.

- **Select four to six likability pictures.** If others are to perceive you as approachable and desirable, you need to include photos of you with friends, children, grandparents, and animals. Doing this makes you seem real, socially skilled, or likable. In contrast, those who don't have such pictures can seem self-centered, fake, or untrustworthy (especially when their images include guns or dead fish and animals). Some of your pictures can have a baseball hat or a less flattering pose. Still, you need at least two good pictures emphasizing your masculine confidence. Body language matters, so if you need to choose between an action picture, where you look less confident but are with great people, that's fine. However, if you have plenty of pictures, always go for the ones that make a better impression. Include between three to ten pictures. If most of your images are not awesome, trust that sometimes less is more. Others will usually fill in the gaps of what they don't see with hopeful possibilities and curiosity that could drive them to action. So stick with three of your best pictures rather than adding unattractive ones.

- **Show others that they can have fun with you.** Because singles unconsciously foreshadow themselves into a picture (at the opera, on a hike, kayaking, or at a family party), they will be more likely to pass on you if they don't see themselves enjoying an activity in your pictures. So, consider others' needs and preferences when picking your photos. You can still use your images at the symphony, a hockey game, or rock climbing (since these may reach those with the same passion), but express in your posts or messages that you have an open mind to discovering new adventures, too. Just as you want others to say yes to you, try finding a reason to say yes to them. If someone uses hunting or fishing pictures, and you know you would never want to join them, consider the outdoor activities you could share. Are you open to ATVing, camping, or visiting national parks? If you don't like football, would you be open to learning more about the game or a favorite team so you can at least share these passions with others? When singles focus on their differences, they disconnect. However, when they acknowledge and build on their commonalities, they create meaningful connections and feel more hopeful.

- **Remember how men and women bond differently and offer what they need.** When selecting your profile pictures, remember that women need to feel safe and secure, and the best way for you to help them feel this way is to demonstrate that you have good relationships with friends and family by including them in your pictures or bio. Contrarily, men tend to bond through doing side-by-side activities. To help a woman feel comfortable joining you in these activities, you may need to meet over a snack or dinner first. You can also offer an activity in a public place. These encourage conversation, which women often want; however, in time, both of you will be better served by engaging in an activity together. High-energy activities increase the possibility of chemistry because of the adrenaline, endorphins, and dopamine that the activities create. Activities are also less pressure, fun, and productive, which is good for both of you. These differences between men and women explain why men often show their hunting, hiking, or boating pictures and share less about themselves or their important relationships in their bios, which is the reverse for women. Therefore, if in doubt, cover all your bases by providing both in your bio, posts, or Instagram stories. This encourages stereotypical and non-stereotypical women to find you interesting and provides meaningful options that could help you enjoy time together.

- **Appeal to your target audience's preferences in a potential partner.** When identifying your target audience's characteristics, you may have identified traits they value most in a partner. If you aren't sure what those are, ask a woman you admire for her perspective. Women are frequently more forgiving of a man's grainy pictures or less-than-ideal image when they see highly valuable traits like ambition, intelligence, hard work, social skills, charisma, and professional success. Thus, it would be wise for you to capitalize on the attributes that make you a good partner and demonstrate your ability to maintain a secure lifestyle. These will help a woman consider you more seriously. Your ability to show you appreciate and respect her successes (versus acting threatened by them) also displays your emotional maturity and confidence.

- **Provide humble brags or hints about your success and lifestyle.** Consider how you can include your career, home, possessions, or accomplishments as a side note in a story or picture. This helps others to know if you have the attributes, they admire so you can stand out. If you fear to do this because you don't want to be exploited or worry about seeming like a braggart, you will shoot yourself in the foot. It's part of who you are. Don't spell it out, but it can be indirectly described as a side note detail. This is crucial, especially if these attributes are included in your personal brand (from the previous chapter) and are essential to your target audience's needs. A woman's desire to see a man's stability or achievements isn't shallow (although some are players looking to exploit men). For most women, this is about their need to feel safe and secure. A woman who fears that she will end up being responsible for all her needs and a man's, too, can't relax, have fun, be feminine, or respect a dating partner. By contrast, a woman who senses that a man can provide for himself and her (in appropriate ways) can do these things and even flirt too. For this reason, most women do not choose a charismatic playboy as a serious partner. They might enjoy a fun night but will not trust that he can offer what they need, so they will not stay for long. Thus, you should include images outside your house, working in your yard, next to your car, at work, or inside your home. You don't need to state these are your possessions; the suggestion of them in the background is enough to attract those who enjoy a similar lifestyle. Then, in the captions, mention something relevant to the image. For example, a picture of you in the kitchen could include, "Tried an awesome new recipe for a dinner with friends at my home." A picture of your grandma in your car's passenger seat could state, "My grandma loves going for rides in my car as she blasts her music. She is truly the coolest." A waterskiing picture could say, "My friend was driving my boat so I could try my new kneeboard." Or a picture of you with colleagues could include, "Me and my team at a trade event. I work with the funniest people." These situations give others a brief indication of your lifestyle and an opportunity to comment or ask questions. Showcasing your achievements as an indirect statement within a social or relationship context makes it less evident that you are bragging. Instead, it presents the possibility that you are simply sharing your life and meaningful relationships. If you enjoy a modest lifestyle, emphasize your hard work, responsibility, and financial security. You can include a picture of yourself doing an everyday activity or spending time with others but with a caption that mentions your work, such as, "Playing pickleball with my best friend after work" or "I enjoyed an amazing run before heading to the clinic. The fall colors were awesome." If you are worried about others figuring out your income (whether great or small), you can keep it simple by saying, "I'm blessed to have a career that meets my needs and many of my wants. Life is good." If you want a partner who will respect your modest lifestyle, take pride in who you are by stating, "I live a simple life and have always been responsible and ambitious. I'm grateful for the stability and security I enjoy."

- **Have a handful of pictures (with potential captions to go with them) ready to upload.** Most dating apps require more than one picture before a profile can be made public. Instagram is an image and video-based platform, and Facebook depends heavily on it, too. Thus, you need to have at least three to ten pictures ready to upload. Very few people will take you seriously if you share little about yourself in your bio and have only one image of you. Not all dating apps allow for captions, but all social media encourages you to describe your photos. So, when there is an easy or familiar building in the background, you can ask, "Can you guess what city I am in?" or state, "My dad and I ran a 5K together in 2023. At 65, I don't know how he can still outpace me, lol." This comment shows that the picture is a few years old and includes an obviously fun and playful connection with your dad, which adds greater likability to your profile.

- **Increase confidence in your appearance by posting the year.** A common complaint of singles is meeting for a date and then discovering that the person doesn't look like their pictures. So, to increase others' confidence in the accuracy of your images, put the date or year in the description of one of your most recent pictures. You can use an older photo or two with an important family member, an interesting event, an exotic animal, a fun vacation, or a hobby as long as you note which picture is a current representation of your appearance and body type. This may seem shallow, but it also helps you feel confident that they are comfortable with your appearance and are interested in you.

- **Present your personality (and brand) in a balanced and congruent way through words and pictures.** After your main profile photo, the additional posts, images, or messages should reveal your goals, personality, or hobbies. If you are musically talented and would love someone who also plays an instrument, include a picture of you during a performance. If you love theater, include yourself at a musical and write a caption (if the dating app provides this option) that could engage others with similar interests. "Can you guess which Broadway show?" Or, if you're a sports lover, a picture of your family watching the game could include, "My dad gets obsessed and depressed if our team doesn't win. Ten points if you can identify the epic game this was." If you love to travel, post a vacation picture and encourage others to guess where you are or ask what places they have visited or want to. And if you have a unique picture (in a cool Halloween costume, riding an elephant, or bungee jumping), post it to see if anyone asks a question or makes a comment. Be sure to keep the pictures or phrases that create the most engagement from others. The goal is to discover what works and leads to action. Since a picture can say a lot about who you are and what's important to you, don't overstate your family values, sports enthusiasm, religious activities, love of the arts, work, or active and fit lifestyle since your pictures already demonstrate these. You don't want to seem preachy or excessive in any one area. So, make sure your pictures and profile descriptions reflect multiple areas of the lifestyle, beliefs, attitudes, and hobbies you want others to associate with your personality.

- **Limit your gym and swimsuit pictures.** Men who post more than one picture at the gym, flexing in the bathroom mirror, or lying shirtless in bed can seem as if they are self-centered, only interested in women with perfect bodies, or are trolling for a hookup. Many women, including the most desirable, view muscle pictures as tacky or lacking maturity and substance. Your clothing can reveal how tone or fit you are, so unless there is a reason to expose your abs in photos (because it is part of your brand or necessary for attracting your target audience), avoid pictures that show too much skin. If fitness is essential to you, consider saying this in your profile instead of using your weightlifting or swimsuit pictures, which might give the right people a wrong impression of your intentions and the wrong people more incentive. Good boundaries show respect and confidence in yourself and others. When you remember to focus on your core values, goals, and target population as you select your pictures, you will be happier with the result. Additionally, if your pictures and profile look too good to be true (or appear too seductive), you may get rejected by the app because you could be a scammer. To avoid this, upload photos with friends and family that show you doing everyday activities. This helps to verify that your profile is authentic.

Create warm, engaging, and exciting profiles

Before you start writing your dating profiles or posting on social media, review your answers from Chapter 4 about the message (or brand) you are trying to portray, the feelings you hope others will experience when interacting with you, and the needs of your target audience. Grab another piece of paper to write notes. The following information is essential and can make you stand out. It will stimulate your creativity, trigger memories, help you craft stories, and provide phrases that make others feel compelled to engage. Additionally, it includes examples of things you will want to avoid so you can edit these out of your profile.

- **Your first sentence and paragraph need to be engaging.** You will now generate ideas for your profile and social media posts. Once you have solidified them into interesting descriptions, stories, or information, you will use the most engaging ones. The longer you keep others' attention, the more likely they will take a chance on you. For instance, if you say, "I love to hike, play pickleball, and run," others may lose interest since describing one's activities is so common that they don't feel unique. Thus, allow your creative juices to flow, and then pick the best one for the top of your profile. You should describe your hobbies; just include them later in your profile. To learn how to post something at the top of your app or social media profiles, an internet search for instructions should be helpful.

- **Describe your positive attributes (avoid being negative, making demands, using profanity, or encouraging sexual comments).** Keep your profile warm, engaging, and positive. Don't introduce yourself by saying, "My friends finally talked me into trying this," or "I never thought I'd end up here." Such statements are negative and even insulting to those on dating apps or social media. Don't use profanity, crude references, sexual innuendo, or disparaging comments about others, the opposite sex, or your ex. On some apps, sexual statements can get you banned. They turn women off and make you seem like a player, creepy, harboring unresolved issues, or potentially toxic and abusive. If you have trust or trauma issues relative to women, save them for your therapist or friends. Remember, the goal is to attract the right people and make it easy for them to say yes to you. Sharing potentially unattractive or vulnerable information not only repels the right people but also makes it easier for manipulators to exploit your issues. It is also not wise to outline what you want in others. For example, "I'm looking for someone who is honest, kind, loves my kids, is financially responsible, and wants to be active and fit"). This can seem demanding and heavy rather than inviting. Instead, describe yourself so others will see who you are through what you value and appreciate. If you want to attract educated, driven, and ambitious women, express how you love learning and encouraging others' passions, education, and ambitions. If you are looking for someone who is attractive, fun, and active, demonstrate this in your profile. If you want someone who is spiritual and has good values, talk briefly about what you're doing in your church ("I teach primary each Sunday) or how you love being around people with good morals and principles. If you want someone who likes the outdoors, discuss the activities you enjoy: "I recently hiked Waterfall Canyon." If you're looking for someone trustworthy, discuss your values and how they guide your decisions: "I've always been blessed with outstanding friends who are honest and loyal." Or, if you want someone with attributes you don't have, share how much you enjoy those with these qualities. For example, "I admire the warmth and compassion of teachers and nurses. They inspire me to be a more patient and understanding person." All these examples motivate others with such traits to feel you would enjoy and appreciate them. Thus, they are more likely to reach out to you.

- **Don't hesitate to list fun facts about yourself or share interesting things you want to do with someone before the end of Spring, Summer, Winter, or Fall.** Sharing activities you want to participate in helps others envision a fun, low-pressure way to get to know you and makes it easier for them to encourage a face-to-face date. Creating a list of seasonal date ideas is a great way to keep your dates interesting. This suggestion isn't just for men, but for women too, since men are always looking for suggestions and would prefer for you to recommend something rather than have to generate all the ideas. Don't hesitate to mention your seasonal ideas in your profile: "I have a fun list of activities and food I want to do before the end of spring, and I love discovering others' favorite activities. Let's exchange ideas and have some fun!"

- **Use humor, wit, and creativity to reveal your personality in a short story format.** Write what you want to share and a few ideas or stories that you think are interesting. Then, play with them to see how many of your values or core personality traits you can weave in. Good storytelling can be fun, playful, and witty. But avoid negative or sarcastic comments as these can land differently than you intend or paint you as someone critical or unkind. For instance, lightly joking about yourself while positively spinning the story can show you don't take yourself too seriously. "I got a bachelor's in English Literature, which set me up for a career in … nothing. I hate it when my dad is right. So now I am a stable, responsible, and well-read accountant. You'll like water skiing behind my boat more than eating Top Ramen while I quote Shakespeare, but if you prefer, we can do both to decide for yourself, lol." This demonstrates your education, career, playfulness, love of reading, and financial success (as evidenced by your possessions) while providing fun questions they could ask relative to your relationship with your dad.

- **Describe your hobbies, sports, vacations, and goals.** Unless you entertainingly illustrating these, describe them in the middle of your profile. Sharing these details helps you, others, and the dating app's algorithm to match you with those of similar interests. They can also lead to conversations about potential dates you can enjoy. Your pictures can illustrate a lot about you and your priorities; however, your bio or posts need to fill in the gaps. This is where you share your hobbies, passions, values, education, and work experiences. For example, "After getting home from the clinic, I'm often rock climbing with friends, going to my nephew's soccer games, or having a blast at my improv class," which indicates a potential medical career, family values, an active and social lifestyle, and something unique that you are exploring. Any of these could create curiosity and be a conversation starter, "Wow, Improv! How fun. How long have you been doing that?" It can also allow someone to share something similar, like, "What a great uncle! I love watching my three-year-old niece at dance lessons. It seriously cracks me up!" When you read others' profiles, you need to look for opportunities to make such comments. Thus, before posting your profile, ask yourself what comments your bio and pictures could elicit as well.

- **Use prompts to stimulate ideas. Many dating apps provide drop-down prompts to help you create your profile bio.** These can be useful in generating topics that make people more interesting, but don't hesitate to craft your profile your way. You can always make changes later. For example, if the emotions you hope others will feel when they read your profile are curiosity, humor, and warmth, you could complete the prompt, "Others would say that I am ..." with the response, "a tease. I once wrapped cellophane over the toilet to prank my brother. But then my grandmother came over. OOPS! You won't believe what it took to avoid being disowned—then again, I am her favorite!" which shows your personality while hitting all three goals. If this includes a caption accompanying a picture of you with your grandma, others will likely comment, "That's hilarious!" or share a prank of their own. Such a post would be great on social media, too. If you don't get any reactions or comments after a few months, look for how somebody could take it differently than intended, or accept it as feedback and try something else next time. Here are other prompts and illustrations to get your creative juices flowing.

  » **A few fun facts about me** (consider interesting or unique experiences from childhood, vacations you have taken, or an unusual experience you've had) …My first kiss was at the ripe old age of five. I got my first car at 16 and then drove it into my neighbor's tree. I love hiking, rock climbing, and traveling with my brothers. They are my best friends. And, since my grandfather passed away, I've become my grandmother's monthly date to local plays, something we both enjoy.

  » **Two truths and a lie** (consider extreme examples to make it difficult for them to know which is the lie) …I nearly died when getting my Boy Scout's merit badge, I narrowly escaped a tsunami, and I am one of 12 children. These may seem extreme, but when you consider the little things you've done or places you've been, you may find details in your life more interesting than you would initially consider. So, take a minute to review some random facts about your life and see if you can create something incredible.

  » **Fun things I want to do this Summer**…Explore a cave, learn to rock climb, go to an outdoor summer concert, experience a Holi Festival, take a cooking class, and discover another person's favorite dessert. Want to join me? This shows that you are active, creative, and willing to go places while caring about others' interests.

> » **My most significant accomplishments are**…Finishing my degrees, buying my dream car, and raising my kind-hearted and amazing kids. This demonstrates a love of education, accomplishment, and family values.

> » **My dreams, hobbies, and goals**…Over the next few years, I hope to travel to Europe, take a cruise, and overcome my fear of heights. To invite others to respond, you could add, I'd love to hear your wish list." The things included in this prompt may seem cliche since many singles have similar travel goals, so be sure to personalize it with more details like, "I want to visit 10 castles in Europe."

> » **My friends would say I am**…quick to crack jokes, have fun, and make time for them (whether moving, having a hard day, or joining them for a run). My mom would also say I am handsome, smart, and the nicest boy you'd ever meet. She might even reveal that I'm secretly her favorite. These statements reveal admirable qualities like loyalty, good relationships, and a sense of humor.

> » **I see myself as**…a class act, who isn't afraid to be romantic when needed—but let's keep that a secret, I've got a tough-guy image to uphold." This can make a muscular guy seem more likable or an average and small guy seem funny and able to joke about his size.

> » **What I love most about my life so far and what's next**…Playing with my siblings and cousins in the family orchard and the time I spent with my younger adopted brothers are my favorite childhood memories. Nowadays, I'd love to buy and update a fixer-upper as a project to do with someone I love. These statements share details about you and provide opportunities for others to ask questions about the orchard and your family. It's personal and warm, so it contrasts nicely against a remarkable success that you could hint at.

- **Review your answers from the perspective of your target audience.** When considering an app's prompts, avoid choosing ones that are potentially negative, critical, or would make others question whether you would be enjoyable to interact with. Sarcasm can seem witty but also mean, so use it carefully.

- **To make your everyday activities stand out, use active (versus passive) language and include your relationships in the details.** If you read these examples and feel woefully dull by comparison, don't despair. You simply need to capitalize on your daily activities in more interesting ways. Use active words instead of passive ones as captions that illustrate your pictures. Doing this will help people to perceive you more positively. For example, using a picture of you reading a book or completing a puzzle is a passive activity. It isn't going to excite a reader. However, saying, "I love doing puzzles with my grandma while she tells me about her fascinating life experiences." or "I have a goal to read a new book each week. Do you have any suggestions?" or "I love doing woodwork on the weekends, binge-watching an old TV series that my friends like, and playing card games with my dad. We both cheat and vehemently deny it." These examples take an ordinary month and turn it into an impressive list because of the active language and relationships woven into the details. Even if these are infrequent activities, they illustrate your values and personality. Make sure you eliminate any messages that are negative and replace them with an active list of things you hope to do, such as "I'm so bored, and it seems impossible to meet anyone" to "I've got a list of fun things I want to do this Summer. Join me!" It is also important not to overemphasize how busy you are at work or with your family, since this will give others the impression that you are too busy for a relationship. Instead, state, "My schedule is pretty busy, but there is always time for a quick call and fun activity."

- **Adapt your profile to fit others' interests.** When you find something compelling in a person's profile, don't hesitate to change yours to include something similar. Don't misrepresent yourself; simply highlight facts about yourself that match these interests. If someone shares something that emotionally impacts you, then sharing something similar may do the same for others. And, if you recognize that someone has interests in things with which you have little experience, express that you would love to enjoy a new activity (sport, book series, recipe, instrument, foreign language, or artistic talent) with a fun and patient partner. You can also state this when sending them a message.

- **Remember what the opposite sex desires most.** As described in Chapter 3, the number one need of a woman is to feel safe and secure, so make sure you include statements that emphasize your values, relationships with others, and hard work. Don't overstate these things (or she will distrust your sincerity), but mention them. Most women want to know that a man has stable employment, is pursuing higher education, or is engaging in religious, cultural, or social activities. If you want women to take you seriously, talk about these things. Don't mention your income level unless you make over $100,000 yearly (and only if this question is included as a drop-down menu option). It can seem boastful to mention a higher level of income, and can set you up for money-diggers; nonetheless, hinting at your success will make you seem more driven, ambitious, and hard-working, which is very attractive to women. Emphasizing your professional success may help you attract more women. However, if you fear being exploited (or undervalued), it would be better not to reveal your income or professional status online. Instead, describe the industry you work in, such as a medical, legal, computer technology, or education field. Let her get to know you for the first few weeks; then, you can divulge whether you are a technician or in a high-level position. This way, she'll know more about you before learning these details. If you want to make a general statement like, "I enjoy a stable and fun career and lifestyle," this can appeal to a larger number of women without making you too vulnerable, since such statements are relative. Instead of outlining all of your possessions, you would do better with a picture of you on your ATV or working in your yard outside your house.

- **If you enjoy self-improvement, talk about it, but don't overemphasize it.** If you want to share your love for self-care and personal improvement (like counseling, essential oils, dietary supplements, a vegan lifestyle, uncommon healing or spiritual practices, and popular self-help books), hint at them, but save the details for later. It can be attractive when people state, "I love learning, and I try to be self-aware," since too many people aren't this way. It can feel refreshing to know that someone has the capacity to be vulnerable and authentic. However, those who share the details of their recovery from abuse, addiction, trauma, or physical and mental challenges too quickly can be viewed as emotionally needy, unstable, overly sensitive, or even manipulative. The simple use of self-help jargon can seem safe enough. Still, if others aren't familiar with it, it may seem off-putting or indicate that you are too high-maintenance. It's not that you are wrong for being human and having real issues (like everyone else). It's just best to select the right time. Only give the best (or most personal and vulnerable parts) of you to those who invest in you. When you share a meaningful connection built on your similarities, they can view your growing revelations about your unique beliefs as a sign of intimacy and trust. Also, being vulnerable too soon can make you a target for manipulators who exploit or use this information to create false trust. Instead, show others (instead of telling them) that you have the gift of emotional warmth, availability, and healthy boundaries. Over time, you can reveal that these behaviors developed through the self-care practices you've invested in. Mature people will often recognize and appreciate your respectful limits and even recognize them as healthy (because they have also engaged in self-help). They will enjoy the fun and relaxation you offer and your willingness to become more open in time. For example, if someone asks you a question, it's appropriate to state, "I'll share the long story as we get to know each other better, but here's the short version (or the valuable lessons I've gained) for now."

- **Spell-check your profile. Spelling and grammar errors can be hard to catch.** Using Grammarly.com or downloading the app will help catch and eliminate your mistakes. With such easy and free tools, there isn't a good reason not to use them. A failure to catch such errors can cause them to question your education, intelligence, or language competency. It's better to make a good first impression. As they get to know you, they will have more information about your strengths and warm personality to balance your weaknesses. So, take a few minutes to have others or Grammarly check your posts, messages, and profile.

- **Use an alternate name or nickname if you are worried about others finding or identifying you.** In the past, singles had to be creative about creating unique usernames, but this is not common nowadays. Some apps use your social media to log in or set up your profile (which gives them access to your pictures). This means they may use your name unless you can restrict it. If you are worried about your safety (which you should be), it is often better to use an email to set up their profiles. You can use a nickname, middle name, or initials to protect your identity and family.

- **Include a call to action that makes it easy and inviting for them to message you.** You need to include several possible and easy ways for others to engage. Some can be indirect, while others are clear and inviting. For example, a picture of you bungee jumping could be easy for someone to comment on or ask about. "Wow. That seems exhilarating but terrifying, too. Was this your first jump, or do you do it often?" However, providing a more obvious way to engage may get better results. "I'm looking forward to experiencing a Lantern or Holi Festival this Summer. Have you ever tried one? Do you have a summer activity or food that you love and recommend? I'm always looking for new ideas." Your profile is incomplete until you offer one clear way for others to engage. This could be done with a simple message at the end of your profile, such as, "If you like what you see, I'd love to hear what fun things you've been doing lately (or want to do)."

- **If you prefer to be succinct by using a bulleted or descriptive list of words rather than sentences, you will get mixed results.** Some people like to spell out who they are in short words or phrases. This can seem efficient, informative, and dry, yet it can work well for some. It won't trigger strong emotions, but it might impress those who are tired of fluff. Thus, it is worth trying as a comparison to other approaches. For example, "Hardworking, honest, parent of two boys, full-time career, have a home, am responsible, play pickleball, and enjoy hiking. Send me a message if you want to know more, and let's meet sooner rather than later to see if we feel a connection." This example shares the important qualifying characteristics of what someone might hope to learn. Still, it is also hard to read their personality or start a conversation. If you choose this approach because you like how simple, straightforward, and direct it is, you need to warm up your first message and provide more details about things you have been doing. Otherwise, others will feel you are too busy and unapproachable and lose interest quickly. Nevertheless, if your list is impressive, others will often be interested enough to engage in a message or two to see what might happen.

- **Your profile is ready to go when you have three intriguing paragraphs of information and one easy way for someone to engage.** Keep your profile introduction short and simple. Very few people will read more than four paragraphs, and can be overwhelmed quickly by them (since it is time-consuming and can make you seem like you're trying too hard or could be needy). Likewise, someone who writes less than two paragraphs (or none) will seem lazy. Many apps limit the number of characters you can have in each section, so editing your thoughts is crucial. With practice, you will improve at including valuable details in each sentence while eliminating unnecessary words. You need to make an effort so that others will have enough information to work with; however, less is often more and creates better engagement. Thus, don't force yourself to put more than you need. Take a final look for any content that does not match your brand or detracts from the emotions you want to create and remove it. This keeps them focused on what is most important. Once you have said enough, take confidence in knowing that leaving them intrigued, entertained, or impressed with a simple way to start a conversation is enough.

- **Keep an experimental and resilient attitude.** Treat your dating apps and social media as experiments that require time to get right. When you find what works or creates the best engagement, always stick with it. To discover what is

Single? It's Not You. It's Your Technique!

most effective, you may enjoy testing two different profiles simultaneously. For example, one could be warm, engaging, and playful, while the other is more business, intellectual, or efficient. If you do this on the same app, use different pictures, emails, and credit cards so the app or social media program won't limit or restrict you. One profile could present you as more focused on family or friends, and the other on your activities, work experiences, or some of your special interests and idiosyncrasies (like love for Comicon, Dungeons and Dragons, or crocheting). After a month or more, compare which pictures got the most comments, posts, messages, and subsequent dates. Then, you can decide how to integrate these approaches or keep them both if you like the contrasting matches they provide. This approach, in marketing terms, is called A/B testing and is a great way to be practical and have fun. The more you view your profiles as an experiment in which the data, information, and results are about your technique, not you personally, the more resilient and playful you may feel. So have fun with it, and don't get too attached to one approach. A typical response rate for someone with a great profile is one mutual match per every ten yeses (or likes, friend requests, and messages). Thus, until you have said yes to over fifty people, you can't adequately measure the effectiveness of your profile. Some people will never see your message because they are inactive on the dating app or social media. Your results are exceptional if you receive more than ten mutual matches after 50 yeses. If you are getting five or fewer, they are below average, and improving your profile would be wise. After making changes, wait a month before you make additional changes. When you switch up your profile pictures, add different ones from your photo shoot, or say something new in your profile bio. Discover what works and do more of that.

- **Delete and create a new profile when needed.** As long as your dating app recycles its members, new pictures will help others who may have previously swiped down on you to get a fresh impression. If this is not the case, and you have been on the app for a year or more, it would be better to cancel and create a new profile with entirely different pictures. You can always pause an account, switch to a different app, and, when ready, return to the first one. However, if you have been on an app before and want to be seen by everyone, canceling the old account and creating a new one may be necessary. Either way, when you return to an old app, use new pictures and change your bio (unless you had great success with it initially). A few months can make a big difference and offer new people to meet. After a few months of being on an app, you will have seen most of the available options, so staying longer won't yield large numbers like you experienced in the beginning. When communication slows down, this can be a good time to jump on social media and send friend requests. Keeping one to two apps and social media in regular rotation will help you engage with the most singles and maintain a steady

- **If you aren't getting the engagement you desire, ask those you respect and admire for feedback.** It is normal to have a feast and famine experience when following the techniques outlined here. This does not mean that you are doing something wrong. Nevertheless, ask a few women you respect to review your profile for possible ways your pictures or posts could be interpreted differently than you intended (especially if you get strong or critical reactions from women). Ask what they would assume you were about if they didn't know you. What would make you seem more desirable? What would they want to know about you? Then, share your brand and target audience and request their suggestions on how to reach others effectively.

Ensure your and your children's personal and financial safety

- **Control what others can learn about you.** Rarely do singles stalk themselves, but since others might, they need to know what others can find through a simple online search.

- **Start with your name, phone number, and address.** Go to Google.com and put your name into the search bar. Try different variations of your name (including nicknames, middle, and maiden) to see if somebody can find your work or home address and phone numbers. Then, do a phone and address search to see what comes up. Your search may reveal nothing, or there may be several pages. Click on every link until you are confident that you have seen it all. Did your telephone, address, age, family, friends, Facebook, LinkedIn, Instagram, or other social media reveal sensitive information? Is your phone tied to your address or name? Did your LinkedIn profile offer any contact information, emails, business and home addresses, or phone numbers? Does your employer share anything about you on their About Us or other pages? Do a search regarding your work number. Does it provide personal information or an address to your office? If so, don't make calls from that number. Do you have a home landline (which is rare these days)? If so, it will provide public information unless you request it be blocked. A cell phone typically doesn't include personal information, but that doesn't mean it is safe, especially if you have listed it for business purposes and used it online or on LinkedIn. If your phone settings allow others to see your name when you text or call, you can search for how to restrict this. With strangers you meet online or in person, only use a phone whose numbers in a search don't reveal your name, work, or address. If your phone number isn't safe, you will need to get a Google number and use it instead, which is easy. Simply Google how, and you will have a new and free number within minutes. You can redirect this number to your cell or computer, so you won't have to get a new phone.

- **Block or restrict sensitive information if you can.** Whitepages.com provides a detailed list of numbers, names, addresses, and even family members. Thus, it is essential to review what is shared there. Some of what is available about you will require a paid subscription, but you can get a one-day trial to explore what others would learn if they were willing to pay to get it. Fortunately, you can request to have some of this information restricted. Search to learn how. Other reputable sites also provide ways to block information or correct inaccuracies. And finally, did you find any public documents posted about you, such as news, divorce, social media, or criminal records? If others can see adverse reports about you, you need to learn how to resolve or remove these records. Be prepared to address what is in them (because once you share your name, others may find these posts). If these are on social media, you can request that slanderous information be taken down if your situation fits their criteria.

- **Until your social media and web search are free of sensitive information, DO NOT give others your FULL NAME or USE PICTURES that are available online.** If you provide your name (even when it is a common one), someone can perform a search with it and then refer to your pictures to determine which account is yours. Suppose you only provide a nickname, initials, or first name. In that case, they can download a picture from your dating app (or screenshot it) and then do a Google image search to find the same picture online. If this picture is in a social media account, it will give your full name, from which they could do additional searches. Although social media doesn't include your phone or address unless you offer them, once someone has your name, they can search for other information. You need to know if LinkedIn provides your work or other contact information. Review all your children's pictures or posts to see if you (or friends and family) reference their school or activities. Remove photos of them in front of their Jr. High or dance studio (for instance). Strangers mustn't know where to find them. If you post (or have posted) events on Facebook that include your home address, they will know where you live. Only share these details through a personal message. Doing a thorough search to discover what compromising or unsafe information is available about you may be uncomfortable. Still, it is essential and will give you peace of mind. Until you are sure that all of your social media is safe, **only offer strangers 1) your first name,** a false name, or initials, **2) pictures that are unique and unavailable anywhere online** (including pictures of your kids), and **3) a safe telephone number**. If they question why, share that you prefer to provide personal information after you get to know someone better. Emotionally mature people will understand that this is a safe and healthy request and will not push you to trust them immediately. End contact with anyone who pressures you to provide your name or address.

- **Social media can increase confidence and trust.** Since women fear assault from men, if you want to instill trust in a woman, you can give her your social media information so she can learn more about you. However, the best practice is to meet at a public place for the first date or two. Since this doesn't put either person at risk, sharing full names and social media isn't necessary until you know you are both interested enough to keep spending time together. Exchanging phone numbers before a date helps prevent miscommunications resulting from being late or lost. When a number is safe, there is little reason not to share it. A full name is different and comes with more risk, but providing it is also a sign of trust that neither has anything to hide. Waiting for a few weeks before sharing your name with a woman isn't unusual, but more than this will trigger alarms (just as it would if she is unwilling to share hers). Once you have the other's name, searching for them on social media is common. Don't post comments or contact their friends or family; you will seem creepy and inappropriate if you do (unless you ask first). Sending a friend request or following someone with fewer than 100 friends or followers could make them feel pressured and trigger awkward questions or assumptions from family. When considering exclusivity, you can share your desire to spend time with friends and family, which provides valuable information and experience. Once she is ready to introduce you to others, you can start commenting on posts and sending these individuals friend requests or messages. It is also important to note that unless you view an Instagram story anonymously (perform a search to learn how), the person will know. Thus, until you are exclusive, limit how often you visit their page, or it may seem excessive and concerning.

- **Use public and private profiles (for when you want to share personal or sensitive information with family and friends online).** Suppose you enjoy posting personal information and pictures for friends and family (which may include vulnerable or sensitive details about you and your experiences). In that case, it is best to have one social media account for dating and socializing purposes and another private account for close friends and family. This private account can have photos and posts others don't see, but only if you mark them private. Only a few social media platforms offer this option. Facebook can make it easy, but you must not mark each post as private and set up your account this way. If you forget, others will see your posts. Search for the best way to ensure your profile stays private. Once you accept someone's Facebook friend request, they will see all your private posts and pictures, which is not wise if you don't know them well. Family won't misuse your information or vulnerability, but they might. Since rejecting friend requests can be uncomfortable, you can accept them on your public Facebook page instead so that your private page remains exclusive to only those you respect and trust.

- **Limit your income, career, or financial information until you trust their intentions.** Don't give others money until you know they are real. If you have achieved economic success or public recognition, you may become a target for money-diggers. Both men and women should fear exploitation and catfishing. Still, they can provide a general impression that they are responsible and financially comfortable. For example, they could state their profession, such as the medical, legal, fitness, labor, or public services, and then state, "I'll tell you more once I know you better." Because women appreciate drive, ambition, and responsibility, it is helpful if you share that you work full-time and have a steady income that meets your needs and many of your wants. Continue to share more over time, but don't hesitate to emphasize that "Everyone wants to be seen and appreciated for who they are, not what they do." Most people will respond well to this answer. If your partner asks for money to meet their needs, move on. Their reaction reveals that their intentions are not sincere. Always say no to requests for money until you have 1) talked with three trusted friends and shared all the details you know about your partner and relationship, 2) you are exclusive with your partner, and 3) you have met their family and friends, and they have met yours during several face-to-face interactions. These steps will ensure they are real people and not catfishing you.

When to pursue (and when not to)

When you are ready, only flirt with those who are on your A and B lists. Whether on social media, a dating app, or interacting with others in everyday encounters, consider whether a person would be on your A, B, friend, or rejection list. Only those with the qualities you desire should be on your A or B-list (no matter how attractive they may be). The difference between A and B-listers is that you are **reasonably attracted to B-listers**, whereas you experience a **higher level of attraction or excitement for A-listers**. **Friends are those you don't feel chemistry with**, and those on the **rejection list would include people you don't enjoy or want to spend time with**. Categorizing people in this way may seem wrong. However, whether you formalize your decision-making or not, you are still rejecting some and not others (and they are doing the same with you, too). No one wants to be on someone's B-list (or outright rejected), but this isn't practical. Fortunately, B-list options can transition to an A-list after a great date. As long as everyone treats each other respectfully, no one gets hurt by spending time together and having fun over a few texts, calls, or dates. An A and B-list designation is not a judgment of the other person's value. It merely reflects what you are looking for in a potential partner and how you feel when with them. Of course, you shouldn't tell others what list they are on since this would be weird and potentially hurtful, but you can engage in ways that respectfully communicate (in words and actions) the nature of your relationship.

To open yourself up to more dating, think about it differently by taking the pressure off yourself and not overthinking potential conversations (or dates). This will help you to focus on having fun, improving your skills, and leaving the door open for chemistry. Unless you say yes to exchanging numbers, texts, phone calls, and dates, you can't get to a better place or the secure, passionate relationship you desire. When you have adequate attraction and sufficient reasons to do so, many benefits come from interacting with the opposite sex. It gives you valuable experience, new perspectives, and potentially fun interactions and opportunities for practicing better techniques and skills. You will never date the people you want to date if you aren't good at attracting and maintaining a date's interest. Singles frequently put too much pressure on themselves and others. Fortunately, you can mitigate your and their overanalysis by communicating that you prefer to go slow, have fun, and limit expectations beyond mutual respect (especially during the first month or so). Keeping affection simple and nonsexual (such as playfully pushing, holding hands, cuddling, or sharing a short kiss) helps you enjoy your shared experiences while ensuring you have no regrets. If you are having a positive experience, go on four to six dates (to see if the person becomes or stays your A-lister). However, don't go on more than six dates if this is not the case. Please note that if you chronically struggle to feel what you think you should (even with those who are attractive and desirable), you are not alone. Avoidant attachment patterns trigger feelings of indifference and doubt in otherwise healthy and compatible relationships. Fortunately, the Lasting Love Academy books and courses can help you break this pattern. Visit LastingLoveAcademy.com to discover additional techniques for breaking this cycle.

When you need to friend-zone someone that you truly enjoy and hope to interact as friends but not more (because you don't feel a desire to touch, cuddle, or kiss them), you need to let them know. You can do this by warmly stating, "I don't feel a romantic connection but would love to be friends because you are so fun."

However, if you are uncertain whether a friend could become something, and you want to find out if you can feel chemistry with them, then dating would be best. To avoid being permanently friend-zoned, you must explore simple affection within the first month to six weeks. Otherwise, one of you may never develop chemistry with the other. Women can more easily fall in love with a male friend and discover chemistry later; however, men usually have to feel attraction and chemistry early on, or it won't develop later. Exploring simple affection should not mean exclusivity, which puts too much pressure on a person's limited (but growing) feelings. Once you explore affection, if you don't feel more than friendship, you can step back and express a desire to remain friends. To do this, be practical and honest with them, which includes congruent words and actions and eliminates physical affection (unless it is clear that teasing touch and warm hugs are not confusing for either of you).

With all these options, you also need to respect your right to say no or simply not engage. You can do this in a guilt-free way when you create a decision-making model for when to flirt or pass on other singles.

To keep it simple, walk away or disengage when:

1. They don't seem compatible with what you desire (as defined in Chapter 4 or your Top-Ten List).

2. You don't believe you could have fun with them and aren't willing to engage in a way that makes them feel great.

3. You see red flags due to their lack of Empathy, Self-control, and Personal responsibility (or E.S.P.).

4. You are not reasonably attracted to them and don't see that changing.

There is no reason to waste your time or theirs under these circumstances. Trying to shame (or should) yourself into dating someone you don't enjoy or can't imagine kissing (even though they are a great person) is a waste of your time and theirs. Instead, go for those for whom you feel a reasonable attraction. It is appropriate to ignore social media messages, friend requests, and dating app matches since this is an acceptable and common practice for showing you are not interested. Similarly, shortening or ending a face-to-face interaction or conversation without an invitation to continue it at another time could indicate your disinterest. Similarly, if you find someone highly attractive but they are regrettably incompatible or potentially unhealthy and toxic, avoid temptation by not engaging. It is far easier to prevent unnecessary contact than to indulge in it, even when you think you can keep your heart in check. Avoiding trouble (even when the feelings are intoxicating) is easier than recovering from heartache.

Why dating B-listers is essential and wise

- **Refine and improve your techniques and confidence through pursuing B-listers.** A true A-lister is someone YOU value most, which means when you love and adore someone (and they treat you the same), they become your A-lister. However, before you discover your personal A-lister, you will find some people less exciting but enjoyable and sufficiently attractive and interesting (i.e., they will be your B-lister). Others will be on your friends' or rejection list. For many reasons, B-listers might move to your A-list, which is why engaging and dating them for up to six dates to discover if this is the case is a wise practice. Dating those on your B-list has other benefits, too. You will not feel as anxious about whether you make a mistake, can get and keep their attention, or might be rejected by them. Feelings of pressure and self-scrutiny can make you act and feel more insecure. Since you won't be as tense about them, this is less of a problem, making it easier to relax and radiate confidence or act naturally. Your behaviors and words will often feel great and cause you to wish you could act in these ways with A-listers. Fortunately, when you remember and become skilled at recreating these behaviors and attitudes and practice them regularly, they will develop muscle memories and skills you can draw upon at will. You can then exude the same confidence under pressure or with your A-listers. Additionally, practicing new techniques is far easier with your B-listers. If you do them awkwardly the first few times, you won't feel as upset or worry about rejection if it occurs. Contrarily, the positive effects and success you experience will make pursuing those you desire easier. Please note that there are still core differences between the physical characteristics of the most attractive and those of average appearance. Without your exceptional success, social skills, and status, or money to gain their attention, you still may not achieve dates with the most desirable women.

- **After experiencing more success and confidence with B-listers, pursue A-listers to discover your limits**. In any society, there are many physical qualities and social skills that are highly prized and often associated with A-list individuals, which is why 90% of men (who by nature are more visually motivated) will express attraction for and pursue the same 10% of women (even though such individuals are out of their league). Likewise, 80% of women are impressed by the same 20% of men and will hold out hope for attracting them (while rejecting those who don't fit this standard). Fortunately, for average-looking men, women find a higher percentage of men desirable because they consider personality traits equal to, and sometimes more critical than, appearance. Because the most desirable have more options, their standards and expectations can be excessive. Thus, those who pursue them suffer a higher rejection rate, no matter how exceptional they are. This (and the avoidant attachment pattern, which is so common among this group) is why highly desirable singles are not all married and struggle like everyone else to find lasting love. Therefore, you must remember your goal isn't the external validation of others but sharing a good chemistry with someone who makes you feel great. You can keep improving your pictures and pursuing skills. Still, in time, you will hit a ceiling that indicates more desirable singles will rarely or never engage or accept dates because you have reached your limit of desirability among this group. Rather than chasing perfection in yourself and others, please consider that at the end of it all, love is a choice, and lasting love is a skill that two people must embrace. Perfection is not what makes someone lovable. In fact, your imperfections help others connect and feel comfortable in your presence (because they are painfully aware of their imperfections, too). Fortunately, pursuing the most desirable singles isn't necessary for achieving a successful outcome, which is good since it won't work for most people. Chemistry and lasting love do not depend on exceptional bodies and facial features. With the right techniques and a willing partner, you can achieve an amazing relationship that is fulfilling, fun, passionate, and meaningful. Looks fade, but these outcomes are what everyone longs for, so don't throw them away when you have them. Nevertheless, if you would regret not doing so, take the confidence you find from dating B-listers and go for those you find most desirable. When they respond to you, don't forget that it is better to be with someone who is good for you and to you. Set limits on how much you will do or put up with to secure the attention of those who are most desirable by society's standards.

- **Consider other personal and relationship skills and get feedback.** If you can consistently achieve first or second dates with those you desire most, but not relationships, don't waste time improving your social media or level of attraction. These are not your issues. You need to consider your communication, listening skills, vulnerability, anxious and avoidant attachment patterns, and ability to physically and emotionally connect. Feedback from dates and others will be essential to the results you desire.

Don't overthink initial conversations and future dates

- **Don't worry about conversations and dates being a big deal.** Many singles resist dating those on their B-list because they fear leading others on and don't want to hurt people. However, singles are not fragile and have enough experience (or soon will) to realize that kindness, warmth, and a few dates rarely end in commitment. So, don't make decisions for others by eliminating their choices before they have them. Don't read their minds. Your assumptions are usually wrong and imply they are sensitive and weak rather than strong and confident. And don't psych yourself out by assuming you will embarrass yourself and won't be able to face them. People rarely pay attention to others because they are too consumed in their lives and problems. All they want to see in others is that they like themselves and make others feel good. Thus, if you act with shame, they will feel bad. If you act confident and happy, they will be happy for you and not think more about it.

- **Take the pressure off by being warm, clear, and direct.** Conversations and dates are nothing more than an opportunity to have fun and get to know each other while exploring whether romantic feelings might develop. Pursuing or encouraging conversations and dates does not create an obligation in others. Trying to anticipate and read their minds is a waste of time. It's wise to be socially aware and use good skills. Still, it is their responsibility to communicate their thoughts and needs. All you can do is offer a good-faith effort and provide a safe space for them to express themselves when they choose. If someone misreads the situation, makes assumptions, or fails to communicate their needs, this is their issue to resolve, not yours. Singles who fail to seize the moment and take action often burden themselves with too much mind-reading and anxiety about reading a situation correctly. Throw off this unnecessary pressure and focus on inviting meaningful and fun communication or contact instead. Whether they are interested or not, they can communicate this to you. Being assertive and inviting is appropriate and something successful people do. If others see it differently, this doesn't make you wrong. You need to be at peace about why you do what you do and that it is appropriate for most people and situations.

- **Make it clear that you keep interactions fun, handle issues well, and are respectful (and deserving of respect, too).** To ensure they know you are someone who can handle rejection well, state, "I treat dates as a fun and low-pressure way to get to know others. As long as we show mutual respect and communicate any needs or expectations, I'm sure we'll both have a good time. I trust you will let me know if there is anything I can do to help you feel comfortable and enjoy yourself. I look forward to having fun with you." This technique can be incredibly liberating for men who feel paralyzed by the risk of doing something that women may perceive as inappropriate. Men need to show women they care about their feelings and safety and will respond to their needs, but they can't read each woman's mind and varying degrees of comfort. Thus, beyond reasonable and socially acceptable limits, it is a woman's responsibility to assert her preferences and boundaries, after which he will be responsible for respecting them. A woman wants to feel comfortable rather than on guard. Thus, show her that expressing her preferences is worthy of your attention and response, and be sure you express yours, too. Empathy is not something that women alone need. Men should also expect and look for it. Everybody wins when both parties treat each other as capable of handling situations well. Dating is an invaluable opportunity to practice such skills, attitudes, and interactions while showing others they are worth your time.

- **Don't overthink their expectations and limit yours beyond having fun and sharing mutual respect.** When a person's expectations are about more than being safe and showing reasonable respect, it is wise to question whether such unspoken demands or criticism are fair or legitimate. A date is not a responsibility or obligation. It's a mutual investment in sharing a good time. There are slight differences between the roles men and women will play and who initially pays; however, if you are dissatisfied with how a person engages, you should look within yourself first. If you didn't request or encourage the behaviors you want, can you reasonably demand or criticize the other for not fulfilling your hidden expectations? If you enjoy phone calls, thoughtful questions, shorter (or longer) texts, well-planned dates, or spontaneous offers to get together, then it is your responsibility to communicate or encourage such actions warmly. If you aren't willing to express such hopes, you can't blame them for disappointing you. In general, you won't go far wrong if you live by the guiding rule: when in doubt, spell it out! If you do this warmly and casually, assuming they would want to know, you will seem confident and desirable. Women respect men who know what they want, seek a woman's suggestions, and take action (rather than being indecisive and passive). Speaking up shows you are this type of man.

- **Show more Empathy, exercise more Self-control, and take more Personal responsibility (or E.S.P.).** When you feel critical of others (unless it is clear they were acting manipulative or abusive), engage in personal reflection rather than blaming them. To do this: 1) give them the benefit of the doubt by empathizing with their perspective and recognizing their positive efforts; 2) ask yourself whether you offered behaviors and communication that would have improved the situation and your or their experience; and 3) accept more responsibility for engaging differently next time. The quality of your dating and relationship experiences will dramatically improve when you offer E.S.P. to others and look for those who do the same. The most undesirable people are those who refuse to take personal responsibility and place unrealistic demands, expectations, and blame on others. When you treat dates as an opportunity to improve your skills, learn more about the opposite sex, and treat yourself and others as having inherent value, you will find dating to be a fun adventure. When you share positive experiences (whether it ends with a couple of dates, a short relationship, or a loving connection), everyone feels more successful and capable (especially when you focus on what's going right).

- **When singles overthink dating, share your relaxed perspective.** Too many singles treat dates as a high-stakes investment and commitment. Social gatherings are often good examples of this since too many singles openly discuss their criticism of the opposite sex, dating, and others' insincere intentions at such events. Fortunately, these conversations also provide an excellent opportunity for you to stand out in a crowd as someone worth pursuing. When you notice a negative discussion, take the opportunity to validate their feelings by saying, "I know many people feel this way. I'm sorry you have experienced this." Then add, "I find dating is a fun and great way to get to know people better. For me, it is a generally positive experience because I don't worry about where it is going or expect too much too soon. Most dating doesn't end in a relationship, so I don't discuss who I am dating unless things get serious. I don't spend much time worrying about it initially, so it doesn't stress me out much." Many singles will be surprised by your approach and respect its simplicity. Of course, you will share specific concerns and challenges with close friends. Still, it is better to have a social reputation that encourages more dating, not less. When you treat it like a fun experience, it becomes so. Those who hear you say such things will also be more willing to take a chance by going on a date with you. They won't overthink the experience because you aren't.

- **Don't worry that you will be seen as a player.** This won't be a problem if you don't make out with multiple people within the same time frame. If you aren't hooking up, engaging in one-night stands, or expressing insincere commitments and feelings, you aren't acting like a player or using them. Those who cheat, lie, and exploit will get a reputation that proceeds and haunts them. However, this is not what you are doing. If you want others to know you are sincerely interested in fun dates, add, "I am open to a relationship if it evolves, but I have reasonable expectations of sharing fun and mutual respect." What can others criticize about that? Instead, you will be known as someone who dates a lot, treats others kindly, has fun, uses good communication, and makes dates feel great. In other words, most people will view you as highly desirable and well-liked. Singles want and admire people who other singles want. Some may be critical, but those who waste their time looking for and pointing out others' flaws are frequently the unhappy, jealous, and insecure types who rarely date (not because they are unattractive, but because they are unpleasant). So have fun and let others be responsible for their thoughts and feelings. It's not your right to read their minds, assume the worst, or worry about whether they are gossiping. Assume the best and do what is right for you; those who care to see the truth will recognize your goodness. In many ways, the law of similarity is real in that you will surely attract those like you. Thus, if you don't like the energy of those you associate with, find and adopt the positivity and energy of those you enjoy, and you will become more like them.

Offer A and B list communication (and understand theirs)

- **Reduce confusion by timing your engagement differently for those on your A or B list (and observe their reactions, too).** It isn't possible or wise to treat everyone as if they are on the A-list. If you text immediately and stay in daily contact, you are sending an A-list message. Please note that this level of engagement may create pressure and anxiety in them if you are on their B-list, so you need to match their response time. If you (or they) text or respond within 12 to 24 hours, you show you are trying to be responsive, but they (or you) are not a top priority. The delay in your responses cools each other's enthusiasm and aligns your expectations for a more moderate experience (which is often wise, balanced, and less pressured, allowing feelings to grow over time rather than rapidly all at once). Those who are emotionally mature and responsible have many responsibilities and relationships that keep them fulfilled and happy. They will respond, but are not needy or desperate, and you need to appear the same way if you want to attract them. Both A and B list interactions show respect and investment. By contrast, if you (or they) wait several days to a week to respond, this shows indifference, friendship, or a lack of interest (unless there are good reasons).

- **Follow up if you don't hear from them.** Although singles often react to a lack of response as ghosting, this implies more of a relationship and abandonment than is realistic for strangers. Additionally, busy professionals and single working parents do not have as much time to check their apps. Thus, assume that others have full lives and mean no offense if they don't respond for a week. Give them space and see what they do on their own. that if they are sincere, once you go on a date, their contact will become consistently engaged.

- **Follow up one more time.** In marketing, someone who is not engaging yet is considered a cold lead. However, a confident follow-up can turn a cold lead into a warm lead. Thus, if you remain interested and want to reach out again, wait a week or two and then send a message stating, "I'm not sure if you got my last message. I look forward to hearing from you and would love to get to know you. If I don't hear from you, I truly hope it is because good things are happening for you. I won't be reaching out again unless you reach out. I look forward to a response, and I truly wish you the best."

Ffinding your match on social media

- **Once you complete your social media profiles, start searching for friends and social pages on Facebook.** Look for singles groups in your area, church singles groups, and local singles events. Find groups that match your interests and see whether they have options or events for singles only. Facebook is usually the best place for social groups and announcements. Meetup is another app that does this, but focuses on local groups, and each event requires a fee to set up. Because Facebook will connect you to a larger audience and it is free, it may be a better option. However, it never hurts to try both.

- **After finding a group that interests you, request to join it.** Once you are admitted, you can view other members and send friend requests, personal messages, or both to those you find interesting.

- **Always check their relationship status since** it could have changed after they joined the group.

- **Review a friend's Facebook page to find their friends and others you know (or want to).** Facebook will also provide you with suggestions for friends and pages that may interest you. The more active you are, the more effective

Facebook's algorithm will become at matching your interests. Through these many options, you can access nearly an unlimited number of people.

- **View your friends' Instagram pages to see who they are following.** It can be harder to determine someone's relationship status on Instagram, but viewing those your friends are following can also connect you with desirable singles. Don't do this with pages that have tens of thousands of followers, as this is a sign of an impersonal relationship with your friend. But for those who are obviously not influencers, you can like or follow their pages and then send a message stating that you know one of their friends. This is far more effective if they are in a picture with this friend.

- **When you send a Facebook friend request, also send a personal message stating how you found them.** Many people do not accept friend requests unless they are attracted to and excited about you, or you have similar friends in common. It can feel creepy if someone from across the world is reaching out. Thus, when sending a friend request, share where you saw them, what you have in common, or why you are reaching out. In your personal message, state, "I noticed you are friends with John Smith (or I saw you on Jewish Singles in Texas), so I thought I'd say hi. Check out my Facebook page, and if you feel comfortable accepting my request or messaging back, awesome."

- **If you want to make your message more flirty and fun, send a private message commenting on one of their pictures or complimenting them.** "This picture seriously made me laugh. You seem like someone I'd love to know," "You seem amazing! I couldn't help but say hi," or "I see that you and I are just friends of friends. We should fix that!" A short message such as this, followed by a winky-face emoji, will ensure they know you're flirting. Don't overplay this. Keep your message brief, and trust that they got the hint and will make the next move by messaging you back. If they don't contact you, respond as you would on any dating app.

- **Experiment and compare results.** If you find that bold and playful messages get better results, keep using them. If not, they may be striking others as odd, creepy, or desperate. Return to more conservative, complementary, and confident messages to discover if this works better with similar singles as those with whom you didn't get a response.

- **If nothing is obvious, use a simple compliment,** such as, "You seem interesting and someone who would be fun to get to know, so I had to say hi. If you feel the same about me, I'd love to hear from you." Add a winky face emoji to ensure a flirty tone.

- **If you want to show that you can handle rejection well and don't want them to feel pressure, you can also add,** "If I don't hear from you, I'll assume it's because great things are happening for you. Have a great day!"

Starting conversations using dating apps

- **I Once you complete your dating app profile, start swiping up, liking, or matching.** Each app has a different user experience. Do an online search to discover the standard way to engage and the available upgrades to increase your success.

- **When possible, send personal messages rather than just saying (or swiping) yes or sending a like.** Until the other person has matched with you, you may not be allowed to message them unless you purchase an upgrade. Apps have different rules about how and when you can do this. Some give you a limited number of free messages. However, using these features to send a warm, creative, or confident unsolicited message may help you to stand out and increase the number of matches you get.

- **Don't send flirts, nudges, roses, pokes, or greetings to women when you can send a message instead.** These features are common in apps, but they indicate the least level of engagement. You can use them if you want, but don't expect a response, and don't take it personally if you don't get one. Such tactics usually provide a low return on investment because women typically see them as lazy and don't know how to respond.

- **Send a private message that is complimentary, warm, and positive.** "Wow, I'm so impressed by all you've accomplished," or "You have an amazing smile." Then add: "I couldn't resist saying hi. If you feel similarly, I'd love to hear from you." Writing short statements such as these (with a few variations depending on the profile) will give you a quick way to make contact without wasting a lot of time.

- **Once you have created a few successful, confident, and positive initial messages, increase your efficiency by saving and reusing them.** If you have to be creative every time you send a message, you will experience unnecessary anxiety, doubt, wasted time, and resentment (when you don't get responses). Instead, create three messages from which you can select, copy, adapt, and send. For example,

  » "I love how creative (funny, smart, efficient, kind, or interesting) your profile was, so I had to say hi. It would be awesome to get to know you!"

  » "Your picture with your friends (dad, dog, motorcycle, co-workers, or running buddies) was impressive (hilarious, cute, exciting, impressive, or fun). You seem like someone with whom I could have a lot of fun (or great conversations, tease and laugh, or enjoy new hobbies)."

  » "I love that you like challenging and improving yourself (engaging fully in your relationships, trying new things, traveling, and learning new languages). I'm impressed and hope to discover more fun things about you!"

  » Or, when you want to be bold, flattering, and cool, be direct and fearless. "Wow! You are impressive AND beautiful (witty and fun, educated and successful, exciting and classy, amazing and responsible, adventurous and loyal). If you feel similar about me, let's connect and do something fun soon." Complimenting others as exceptional while asserting that you feel the same about yourself shows you aren't afraid to pursue, take chances, and experience rejection. This approach shows that you understand how to date, and it's about having fun. Just make sure you maintain your assertiveness by requesting her number and offering to call or plan a date sooner rather than later, "because you know that both of you are busy and would prefer a fun, meaningful interaction rather than merely texting."

- **With these options available, you can efficiently swipe through profiles, send messages to 5 to 10 women who fit your A and B lists, and get back to your day.** If you never hear from them, it won't bother you because you spent no more than 2 minutes on each profile, so you aren't preoccupied with them anyway. The more time you invest in a message, the higher the stakes you place on yourself to be impressive. This can also make you worry about whether they noticed, read, liked, or felt annoyed by what you wrote. Sending a confident, fun, and assertive message and not worrying about their reaction proves that you really can be cool and nonchalant when they need to reject you.

- **If you worry that using the same "pickup lines" with multiple women will eventually lead to friends comparing notes and taking offense, you are right.** Women frequently share notes and talk about the guys they meet. Men rarely do this with friends. Thus, it is critical that you personalize your adjectives and descriptions to a woman's profile rather than copy and paste the same exact phrases.

- **If a woman sends you a flirt, nudge, poke, rose, or like, check out her profile and send a message in response (if you are interested).** Craft your messages in a similar way to any first or second message you might send. Don't respond with a thumbs up, heart, "What's up?" or "Hi." It's not just lazy. Such responses make women feel dismissed, burdened, and annoyed because they want you to show interest in them or share something they can follow up on. So respond enthusiastically by commenting on her profile, saying something flattering, sharing something about your day, or asking about her day. Since she sent the first flirt, she should continue to respond and do her part to maintain the communication. If she repeatedly responds with minimal effort, despite your efforts, unmatch her.

When you are NOT interested

- **If you are NOT interested, remove her message from your inbox or don't respond.** It can be painful to have a message ignored, but this is how dating apps work. Most people learn not to take it personally. You may desire to send a thoughtful message stating you're not interested; however, this is usually not appreciated. It is better to get no message than to become excited about someone new who is just writing to say they don't want to write to you. So, if you're not interested, merely delete their message. Your inbox needs to be a happy place, not a depressing reminder of all the people you don't want to date. Keep your message board clean, and you'll find it easier to maintain contact with those with whom you are excited. Some apps have options for deleting messages; others allow you to archive your messages. Sometimes, you will have to unmatch to remove the message history. You will need to learn how your app works to maintain efficiency and prevent losing track of those with whom you want to continue communicating.

- **Never talk sexually or include anything sexual in your messages.** Most women are deeply offended and turned off by such things. It makes you look like a player, a jerk, or a predator, so don't think you can get away with it for very long before someone complains, resulting in you being blocked or removed from the site. Additionally, women are notorious for sharing bad experiences with each other, which may result in a problematic reputation or gossip. Furthermore, it's not just women who need to be cautious online. Men can be stalked, harassed, exploited, and extorted, too. Dating apps can attract sex workers and scammers. Most women will not immediately engage in sexual conversations, offer unsolicited images, or be comfortable inviting you to their house or going to yours. If someone is eager to engage in these encounters, they may only be looking for a one-night stand, but you can't be sure if that's all they have planned. Images can be used against you later, and once you become sexually entangled, you may feel more obligated to help them financially, especially if they exploit your emotions and appeal to your vulnerabilities. Is a sexual dalliance worth the risk of regret, STDs, pregnancy, child support, exploitation, or toxic manipulations? One thing is for sure: her intentions are not sincere. When engaging with women who have healthy boundaries and limits, your risks are minimal. Holding out for a real connection and investment will be worth waiting for.

- **Don't hesitate to delete and block people who ask pushy or inappropriate questions or request money.** Don't share your full name (unless you want her to feel safer and comfortable), place of work, or home address until you've had enough contact to trust the person. If someone pushes you for these details, stop talking with them, and if needed, block them. Blocking someone is typically reserved for those who act disrespectfully or inappropriately, so use it sparingly. People can tell when they've been blocked, which can be hurtful, especially if they don't know what they did wrong. Unmatching isn't as offensive as blocking someone, even though it is virtually the same. When you have other options, but you choose to block someone, doing so can make you seem easily offended, insecure, or overreactive.

Send engaging messages that progress to phone calls and dates

- **Keep your messages short and sweet while encouraging engagement.** Messaging through dating apps can provide you valuable practice and experiences with initiating contact, starting conversations, acting strong and confident, asking questions about their day, and sharing your experiences. However, if your messages extend beyond three exchanges each without leading to sharing numbers or planning dates, you will lose their interest.

  » **To make messaging others easier, create three possible first messages** and then copy and paste one of them to fit the person you're messaging. These could include a few facts about where you grew up, what you like to do, a little about your family, what brought you to your new city, the universities and fields of study you've pursued, a favorite hobby, activities you want to do during the upcoming season, a vacation you recently took or want to.

  » **Make it easy for a woman to respond to what you share or to answer a question.** "I love taking one good vacation every year. Last year, it was to the Grand Canyon. How about you? Where do you like to travel (or want to)?"

  » **To be bold, fun, or playful, get to the point, tease, or share something unique.** For example, "I grew up in the middle of my grandparents' orchard with my cousins and grandparents on the same street, and a demon cat lurking at the bottom of my stairs to chase me every morning. Tag. You're it. How about you?" or "Here are three questions. Answer the one you would enjoy, and then send me three, and I'll answer one, too. Sound good?" "I created a list of five new activities I want to do this summer: Try a new hole-in-the-wall restaurant, learn pickleball, attend a local baseball game, go ATVing, and kayak around a lake. What about you? Any fun goals?" Or you can try jumping to the point: "I know it is hard to get to know someone this way, and it is more fun to meet in person. Do you have a list of things you like to do, topics you enjoy, or foods you want to try? If so, let's discuss a few options and then meet to enjoy one. Sound good?"

  » **When you ask questions, make sure you share similar information about yourself.** If you ask how a woman enjoyed her holidays, share something you did. If you ask about her family, talk about yours. Engaging in this way personalizes her experience and makes it easier to be slightly vulnerable or ask follow-up questions.

- **Don't make your message longer than two to three short paragraphs.** Long messages require too much time to read and can appear needy or desperate, which adds pressure. Instead, encourage the idea of exchanging numbers and talking on the phone to share more fun and interesting details about their questions.

- **Comment or respond to what she shares, ask follow-up questions, and don't ignore her questions.** A common complaint singles make when using apps and texting is not getting a response to their questions, statements, or experiences. Responding with an emoji or thumbs up is at least a response, but when possible, provide a short thought or reaction instead. For example, if a woman shares something personal or important, state, "Thanks for sharing that," or "That made me smile (think, feel closer to you, or impressed me)." Ask one or two follow-up questions like, "What happened next?" "That must have made your parents so proud," or "If you would like, I'd enjoy calling you to hear more about this. Can I get your number?" If she asks you a question, respond or share that you will answer it later that day when you have more time. If you forgot to respond, comment on that too: "I just realized that I never got back to you on that question. Sorry about that." Then, provide your answer.

- **When responding to her messages, use emotional words to demonstrate good listening and communication skills** while limiting your use of emojis. Sadly, men who use a lot of emojis can seem immmature. Similarly, men who describe themselves and their experiences with lots of emotional words can be perceived as effeminate or too sensitive. Once a woman gets to know you (and has established sufficient chemistry and confidence in you), then she will want a deeper exchange of your feelings, needs, and vulnerabilities (since these are necessary to strengthen your connection). However, in the beginning, she must see that you can handle her emotions skillfully if she is to trust and respect you. Women are attracted to strength and confidence because it helps them feel safe and secure, but this also must include showing them your emotional maturity and compassion. Likewise, for you to feel chemistry, you will want to see her be feminine and fun with you before you are burdened by her fears and insecurities. In time, your mutual empathy, investment, and connection will allow for the reality that you are both human and need support and encouragement.

- **Avoid self-deprecating statements.** Be witty, playful, fun, informative, or direct while also avoiding negative, critical, or pessimistic remarks. You can show a little vulnerability and briefly mention a difficult life experience while also emphasizing the positive, healing, or transforming experiences related to it. Referring to yourself as dumb, naive, forgetful, or a nerd and using other deprecating remarks will not make others feel impressed or excited about seeing you. They may act reassuringly or dismiss the remark but also feel manipulated and repelled. This isn't the same as sharing your hero's journey through a difficult time, which is positive. Self-deprecating remarks are negative characterizations about you as a person, such as, "I'm broke," "I suck at relationships," or "I'm not brave like you. I could never travel to a foreign country." Many people say such things habitually, humbly, or jokingly, but you need to recognize and eliminate such phrases in general. Building others up by putting yourself down doesn't serve either of you. Instead, make others feel great and show you feel the same about yourself.

- **Use good grammar, spelling, and punctuation, especially during the first few messages or texts.** Some people may feel that basic writing skills are inconvenient or less essential when meeting through apps or texting; however, the opposite is often true. The other person must draw from the few things they can learn about you to determine their interest. Poor grammar and punctuation may make them think you're uneducated, sloppy, or lazy. If grammar and spelling are weaknesses for you, download an app like Grammarly, which will help you proofread your messages before you send them. If you recognize that your message has typos or errors, you may be able to unsend a recently sent message. If not, simply state, "Oops," followed by the corrected statement. When you use good writing skills at first, you can become less formal later, and they will think little of it since it's apparent that you are literate.

- **Avoid immediate responses and late-night messages.** You may look less busy, confident, and capable if you're sending messages all day (which can become annoying or cause pressure). Instead of responding immediately, allow time in between texts (so you don't appear desperate, needy, bored, or lazy). Waiting twenty minutes to two hours (or the next morning) demonstrates an A-list engagement. You need to leave them wanting more by offering encouragement (rather than indifference) and being reasonably responsive (rather than being excessively available). Emotionally mature people are busy, too, and will understand and expect a delay (of up to a few days, which is a B-list response). As long as you also act enthusiastic and supportive in your responses, they will feel sufficiently encouraged and curious about meeting you. Relative to late-night messages, it's important to note that a woman can't know you well enough to interpret your intentions, personality, or daily patterns accurately. If you send messages after midnight, she could conclude that you are irresponsible with your time or don't respect her need for sleep. She may wonder whether you are looking for a hook-up, could be intoxicated or high, or anxious and desperate. Late-night conversations can be common and a lot of fun for those who are younger; however, those with jobs and responsibilities won't appreciate them as much. Additionally, when you are tired, your inhibitions will be lower. If a fun conversation turns sexual, you or they may feel regret, shame, or used later (even if it seemed fun at the time). There is never any harm in playing it safe. Good boundaries turn off the wrong people and encourage the right ones. Thus, if you have had a crazy day and didn't get to respond earlier, just wait till the morning. She isn't going anywhere, and if she's anxious to hear from you, she will still be excited (and even relieved) to get your response after a reasonable delay. When you feel you must respond after midnight, keep it brief. To do this, state, "I am so sorry that it was such a busy day. I am just checking my messages before going to bed. I wanted you to know I was thinking about you, and I didn't want to keep you waiting. It's hard to check the app, and texting is more efficient for me. If you would like to exchange numbers and communicate that way, I'll probably respond more quickly. If so, I'd love to get your number." Then, answer their questions or let them know you will respond the next day with the requested information. If you get an immediate response, state, "I just have a few minutes before heading to bed. I have a busy day tomorrow, so I will need to say good night, but I'd love to chat some more tomorrow."

- **If you are over thirty, limit your use of shortened phrases and slang commonly used by teens** (such as OMG, TTYL, bro, or bae), or you may seem immature.

- **Don't make your message longer than two to three short paragraphs.** Long messages require too much time to read and can appear needy, desperate, or overwhelming, which adds pressure. Instead, encourage exchanging numbers sooner rather than later so you can share more fun and interesting details by text, phone, FaceTime, or during a date.

- **Send and respond to messages at least every few days.** There is no point in messaging someone if you aren't going to follow through. If a woman takes a few days to respond, don't get frustrated: it just means she is busy and has a full life (which makes her more desirable).

- **Don't respond to, ask for, or engage in sexual conversations or the exchange of sexual images** since these significantly increase your risks for a regretful one-night stand, sexual extortion, catfishing, or prostitution. This is not a typical female behavior (no matter how common it appears in movies and TV). Women rarely enjoy the regret they feel after a hookup or one-night stand, especially if it went farther than they wanted, for which you may be accused later. Thus, women who initiate these interactions and pressure you to participate should be viewed suspiciously, especially if they are exceptionally beautiful (which is a typical red flag that their profile is fake).

- **Be realistic and patient with the process while encouraging you both to exchange phone numbers or schedule a date to meet up.** Sending brief messages back and forth is hard for everyone, so acknowledge this and then offer to progress the conversation to something more meaningful by stating, "It's so hard to get to know someone this way. I'd love to exchange numbers and text or call to answer those questions and learn more about you. Can I get your number? Or, if you prefer, we could meet for a short, fun date, too." The sooner you get off the app, the better, and until you get on a date, you can't really know if you want to continue communicating. Being efficient, direct, and interested in getting to know her is going to make a better impression than creative questions and numerous back-and-forth messages on the app.

- **Leave them wanting more so they will take action.** If you share your best chit-chat material by text, you will have less to talk about later, so don't hesitate to leave them with a cliffhanger or dangle details that are best shared later. For example, when they ask about your work, say, "That is a story best shared over dinner," followed by a winky face emoji or smile. When they press for details about something more mundane or personal like your family, career, education, or a challenging experience, state, "That topic will take some explaining and a good dessert (to make it enjoyable). You suggest the restaurant or activity, and I'll provide the exciting details over dinner (provided you are willing to share, too). You game?" or "Instead of texting about this, let's jump on a short call. It will be more fun to talk about it that way. Can I get your number?"

- **If you don't hear back from her, assume it could be your mistake.** Women often wait to reach out until the other person responds or engages. Rather than lose contact, you should consider bridging the communication gap. If you believe a woman needs to share 50% of the conversation, this unspoken expectation could result in a stalemate. So, check your texts or messages to see if there could be a missed communication, response, or question that requires your attention. If she was the last to message you, the next move is yours. However, it never hurts to follow up, even when it is clear that she dropped the ball. To do this, you can say, "I'm not sure if you got my last message. Just in case, I wanted you to know I was thinking about you. How are you doing?'

- **If it has been a while since you messaged her, apologize and explain.** Sometimes, singles are unsure about someone, they get busy, or they simply forget, become sick, or feel too depressed to reach out. When this is the case, re-engage (even if it has been a few weeks). They might be glad to hear from you and willing to pick up where you left off. "I'm sorry that I went silent for a bit. Things got crazy here. I'd love to continue getting to know you and catch up. Let me know if you would enjoy that too. And I promise to be more consistent or explain any delay next time."

- **By the third message, encourage the conversation to move to phone or face-to-face contact.** Talking online can be very limiting and even waste your time if it persists. You do not need a lot of back-and-forth messages before exchanging numbers. As a matter of fact, the longer you message, the more disinterested she or you will become. Messaging is too limiting and leaves too much unsaid. Furthermore, it is easy to misunderstand or read too much into messages. Telephone, FaceTime, or in-person contact are the most reliable ways to facilitate and maintain a connection. So, by your third (and definitely no later than the fifth) message, state, "It can be hard to get to know someone this way. If you're up for it, I'd love to call or meet you for a quick bite to eat. If not, we can continue communicating this way for a little longer. Your thoughts?"

- **When she provides her number, offer yours, too.** When you get her number, send her a text or respond to her message by stating, "Thanks for your number. I'll reach out soon. Here's my number so that you'll recognize me when I call or text." Make sure the number you provide can't be linked (through a Google search) to your name and work or home address. Men do not need to reveal their full name and personal information to strangers any more than women should. It is your right to protect your identity and social media accounts from potential stalkers and scammers who could harm your reputation or threaten you.

- **If she continues to resist giving you her number, after a few more messages, end contact.** Send her a final message stating, "I'd love to get to know you better, but messaging this way is pretty limiting. Let me know when you're ready to talk on the phone. Until then, please know it was a pleasure getting to know you."

- **Share your communication preferences so she can anticipate what to expect.** Some singles prefer texting versus calls because maintaining phone conversations (especially long ones) can feel stressful. Texting is okay for scheduling a date if you both are okay with it; however, if you call and leave a message, you also need to text her (since voice messages are often ignored). Be sure you ask her to call you back. If you don't, she may feel anxious about whether you will call back or if you dialed her by mistake. It is more courteous for her to return your call than to merely text a response. If you prefer a phone call before scheduling a date, you need to let her know. If you like spontaneous calls rather than scheduling them (since this causes less pressure and anxious anticipation), state, "I've got some free time. Are you available for a quick call?" or when texting about something, state, "I'd love to chat on the phone about this rather than text it. I'll give you a quick call." Longer, scheduled calls are ideal when dating long distances or setting up a Zoom or FaceTime date. If this is your preference, offer times that work for you and suggest topics or activities you could enjoy. It is also wise to explain your texting patterns and preferences so your responses don't confuse them. For example, "Just so you know, I'm not much of a texter during the day since it's hard to respond at work. My days are usually busy, but I can fit in short calls after work. What about you? Do you prefer calls, FaceTime, texts, or meeting for a date sooner rather than later? I'm flexible, but I'd love to know your preferences, too."

If you lose contact, follow up

- **If you lose touch, send a follow-up message.** You need to view dating as similar to a sales-generation process. Each person you send initial messages to is essentially a cold lead, whom you want to make a warm lead through messaging and then a hot lead that converts to a date (or sale). The less contact you have, the cooler you both will feel about the other, thus losing an opportunity. So, rather than letting a contact passively die, follow up.

- **Whether you or they dropped the ball, send a text or message (a week or two after the last message)** saying, "I'm not sure how we lost contact, but I'd love to keep chatting." If you desire, you can share something about your recent activities and ask about theirs. Then, state, "It will be easier to stay in touch and get to know each other if we exchange numbers. Or we could meet up for a quick bite to eat. I'm game if you are. Your thoughts?"

- **When you don't hear from her, either delete her messages** (if she is on your B list) **or reach out one last time** (if she is on your A list and you would regret it if you didn't). It can be hard to know why communication goes silent. An old boyfriend could have reentered the picture, she might have stopped getting on the app, or she could have been on vacation or gotten sick. Thus, reaching out after another few weeks might recapture her attention (if her situation has improved). You can send a similar message as before, but this time, show that you can handle rejection well. To do this, state, "I enjoyed getting to know you. I hope you are doing well. If you still want to chat, let me know. Unless I hear from you, I'll assume you've lost interest. If that's the case, no worries. Either way, I look forward to hearing from you, and I truly wish you the best."

- **Show her you can confidently walk away on your terms** (rather than merely avoiding the situation). Whether on the first or second follow-up, you can be warm, clear, and confident. Doing this can show mutual respect but also increase the possibility that she will take action (for fear of missing out). To do this, state, "It's been a while since we chatted. If you want to continue engaging, let me know. I won't reach out again if I don't hear from you, but I'll be hoping good things are happening for you! Either way, I truly wish you the best." You never look more desirable than when you confidently walk away. Additionally, using this technique makes it easy for you to see her in the future since you ended contact on your terms.

When you or they lose interest

- **It is common for someone to stop messaging if they lose interest, but you can't be certain unless they say something (or unmatch with you).** Since you won't know if she lost interest or there was a misunderstanding, following up can be appropriate, especially if you would regret not doing so.

- **If you prefer, let them know you lost interest and won't be reaching out again.** Although you are entitled to stop messaging (and can simply unmatch with them), if you would appreciate someone telling you rather than disappearing, consider how to do the same. For example, "It's been fun chatting, and I don't want to leave you hanging. I do not feel we are a romantic fit, but I genuinely wish you the best.

- **Keep your inbox clean, so it is a happy place.** When you or they lose interest, delete their messages, unmatch, or archive the conversation so you can easily see and respond to others. When your inbox of messages only includes those who are actively engaged and fun, you will enjoy checking it. When it's littered with those you have rejected (and vice versa), visiting your inbox can be unpleasant and depressing. Thus, learn how best to use your app features and delete the excess waste in your messages.

Pursuing skills during live interactions

For your convenience, this chapter highlights each technique (i.e., action or behavioral strategy) by using a bullet format. Consider each bullet as a potential goal or technique you can apply. No one can work on more than three goals or behaviors at a given time, so choose the most appealing options first and leave the others for another time. Remember, making a meaningful connection is the goal, not perfection.

Influence versus manipulation

Eventually, all digital communication needs to transition to face-to-face contact, which means your skills for confident body language are essential. Since 40% of the adult population is single, you can't afford to miss opportunities to make a great impression when starting a simple conversation. When you practice behaviors that exude warmth, self-respect, and an ability to make others feel great, they can develop into muscle memories and habits that are available whenever you need them.

Skills for confidently and respectfully pursuing a conversation while appearing confident and trustworthy can transform your social, professional, and romantic relationships. Sharing a friendly interaction, whether for dating or enhancing your personal or employment opportunities, is not insincere (even when you are doing them on demand). This is no different than using the right tool for the job. As long as you are warm, clear, and direct when encouraging more contact (and are not excluding important information that benefits you while harming others), then you are merely influencing others, not manipulating them. It is not your responsibility to read others' minds and prevent every possible misunderstanding, especially when your words and actions are clear and congruent. They are responsible for listening, asking questions, and seeking clarification rather than making assumptions.

When you can easily and efficiently manage expectations, prevent and avoid common dating challenges, misunderstandings, or unintentional pressure, and handle rejection well, others will recognize and respect your strength and confidence. Thus, it is essential that you practice these strategies without overthinking them and taking too much responsibility for others.

Achieving mutually respectful outcomes and win/win interactions is possible when you know what to do and say during live interactions. The strategies that follow can be applied (with appropriate changes) to many situations, so incorporating them into your everyday circumstances will serve you well.

Think like a woman. Act like a man.

- To think like a woman and act like a man, **you need to know that women thrive when they feel safe and secure, and men seek out relationships that make them feel trusted.** When a man is with a woman who makes him feel like a man (and vice versa), they tend to bring out the best in each other. Too often, women feel that they need to cast off their femininity because it makes them vulnerable to or exploited by the worst men. Likewise, too many men feel rejected and mistrusted at the slightest offer of help, support, or simple affection. Their thoughtful gestures are frequently brushed off with, "No, thank you. I've got it." In the absence of meaningful connections, both grow increasingly independent and play a cat-and-mouse game of not needing the other (while longing to be wanted). Each wants to belong and experience companionship but fears being vulnerable or appearing weak, needy, or desperate. Fortunately, as you understand the power of your confidence and masculine or feminine energy for making the opposite sex feel great, you gain the ability to skew the odds in your favor (whether in the written word or direct face-to-face contact). The secret to success in getting more attention on the apps and before or after dates is through seeing the other as similar to yourself and interacting in ways that would be meaningful for them, just as you would hope they would do for you.

- **Recognize how femininity builds chemistry.** To achieve this, you need to understand why men desire faith and trust from a partner and how this helps them to feel needed, appreciated, and successful. It is a woman's soft and feminine response that makes him feel like he's reaching her and that his efforts matter. Men are visual by nature and often drawn to the same feminine physical features (including curves, breasts, hips, butt, legs, and long hair). However, other visual cues also draw their attention and emotions, such as smiles, laughter, soft and feminine movements, and open and engaging body language. Whether they register these gestures consciously or subconsciously, they make a difference in how he feels. When a man feels sufficient chemistry or connection, he often desires to pursue closeness with her and hopes to succeed (rather than experience rejection). When a woman has the self-respect to ask for meaningful engagement rather than immediate gratification, all while acting warm, playful, and confident, he feels encouraged rather than repelled. He values her more because she values herself, which increases his willingness to sacrifice (in the hope of acceptance or success). Thus, for men, the perfect combination in a woman is femininity (i.e., her visually stimulating features, softness, mannerisms, confidence, and curves), emotional encouragement (i.e., warmth, kindness, touch, vulnerability, and thoughtfulness), and faith in his goodness (i.e., her openness to spend time with him and treat him as worthy of her investment). These things help him to feel like a success and keep him coming back for more.

- **Recognize how masculinity builds chemistry.** A woman needs to feel safe and secure (emotionally, physically, and sexually). Those who help her to feel this way are often valued and appreciated above others. It is a man's empathy and self-control that win a woman's trust and respect. Unfortunately, this is not enough to ensure chemistry, too. For this, she needs to experience masculine strength and confidence in his words, actions, and pursuit behaviors. Women want to be wanted and like feeling special. Without a man risking the possibility of rejection and boldly pursuing her, she is often left feeling uncertain and anxious. She can't relax and be soft or feminine when she is the one doing all the work to make a connection possible. Likewise, she can't act feminine and flirtatious when she feels attacked and on guard. When a man shows that he has the confidence and strength to manage difficult situations, anticipate her feelings and needs, and be undaunted in his pursuit of her affection, a woman's excitement and enthusiasm grow. She feels seen, appreciated, and wanted. This is why a woman wants a man to be active (which shows personal responsibility) rather than passive about spending time with her. His pursuit behaviors help her to worry less and enjoy herself more (because his presence is calming and exciting). Often, women fail to see how their feminine encouragement is essential to this process and that their expectations are unrealistic without their active participation in his needs, too. Nonetheless, it is a man's consistent, confident, masculine, and non-creepy pursuit that makes him irresistible. Thus, for women, the perfect combination in a man is empathy and self-control (for the safety she needs), personal responsibility (for the pursuit she wants), and masculine strength and confidence (for the chemistry she desires).

- **Recognize the toxic counterfeits of femininity and masculinity in exploiting emotions.** Unfortunately, jerks (i.e., those men and women who lack empathy, self-control, and personal responsibility) can easily bypass such time-consuming and selfless traits. To do this, a man will counterfeit strength, confidence, and meaningful pursuit behaviors with arrogance (i.e., flashy clothing, muscles, and symbols of success), selfishness (i.e., intermittent and unreliable acceptance and rejection to reward and punish until they get what they want), and insincere words (with little real action, commitment, or follow through). Likewise, women will counterfeit femininity, emotional support, and faith in a man's goodness with seduction (i.e., visually revealing clothing and promiscuously aggressive behavior), neediness (i.e., exploiting a man's desire to protect, be a hero, and feel needed), and fears of failure (i.e., emotionally and sexually praising, rewarding, and punishing him until she gets what she wants).

- **Level the playing field by ramping up your masculinity and pursuit behaviors while anticipating her needs.** Fortunately for women, there are not just good men and other men because men, by nature, are good and in the majority. Thus, there are men and jerks. Unfortunately for men, jerks get far more attention because they know how to masterfully manipulate, excite, and exploit women. However, you can gain back your power and level the playing field when you know how to wield your masculine body language (i.e., posture, tone of voice, and words), show strength (i.e., your self-respect, support for your needs, and healthy boundaries), and display your trustworthiness (i.e., empathy, personal responsibility, and self-control). This may seem like a daunting task, but each of these traits is one you already possess. You just need to showcase them more effectively. After all, *it's just technique!* You can change your behavior and get a better result when you know what to do.

Use confident, calm, and masculine posture and body language

- **Appear cool, calm, strong, confident, and masculine.** There are several ways to determine if a woman is open to having a brief conversation or interaction with a man she doesn't know. The first is to look for eye contact. If she is looking at her phone or distracted by the task or environment she is in, she will most likely not recognize or acknowledge you. If she looks in your direction and then quickly looks away without acknowledging or smiling at you, this could be due to a variety of reasons. She may be married, preoccupied, in a hurry, unavailable, single but not interested in dating opportunities, not attracted to you, or feels less safe and uncomfortable due to how you present yourself. Since many of these variables have nothing to do with you, it's best to focus only on the ones that you can control: being attractive, confident, and casual (so she feels at ease). You will be less likely to act and feel confident if you don't look and feel good before you leave the house (as encouraged earlier in this chapter). Nevertheless, as long as you are reasonably presentable, your confident and casual behavior will greatly improve your chances of getting and keeping her attention.

  » **When sitting, spread out, lean back, and maintain good posture.** You look stronger and more confident and casual when you are leaning back slightly, keeping your elbows away from your body, and straightening your back (so your shoulders appear more square instead of rounded or slouched). If your shoulders are stiff or elevated, you will seem anxious or insecure, so make sure you relax them. A man's strong shoulders and chin add to his perception of masculinity, so good posture is essential. The more you spread out, the more confident and relaxed you will be. Avoid dropping your chin, crossing your arms, covering your belly, slouching, or bringing your arms or legs inward to your chest. This makes you look small, defensive, anxious, or insecure. So spread out. Keep at least one elbow away from your body. Put an arm on the back of your chair or rest a hand on the side of your thigh or hip. Don't cross your legs or ankles, but you can place your ankle on top of your knee. From this position, you can put a forearm, hand, or elbow on your knee, which encourages good posture (especially when you are leaning in during a conversation). Keep your feet and ankles strong (rather than shaking a foot anxiously or bending your ankles inward, which looks insecure). Keep your feet pointing forward or outward (rather than inward toward each other).

» **When standing, keep one foot slightly forward while resting your weight and posture over your back leg.** This will cause you to lean back in a cool and relaxed way. It helps you to look and feel calm and controlled. Leaning forward on a front leg adds intensity. There is a time and place for shifting onto the front leg—to test her interest—but for the most part, you will look more confident and masculine and less intimidating when you lean on your back leg. To achieve this, make sure your shoulders, hips, or feet are at a slight angle so one is behind the other. This can include one heel of the foot at roughly the position of the other foot's toes, with a width of about nine inches (or a comfortable distance) apart. The torso will naturally match your hips and shoulders. Bigger and taller men need to angle their bodies since this makes them seem less intimidating. Facing someone straight on is usually an aggressive gesture to be avoided; however, smaller men can do this when they want to seem bigger or more confident. To ensure good posture, straighten your back and square your shoulders (without lifting them). Your shoulders need to be relaxed (not stiff), and this is achieved by straightening your back, not pulling your shoulder blades together. Rather than putting both hands in your pockets (which raises and rounds your shoulders and places your arms and elbows too close to your body), put a thumb in the top corner of your front or back pocket or in a belt loop. This loosens and squares your shoulders and forces your elbows to point outward and backward, making you look more casual and broad. When standing near a wall, you can use it to support your weight as you relax. To do this, rest your shoulders (and head as desired) against it.

» **Provide opportunities for eye contact.** When you are sitting or standing with a confident, open, and leaned-back posture, you will appear more desirable. However, to encourage conversation, you must make eye contact, too. To do this, you need to keep your eyes roaming around the room. If brief eye contact is achieved, you should nod your head up, add a smile, and then look away. When you are at a distance from someone, and you achieve a second and longer glance (if you are interested), you need to maintain their gaze for a second or two longer and brighten your smile. When you receive a longer glance from a woman (and especially a third glance) that includes a head tilt, a coy smile, or a wave, this indicates that a conversation would be welcome. Look for an opportunity when she is away from her friends and seize the moment. If nothing else, the experience will be good practice. If it doesn't go well, you'll probably never see her again anyway, so what do you have to lose? You can also walk across the room to introduce yourself to her or her friends, as taught in this chapter for breaking into groups.

Starting conversations using daily interactions

- **Prepare to start conversations in any situation.** Look for singles everywhere, not just at school, singles events, or in dating apps. Over 40% of the adult population is single; thus, they are at the grocery store, baseball games, parks, and doctor's offices. The biggest difference between those who date a lot and those who don't is that the former act single: they keep their eyes up, notice others around them, make eye contact, smile, and start casual conversations. This is a daily habit that you can develop, too, especially as you consider and practice the many options for casually beginning conversations.

- **When initiating a conversation, you need to feel confident and capable of making a good impression.** Whether it is someone at the store, a singles event, a party, or on a dating app, you are less likely to pursue when they look good and more likely when you look good. This is why so much attention is dedicated to your skills for making a lasting impression through an updated image in your live presentation, dating apps, or social media. Nevertheless, making first contact can be nerve-racking even when you look great. You may feel vulnerable, self-conscious, or worried about saying something that makes you seem anxious, unnatural, or weird. Fortunately, the same techniques and considerations for initiating conversations in live interactions also make a great impression when sending messages, so the practice you do on apps can translate to more confidence in live interactions. There are several important variables in creating a good impression in your written words, vocal tones, or body language. Like playing a musical instrument, if you practice each of these elements individually, it will become easier to bring them together.

- **Use the simplest and most effective techniques for starting a conversation.** The best way to make others feel great while looking casual and confident is to introduce yourself. You don't need to be witty, as this can make people uncomfortable, especially if they don't know how to respond. Instead, keep it simple and socially on point and build from there. **From four or five feet away from others, observe what is around you and comment on it.** Depending on the situation, use one of the following options:

  » At a party, event, or church group where you know several people, simply approach them and say, **"Hi. I don't think we have met before."** Then, introduce yourself and ask her name.

  » In an everyday location (like the grocery store, while walking your dog, on the subway, or at a sporting event), **find something neutral to comment on or ask about** (such as their shoes, colorful clothing, and satisfaction with an obviously new iPhone, or comment on the exceptionally cold day, a magazine cover they are reading at the doctor's office, how adorable her pet is, or what they recommend while standing at a taco stand).

  » **Ask for their opinion or get advice about something relatable.** For example, at the grocery store, stating, "Can you tell if a pineapple is ripe?" or

"Do you recommend that brand over this one?" If you are somewhere new, state that you aren't from the area and ask if there are any good restaurants the person would recommend. At a singles event, ask about some of the activities they are attending or other events that they might know about.

» When in the neighborhood, **approach others and introduce yourself first** rather than drilling them with questions. For example, **ask yourself what you would enjoy learning about them and what you would enjoy sharing about yourself.** Then, offer this information to encourage them to respond likewise. This helps them to see that you are willing to be vulnerable and puts them at ease. Keep your questions simple and reasonable. If you want to ask where they live or who is in their family, first ask yourself if you would feel comfortable sharing this. For example, if they have a dog, say, "Your dog is so cute. I've got a Cavalier King Charles. He is so much fun. What kind of dog is yours?" Or "I think our kids are in school together. My son is Johnathan, and he's in the 2nd grade. Do you have a second grader, too?" Then, offer your name before asking theirs. Share how long you have been in the neighborhood (how frequently you engage in local activities or what you love about the area), which helps them to do the same. This can lead to questions about other places either of you has lived (people you both know or local foods you enjoy).

» **If you can, provide an appropriate comment or compliment,** such as, "You have a fun laugh (or great smile)." Just be careful about pickup lines, which usually fail to impress, especially when they are confusing or don't fit the situation (since this can seem unnatural or make you appear to be trying too hard). Trust that a safe, respectful conversation is enough to get her attention and interest. She is not looking for originality as much as she is looking for behaviors that make you appear confident while also providing an option for comfortable conversation. You can practice giving others compliments (whether male, female, young, or old) since it is simply kind and makes others feel great. So, make a habit of looking for and making brief remarks about what you see or experience. When you keep your compliments short and non-sexual, you will not appear creepy, desperate, or inappropriately aggressive. For example, imagine how you would feel if a woman at work said that you did a great job versus commenting on how your clothes accentuate your muscles. The first statement is flattering; the other is uncomfortably too personal (especially when said to women). If the first compliment were given with a sincere and respectful tone, you most likely wouldn't feel she was coming on to you, especially if she didn't linger. Likewise, a married woman won't think much about it if you give a short, appropriate compliment and then walk away. Since you can't always know who is married or not, this is enough to encourage the right people, since single women will try to keep the conversation going if they are interested. As long as you don't repeatedly give the same woman compliments every time you see her, you will not look too aggressive.

> » **When needed, use a white lie approach.** Many men have found great success with the white lie of, "You look familiar. Have we met? What school did you go to?" Often, she will respond by answering and asking several questions to confirm the possible ways you may have met. She may state, "I hear that all the time. I must just have one of those faces." If this is the case, don't let the conversation die there. Say, "Well, it's nice to meet you." Then, offer your name and learn hers. If she shows interest in continuing the conversation, maintain it for a few minutes.

- **Give a bright and warm smile that shows your teeth.** The difference between a big, close-mouthed smile and a warm, open-mouthed smile can be dramatic. People who give closed-mouthed smiles often don't realize how much it scrunches their face, flattens their lips, and closes their eyes. Close-mouthed smiles are often given to strangers as part of a general nod hello. Thus, these smiles seem businesslike and impersonal. An open-mouthed smile, however, drops your jaw, elongates your face, keeps your eyes open, and shows more enthusiasm. Sadly, many men do not smile enough. Although too much smiling and laughing could make you seem less masculine, it will still make others feel better than when you never show emotion. Thus, if in doubt, make sure you smile and laugh when possible. You will seem far more approachable if you do.

Identify their interest (or lack of) and help them feel comfortable

- **If someone seems limited in their responses when you initiate conversation, you need to pull back while remaining confident.** If they are not maintaining eye contact, are looking at their phone, stepping back, leaning away, looking around, talking with others, or saying they need to leave, this is a sign of their disinterest in the conversation, anxiety, or preoccupation with something in their life. If you don't provide a timely and respectful way for them to disengage, you will be viewed as less socially aware or appropriate.

  > » **When these behaviors occur,** always step or lean back, slow your breathing, drop your tone of voice to a deeper and more confident resonance (or chest voice), and say, "I better get back to my messages (friends, work, or podcast). It was a pleasure talking with you." Smile and redirect your attention.

  > » **Do not apologize or assume you did anything wrong.** Their reaction may have nothing to do with you. They can make the next move and continue the interaction if they choose. Assume the best, but respond in a leaned-back and casual way until they reengage you.

  > » **If you forgot to introduce yourself during the conversation, make sure you do so now.** To do this, step forward, offer to shake their hand (with a moderately firm rather than limp grip), and say, "I'm sorry. I haven't introduced myself. My name is _______. It was a pleasure meeting you."

» **Smile and prepare to say goodbye (or say nothing more) unless they seem eager to continue the conversation.** This is a confident and socially skilled way to bring the interaction to an end without dismissing her or reacting awkwardly.

» **When walking away, assume a casual pace, keep your chin up, and walk on the heels of your feet.** Walking on the balls of your feet will force your body into a more forward and fast momentum and possibly make you look like you are fleeing rather than casually leaving. Likewise, keep your chin straightforward or slightly up. This helps you maintain better posture and shows that what others do doesn't change the way you feel about yourself. By contrast, dropping your chin often simultaneously causes your shoulders to slouch, which looks like shame or regret.

- **If someone responds more cautiously but gives you their attention,** continue talking about the situation you are in or share something about yourself, followed by a relatable question, such as "I live around here. Are you from this area?"

- **When they show enthusiasm and engage fully, be sure to match their engagement.** You will know you are on the right track, and a man is interested in conversation when he asks questions, shares unsolicited information, and leans forward or comes closer. When a woman encourages and maintains the conversation, make sure you note what she is sharing and ask questions or make comments such as:

  » "Wow. That's impressive (funny, amazing, interesting, awful). What happened next?"

  » "That makes me think about something similar. After you are done, I'd love to share it."

  » "That's fascinating. How did you develop an interest in this?"

  » Ask open-ended questions that include who, what, when, where, or how questions. Asking why is usually more difficult for people to answer. "Who did you go on your trip with?" "What drew you to the idea of being a teacher?" "That is so smart and insightful. Where did you learn about that?"

- **Learn and use their name.** When you introduce yourself, they will most likely do the same. You will be more likely to remember their name if you use it twice during the conversation and when saying goodbye. If possible, note what you remember about them, their name, or their social media profiles (if you can find them) and store this information in your phone for future reference (within your contacts or notes). No word causes a more positive reaction in others than hearing their name. Thus, flatter a woman by learning and using her name each time you see her. Don't send a Facebook request unless a woman seems to be engaging in voluntary contact and the conversation is enthusiastic enough that you believe she will remember you.

During a conversation, bridge the gap, lean back, and match her

- **When a conversation is initiated and maintained, bridge the gap between you while leaving space for them to lean in.** One of the best ways to bridge the distance between you and others is to offer to shake their hand as you introduce yourself. However, most people will step closer during a conversation. Just be sure to stay in comfortable proximity, which is often about three feet apart (or roughly one arm's length). After introducing yourself, shift your weight to your backward leg (which provides an additional six inches of space between you and the other person). You can transition from your backward to your forward leg occasionally, but it is essential that you give others space so they can lean forward, too. When others participate in bridging the gap between you, they show their comfort and interest in the conversation. They can't do this, however, if you are always in the leaned-forward position. Likewise, they won't bridge the gap if you are consistently positioned four feet or more away. Being too distant makes you seem disengaged, uncomfortable, or shy. So step forward, assume the best, and then lean back casually by resting your body and weight on your backward leg. If they bridge the gap occasionally, match their efforts, and keep the conversation going.

- **When talking with others, align your eyes and chin with theirs.** Infrequent eye contact, especially when they are talking, appears disinterested or anxious. Similarly, a chin that is elevated appears arrogant, and one that is tucked in or down appears sheepish or ashamed. Instead, imagine that your eyes and chin need to align as if two rulers would connect them. These two points of contact will prevent you from looking down on others or up at them. Maintaining eye contact should not be constant or nonblinking, which is creepy. When speaking, it is natural to look up and around and then back to the listener (who should be maintaining their gaze on your face and eyes). If the listener is looking around, it shows disinterest, boredom, or discomfort. So, be sure that you offer consistent eye contact when someone is talking. Although this varies occasionally, it is typical for both eyes to look at the other person's right eye (which, from your orientation, would be on the left side of their face). You also need to read their eye contact correctly. Their eye contact (or lack thereof) and the position of their chin also reveal their confidence and curiosity (or boredom, dislike, and insecurity). With this insight, you need to respond in a way that resolves their needs. To achieve this, either match their behavior or address it directly. For example, if they are looking around or stepping back, this could indicate that they are uncomfortable, in a hurry, or need to end the conversation. To address the situation, say, "Am I keeping you? I understand if you need to leave or get back to what you were doing."

- **Read a woman's body language and match it.** The leaned-back position is essential when engaging with women because it helps them to feel more relaxed and safe. Men who lean into a woman's personal space for more than ten seconds, continue to close the gap when she is stepping back, and follow her to maintain a conversation when she is saying she needs to go (as she is walking away) will make her feel uncomfortable, pressured, intimidated, and even dominated. Thus, when a woman turns her body or steps backward, you need to give her even more space by leaning back or stepping back, too. This shows that you recognize when the natural flow of a conversation has transitioned or needs to come to an end while also allowing her the opportunity to lean in or continue the conversation on her terms if she would like. Stepping physically back is easy to do with your body language, but it can also be achieved conversationally by saying, "I know we are both busy (or should mingle). If you would like to continue this conversation, please let me know (or catch me again before you leave). It's been wonderful chatting with you." Both verbal and nonverbal recognition of her needs, words, and actions is critical. Being socially aware and sensitive to her nonverbal cues (without reacting negatively) encourages her to come back when or if she would enjoy doing so. If she returns, she's probably interested. If not, she will still think highly of you. Either way, continue to maintain confident and masculine behavior while mirroring hers. If she approaches you, respond. If she stays distant, approach briefly (to show you are assuming the best in her and yourself) and then engage others and walk away, too. Matching and mirroring a woman's behavior does not mean replicating her every move. Instead, it's an offering of similar gestures for the purpose of tuning into the other to make them more comfortable. For example, when she crosses her arms, casually cross one or both of yours for a few minutes, then relax your posture and open it up again. This matches where she is at and then guides her to a more open position. When she sits down (or is standing on a step), then sit down too (or position yourself on a lower step). This not only encourages better eye contact but also matches her position and shows you are aware of her. Likewise, when she leans forward (and you lean in slightly, too), you get to see if the added closeness triggers her to move back or linger. If she lingers, she is comfortable with you and the new closeness you share (because no woman will lean forward when she is uncomfortable). When she talks in a fast or enthusiastic tone, match it for a moment. When she becomes energetic, do so, too, but return to a more masculine pattern (rather than appearing too eager). When you slow down your speech or speed, and she mirrors you as well, take this as a good sign that you are syncing with each other (especially when she fills a lull in the conversation). These examples illustrate why staying predominantly in the leaned-back position is best for both of you. Doing this helps you to appear confident, strong, and masculine and encourages her to be more engaged, feminine, and encouraging (rather than merely reactive or feeling cornered). Until a woman is engaged in filling the gap between you by leaning in (or asking questions), you can't know if she is interested and wants more contact. Women only lean forward when they are comfortable, so observe her body language. If she leans or steps forward while maintaining eye contact, smiling, and encouraging the conversation, she may be interested. Certainly, women lean back naturally during conversations, but when they are enjoying an interaction, they will return to a more forward or engaging posture (if you are leaning back). Doing this for them not only provides her a comfortable space from which to engage with you, but it helps you avoid the squeaky voice, nervous talking, and insecure posture or neediness that comes when a man leans in for too long. Continue to lean in occasionally and for short periods. This will help her feel encouraged by your interest. Just keep returning to a confident posture. Leaning back is cool and casual. It shows you are not in a hurry, you understand social dynamics, and you can handle any situation appropriately while anticipating and respecting the needs of women.

- **Show comfort with touch while minimizing your own outreaches based on her actions.** In social exchanges, shaking hands is typically an appropriate and rarely misunderstood interaction. However, a handshake needs to show confidence. If a man grasps a person's hand in a way that is too limp or too firm, it will make him seem insecure or dominating. A limp handshake is one that is loose, weak, or just around the fingers (rather than being palm to palm with the fingers curled over the sides of the hand). One that is too firm includes seizing the hand and forcing or compressing the bones inward. A good handshake is a soft but connected grasp that provides some grip (or resistance) if it were withdrawn unexpectedly. Alternatively, it is also socially acceptable among friends and comfortable acquaintances to briefly pat or grasp the upper arm (from the mid-arm to the elbow, but not higher). This is often done when greeting, teasing, congratulating, or saying goodbye to other men or when engaging in a friendly, playful, encouraging, or flirtatious way with women. This gesture is more confident and warm than a handshake or a fast hug since it encourages eye contact and allows both parties to read the other person's facial expressions (which often communicates more than a hug can). It shows cool confidence, especially if you sustain a laugh, smile, or sweet expression during the exchange. However, just make sure the action begins from a downward (near your leg) position that comes up (rather than swinging out and around in a sideways or swooping motion, which may appear dramatic or feminine). In other words, you are simply lifting your arm to touch theirs with a sure and fluid thrust (that is similar to offering a handshake. You will aim for a few inches away from the side of their arm so that the open palm can execute a solid but nonaggressive pat that closes the distance (with the arm returning to its previous position).

- **Control anxious behavior or nervous talking by using a leaned-back posture, slower breathing, and maintaining positive, calming self-talk.** To help you calm down or to conceal your excitement, slow your breathing. Take deep abdominal breaths, and avoid holding your breath. Maintain a constant and slow intake and exhale of breath. Get in a comfortable position and stay in it for a while. Shift from time to time, but show you are at ease with yourself and the situation by acting casual rather than fidgety. You will seem more calm, casual, and sincere when you slow the pace of your speech and lower its tone to resonate more from your chest (rather than from your throat or nasal ranges), calm your hands (with actions at the abdominal or lower level, which is more masculine and prevents the possibility of nervously covering your mouth or face) and slow all your movements (which shows you are at ease and relaxed). Talk with your hands occasionally, but keep your hand motions more tame, with fingers together or just one finger pointing. Avoid fluttering your fingers or hands (which is a feminine gesture). It is better to have a thumb in the corner of a pocket or belt loop than to put one or both of your hands in a pocket. All this being said, don't worry about appearing a little nervous or excited because women are often flattered that you are excited about them. Just square your shoulders, focus on calming down and breathing, and return to a confident position. To help you calm your mind, remind yourself of what a great catch you are and how much you have to offer.

Use wit, humor, and playfulness (not sarcasm)

- **Find simple phrases that work and stick with them** (rather than pick-up lines). Men frequently look for something witty, interesting, or funny to say. When this is a random fact or a pick-up line, it will appear awkward and less confident. Such phrases can make a woman smile or respond kindly, even including a forced laugh, but often, such gestures make her feel uncomfortable since she doesn't know how to respond. Being kind is a woman's go-to and is not an indication that she is interested. Most women will relate to this and can provide many examples of how they have felt this way, which validates why being too clever is unnecessary and even undesirable when it is something random.

- **When using charisma, wit, and humor, relate it to yourself rather than using a random fact, commenting about her, or criticizing others.** Avoid self-deprecation unless you can describe your experiences, issues, or quirks (with a confident tone, posture, and smile). Charisma and humor can be impressive, especially when you add pauses for effect. Comments that include a pause before delivering the punch line get others engaged and curious. It shows confidence and playfulness and can trigger a gentle nudge. Charisma is hard to learn and usually relies on both parties vibing well with each other, but you can watch video instructions on YouTube for suggestions. Many actors and comedians demonstrate subtle body language, timing, smiles, and coy expressions that are worth experimenting with.

- **Remember that entertaining others is good, but connecting is better.** Your humor shouldn't make you the center of attention or disconnect others from you. Your comments need to be interesting (not sarcastic), make you and others seem desirable (not anxious and insecure), and create a disarming effect (rather than causing alarm or confusion). When you make others feel great, and your situational humor adds to the conversation, others can relax and enjoy the moment. Your humor needs to enhance the mood and show that you are listening, not distracting others from what they are sharing, unless you say, "Please continue with what you were saying." Keep the interaction focused on them or between you so they feel special and interested in more time with you.

Show emotional and social awareness (keep them wanting more)

- **Recognize and use one or two emotion words during your conversation.** In general, emotional words add enthusiasm, show empathy, demonstrate active listening skills, and indicate social and emotional maturity. So, look for and practice emotional words in a variety of situations. This will help you to be ready to recognize and use them appropriately. For example, "That must have been disappointing (exciting, lonely, hilarious, encouraging, satisfying, a dream come true, amazing, confusing, frustrating, annoying, or triggering)." Emotion words like sad, mad, and glad are not enough to indicate your empathy or emotional maturity. To broaden your awareness and use of emotion words, refer to Appendix C and the activities there. This advice is essential for both men and women to find greater success and engagement from others. Women can do this in abundance, but men need to be cautious about overdoing the use of emotional words, or they may seem too nice and intense or effeminate. Similarly, women often think they are warm, inviting, and emotionally expressive when, in fact, they do far less of this than they realize. Thus, in general, having a goal of using one or two emotional words in each interaction is essential for both genders.

- **Avoid grilling others with a shotgun approach to questions in which they are always on defense and solely vulnerable.** It is uncomfortable to be the only one being vulnerable or grilled for information, which is why sharing information and then asking is a better approach. "This summer, I went to one of my favorite camping spots in the Rocky Mountains. What outdoor or summer activities are your favorite? Do you have any suggestions?" It is critical to maintain balanced conversations. Grilling questions and dominating conversations are common turn-offs for singles, and both men and women can be criticized for doing this. So, don't hesitate to get the conversation back on track with a gentle redirection to a better topic. If the other person does not respond to your efforts to shift the conversation, this may be an indication of a potential social learning challenge, lack of empathy, or a mental health episode (in which racing speech and disjointed thoughts are common). Fortunately, redirecting a conversation usually works because, most of the time, others respond well and appreciate your efforts to create a more balanced, casual, and enjoyable connection.

- **Give others time and space when asking questions and sharing information.** If someone continues to raise questions or make comments, then they are comfortable and interested in maintaining a conversation. This is a great sign. Just make sure you are providing a balanced discussion by regularly answering the questions you ask them (and vice versa). For example, "Where did you grow up? I've spent most of my life near here." If they keep asking you questions but aren't volunteering or reciprocating, don't hesitate to say, "Thank you for being interested in my thoughts, but I'd love to learn how you feel about this topic, too."

- **Use decisive language, avoid unnecessary apologies, and never make self-deprecating statements.** It is important that you don't put yourself down or act as though you are weak or incapable. This is not being humble; it is being self-deprecating and is very unattractive. If you don't make an issue out of your faults, most other people won't either. Also, show that you have confidence by expressing your opinions, thoughts, or needs decisively. To do this, you need to recognize those words and phrases that disqualify or weaken your feelings and needs, such as, "I kind of like_____," or "I guess that's okay," or "I sort of think _____," or "I don't care." Others can't get to know you when you minimize or avoid having an opinion. Other forms of hedging include using a weak, soft, or fluctuating voice (or mumble), using contradictory facial expressions, or making a statement while elevating your tone of voice so it sounds like a question rather than a comment. When your tone of voice is strong and low, and your chin is raised a little, you show conviction and certainty. Although women appreciate men who can admit when they are wrong or don't know something, if this is a constant pattern of indecision, it can be unattractive. Women like decisiveness in men. It makes men look strong and competent and prevents them from falling into the too-nice trap. Therefore, make it a general rule to express your opinion, preferences, feelings, or needs at least once during each encounter with a particular woman. You can still change your mind later. This way, when you occasionally need to ask for help, admit you were wrong, ask for directions, or solicit suggestions, you seem like a competent man who is also more likable, human, and sincere, which makes women feel more comfortable and emotionally safe around you.

- **Be a little more expressive about yourself.** This shows her you know your worth. Don't be afraid to share who you are, what you do, the things you enjoy, or the things you are good at. Being able to talk about yourself and your strengths is not boastful, arrogant, or self-centered. It says that you like yourself and have confidence in your worth. It also gives you an opportunity to see how she'll respond as she learns about you. If she quickly changes the subject, seems offended, or acts insecure, you will have learned a lot about her possible lack of empathy or interest in you. Remember, however, that your situation does not define your worth, so do not set yourself up for money diggers by talking about your possessions, education, or career as though you have to prove your value. These things are a part of your life and experiences, but they are not who you are. Don't be afraid to casually discuss these things when the time seems right, but make sure you emphasize other truths about yourself much more. Furthermore, it can be fun for a woman to discover new things about you as she spends more time with you. It adds intrigue, mystery, and excitement, leaving her curious about what more there is to discover. On the flip side, if you lack great possessions, feel your current "status" is in question, or believe you have a lackluster job, remember again, your situation does not define your value. Do not believe that you are uninteresting and undesirable to women because of your financial status. Most women are looking for qualities in men, not status alone. They are looking for men who are hardworking, driven to succeed, and active in improving their situation—in other words, men they can trust and respect. A woman knows that a wealthy doctor who is a louse and berates her has no value to her in the end. A hardworking man who makes a modest income but treats her great, cares about her needs, and makes her feel safe and secure is by far a better prize. A woman's number-one need is not money. It's safety and security. Don't make your financial status an issue when you can offer her so much more. Don't keep yourself from pursuing a woman because of your situation. Know your worth and all you have to offer that will make her feel great. Act strong and confident. Pursue her and let her decide for herself if you have the qualities she is looking for, just as you will be doing with her.

- **Comment on or complement her opinions or ideas.** Just as it is important for you to show you like yourself, you need to be expressive about things you enjoy or appreciate relative to her statements. Compliments that are too global will seem untrustworthy, such as "You are so amazing." Instead, express something specific, like "That's smart (impressive, interesting, fascinating," or "Wow, that makes me think," or "What a unique (great, cool) idea (or perspective)."

- **When feeling awkward, just rely on your techniques to make you look strong and confident.** If you say or do something that you feel is stupid or awkward, don't obsess about it. Instead, focus your attention on your posture. Straighten your back, relax your shoulders, keep your chin forward, lean back or (spread out), and use confident statements while repeating in your mind: *What I said or did does not define my worth or value. I don't need to be perfect. I just need to act strong and confident. If I don't make an issue out of my mistake, it will quickly be forgotten.*

- **When in social gatherings, church, the neighborhood, or singles events, showcase your group connections by introducing others to those you are meeting.** You can do this by including those nearby in the conversation. "Jane, have you met Sara? She is a graduate student like you." This is a great way to make others feel comfortable and important, and can keep conversations from going stale by building on group dynamics.

- **Keep most initial conversations under ten to fifteen minutes at the most.** Meeting new people and enjoying a fun and engaging discussion can be exciting. However, it is better to leave them wanting more than to linger too long. Recognizing the high point in a conversation (whether two or ten minutes into a conversation) and then transitioning to an invitation for more contact and further discussions is far more effective.

Convert conversations to numbers

- **Don't linger too long.** Remember, when starting a conversation, your goal isn't to run out of things to say but to leave them wanting more because they couldn't get enough. By being someone who is going places, doing things, and engaging in productive activities and relationships (yet willing to spend time continuing a conversation later), you appear more desirable. So don't hesitate to prepare them for the ending of the conversation by saying, "I apologize. I have to go (or get back to work, return a call, connect with a few friends before they leave), but please finish what you were saying. I just wanted you to know I need to leave in a minute." This keeps you from cutting them off or abruptly ending the conversation, and it makes you look more confident, outgoing, productive, and desirable

- **If you have decided you aren't interested,** you can use the "I have to leave soon" technique to provide a respectful exit to the conversation without encouraging more contact. Make sure that you provide a friendly but less enthusiastic vibe. Don't show as much warmth, encourage additional conversation, ask as many questions, or offer personal information. Also, don't engage in or encourage touch beyond a simple handshake. Simply say goodbye and leave it there.

- **If the conversation is going well and you sense they may be interested, make sure you assess their relationship status (when possible).** To do this, look for a ring, ask questions to reveal their situation, and be prepared with a casual compliment. It can be uncomfortable to misinterpret a conversation as being flirtatious when the other person didn't intend to convey interest. Looking for a ring on someone's ring finger (i.e., left hand on the finger next to the pinky) is always a good practice. However, not everyone wears their ring (when at the gym, at work, or because it has been forgotten), so if it isn't present, there is no guarantee that they are single. To confirm their relationship status, ask follow-up questions relative to something they mention. For example, "Your husband (or boyfriend) must be proud of you," or when talking about something fun they did, asking, "Did you do this with friends, family, a boyfriend, or on your own?" This provides a gentle assumption rather than an awkward question. They may still struggle to provide a response, but either way, you will get valuable information. If they are potentially interested in you, they will clarify their relationship status with comments like, "I don't have a boyfriend" or "I went with my ex." If they ignore the reference and only refer to friends, family, or doing something alone, this is a good indicator, too. If they pick up on the hint and are married or in a relationship, they will reference their partner from there forward. When this is the case, casually reduce your enthusiasm and investment in them and end the conversation without commenting on their relationship status. Having a fun conversation is not inappropriate or something you need to apologize for.

- **If the interaction is going well** (because when you pause, they ask more questions, continue the conversation, or encourage the idea of talking again in the future), **offer to exchange numbers**. There are many nuances to encouraging social interaction and future contact in different situations.

- **When you have had several interactions (or you don't anticipate seeing someone again)**, seize the moment with confidence and state, "I could talk with you forever. I wish I had more time. I'd love to continue this conversation, but I'd better go (get back to work, finish responding to my texts, get back to my studying, find my friends, or get lunch). However, it would be awesome to exchange numbers so we can continue to chat about this at another time." If you have irregular contact or have interacted a few times and are unsure of their interest, this is a great opportunity to discover their interest level. Be prepared to act like you are ready to walk away, either with or without their number. This takes the pressure off and requires that they engage further (and be more vulnerable, too) if you are going to share numbers. Saying this as you prepare to shake their hand, smile, and walk away helps them to fear missing out. If you are somewhere you can't leave, then lean back in your chair, pick up your phone, or continue your music with only one earbud in the opposite ear from them. If they are interested, they will stop you or bring it up. When they participate in and encourage the idea of exchanging their number, they are more likely to follow through.

- **When they seem to be fully engaged in the conversation** (as evidenced by their questions, leaning forward, animated body language, and enthusiasm), **reward their investment** (or A-list interaction) **by showing you will make time for them** (while still leaving them wanting more). When both parties are enthused about the other, they experience more excitement and hope for contact. You can build on this energy without overplaying your enthusiasm by saying, "I'm going to need to leave in a minute, but I think I can spare another ten minutes. I really want to hear the rest of this, and I hate to go." Doing this with a smile or playful wink will encourage them. This also helps you keep the conversation from running dry and creates a great segue for exchanging numbers.

- **If they are on your A list and you sense that you are on theirs,** don't hesitate to compliment them and show enthusiasm by saying, "I have to go, but I know I would regret it if I didn't ask. I'd love to exchange numbers and continue this conversation or do something fun together."

- **When you are unsure of their interest, don't hesitate to encourage more contact by using the MOST OBVIOUS and CONVENIENT TRUTH about the situation.** It is often hard to know how to transition from a conversation to encouraging more contact, especially when you have had very little contact so far. However, there is one technique that is natural, socially relevant, and provides a cool and casual vibe in EVERY situation. All you need to say in these circumstances is, "It is so hard to get to know someone at these events (on an app, in a college class, at the store, in the neighborhood, at a party, or when with friends). I'd love to exchange numbers so we can finish this conversation by text or on the phone."

- **At any point in a conversation, you can use a question or topic as a jumping-off point for exchanging information.** Whether you are messaging on an app, texting, or talking while in line for food at a major league game, you can state, "That is an awesome question, and it would be so much more fun to share over a quick bite to eat or an activity. Plus, I'd love to hear more about your trip. Let's exchange numbers (get on a phone call or plan something fun) and talk about this more soon. I'd love to continue this conversation if you would enjoy that, too."

- **When you ask for her number, be sure you do so from a leaned-back position so you don't look intense or too vulnerable.** Leaning back relaxes your abdominal and throat muscles. Leaning forward tightens these muscles and increases the risk that your voice will squeak or tremble. Men who are in the leaned-forward position also tend to be less direct (i.e., they ramble) as they ask for a woman's number, whereas men who keep their weight on their back foot appear more casual, confident, and direct (probably because they feel more relaxed). Also, be sure you make eye contact and keep your chin forward.

- **Don't forget that the number-one need of a woman is to feel safe and secure.** Men who lean forward, who tower over her, or who lean into her space while asking for her number or a date create too much intensity and look creepy. It's not that they are asking for her contact information, but how they are asking for it that turns her off. It's all about their posture and stance. So, if you ask for her number and she responds with hesitation or uncertainty and explains that she is excessively busy, give her a little more space. To do this, keep your chin forward, maintain eye contact, and shift your posture by simply transitioning to your backward leg, a small step back, or leaning back in your seat. By giving her a little more physical space to think, you increase the chance that she will feel more secure and safe, and you will look more attractive, confident, and socially skilled.

- **Make sure you choose words that show you are asking without pressure or expectations.** Saying,

- "I would *regret not asking. Can I get your number?*" is different than saying, "I'd *regret not getting your number*" or "*We should exchange numbers.*" The first shows bravery and personal responsibility, from which she can say no without diminishing your courage and confidence. It is easy to respond to a woman's rejection with, "I appreciate your honesty. It's hard to say no. I'm even more impressed, and I'm glad I asked. I truly wish you the best." This is classy and shows you can walk away feeling successful by seizing the moment, which is a personal accomplishment. By contrast, the second approach creates pressure and expectation because saying, "*I'd regret not getting your number,*" or "*We should* exchange numbers," implies that her reaction is tied to your feelings. "Should" statements impose an expectation or command. "We" statements create an assumption that she should act or that she is already in agreement with your desires. This bypasses a request and burdens her to have to agree or reject you. Her agreement isn't a gift but an expectation. Thus, your statement is not a request that took bravery but an imposition. The only positive outcome for you is if you get what you want. If you read her interest accurately, she will have a positive response to these poorly formed statements, but since you can't know for sure if she is interested, using a request is more attractive and desirable, which allows both of you to save face and shows greater respect. The secret to navigating this is to always start with "I" statements, followed by a feeling or hope, and then a request. From this, you can express your gratitude for her answer (either way) and your shameless relief for having no regrets.

- **If in doubt, ask for her number anyway.** Don't ask if you aren't interested in texting, calling, or getting to know her better, but also don't hesitate just because you aren't sure you'll have the confidence or courage to call later. If you like her and think you might want to call, keep the option open by going for her number. With the right techniques, you can always manage and reduce any pressure or expectations that may arise later. So, don't overthink the situation. You will look more confident, strong, and attractive to others when you fearlessly seize the moment. Whether she is interested or not, if you handle rejection well, she will still feel flattered by your courageous interest in her. Furthermore, you feel better knowing one way or the other if she is interested. Taking action creates more confidence than passivity and overanalysis. You are prepared—you can manage rejection well, so you have very little to lose. Furthermore, most women will not reject you, and if they do, they will be kind.

When you exchange numbers, create a contact (and a lasting impression)

- **When a woman provides her number, pull out your phone and create a contact.** Enter her name and phone number and confirm that you have it right. Ask if she would like your number, too, so she will recognize you when you call.

- **After getting her number, tell her you will reach out soon, but don't lock a woman into any plans at that moment.** It is always best to leave others feeling curious rather than feeling pressured. If you immediately ask her when a good time is to call, this can feel like pressure or trigger anxiety. Instead, just say you will be in contact and are excited to continue chatting or getting to know her.

- **Show confidence as you casually walk away.** No matter how smoothly or awkwardly the experience progresses, you need to show strength and confidence. To do this, always keep your chin forward or slightly up, which will naturally straighten your back and square your shoulders (whereas dropping your chin will make you slouch and look sheepish or ashamed). Slowly walk on the heels of your feet (rather than on the balls of your feet, which will cause you to look like you are fleeing anxiously). Pull your elbows slightly back and away from your body, which will make you look broad, or add a little swagger. And finally, solidify the overall effect by silently repeating to yourself, *Dang, I look good to her right now!* because it is true.

- **After walking away, take a minute to update and organize her contact information.** Before you forget the details, you need to add important information into the note section of her contact information with descriptions of what she looked like, what you talked about, and how you met her. You don't want to embarrass yourself later by not remembering these details. It's essential that you create a section in your contacts that is dedicated specifically to those you are dating. If you don't do this, you will struggle to track and maintain contact with them, especially if they get lost among the many other contacts you have on your phone. Follow-through is absolutely essential at this point, so take a few minutes to do this before you get busy with other things. This is also a great time to add any social media links or pictures you can find to the contact, so you will recognize her face.

- **After you walk away, text her with a relatable question.** For example, "This is John from _______ (the place you met). It was great talking with you today. I forgot to ask whether you prefer texts or phone calls." Reminding her of where you met can help her recall the details and your identity. By asking a follow-up question, she is more likely to respond (which will confirm for you that you have the right number. You can ask a different question if you prefer.

- **If a woman doesn't respond to your calls or texts, give it a few days before reaching out again, and don't react negatively.** It is possible that she gave you a fake number. Women do this as a seemingly kind option rather than directly rejecting a man. Of course, this can be discouraging, hurtful, and insulting (to some men), but try to see it from a woman's perspective. This is less often meant as something hurtful but reveals her own discomfort, fears, and difficulties with being assertive or saying no.

- **If she quickly sends a response, question, or message,** it's likely she is sincerely interested and will keep responding.

- **If she acts sheepish or uncomfortable after providing her number, reassure her and take the pressure off.** Even when a woman is initially excited about you, she may have doubts or express concerns (since she doesn't know you). Don't take this personally. Instead, see it as an opportunity to put her at ease and show self-respect. To do this, say, "I get it. It's important for women to feel comfortable and safe, especially when they don't know someone well. No worries. If you want to think about it, you can reach out any time, and when we meet, we can do it somewhere in a public place or as part of a group activity as friends. And if you want to say no, I respect that, too. Dating is fun and doesn't need to feel like pressure. I can handle hearing no. I just want to have fun and get to know you, but I'm truly okay with whatever you feel is best for you."

- **If you feel it may help her feel more comfortable meeting you, share your social media pages (which will also help her remember who you are).** It can be difficult for a woman to remember all the people she meets through just their number or texting history. Thus, help her to have a positive, lasting impression of you by texting a picture or sending her a link to your social media. To do this, state, "Just so it is easier to recognize me with my number, here's a picture," or "Since you don't know me well, here is my social media. I thought sharing more information might be comforting or help you learn a little more about me. I look forward to chatting some more soon."

Maximize your social opportunities

- **Don't overthink the situation.** Do take action, assume the best, and make others feel great. When tempted to believe that others know everyone while you awkwardly sit alone, take confidence in knowing that this is rarely true. In a social setting, many people have superficial relationships at best. They just enjoy being a part of the group, and the bigger it is, the better. Additionally, they are too preoccupied with the event or their own lives to bother noticing you. Unless you demand their attention in negative and draining ways, the only thing they will remember about you is how you made them feel. If you don't make a meaningful and positive impact on them, they won't remember your small mistakes or social missteps after a few minutes (especially when you laugh it off or confidently recover). You simply aren't that important. It may hurt to realize this, but it is freeing, too. Instead of worrying, be glad you aren't actually the center of attention (no matter how much your anxiety attempts to convince you otherwise). Let loose, have more fun, speak up, give compliments, and be more enthusiastic when listening to others. The energy you add to the group or during individual conversations makes you look great while making others feel great, too. So relax! After all, you really have nothing to lose (by getting out of your head) and everything to gain (by making others feel great).

- **Focus on connection and service.** Instead of letting your mind and anxieties go wild, remember that social discomfort is normal. If you are unsure how to add to an event, connect with others through simple acts of service. If you sit at a table where others have run out of water, offer to get them more. If you see others staying late to clean up, jump in and help. When a small group is talking about grabbing ice cream, and you aren't included, look to see who else is alone and suggest that you each invite a few people and go to Applebee's for a dessert or drinks. And when you can't find any other way to be helpful, ask who set up the event and share how much you appreciate their efforts and would love to volunteer to help next time. You can be a memorable, useful, and reliable group member. For those who identify as shy, service provides a great way to show you are kind and supportive. Additionally, conversations are easier to engage in and maintain when you and others work side by side. Happily engaging in a group makes you appear confident, trustworthy, socially aware, and empathetic. Likewise, you benefit from knowing you are needed and appreciated.

- **Focus on your strengths, successes, and growing connections.** Pure and lasting change always flows from a person's strengths, not their weaknesses. So, identify your skills, recognize what went right, participate more fully with those who engage you, and count your blessings. In time, you will feel more successful, resilient, likable, hopeful, and valuable.

- **Save your issues, anger, depression, and resentment for close friends or therapists.** The only people a group never wants around are those who complain, make demands, compete inappropriately for attention (with random and irrelevant details), get easily offended, and expect support and recognition while providing very little value and enjoyment for others. Groups exist to provide entertainment, fun, and shared positive experiences. Groups that don't maintain a vibrant and energetic population usually develop less attendance or die out. Certainly, a one-on-one conversation can include a few personal details. Still, you need to wait until a relationship has deep roots and a strong foundation before putting too much pressure on the emerging friendship. If you are depressed, rather than weighing others down, focus on having fun and finding joy in the moment. Doing this will lift your mood. In many ways, *faking it until you make* it is a good technique for distracting and managing your problems and stress.

- **Develop individual connections with group members and then jump into the larger group.** As explained in Chapter 4, look for the transitional or supporting characters in a desirable group. Approach them when they are nearby or alone. Learn and use their name and encourage a conversation that discovers and builds on your common interests. When they are in a group later in the evening or during a different event, approach them and the group confidently. Stand next to them and say hello without demanding their attention. Listen, laugh, smile, and nod as you stay near your new acquaintance.

- **Notice if the group expands to include (or retracts to exclude) you and respond appropriately.** If those near you step back or turn their bodies toward you, thus expanding the circle, you have been unconsciously included in the group. Stay, participate, and assume the best. Introduce yourself to others and compliment a few of them (for their hair, clothes, comments, smiles, or humor). If, instead, those near you turn their backs or step between you and others in the group, thus closing the circle, confidently touch your acquaintance on the arm and say, "I'll catch you later. It's good seeing you." If your acquaintance engages you in conversation, stay and observe how others engage or don't. Remember that what others do or say reflects on them and their needs or issues. It's not your right to read their mind and falsely assume they have nefarious intentions and are critical of you. It's a waste of time and energy to assume the worst. You can always join other groups or build a one-on-one connection with your new friend or others. The most important question isn't whether you can get this group's acceptance, but whether you would want or enjoy it. You don't have to judge or fear others. Just do your part and follow the joy and fun you experience until you find your preferred group of friends.

- **Observe the group and ensure you add value before attempting to hold their attention.** Laughing, making a brief comment, or asking questions is a great way to show that you understand the role of a supportive character in a group dynamic. Standing or sitting while providing intermittent smiles, occasional nods, and consistent eye contact is enough for you to remain a transitional character, especially if you act comfortable and unapologetic. Make sure you learn others' names and offer yours when appropriate. "Oh, I'm sorry. I haven't met you yet. My name is Jane. I love your hair (comment, laugh, smile, or fun personality)." Until you have learned three to five people's names and assessed who the existing leaders (i.e., captain or manager) are, don't challenge their position. If you develop a good vibe with them and they actively engage, laugh, and encourage your comments, avoid being too assertive or attention-seeking. If the whole group seems to be enthusiastically engaging with you, then you may be perceived as a potential leader. In this case, support and encourage their participation and provide positive reinforcement to make them feel recognized and valuable. Ask for a few numbers while sharing how fun and awesome these individuals are. Don't linger too long. Instead, leave them wanting more and express a desire to plan another activity or do something fun soon (whether one-on-one or as a group).

- **When the night is early, and you won't be leaving an event for a while, encourage others to catch you later** so you can keep chatting (dancing or hanging out) then. When you need to mingle but want to make others feel great and continue to connect with you, express, "I am sorry. I need to get back to my friends (grab something to eat, catch someone before they leave), but I'd love you to find me later so we can continue this conversation."

- **When in a group situation, take opportunities for a personal connection so you can offer to exchange numbers.** The simplest and easiest way to get someone's number is to speak frankly about the situation you are in. When talking more privately, it is appropriate to gently touch someone on the arm and say, "It's so hard to get to know someone at church (in the store, at a game, or during a party), but I'd love to continue talking with you. Let me know if you would enjoy exchanging numbers so we can chat later." Make sure you say, "I'd love to see you again." Do not weaken your emotional words from being bold and confident to merely friendly. Doing so is less flattering for women, confusing, or can be interpreted as a polite way to brush them off. It is common for others to hear, "It would be nice to see you again," or "It would be fun to talk when I see you at the next party," which rarely includes any follow-up. A woman doesn't know if she should act friendly or flirtatious in such situations, which is why she prefers to hear, "I'd love to call you or do something fun to continue this conversation," or "I hate to leave and wish I could get to know you better. I'd love to exchange numbers." When you do one of these while preparing to walk away, she will feel flattered, especially if she doesn't feel pressured or uncomfortable.

- **If you recognize her hesitation, comment on it to alleviate the pressure while remaining confident and assertive.** To do this, state, "If you aren't ready to exchange numbers because you don't know me well enough, I understand. We can chat or hang out in a group until you know me better if that feels more comfortable." Alternatively, you can offer to give her your number so she can reach out when she is ready. Both of these responses can be used to take the pressure off, but they need to appear confident and non-apologetic, too. A good way to approach this (if it is true) is to provide a flattering qualifier before transitioning to your request to exchange numbers. To do this, add "I don't normally do this, but I'd regret not asking," followed by, "It's so hard to get to know someone in this situation. Can I get your number so we can keep chatting about this later?" As long as you don't use this technique in the same social circles with multiple women, it will make her feel special while opening the door for your lower-pressure alternatives.

- **Be prepared to respectfully reject a woman with whom you are not interested.** If a woman at a party or event suggests exchanging numbers and you know you are not interested in her romantically, you can communicate this rather than brushing her off (which may cause you to look like a jerk). Rather than giving a fake number, faking interest, making promises you don't want to keep (or will cancel), lying about being in a relationship, or providing a different excuse, say, "I'd enjoy a few more friendly exchanges or doing something as a group. Sure, let's exchange numbers or chat through social media to stay in touch periodically. Thanks for asking." This redirects her to the types of engagement you would be open to without shutting her down entirely. She should recognize the hint, but your response time relative to her texts or social media messages can also reveal your less-than-A or B-list interest. If you respond a few days after a text, only provide a thumbs up, or redirect her to group activities rather than one-on-one encounters, she will know you are not interested in being more than a casual or friendly acquaintance. If needed, however, you can also clarify your intentions by stating, "I respect and appreciate you as a friend, but don't feel a romantic connection." If you would enjoy becoming friends, you can also add, "If you feel the same and want to enjoy that activity as friends, I'd enjoy that, too." It doesn't hurt to add a flattering compliment to ease the pain of rejection, such as, "You truly are amazing, and I am flattered you felt impressed enough by me to want more time together."

- **Always walk away with confidence and faith in yourself and her**. Whether you exchanged numbers or not, make sure you keep your chin up (which prevents slouching and helps to straighten your back) as you slowly walk away on your heels. Use positive self-talk, especially when either of you rejects the other. To do this, repeat to yourself all the things that make you a great catch, followed by: *I have just proved to her that I am a smart, kind, respectful, and courageous man. If she values and appreciates such things, she will invest in me, too. Either way, she is not my only chance for happiness, but she is good practice.* And when you need to reject her, repeat to yourself: *She is smart, strong, and capable. How she feels about herself is not dependent on or changed by one person's rejection. She will be okay. I have faith in her resilience and future.*

- **When you can't ask for her number (or provide yours), leave a hint for how she can get ahold of you later.** When you are unable to get time alone with someone (thus, exchanging numbers isn't possible), act strong, masculine, and approachable by dropping a hint as to how she could contact you. For example, when in a group setting, you could say, "If you would feel more comfortable, I can walk you to your car since it is dark (or a sketchy part of town)," which opens an opportunity for her to accept time alone with you. You could also mention something about being on Facebook, Instagram, X, or LinkedIn after ensuring she has learned your full name. If she mentions her social media, you can ask how best to find her account or pull out your phone to find her. If you don't want it to seem too obvious that you are singling her out, ask to find others' accounts, too, but then message her privately. You can also encourage the group members to share their numbers so you can stay in contact, thus guaranteeing you get her number and vice versa. Likewise, she will have yours and can do the same. Please be aware that group texts can become annoying when others message individuals through the group text rather than individually. The delivery of group texts can also be inconsistent for those who have Androids versus iPhones. This is why GroupMe can be a better resource for collaborating with group members about events. After getting this information, wait a few days before sending a private text or social media message that states, "I wish we had had more time at the party to chat. You seem sweet and fun. I'd love to get to know you better." If you don't get a response a week later, you can send a social media friend request or a like to see if this garners a reaction. Don't do more than this for now, or you may seem creepy. Wait until your next opportunity to connect at a social gathering. When there, act confident, warm, and engaging while reading her body language and other cues to see if she pursues more contact or keeps a distance. It's important that you don't create a reputation for aggressively pursuing women who are not interested and haven't volunteered their number. It is less socially acceptable or confident to use social media if direct one-on-one interaction is available (because it is too passive and common for men to reach out with unsolicited interest). This can be flattering when it is clear that you both were interested, but the opportunity to exchange numbers was not convenient (or could have been hurtful to others at the event). Thus, a short message and friend request are appropriate as long as you don't push for more if she doesn't reciprocate.

Be emotionally responsive while preventing vulnerability

- **Use good boundaries relative to your personal issues and how vulnerable you are willing to be until you know someone better.** Women often build relationships by talking about the people and problems in their lives. Being vulnerable and problem-solving their issues together can feel like a relaxing and meaningful bonding experience for women; however, for men, they bond through doing things and activities together. Men are often willing to discuss difficult topics and emotions that someone they care about is experiencing, but this is heavy and taxing for them. Thus, women may appreciate you sharing some challenging experiences or emotions with them, but since this would be quite unnatural from what they experience with other men, they may see it as a warning sign. Some women will also feel it's a sign of intimacy or believe you are offering a more meaningful interaction (whether as a friend or romantic partner), especially if you also say things like, "I feel so naturally close to you as if I've known you before." This may seem flattering, but it also makes them feel prematurely responsible for you or hopeful about a relationship. Be careful about how emotionally vulnerable or interconnected you become with someone too soon, since this can make either of you vulnerable or easily manipulated. More experienced women will be turned off by seemingly insincere and premature emotional expressions, and it would be wise for you to see these as red flags, too. Most people, during the initial first few weeks, will get discouraged by heavy topics and deeply personal or traumatic experiences that a person shares. They may desire to prove themselves to others and be supportive, but most women who are in a good place in their lives want someone who is also in a good place. Overly nurturing (and younger) women or those who are more toxic may embrace you and your vulnerabilities either because they like to be needed or they can use your vulnerabilities to blind you from their problems and manipulations. Unfortunately, healthy women will distance themselves from you because your problems overwhelm and burden them, and they know you aren't in a good place for a relationship. Although you may be trying to connect by being personal and vulnerable, you will get better results if you use fun and engaging emotional words while listening to a woman's experiences and discovering her hobbies and interests. In time, you can go deeper and develop greater trust and emotional investments.

- **Make her feel safe and secure (while recognizing warning signs).** When a woman shows vulnerability or weakness, apologizes for a mistake, or shares something personal about herself, you need to respond with warmth. When a woman mentions a sad or deeply personal event or issue in her life, do not ignore or pursue it more deeply. Instead, choose to act confident, happy, and interesting while either briefly empathizing and complimenting her (by saying, "I'm sorry. That sucks," or, "You seem to be doing really well given all you've gone through"). If the problem is common enough and you want to make her feel comfortable, add, "I've made mistakes like that before, too." If she shares something that is deeply personal, vulnerable, sad, or tragic (and pushes you to be vulnerable, too), she may be coming out of a bad experience (and, as such, is not in a good place for dating), or she may be trying to manipulate you.

- **Redirect the conversation, and observe how she responds.** If you briefly empathize (to help her feel you care) and then say, "I'm sorry you have gone through that. I'd love to learn more once we get to know each other better. For now, I'd love to help you escape that for a few hours. Would you be interested in enjoying a fun activity together?" This redirects a woman to a more socially and emotionally appropriate way to engage (which many women will immediately recognize and appreciate as a healthy and more positive shift in the conversation). Those who continue to talk about the details of their situation while also pressing for you to see them right away, help them (financially and emotionally), or use seduction are manipulating you. Do not drop a boundary or agree to something she wants just because she shows vulnerability. Expressing and keeping a boundary (by saying, "I don't think that will work for me," or, "I wouldn't feel comfortable getting involved in this situation since we don't know each other well enough yet") will quickly reveal her insincerity (and anger, manipulations, or victim playing). Always trust your gut. Don't engage in conversations or exchanges of money, sexual contact, or anything else, especially when someone is pressuring you (which is always a clear warning sign). It is not normal or socially appropriate for a woman to talk sexually to you or about you when with a near stranger, especially after you show or express discomfort. Such behavior is not flattery. It is a clear warning sign that she has significant self-control issues that will prove problematic later.

When (and how) to reject or reconsider

For your convenience, this chapter highlights each technique (i.e., action or behavioral strategy) by using a bullet format. Consider each bullet as a potential goal or technique you can apply. No one can work on more than three goals or behaviors at a given time, so choose the most appealing options first and leave the others for another time. Remember, making a meaningful connection is the goal, not perfection.

Identify potential red flags (due to their lack of E.S.P.)

Ensuring your and your family's financial, emotional, and sexual safety and security often depends on early detection of those who are potentially abusive and manipulative. This can be a tall order since you are unlikely to see anything more than small hints, confusing behavior, or passing comments that they or you could easily justify or minimize. However, when you sift out these incidents through the perspective of normal human error versus significant signs of a lack of Empathy, Self-control, and Personal responsibility (or E.S.P.), you can confidently determine if it is wise to reject them or allow more time to get to know them. When engaging in only a few brief exchanges, you can't know if their lack of E.S.P. would indicate an active addiction, unlawful behavior, infidelities, toxic manipulations, or other abusive behaviors, but you don't need to wait to find out. A lack of E.S.P. is at the heart of the unbearable problems that most partners complain about once in a relationship. When you recognize the red flags of a lack of E.S.P. early on, you save yourself unnecessary heartache.

No person is perfect, so waiting for the best relationship or individual is fundamentally flawed and a waste of time. At the end of the day, you will only have the option to choose real life, real people, and real love. The best doesn't exist (especially once you know the person and their flaws), but you do need to distinguish the difference between those people and relationships that offer bad, good, and better outcomes. If you doubt the red flags that you see and wait for more information, you may struggle to disconnect later, especially after you develop feelings of attachment (since manipulators excel at exploiting emotions while creating false trust). Thus, your best chance for a better relationship requires exercising and trusting your skills to identify others' (and your) challenges and strengths with E.S.P.

To ensure a better outcome, follow these **4 Steps to the 3 Date Rule** for exposing the potentially abusive and manipulative.

1. **Know the warning signs of a lack of Empathy, Self-control, and Personal responsibility** (or E.S.P.).

2. **Express a feeling or need, say no, set a boundary, share an opinion, or be imperfect, and then watch their reaction.** A person's challenges with E.S.P. are not exposed when you give them what they want, act kind, or make everything easy and comfortable. A person's ability to see another's perspective, admit when they are wrong, and take action to improve, or exercise restraint for the benefit of others (and as a reflection on their core values) is only evident when the focus is on someone else, and they can't obtain immediate gratification. Kindness is not the same as empathy. Empathy is inconvenient and requires self-control for the benefit of others. Being responsible (i.e., paying bills, going to work, and improving one's social or personal status) isn't the same as personal responsibility (which requires the ability to engage in self-reflection, admit when they are wrong, and take action to create change over a prolonged period). Likewise, significant problems with self-control issues (like drug, alcohol, and sexual addictions, illegal behaviors, verbal and physical abuse, and reckless spending that have life-changing impacts) are not just something you can love someone out of. They have to be resolved and sustained over time by the perpetrator with an ongoing openness to receiving help.

3. **Ensure you are being honest with yourself by being honest with others who will help you to see the truth (in yourself and those you date).** When you share every detail of your dating and relationship experiences with a few trusted friends or family members who are healthy examples of the life and relationships you desire, you will feel more confident about why you stay or leave a potential relationship. Charming people who are impressive and flattering toward you won't have the same influence over outsiders (since these individuals are not caught up in the person's manipulations). Thus, your friends, family, or counselors will see through the fog that the manipulators create and recognize potential inconsistencies or deceptions. Thus, if there is something you don't want to share because you fear your friends or family will judge your partner, this indicates you already know something feels off. Saying it out loud will help you get in touch with what their words or behaviors actually mean. If those in your circle of trust don't see the issue as a big deal, then your anxiety will be resolved, and you can put the issue to rest. If they do see concerns, you will feel empowered with ways to get more information, address the issue, or walk away. Either way, the truth will set you free because facing the facts either becomes

comforting and empowering or alarming and motivating. Now, you can respond accordingly.

4. **Trust your gut.** Whether you have all the information you need or not, stomach discomfort, anxiety, difficulty sleeping, bad memories, fears, and a desire to avoid a situation (or desperately clinging to a person or relationship) might mean something. Talking with friends, setting boundaries to observe your partner's reactions, or canceling a date are appropriate whenever you feel uncomfortable. You are the only one who can know what is right for you. If your gut feelings can be dissected into specific experiences that also fit with a lack of E.S.P. in a dating partner or your interactions, then you definitely need to act on them. You do not need to go on another date or share your concerns. Don't consider their feelings or be more loyal to them than you are to yourself. Your only job at this stage is to know what is right (and wrong) for you and to act accordingly. Once you get in the habit of dismissing your gut feelings, you will stop recognizing the wisdom that your body offers. In time, dismissing these impressions will lead to you only telling yourself what you want to hear rather than discovering what you need to see. A manipulator excels at isolating their victims, telling them what to think and feel, making them doubt themselves, and getting them overly committed so that when the truth comes out, they will have a hard time responding to it. To avoid this, follow the timing and pacing guidelines for dating as outlined in Chapter 8, and always communicate with the three to five people you have selected to be in your circle of trust. You will never regret slowing a relationship down, but you will probably regret not doing so.

When to NOT accept a date

Do not accept dates in any of the following situations:

- **If they pressure you to meet them right away,** they may be potentially abusive, manipulative, or exploitative.

- **If they seem quick to talk about their problems and ask for help financially**, emotionally, physically, or sexually, they may be irresponsible, in chaos, manipulative, or looking for someone to take care of them.

- **If they show a lot of interest in your kids, pry for information about where you live or work, or ask you deeply personal questions,** they are crossing a critical boundary. This could indicate issues with empathy and social skills or a manipulative desire to exploit weaknesses and problems within your situation to gain access to you, your children, or your money.

- **If they talk sexually to you, about you, about themselves, or attempt to exchange sexual selfies,** they are revealing their motivation as a player or sexual predator.

- **If they talk as if they abuse substances, view pornography, are sexually addicted, or are frequently angry,** they definitely have issues with self-control and possible addictions.

- **If they have had multiple affairs, insist on a swinging lifestyle, and demonstrate a history of secretive, selfish, or dishonest behaviors that have hurt others in relationships, but continue these behaviors,** they do not have sufficient empathy, self-control, and personal responsibility, and may have a personality disorder or addiction.

- **If they talk casually about abusive, unkind, or illegal behavior, criminal activity, assault charges, or restraining and protective orders,** they have self-control and empathy problems that will affect you, too. Take these seriously, no matter the excuses or justifications they provide.

- **If they are currently married (which includes being separated), recently out of a bad breakup or divorce, or struggling with trauma or death,** they are not in a good place and will not be ready or able to offer love or commitment for a while.

You don't owe anyone a first date, no matter what friends or family may say. No one has ever regretted trusting their gut feeling, but many people have lamented that they didn't. If you sense that a potential date is currently struggling with some of these issues, walk away immediately. Past and present behaviors are a strong indicator of future behavior.

If these issues were a problem well in the past, pause and give serious consideration to what they did to overcome and correct these issues as well as how long it has been since they abandoned their problematic behaviors.

As a general rule of thumb, there is less reason for concern when they:

- have obtained and maintained **sobriety for five years**

- have abstained from sexual **addictions for two years**

- have been **divorced** (and dealt with the fallout effectively) **for one year**

- have confronted and resolved a **death or trauma for at least one year**

- **have a history of sustained** counseling, law-abiding behavior, and steady relationships and employment of **over ten years**

In such cases, look for signs of empathy, self-control, and personal responsibility in how they have managed their issues. Give little to no credit for time spent away from the problem that was actually due to an external source (for example, time spent in jail or on probation, in drug and alcohol treatment, or on a religious mission). You need to see how they handle their issues when they are on their own.

Also, look for evidence that they made restitution for their wrongs. Making restitution is the best indicator of remorse and a desire to abandon hurtful behaviors. If you see positive signs (not just their verbal claims), consider getting to know them further (with a commitment to not becoming engaged for at least one year, so you can make sure they have overcome their issues).

Otherwise, walk away. You will not be the exception to the rule. The relationship will end disastrously within a few years. By not going on the first date, you will have avoided any temptation, weakness, or patterns you have relative to these kinds of relationships. Although people are more than their problems, you have the right and obligation to know what is good for you. You don't need to judge them, but you do need to know yourself, what you are looking for, and what issues are deal breakers and those you can accept.

When to reject or say yes

It can be challenging to know if you feel uncomfortable because your gut feeling is telling you something is off (i.e., the person is exhibiting red flags) or if your anxiety and avoidant tendencies are shutting you down. No one wants to pass up on a good opportunity or potential relationship when that is what they ultimately want. However, when faced with real people and real life, it is easy to worry, get turned off by a flaw or social misstep, or fear missing out on something better. What do you do when you just aren't feeling it or as excited about someone as you have felt for others in the past?

To help you determine if you should stay, engage more fully, allow more time for your feelings or a connection to develop, or walk away, ask yourself the following questions.

1. "Am I safe?"

Yes/No **On three separate occasions (or in three distinct ways), have they demonstrated a moderate or high lack of Empathy, Self-control, or Personal responsibility?**

> *If these challenges are significantly problematic in one area or problematically lacking in all three areas, walk away sooner rather than later. If you want a positive, healthy, and loving relationship, you need to be true to yourself and the truth (not them). Don't feel guilty. Be respectful (when appropriate) and end contact with them by either text or ending communication (if they want to argue or try to manipulate you to change your mind).*

2. Are we compatible?

Yes/No **Do they seem to have many of the qualities from your Top-Ten List?**

> *You can't improve your skills for attracting and dating the types of people you desire if you are not spending time with them. There is no harm in going on a few dates, making someone feel great, keeping the pressure off, and having fun. Go on up to four dates and possibly six to see if you enjoy time with them enough to explore simple affection and continue more dates. Be active rather than passive, or your feelings and connections will not grow. Apply the techniques you are learning*

and manage your expectations and avoidant (or anxious) attachment behaviors. You do not need to go on more than six dates with someone who is on your B-list. If your feelings start to increase and you think they could maybe go more to your A-list, then another month of dating after the first six dates (while engaging more fully) may be appropriate. You can play it by ear until then. Remember, you are just taking dating one stage at a time, and making a long-term commitment and being serious about your feelings and compatibility with this person isn't realistic at this stage. You don't need to rush a decision when you don't have enough information or experience to accurately assess their or your compatibilities or ability to create a secure attachment or solve problems together. Attraction and chemistry are important, but chemistry can be achieved in many satisfying ways. Take your time and reassess these considerations later. Avoid commitment but invest, communicate, have fun, and make them feel great for now.

Yes/No **Are you highly attracted and excited about them, but they lack significant things you'd desire on your top-ten list or exhibit issues that are on your deal-breakers list?**

It's amazing how desirable someone can be when they are unavailable or a relationship with them seems impractical or forbidden. Those with an avoidant attachment pattern long to feel excited and infatuated with a partner, but they rarely feel this way unless the other person is in a relationship, not a good fit for them (so they shouldn't pursue them), long-distance, too busy, or inconsistently and unreliably engaged (i.e., acting more avoidant than them). If you struggle with an avoidant attachment (as evidenced by your frequently indifferent or numb feelings, doubts about the relationship, and anxiety about being trapped or missing out on something better), the solution to your problem isn't seeking out those who are unavailable or bad news but resolving the triggers that turn you off from the attractive and good people you struggle to maintain your excitement about. You have an internal switch that keeps flipping you into the off position, but you can gain control over this tendency and enjoy a mutually engaging and satisfying relationship rather than switching positions in the never-ending cat-and-mouse game that keeps you from being happy and intellectually capable of committing (because inwardly you know the relationship is profoundly unwise).

3. Am I willing to be Available, Responsive, and Emotionally engaged (A.R.E.)?

Yes/No **Are you willing to have fun, make them feel great, invest, participate, communicate, and enjoy the moment (for now)?**

If you are willing to engage in these ways, then there is no harm in going on a few dates and sharing a positive experience with them. The likelihood of both of you continuing to be interested beyond three dates is fairly low (for a variety of reasons). Often, one of you will simply stop engaging, no matter how fun the date was. So, just do your part and let the process evolve appropriately. Instead of overanalyzing your feelings (or anticipating their feelings or unexpressed expectations), create a list of fun activities or foods that you want to try, and appeal to both of you. Enjoy the moment and the adventure of exploring your interests while getting to know them. When the focus of your dating is having fun doing things you enjoy (rather than eating frozen yogurt on every date), you will stop worrying about whether you feel a connection and start enjoying dates and new connections. If you are both keeping a good time, showing mutual respect, and expressing interest in dating beyond three dates, great! There's no need to overthink your feelings right now. As long as you can freely participate in having fun, acting fairly, and doing your part, there is no reason to pass on a mutually enjoyable activity. If you aren't having fun and enjoying your time with them, or if other emerging relationships are a better fit and you don't want to overburden your time, then you can say no to further dates. If you rarely date and are willing to continue more dates to see if your efforts improve the experience, then it is always best to err on the side of personal growth and progress rather than limiting your options. Just don't go on more than six dates if they are solidly only on your B-list, and don't go on more dates if they aren't at least on your B-list. In other words, have fun, do your part, and be practical. If you both focus on making the other feel great, you will feel good about the overall experience and have little to no discomfort when you see the other socially after you stop dating.

4. Do I feel a strong desire to say no, but I am not sure why?

Yes/No **Are you regularly willing to say yes but can't bring yourself to do so this time?**

When you have a habit of being open-minded, willing to engage, and sacrificing sufficient time to support real dating or relationship practices, but you dread going on a date with a specific person, then say no. If the problem isn't an overall avoidant tendency or refusing to prioritize short dates and texts every day or week to encourage a healthy priority for your social and dating relationships, then "not feeling it" and needing to say no sometimes is totally justified. You can not freely say yes if you never say no. Just be honest with yourself about your avoidant tendencies, and don't overthink what a date means. If you feel this isn't your problem and you know you would struggle to engage on a minimum level or would resent your time spent on the date, speak up and don't feel guilty about it. Focus on what is working and all your efforts. You are doing enough. Respectfully say no so that you can freely say yes to someone else.

When you need to reject a woman or date

- **When you need to reject a woman, be warm, clear, grateful, and direct.** Trust that, as a woman, she is strong and capable of handling rejection and that she will be fine. When you fear devastating others (you barely know), you undervalue their resilience and overvalue your importance. Your rejection (especially when communicated respectfully) is quite small in the overall impact of their life experiences. So, rather than lying to them, making up a girlfriend you don't have, exchanging numbers and then never contacting them, making promises you won't keep, or resentfully taking them on a date, simply state, "I'm flattered that you think highly enough of me to ask. Thank you. You are a great person, and I respect you so much that I want to be fair. I don't feel a romantic connection, and so I need to say no, but I truly appreciate you asking and want only the best for you." When you say this with warmth, confidence, and respect, she will feel your sincerity. This type of response is classy, compliments both of you, and leaves the interaction with a clear no and mutual respect. Say, "I don't feel a romantic connection," rather than saying, "I don't feel any chemistry." Women prefer hearing it that way because it seems less of an affront to their attractiveness or charisma and more about personal compatibility.

- **If you are willing to go to an event, but only as a friend, and don't want to confuse her,** say, "Thanks for asking. I'd love to go with you, but in fairness, I only see you as a friend. If you are okay with that, I'm sure we'll have a great time. But I also understand if you would prefer to ask someone else. Do you want to think about it and let me know?" Once you have said this, walk away, repeating in your mind: *She is resilient and capable, or She is more than this one experience. She will be okay.* As you say this, it will calm your anxiety because it's true.

- **If she continues to press you for details about why you are saying no, tries to shame you, cries, or engages in lectures,** simply state, "I need to go. Thank you for thinking of me, and I truly wish you the best." You can use this technique as a broken record rather than engage in defensive or kind explanations to help you save face or to resolve her fears, anxieties, anger, or tears.

- **If she becomes belligerent, won't let you leave, keeps pressing you to agree, or badgers and harasses you,** then state, "This isn't respectful. I don't want to get angry. I'm trying to be kind. I won't be responding or engaging anymore." She can't have an argument with you if you won't engage. The sooner you stop participating, the sooner she will accept the reality of your no. As long as you are willing to engage, you are rewarding her actions. Your words may be saying no, but your interactions are saying that she can get to you because she is important to you. The most powerful way to show others that you mean business is not to tell them but to show them. A true no, especially when another person is acting inappropriately, is more than words but a lack of participation. The opposite of love is not hate but indifference. You do not need to respond to her texts, disparaging social media posts, or friends who want to press you for details. If you starve a predatory animal, it will eventually look for food elsewhere.

- **If she engages in unlawful behavior, such as threats, trespassing, property damage, violence, or harassment, you should talk to local law enforcement for advice on the best way to proceed.** Often, you will be told you need to warn someone that you will take action if they do not stop calling, harassing, or threatening you. This typically needs to be done in writing (which can include text or email). If the behavior persists, you can then file a police report and pursue a no-trespass order or stalking injunction. Both men and women can experience abuse from strangers and romantic partners, so don't ignore harassment. You need to show them that you will not let them get away with abusive behavior, or they will keep pushing your limits (especially if they have a personality disorder). You can't reason with some people. In these cases, no interaction and engagement is best with legal action when needed.

Techniques for breaking a date with a potentially abusive or manipulative person

- **When breaking a date, be clear, direct, and consistent.** If you feel that someone is potentially abusive or manipulative or would not be good for you right now, don't accept a date (and if you already have, break the date). To do this, tell her, "I don't feel good about proceeding with a date, but thank you, and I hope you have a good day." If they respond with guilt trips, anger, continued pressure to meet, manipulation, or personal attacks, do not respond or engage in further discussion; simply repeat, "I don't feel good about proceeding with a date. But good luck and goodbye." If you feel tempted to give in, do not commit to anything; instead, state, "I will need to think about this and get back to you." Then, call a friend who understands abuse and manipulation so they can strengthen your efforts and help you address and manage the effects of this person's manipulations. If you need to get back with the person, do it by text or email (which is the best way to minimize their ability to manipulate you), keep your text short, and do not respond if they keep trying to talk to you about your decision. If needed, block their email, phone number, and online profile. If you talk on the phone, keep the call to two to five minutes or less and keep repeating the same sentences (e.g., "I just don't feel good about meeting you. I have made my decision. I need to go.") rather than attempting to reason with them (which only gives them more information and ways to manipulate you). If you know that you will have to see the person face to face (because you see them in your social circles, you work with them, or they know where to find you), make arrangements for a friend to be with you or to be available by phone before and after you have to face them. Keep all face-to-face contact to five minutes or less and repeat the same phrase, "I just don't feel good about dating you. I need to go." If you fear that face-to-face contact may become aggressive, use an excuse to delay the conversation until you are away from them and can message them instead (e.g., "I need to go, but let me call or text you about this later today"), which makes it safer for you to leave. Then say what you need to say later.

Handle rejection well, take the pressure off, and overcome their concerns

Since your confident and assertive engagement may seem surprising (even if it is exciting to them), they may not be prepared with a response when you offer to exchange numbers. Some may immediately respond with enthusiasm. Others may boldly state that they aren't interested or are married. However, many may hesitate, make excuses, or show that they are struggling to say yes. This latter group can feel impressed or comforted when you offer a safe and respectful way to reengage when they feel ready. In all of these cases, you will appear more confident and desirable when you are prepared with strong and casual body language (through shifting to a leaned-back and confident stance) and offering a mutually respectful response. Believe it or not, from a woman's perspective, men who handle rejection well are suddenly more attractive. A man never looks stronger and more confident (to either a woman or her friends) than when he acts as though rejection does not define his value. Also, you never know what impression such confident behavior might make on her and others. And others will also be intrigued by your strength. Therefore, plan for the possibility of rejection. Pursue more women, and be prepared with a gracious response in the event that a woman says no.

- **To handle rejection well, square your shoulders, look her in the eyes, keep your chin forward, and give her a sweet and sincere compliment.** Saying, "I like it when a woman has the courage to be honest and say no. I am even more impressed (while offering a handshake and adding a wink or smile). I hope you have a great day. It was a pleasure meeting you." Other options can include, "You are an impressive woman. I would have regretted not asking. I truly wish you the best." or "It was a pleasure meeting you, and I hope you have a good day." Having the clarity of mind to handle yourself well while complementing those who reject you is a skill few men demonstrate. This will definitely leave a lasting impression. It proves that you can value and respect others without losing respect for yourself. Sure, a woman's rejection may sting or embarrass you at first, but she doesn't have to know or see this on your face, in your eyes, or in your behavior. Acting cool and confident in the presence of rejection will always make you feel better, too.

- **When a woman says she is in a relationship (which may be a lie) or is married, acknowledge this with a compliment and end the conversation soon after.** Making up a boyfriend to let someone down easily is common. However, it is also a screen for anxiety and discomfort. Rather than taking this personally (or commenting on the possibility that a woman is lying), recognize that her deception reflects her fears and issues and choose compassion. Reply by saying, "I'm not surprised. You are awesome. He's a lucky man." Add a pause and then smile as you say goodbye. If you want to add an additional compliment, include, "By the way, I'm impressed by your loyalty. You're a good woman. I truly wish you both the best." Don't act apologetic or embarrassed. There is no reason to make either of you uncomfortable from the experience or to act awkwardly. Your ability to handle rejection well (with a compliment and confidence) says a lot about you while flattering her, too.

- **As an advanced technique, show that you have the confidence to handle rejection well, be persistent, and address her concerns.** Depending on her uncertainty, there are several ways that you can recognize and overcome her concerns. Not all men may feel comfortable with being persistent, but that is why persistent men get more dates—they look more confident and driven than most men. Some women may feel that persistence is creepy, but this approach should not have such an impact, especially if you lean back and are calm when offering her one of the options below. After all, many of these options clearly put the power in her hands.

  » **If she seems hesitant, stalls, or seems uncomfortable,** state, "We don't know each other well. Seriously, there is no pressure. If you feel comfortable exchanging numbers, great. We can chat a little by text so you have time to decide what feels right for you. I also won't feel hurt if you need to say no. As a matter of fact, I really respect and admire the strength it takes to reject others. It's super hard and attractive, actually. (Add a smile) Would you prefer to say no, exchange numbers, or get mine so that you can reach out on your terms?" You could also add, "If you prefer to learn more about me on Facebook or Instagram, you can contact me there, too. I just want you to do what feels right for you."

  » **If she shares that she is coming out of a bad relationship, too busy, or not in a good place to date right now,** state, "I totally get it. You've got to do what's right for you, but if you want to exchange numbers and reach out when things change, I'd love to hear from you then. There is no pressure either way. I don't expect anything more than mutual respect while doing something fun. It would be great to get to know you better. I need to go. If that feels good to you, I'll give you my number. Either way, it was a pleasure talking with you."

  » **As a general rule of thumb, it is important that you take the pressure off and redirect a potential date's attention to the fun she will have when with you.** To do this, show her that you are a person who is going places and doing things that you enjoy by saying, "I've got a list of fun activities and things I am planning to do or try over the next few months. How about if I share a few ideas, and you can share some, too, so we can find something we both would enjoy?" This helps her to worry less about what she is feeling (or not feeling) and think more about the activity and potential fun she may have (or what she might miss out on). You can also share, "Oh, and by the way, I don't overthink dating. Instead, I simply focus on having a good time while getting to know people I think are fascinating. If that sounds good to you, let's exchange numbers."

- **Whether she accepts or rejects your offer, show that what others think or do does not change how you feel about yourself by keeping your head**

and chin up and your shoulders square and walking away with strength and confidence. Keeping your chin straight forward or slightly up naturally straightens your back and squares your shoulders (whereas dropping your chin makes you slouch and look sheepish or ashamed). Make sure that you walk away slowly and on the heels of your feet (rather than on the balls, which will cause you to speed up and look as if you are anxiously fleeing). You can also add a little swagger as you repeat to yourself: I've just proven to her that I'm a confident, controlled, secure, and respectful person. The kind of woman that I am looking for will recognize and appreciate what I have to offer. I really am a good catch, and she is not my only chance for happiness, but she is good practice!

- **Remember that handling rejection well only makes you look more desirable.** For good and for bad, women talk. If you handle rejection poorly, they may feel bad, but you will definitely look bad to them, too. If you act like a jerk, they will definitely tell others. If you make them feel bad for you, they will also tell others (which isn't going to make you more desirable to their friends). However, if they think you are impressive and flattering, they will share this, too! Thus, practicing these techniques is one of the most powerful things you can do for yourself and your reputation.

- **If you see her again, don't hesitate to make eye contact, smile, wave, or say hi.** When you can handle rejection well, and you both act respectfully, there is no reason to shy away from future contact. Additionally, she may reconsider her answer and hope for a second chance.

- **Rejection techniques are valuable skills to practice and use in a variety of situations.** Those who face challenges with class and respect (whether socially, professionally, or personally) will accomplish and succeed in all areas of life. The body language, words, and mental resilience within these techniques can be appropriately adapted when pursuing a promotion, selling products, or managing a difficult conversation. Thus, mentally practicing individual elements of the technique (with the appropriate words to fit your situation) is a great first step. As you do this, you will gain greater confidence and ease until they fit you more naturally. Discovering the emotional benefits and results can feel empowering and life-changing. In time, these skills will develop into muscle memories and attitude adjustments that habitually take over when needed. Incorporating them when interacting with those on your B-list will be easier than trying them for the first time with those on your A-list. Once you feel greater confidence in your skills, you definitely need to take it to the next level. You can't know what is possible until you pursue those on your A-list. These techniques will help you engage with less anxiety and overanalysis (because you are prepared to handle rejection with class and confidence).

- **Pursue rejection.** When you seek rejection, you will discover that it happens less often than you would anticipate. Being prepared for it makes it less frightening. Additionally, expecting it while staying in the leaned-back head-up position changes your overall aura and makes others curious. So, what do you have to lose?

Over the next few weeks, practice these techniques by pursuing three women. If you don't get rejected at least once, pursue two more women. Keep pursuing others until you have been rejected at least three times. You'll be surprised by how many numbers and dates you receive and how little rejection will matter after this. Either way, you will win. You will get the numbers of the women you really want to date, or you will get valuable experience in mastering your skills for handling rejection well, which will serve you well in all areas of life.

When tempted to blame others or give up, be resilient, open-minded, and realistic

- **Take the pressure off and have fun.** The more positive experiences you have, the more attractive, happy, and confident you will become. The less pressure you put on yourself and them, the more you both will relax. When you treat dating as an adventure and set reasonable expectations, while letting a commitment evolve along with a deeper connection over time, you and your partner will be less likely to overthink or freak out prematurely. Without spending time together, it is unrealistic to expect that either of you can know if you are right for each other (or "the one"). As long as you both are willing to enjoy the process, show mutual respect, and offer clear and fair communication, you aren't wasting anyone's time.

- **Resist taking rejection personally.** There are dozens of reasons someone won't respond online, and most have little to do with you. Many dating apps feature singles who don't have active profiles or are rarely on the app. Taking rejection personally when they never saw your profile is impractical. Just do your part, and don't focus on those who aren't engaging with you. They don't matter. Focus instead on those who are participating and showing appreciation for your investment. To avoid wasting time, search the internet for ways to discover who has recently logged into the app you are using (versus those who are inactive). If the app offers such features or uses an algorithm that applies this principle, you will be able to interpret others' reactions (or lack thereof) more accurately. The app may offer upgrades that provide other invaluable insights, too.

- **If you aren't getting the response you desire, consider investing more in your image, pictures, and profile.** It never hurts to up your game. Remember, you are experimenting to see what works. A lack of engaging responses is merely an invitation for further exploration and creativity. After all, they aren't rejecting you, just your technique (which is all they see). Take this opportunity to request feedback or try side-by-side comparisons to see what combination of pictures and profiles gets the best results. To do this, create two or more online accounts. One can represent you as fun and active, another as smart and hard-working, or religious and family-oriented. Expressing yourself in fun, creative, and honest ways can shake things up and provide unique results and options.

- **Remember that you are rejecting others, too.** It's just part of life. For every person who dismisses you, you are doing the same to others. So, hang in there and keep applying what you're learning. Avoid taking offense and focus on what's working or getting better results.

- **Ask for feedback or schedule an individual coaching session if you're not getting the success you desire.** Until you practice most of these techniques, you won't know if they will work for you. However, if (after a period of experimentation and change) you still struggle, you need to get direct feedback from others, former dates, or one of our coaches. Seek advice from those who are dating frequently, in loving relationships, or happily married, or offer dating and relationship expertise. Counselors are great, and their advice relative to your mental health can be life-changing, but most counselors won't have experience or training in effective and time-tested dating strategies. Do your research to find the right options for you. As long as you are willing to improve and change, you will succeed, so keep an open mind and be willing to ask for help.

- **When asking for feedback, don't be afraid to set healthy limits.** Instead of reading minds or drawing unhealthy negative conclusions, let others know you are open to feedback and trust that they will share their thoughts when needed. This can be empowering, especially when you observe others gossiping or acting critical of those they date. You can show an open-minded and confident attitude while expressing faith in others. To do this, state, "I believe we are all concerned about improving ourselves, especially when others kindly express a problem. Since I can't read minds, I trust that others have enough faith in me to share their thoughts and ask for mine. Unless they do this, I assume we are good. This makes my life and relationships so much easier and worry-free." If they offer suggestions, be sure to ask for specifics. For example, "I do best when given a few ideas and specific or behaviorally clear observations that focus on what is going well or works better. If you have a general idea, that is good too, but try to think about specifics and solutions and offer them as often as possible." Targetless feedback is usually less effective. Thus, if you let them know that you would appreciate suggestions about clothing, body language, pictures, or what to say in a situation, you will find their advice more meaningful. If they start to bombard you with feedback or criticism, pause them and state, "Thank you for being willing to share. That can feel uncomfortable or risky for some people. Can you text me with the specific possibilities of feedback you would have, and then I'll choose which ones I would want to focus on first?" There is never any harm in taking some time rather than diving in, as this can help them formulate their ideas to make them more constructive, and you will be more prepared to receive their feedback. If someone gives critical or disrespectful feedback, you can simply restate, "I am open to feedback when it is respectful and balanced with positive insights. This doesn't feel that way. If you want to redirect your feedback more positively, I'd love to explore this for a few more minutes. Otherwise, I'll think about what you said, but I'm not interested in continuing the conversation."

     Single? It's Not You. It's Your Technique!

- **Explore your hang-ups, increase your flexibility, or grieve your lost opportunities.** If you are to embrace the good options in front of you, you need to let go of your past mistakes, unrealistic dreams, and imbalanced expectations. Being too particular can be a sign of an avoidant attachment pattern, thinking errors, perfectionism (resulting from anxiety or OCD), and inexperience with normal relationships. So look at yourself and make a change rather than waiting for the best option to knock at your door. Whether you know it or not, you are not the best, and neither is anyone else, but two good people can create something that is better, and even best, together.

- Rather than giving up, **consider increasing the number of people with whom you're willing to communicate and become more actively engaged** in your dating and relationship experiences with them. Attractive but less stunning people may prove to be more responsive, fun, and engaging. Creating a meaningful and passionate connection is about more than just attraction, so don't get too hung up on one type of personality trait or physical feature. Passiveness creates passionless feelings. Meaningful connection and chemistry depend on more than someone's status or sex appeal. Until you become vulnerable, emotionally engaged, and invested, you can't develop a deeper connection. Until you are willing to engage in simple affection, you can't discover if you will feel chemistry and experience a sufficient sexual response. Holding off on non-sexual touch (including holding hands, cuddling, and kissing) will ensure that you both feel passionless and insecure about your relationship. So, take more risks and explore a few dating or relationship situations to discover if they become fulfilling in unexpected and satisfying ways. This doesn't mean you need to be sexual with them (which will complicate the experience), but do engage in more affectionate exchanges. If your feelings and chemistry don't grow, then you will know that you did what you could and can walk away with confidence. As long as you are always willing to do something new, you can anticipate getting new and better results that eventually end in love and connection.

- **Stay engaged, be consistent, and choose to have faith that your efforts will make a difference.** Most people who are successful in finding a relationship are reliably engaged in doing their part, whether with dating apps, social media, or live interactions. They don't take extended breaks from everything. Instead, they redirect their efforts and skill development to related but different areas. For example, they shift from dating apps to more singles' events or social gatherings for a time. Instead of focusing on dating skills, they learn about and practice more relationship skills (with friends, family, and colleagues) while trusting that these skills will translate well into their dating or emerging relationships when needed. A flexible and growth-minded attitude and focus are empowering. Being proactive reduces discouragement and feelings of powerlessness. Unless you are taking action, you can not hope for a different outcome. So, engage in a different dating app, try a new profile approach, encourage a friend to introduce you to other singles, or attend a singles conference, cruise, or travel group. Practice new assertiveness and conflict resolution skills at work or in your personal life. And, when you feel you need a break, take it, but only for a few months. If you take a longer break, you will lose momentum, or you may develop unhealthy patterns and thinking errors that separate you from others rather than bridge the gap between you. If you regularly participate in the Lasting Love Academy content, this will be less likely to happen.

- **Develop a positive and active support system.** Singles experience more attachment losses and injuries than those who are in long-term marriages, not just from broken relationships but also from peers and friends who get married or move away. Feelings of loneliness and isolation are detrimental to your emotional well-being. Thus, look for others with whom you can relate and engage more fully. If they are single, too, share support and encouragement (even while empathizing with their frustrations). Encourage, uplift, and inspire each other's dreams rather than focusing on what is going wrong. Pure and lasting change will flow from your strengths and progress, not your weaknesses and failures. Empathize but seek new and better ways to motivate and change together. Friendships (like seasons) change (due to the demands and unavoidable transitions of life), but trust that each relationship can provide a beautiful and healing season along your mutual journeys. If you fear loss or abandonment, you will not develop secure attachments. For this, you need to remember that you are capable, resilient, strong, and loving. You do not need to fear the future when you remember that good people and experiences are all around you and will continue to surround you throughout all the seasons of your life. You are meant to love and be loved. It is your present and future reality (when you look for and embrace its varied opportunities).

Have realistic expectations about attraction, age, and fertility

- **Have realistic expectations, especially when pursuing the most attractive women.** More attractive women get dozens of new messages every day and will rarely respond unless a person stands out as exceptional. This includes being attractive AND educated, successful, witty, fun, outgoing, and well-liked by others. Thus, you will need to make a great impression, be patient, and regularly improve your techniques until you get the results you want (or hit your personal ceiling of desirability). Because beautiful women get overwhelmed by the volume of messages they receive, they usually don't check their apps or cancel their memberships. If they can meet others on their terms or in their everyday life, they will prefer this to wasting their time on unattractive profiles that make them feel like a bad person (due to the repulsion, pressure, and guilt these apps and rejecting others create). Nevertheless, if you think you can compete with the best of them and your pictures and bio make you stand out, don't be afraid to send the most desirable women occasional messages every month or so in case one of them happens to see it. If it has been over a week, your message will drop to the bottom of a long list, which is why you need to keep sending more until she either unmatches you or responds. It is also possible that she doesn't have a current account and will never see your message, so don't take this personally. If she does see your messages and isn't interested, she will swipe down or unmatch you, so don't worry about sending short messages a month later as long as they are positive and appropriate. Alternatively, you will have a better chance with her if you find her on Facebook or Instagram and discover that you have mutual friends. If you are able to get a personal introduction or live interactions, you are far more likely to get results. After attempting this for a while, you need to consider the possibility that you need to alter your expectations since ongoing and repeated failure among certain women is a strong indication that they are out of your league.

- **Have realistic expectations, especially when pursuing women who are more than 10 years younger than you.** Women of all ages believe that men who pursue significantly younger women are creepy. For women in their twenties, an age disparity of five years may not be too concerning. For those in their thirties and forties, a ten-year gap is still uncomfortable. And this doesn't change much for those in their fifties or sixties. Perceiving older men as predatory when they pursue women fifteen years their junior isn't fair, however. A 65-year-old who pursues a 50-year-old is less likely to be doing so because of the manipulative advantage it offers (which is often the case when a 35-year-old pursues a 20-year-old). When both parties have valuable and similar life experiences, they can relate and connect appropriately. Nevertheless, middle-aged women are often unwilling to consider a man more than 10 years their senior since they fear becoming a caretaker or a widow while they are still relatively young. When women are willing to consider such men, they often prefer being the first to encourage dating since this causes less pressure and avoidance on their part. A woman's tendency to reject older men is increased on dating apps since they assume that most men are using outdated pictures and are not as youthful as the men present themselves to be. Thus, to buck this stereotype and increase a woman's interest, you would be wise to get current pictures and include the date when the images were taken. An updated style and clothing will also help you appear youthful. Clothes that were expensive and fashionable five years ago will still make you appear outdated now.

- **Have realistic expectations when pursuing women in their 20s or 30s.** If you are in your late 30s or 40s and pursuing women in their 20s or 30s (respectively), be prepared to be dismissed. You may believe that younger women provide better opportunities for having children (if you want them). However, beautiful, younger women can have the pick of the litter. If you are not as attractive, successful, socially skilled, and well-respected as men who are a woman's age, she won't feel any need to consider you. If you succeed in getting and keeping her attention, you can be assured that she will probably want children (or already have them). So be honest with yourself about whether you want to raise children (for twenty years or more) or would prefer to be with someone whose children are nearly raised. If you are holding out for an ideal woman who's willing to have kids with you, and yet your age, appearance, and life accomplishments are merely average, you will experience a higher rejection rate and even gain a reputation for appearing immature and creepy. No matter what TV and movies portray, most women believe that older men who pursue 20-year-olds are doing so to exploit their naivety and mask their controlling, manipulative, or narcissistic behaviors. Likewise, they assume any woman who considers doing so is naive, insincere, or a gold-digger. From a man's perspective, he will usually state that if he can date a younger woman, why wouldn't he? The questions you need to ask are: If you succeed, how satisfied would you be if a partner doesn't share your interests, goals, life experiences, and energy? Do you desire to have children with her and play an active role in family life for the next two decades? Do you have recent evidence (within the last two years) to prove that younger women sincerely engage in both dating and exclusive relationship behaviors with you? If you answer yes to all the above, then investing another year or two toward this goal may be worth the risk.

- **If you are concerned about dating women between 38 and 45** because you want kids and they may not be able to have them, **have confidence that this won't be a problem**. Men and women who are interested in having a family will find there are many ways to fulfill their dreams. Those who need alternative options (due to advancing age or medical issues) can benefit from egg retrieval, egg donors, artificial insemination, IVF, surrogacy, adoption, and foster care. The cost for these services can be minimal (when considering foster care) to tens of thousands of dollars, but the benefits will be great, too. The more important and primary consideration (for your and your children's mental health) is the partner you choose. Thus, although it may seem more desirable to date and marry younger women, keep all of your options open (including women your age or a little older). Holding out for an ideal situation (that hasn't yet happened and may not exist) will only add to your advancing years. Instead, find a loving partner with whom you have a joyful relationship and begin exploring the many ways you can fulfill your dreams together. If needed, research your family planning options to increase your confidence and preparation for these procedures. The more you understand what's available, the more empowered and assured you will feel. Additionally, if you want several children, the probability of twins is an added benefit.

To achieve lasting love, be frequently and consistently engaged

- **Establish patterns of being Available, Responsive, and Emotionally engaged (or A.R.E.)[5] in secure (rather than anxious or avoidant) ways.** Creating secure attachments requires that you AND your partner are able to depend and rely on each other because you both choose to be accessible to the

---

5   Johnson, S. M.: (2008). *Hold Me Tight: Seven Conversations for a Lifetime of Love*. New York, Little, Brown & Co.

other, participate in meeting the other's needs, and do more than show up, but actively and emotionally participate in the relationship (with growing vulnerability and trust). Without this, one or both partners will become anxious or avoidant (silently suffering or needy and disconnected or withdrawn) in their attachment behaviors. This reality occurs in family and friendships as well as relationships.

- **Commit to daily and weekly attachment behaviors.** For you to have hope for a secure attachment in a romantic relationship, you need to maintain a consistent pattern of being available, responsive, and emotionally engaged in the dating apps, with those you meet, and in your significant relationships. Through scheduling and prioritizing your efforts to engage in a timely manner (with friends and family and when messaging through apps and texts or encouraging dates), you will develop and maintain the required skills for a secure attachment.

- **Schedule reminders and prioritize your day and week so your daily routine doesn't starve your relationships.** To succeed in dating and lasting love, you must spend 5 to 30 minutes daily or at least three times a week building your relationships. Whether this is achieved through swiping on dating apps, following up with texts and phone calls, or communicating with a potential date for an upcoming activity, you need to be in regular contact with important people in your life. So, set reminders and create habits that ensure you don't forget about your relationships, friends, and family, so they know they can depend on you (and vice versa). To do this, list those you can call, text, and spend time with. Find out what is happening in their lives and share updates with them. Create a list of at least five people you can call when in the car, text when lonely, and spend time with during the evening or on weekends. If you aren't planning dates, schedule something with them and follow through each week. Let them know you appreciate having them in your life and want them to know you are there for them, too.

- **Manage your anxious and avoidant tendencies. Make sure you are Available, Responsive, and Emotionally engaged.** Some singles compulsively check their apps and texts, which increases their anxiety and makes them appear needy, especially when they quickly respond to messages or become frustrated by others' slower responses. Other singles can ignore, avoid, or forget to get on the app, respond to texts, or progress their communication to calls or dates. This avoidant or absent-minded pattern will waste their potential opportunities and cool others' interest in them. To avoid this, make sure you are pushing yourself to have a reasonably engaged pattern of timing and pacing your interactions.

- **Regulate your emotions and attachment behaviors by sticking to a reasonable pattern of engagement.** During pre-date interactions, checking your apps and texting or messaging three times a week is sufficient to ensure you are doing your part to build relationships and are not missing others' messages. If it is comfortable and appropriate to check the app or message daily, ensure you are not compulsively or anxiously doing so. If you find yourself frequently looking at your phone or using the app throughout the day, you are probably doing so obsessively. When this is the case, close the app and don't open it until an appointed time. This will help you to regulate your emotions and anxious thoughts. Likewise, when you feel irritated, critical, and repulsed by the idea of getting on the app or sending and responding to messages, push yourself to do this three times a week when communicating with someone or at least once to twice a week when searching for new matches.

- **Regulate your emotions and thoughts by engaging during high-energy times of the day and week.** If you tend to feel anxious, worried, frustrated, annoyed, withdrawn, avoidant, or discouraged relative to getting on apps, texting, answering calls, or going on dates, then you need to consider the other variables that are influencing your moods and thoughts. Negative emotions will alter your and others' experiences when you accept them as meaningful instead of recognizing the natural fluctuations and patterns of your brain experiences throughout a day or week. You can be a scientist who observes yourself more objectively. You are not a slave to your emotions, a victim of your thoughts, and limited in your options for getting results. You can experiment with what works best and create more meaningful and fun experiences. To do this:

  » **Analyze your high-energy and resilient times of the day (versus your low-energy or depressed and irritable patterns).** Take notes during the day relative to the following questions:

    Are you more energetic and happy in the morning, afternoon, or night?

    Do you think about and call people when in the car, before bed, or on the weekends?

    Do you feel more depressed on Mondays or the weekends?

    Do you get angry when others text you at work, but enjoy messages in the evening?

    Do you need eight hours of sleep and lash out or shut down without it?

    Do you feel needy and desperate when you are alone, but are you more confident and relaxed when around family and friends or in public spaces?

    How do music, movies, or background noises influence your moods in positive or negative ways?

    What music or environments are most commonly associated with your best times of day, exercise routines, or a positive and happy attitude?

  » **Write your observations down and plot the most effective, bonding, and high-energy times of your day and week.** With an understanding of your high and low energy influences in mind:

    How can you increase your use of these variables to maximize your mood daily?

When would be best each day or several times a week to schedule a reminder to check the apps, follow up on texts, or reach out to others to plan dates or get together?

How can you prioritize your weekend and free time for more interactions, connections, and bonding experiences?

What times of the day or week are more likely to be fun and exciting for you versus stressful and depressing (thus increasing your risks of canceling your plans at the last minute)?

When tempted to cancel or reschedule, how can you power through these emotions and become more dependable?

How will showing up and being A.R.E. in your relationships (whether you feel it in the moment or not) improve your life and relationships?

What can you do and say to yourself to help you endure or change a temporary emotion and thought for a long-term benefit?

Make a good faith effort, let go, and have fun

The process of practicing your skills, dating, building relationships, and getting married needs to be viewed as a marathon, not a sprint. Like everything, dating and relationships take time and patience. If you are to maintain your focus, faith, and energy throughout the race, you need to change the way you think about dating and pace yourself and your efforts. If you rush in and give everything all at once, you'll exhaust yourself and get injured. You cannot expect dramatic results immediately; if you do, you'll get discouraged and want to quit.

Trust and relax

Janice was a twenty-eight-year-old redhead with a fun and spunky personality, but surprisingly, she had never been in a serious relationship. She frequently hung out with men and experienced many friendships, but none became anything more, and she dated very little. When she began meeting with me, she was excited about trying out the new techniques and quickly began experiencing more attention from men. Nonetheless, within a few months, she called me again, exasperated and confused. In spite of the fact that she was now giving out her number to many men, few were following through and calling her. She felt frustrated and worn out. She was flirting and playing her role. What more was she to do?

I reminded Janice of several of the Be-Effective Facts from Chapter 1: #1—*your situation does not define your value,* #2—*confidence matters,* #4—*the more you practice, the better you get,* #5—*faith works,* #7—*the more deeply you sacrifice, the more deeply you love,* and #8—*if he doesn't respond, someone else will.* I reviewed her My Truths box from Chapter 2. I pointed out her flirting skills from Chapter 3. I encouraged her to recognize how much success she was obviously experiencing as a result of her flirting (e.g., how frequently men were asking for her number). I encouraged her faith, and then I reminded her of a crucial part of the process: *to trust and relax.*

I pointed out that her flirting behaviors clearly showed that she was willing to make a good-faith effort. Now, she just needed to trust in the process and in God (Karma, positive energy, the laws of attraction, or the spiritual world) to help it along. I encouraged her to believe that her actions did have power and would attract the type of men and relationships she desired. She needed to do her part but then relax, trust, and let go, which is far more attractive, fun, and freeing than worrying, waiting, and doubting men and her future.

Janice struggled to accept this advice. She feared that a more invested and passionate man wouldn't come along. She'd had so many experiences with men who just wanted to hang out, said they would call and then didn't, or seemed passive and had to be prodded along in relationships that she wasn't sure she could confidently stick with the plan to keep practicing. I reminded her that being in a relationship with someone so passive was hardly worth her time. She would forever be at the mercy of such a man's minimal interest and investment. I encouraged her to let go of her expectations about how and when relationships were to develop and just trust that God (whom she said she believed in) would help her meet others who would do their part as well.

Although this was difficult advice to accept at first, Janice decided to let go of trying to control the outcome. In time, she found it easier to have fun, stating, "I know God is invested in both the men I date and me. We are not meant to be alone. We are meant to love and be loved, and God wants us to be successful in love and family life. I don't have to worry about this alone. I'm not alone. And the men I'm seeking care about this, too." As she practiced patience and learned to relax, she was able to let go of relationships that made her feel burdened, angry, frustrated, or neglected, and she began to see that invested men and better experiences were more common than she'd thought.

Let go of control by making yourself truly available

Learning to make a good-faith effort, let go, relax, and trust others and the process is the ultimate sign of your faith in the truths you developed in Chapter 2. Until you learn to do your part, let go of control, and relax, you will never enjoy dating and relationships. Usually, the things people want and need the most escape them when they over-focus or obsess about such things. To avoid this trap, you must focus elsewhere.

Steven worked a lot and was very busy, so he joined a dating app. He did his part and pursued many women. He messaged several of them for multiple weeks, worrying that it would be rude if he asked for phone numbers too soon. Eventually, he exchanged phone numbers and called a couple of the women. He had many great conversations. He was particularly excited about one of them. However, when he met these women, he felt many of them did not look like their pictures, especially the one he really liked. Some of the women looked older, heavier, or plainer to him. And some of their personalities seemed very different from what he had perceived when messaging or over the phone. He felt frustrated and discouraged about how much time he'd spent investing in dating apps.

Steven knew that I often encourage using social media and dating websites and apps as a tool for meeting other singles, so he was quite surprised when I stated, "You need to focus outside of these resources. You're in the presence of singles all the time. If you don't recognize this, then you're not actively looking. Approximately forty percent of the adult population is single. Granted, that includes many singles who are older or younger than you, but you still need the skills to recognize those around you who may have the qualities on your Top-Ten List. Singles are at the grocery store, your nephew's soccer game, the park, the library, pro basketball games, your doctor's office, and everywhere you go. You don't need to flirt with everyone of them, but if you do not look for and recognize them and then actively engage when a situation arises, you will miss out on some of your best opportunities to meet singles."

To this, Steven simply stated that he was too busy to find women in his everyday life. I pressed forward nonetheless, replying that he often ignored and dismissed his social needs and potential relationships. If he were to succeed in relationships, he needed to start now by prioritizing his social needs. He needed more interests, friends, relationships, and boundaries around how much he worked—otherwise, he would likely fail once he did get into a relationship. He was not prepared to sustain a relationship with his life so out of balance. It simply had no room for someone else.

He believed that he would make the necessary changes, once he met that certain someone, but I insisted that his habits would prevent him from investing the necessary time to discover who might be worth it. Even if he met someone, he would be willing to make quick changes for, he might discover—as many do—that old habits return quickly and he'd become a workaholic again, sabotaging his relationship.

Steven's inability to find that special someone would not be eliminated even if he did meet a woman whom he was attracted to after he met her in person. Contact through dating apps has to eventually evolve into real-life dating, and Steven needed more real-life and relationship skills.

Being successful in relationships is not just about developing new yet temporary techniques; it is also about developing *lifelong skills that support good relationships.* If Steven was going to succeed, he needed to do more than make himself available on apps—he needed to make himself available everywhere in his life. Doing this would also allow more options for God to bless his efforts and his life. Steven believed in God and was actively praying for help, so if he refused to do this, it would be the equivalent of dictating to God how, when, and where he was willing to meet women and in what way God should respond. This is the opposite of letting go and trusting God to advance the process.

I encouraged Steven to continue meeting people through dating apps and social media, but his specific goals for the next few months were all focused on increasing his real-life interactions when at singles events, while at the grocery store, when waiting for the train after a pro basketball game, and while picking out dog food. These were great opportunities for starting conversations with people he might already know, as well as new people. He didn't need to control where the conversation went from there. He simply needed to get the ball rolling and let the other person and God lead the next step.

Enjoy the garden of life rather than watching the flowers grow

Angela was in a new relationship with a man who seemed to value, appreciate, and invest in her. Nonetheless, she obsessed about whether or not things would work out. She analyzed everything he did or said in fear that he wasn't truly interested, and she often felt tempted to tell him they should just be friends simply because she couldn't handle the stress. She liked him a lot, but she felt anxious and insecure in spite of his efforts. She felt overwhelmed by the possibility of getting hurt.

To help her control her anxiety, I explained, "Relationships are like gardens. You can till the ground, plant the seed, fertilize the soul, and pluck the weeds, but you cannot make your seed grow. You can only do your part while trusting the seed and natural goodness inherent in the design of the world, God, or the Spiritual World to do the rest. You need to trust that the sun, soil, and seed will do their part from there. There is a natural order to predictable and consistent things, and you are not the exception to this rule."

"Your current behavior," I continued, "is the equivalent of spending twenty-four hours a day overturning the dirt, pulling at the new stock to see if the roots are developing, and measuring the plant to see if it's growing. Obsessing in this way hinders your progress and shows little faith in the men you are dating and the effectiveness of your actions. It makes you miserable. You need to do your part, but then leave your garden to have fun."

"Focusing on other things will settle your mind and help you be patient. So get busy, spend time with friends and family, and pursue your interests. A day or so later, come back, water the plant, pluck the weeds (i.e., give attention to him and the relationship), look for signs of progress (trusting that you will find it), and have more fun. This is the best way to show the men you're dating that you have faith in them and yourself."

I instructed Angela that whenever she felt anxious, she needed to repeat in her mind: *It's not fun watching plants grow. I need to do my part and then let it go.*

Unless you learn to let go, relax, and play, you will also be prone to obsessing about your new relationships. You will feel vulnerable to your fears and tempted to quit. Instead, take deep breaths often. Plan lots of activities with friends and family. And redirect your attention away from your new relationships each day. Choose faith, not fear, and get busy. It is the only way to train your mind not to obsess about your relationships.

Single? It's Not You. It's Your Technique!

Be assertive about your needs but open and patient with slow-moving processes

Becca's biggest complaint about dating apps and texting was that none of it made her feel great. She was ready to give up on dating sites and all the technologies that went with them. Her experiences thus far had failed to match her expectations. For example, she spent two months messaging, texting, and then talking with one man she met on Facebook. She really liked him and felt they had a great connection. They talked every day, shared their life stories, and expressed mutual affection. But after she made the 600-mile drive to see him, everything changed. He stopped calling as much, and when she called him, he seemed lackluster and not at all as he once had. It didn't take long before she got the hint that he wasn't interested anymore.

Now, even though she'd met someone she liked—Jason—and been on a few dates with him, he only communicated through text. He never called, and phone calls were what she wanted most. She appreciated that Jason was trying, but a brief text twice a week—one to say hi and another to ask her out—was not enough to keep her interest. Although he was fun, polite, and respectful on their dates, texts left so much unsaid and undone that the relationship wasn't progressing much. His tactics seemed too impersonal and safe. She couldn't tell if he was genuinely interested or if he was just fitting her in as a good-for-now girl when his A-list girls weren't around. She didn't know him well enough to determine whether he was shy and uncomfortable with phone calls or simply lazy. What she did know was that she was losing interest fast. Why wouldn't Jason just pick up the phone and call?

Finding the kind of person you're looking for is essentially a numbers game. Dating apps offer many advantages, especially for singles over thirty. Though Becca needed to be more assertive about her needs, she also needed to stay open to available opportunities and expose herself to as many singles as possible if she wanted to increase her odds of meeting the right person. Pursuing several potential relationships through live and dating apps would also help her feel less desperate and anxious when she is in the early stages of dating someone. Singles need to remember that most dating relationships won't last past the first six weeks. So, it's best to keep your options open to remind you that the person you see isn't your only chance for happiness. In Becca's case, by continuing to make herself available through dating apps, social media, and websites, she would remain open to other men, showing a good-faith effort and giving her more ways to feel empowered. She needed to change her approach to dating apps while also hanging in there and letting technology work for her.

I encouraged Becca to be more assertive. The next time she was with Jason, she needed to touch him on the arm, tilt her head, smile, and warmly explain, "I would love to get to know you better. Texting is not my favorite. I enjoy phone calls so much more, including short ones. And if you call at a time when I can't answer, I promise I'll call you back. I look forward to hearing from you. Thank you!" By saying thank you, Becca would show she trusts him to respect her wishes.

If this did not work and he continued only texting, she should reinforce her words by writing back, "I would love to discuss that with you on the phone. I have a few minutes to talk now or after three today. Will that work for you?" She should continue responding this way until he starts calling. And she should continue doing this with every man thereafter, as necessary.

To combat her anxiety while doing this, Becca's goal was to repeat each day or as often as needed: *If he is interested, he will hear my feelings and needs and will invest in meeting them, or someone else will.*

Focus on being emotionally open and fair and only playing with others who do the same

As you learn to trust, let go, and have fun, you also need to become skilled at recognizing others who are doing the same. To help illustrate this point, consider for a moment that you are a child on a playground looking to have fun and build new relationships. As you look around, you see many children, including a girl at the edge of the park and a boy sitting on a seesaw alone. You decide to approach the boy on the seesaw. He quickly agrees to have you join him, but as soon as you take a risk and push off the ground, he reveals himself to be a bully. He plants his seat firmly on the ground and taunts you as you sit helplessly with your feet dangling from the top of the seesaw. Your pleading, begging, whining, and complaining fail to convince him to play fair and make the experience mutually fun. When he finally gets bored with torturing you, he jumps off the seat, causing you to crash to the ground below. He laughs and points, then saunters away.

Embarrassed, bruised, and battered, you realize you can curse the situation and the bully, give up trying, and go home, or you can trust that what matters most is finding not the one bully on the playground but the many kids (all around you) who are willing to have fun and play fair. You decide to brush the situation off, ignore the bully, square your shoulders, and approach the girl at the edge of the park.

The girl quickly reveals herself to be shy, cautious, and reserved. Thus, you try extra hard to show her you will be gentle and fun. You attempt to make her smile. You say several nice things and show your patience. Finally, she warms up to you, and after much coaxing from you and her mother, she agrees to play on the seesaw with you. At first, the experience seems to be fun, and you two are doing well, but you accidentally push off too fast. Her feet slip when she comes down, and she hits her seat hard on the ground. She falls off the seesaw, and you come crashing down as well. She storms off to her mother, and you are left to pick yourself up, rub your bruises, and walk sheepishly to her so you can apologize. She seems indifferent to your apology, but finally agrees to play again. This time, she dictates what she is willing to do and what she is not. It doesn't take long before she gets offended again and storms off, leaving you alone on the swings.

You aren't having much fun. You know that you could quit now and go home, but instead, you feel inspired to look within yourself and recognize everything your behaviors say about you. You are hard-working. You care about having fun and playing fair. You are willing to invest, risk, and try. You admit when you are wrong and are committed to working things out. You have a lot to offer and are a great friend. All of your behaviors at the playground have proven this. As you ponder these things, you feel inspired to just relax, let go, trust others and the process, and believe that fun will come.

You start swinging with your shoulders square and a smile on your face. You enjoy the moment, the cool breeze, and the sand under your feet. While swinging casually, you happen to notice a group of boys playing soccer and having fun, as well as a couple of girls laughing, sharing, talking, and sliding. You like what you see and begin to feel confident that several of these kids would respond well to you. You offer to build a sandcastle with a girl swinging near you, and she happily accepts. Twenty minutes later, you notice that a boy leaves the soccer game, so you confidently offer to jump in and play his position. The other boys respond well. Before long, you discover that it doesn't matter that things were going wrong for a time. It only matters that they are now going right.

The techniques of the quiet girl and the bully are not too dissimilar. They both exercise control in the relationship by using the principle of least interest: the person with the least amount of interest, investment, or vulnerability in a relationship has the greatest amount of control.

The bully risks nothing, gives little, cares little, and aggressively maintains control; however, he pays a high price to maintain this control. He cannot let go, trust, relax, and enjoy. He must always worry about retaliation. He must cautiously guard himself against being vulnerable because he cannot trust that others will be respectful or kind when he is in need, since he was not respectful and kind when they were in need. He is not free, and he is plagued by many fears, which is why he acts the way he does. He cannot love or be loved because he does not sacrifice enough to experience, feel, and enjoy love. Whether he bullies others into relationships with him or not, he always feels alone and threatened that they might leave. In the end, he neither feels great nor makes anyone else feel great.

The quiet girl also risks little, gives little, and maintains control, but she does so passively. She uses sadness and her withdrawn behavior to entice others to feel sorry for her. She enjoys the experience of having people care enough to coax her out of her shell, but she only feels loved and important when they are pursuing her. She quickly begins to distrust that they will be around for long and so withdraws, hoping they'll once again reassure her of their commitment and interest in her. This keeps her caught in a constant game of being passive or withdrawing so others will pursue her. No matter how much they pursue, however, she never feels loved because she doesn't sacrifice enough to feel love or to feel deserving of their love. She feels insecure and afraid they will hurt, disappoint, or leave her. In time, they eventually do something that confirms these fears. If they then try to regain her trust, she often tests them by withdrawing more, so they have to work harder to get her to play. When she does play, she retaliates by setting limits on what she will do for them in return. She does all this in a passive rather than aggressive manner. She acts as if she is weak, vulnerable, needy, sick, sad, and powerless, and as if she has no control, but in fact, she has tremendous control. She is the one who gives and does the least, and she only risks after others invest ten times more energy than she does. The relationship is at her mercy.

The quiet girl and the bully are not consciously aware of everything they are doing, but they are aware that they are often alone and sad or angry. They really do want to play and have fun, but until they are ready to change their ways and put in a good-faith effort to play fair, be nice, invest, risk, and share equally with others, they will burn out the few relationships they have and will always be under the threat of rejection.

Which child are you in this story? Do you act aggressively, demandingly, or powerfully in relationships? Do you act passive, disengaged, and unwilling to invest in others until they win you over? Or do you extend yourself to others, make yourself open, and play fair? Most people do a little bit of each of these things, but which of these do you do the most in your relationships? Which of these would your ex say you did with him or her?

If you are to be successful in dating and relationships, you need to be open, ready, and willing to love and be loved. You need to extend yourself to others. You need to trust, risk, invest, try, and be a little vulnerable like the kid on the playground who consistently did his part. While you do this, you need to look for others who respond in like manner.

Being open and putting yourself out there to date means you will face numerous situations and circumstances that will feel frightening and uncertain. You will wonder if you should approach someone or not. You will worry about doing the wrong thing. You will question whether you did something that ruined your chances with a specific person. You will sometimes doubt your worth or the process.

What you need to realize is that you do not need to be perfect to obtain success. You do not need to respond to every situation with textbook certainty. You need only focus on playing your role, trusting that it will all work out eventually and that you will attract others who care about doing the right things, too. Faith is a powerful antidote to fear. It builds confidence, and it attracts others of a similar nature—birds of a feather will flock together once they learn to recognize each other.

Many religious people believe that marriage and family are sanctified by God and part of His plan for their happiness, progression, and well-being. If you have such beliefs, trust that God is on your side and wants you to get married and remain happily married.

If this doesn't describe your beliefs, do you have experiences in which an unseen power, influence, comfort, or love has reached you in a time of need? If so, have faith that such influence and power for good exists and do your part with the hope that karma or the laws of positive attraction (i.e., those of a feather flock together) will match your efforts.

To help you see the unseen power that is matching your efforts, redirect your attention from what is going wrong to what is going right. Yes, there are many bullies and passive manipulators out there, but there are even more people who play fair, live by the basic rules of decency, reciprocate, and share. Learn to recognize these individuals and their efforts in your life. Give your time and attention to them, and soon, you will discover that relationships can be fun and easy.

In spite of all the techniques you are applying, there can be no assurance that relationships will develop in the manner you desire. Therefore, you need to build and strengthen your faith in yourself, the opposite sex, and your future. Setting goals to help you let go and have fun, as taught in this chapter, will prevent you from losing hope and feeling despair. So, take some time to outline how you will apply the concepts here until you reach your goal of a happy marriage. You can do this!

Get first dates and avoid common traps

Everything you desire, every blessing you hope for, and every need you have can only be met if you live by the laws that govern that blessing and accept the processes that lead to success. There are rules and laws that govern everything on this earth, from the speed at which things fall (gravity) to electricity, aviation, and chemistry. If you want to be successful in a specific career, if you want to learn how to make and keep money, or if you want to lose weight, you need to understand the steps necessary to obtain *that* goal, as the steps are—and not as you think they should be.

Likewise, if you want to be effective at dating and relationships, you need to know what works for the culture you are in, what steps increase your chances for success, and what red flags indicate the greatest probability of complications or disaster. You need to obey the "laws" that govern good relationships and avoid the patterns that predict bad or dead-end relationships. You need to understand all of this before you begin a new relationship, not after. The first six weeks of dating are the best time to set yourself up for an increased probability of success because the patterns you establish early in a relationship can bless or haunt you for years to come.

There are many different types of relationship traps that you could fall into, any of which could result in abuse, manipulation, neglect, abandonment, infidelity, or exploitation months or years later. For the purposes of this chapter, I've highlighted a few dating traps that you would be wise to avoid during the first six weeks of dating. It may not seem obvious at first how these common traps could end in disaster (because you may not yet recognize how they set you up for those who lack empathy, self-control, and personal responsibility), but you can at least be assured that such patterns will, at a minimum, waste your time and emotional energy.

The too-nice trap

Peter was an attractive, fit, and successful man in his thirties; nonetheless, he struggled to develop relationships. He had no problem getting dates, but most of his relationships didn't last past the first six weeks. He couldn't understand why. He

Alisa Goodwin Snell, M.A.

treated women well, called them twice a week, planned great dates, was quick to date only one woman, and even bought thoughtful gifts. "Isn't that what women like?" he asked. Others often told him he was simply "too nice," like being nice was a disease to be avoided. He couldn't see how becoming a jerk would improve his chances. "How could a woman want to be with a jerk instead of appreciating nice men?" he questioned.

Peter fell into the too-nice trap and kept experiencing early rejection because he acted "too intense" too early in the relationship. He was willing to become exclusive too quickly. He gave too many compliments. And he invested too much without having enough investment from the women in return. He never said no. He was quick to please and eager to make whoever he was dating feel great. All of this made him appear too vulnerable, thus making him look less strong and confident. This was why everyone said he was too nice; being nice wasn't wrong, but doing *too* much *too* early created *too* much pressure, making women prone to reject him even though they saw him as a nice man.

His heart was in the right place, but he needed to hold back some of his efforts, especially in the first six weeks. He needed to express more of his thoughts and needs, and he needed to learn to be more careful about who he invested in. The women he chose to date consistently acted passively in the relationship. He needed to look for women who had a pattern of playing fair and investing in others, just as he did.

The "I'm the exception to the rule" trap

Maria felt an immediate connection with a recently divorced man. He expressed the same amount of interest and affection for her, but she feared that because she was the first woman he'd dated since his divorce two months before, she would be a rebound. However, he frequently repeated that he knew what he wanted and he was not like other men. His warmth, patience, and commitment won her over, and they were engaged within four months and married six months later. However, a month after their wedding, when the first significant issue presented itself, he said he wasn't sure he was ready to be married, and he moved out. He didn't seem to miss her or even look back with regret afterward. He was just done, and the relationship was over. She was devastated.

Most people, after a breakup, divorce, or painful loss, want the benefits of being loved. They want attention, affection, validation, comfort, companionship, and support, yet they are not really in a good place to commit and love back in the long term. Thus, they are a poor bet to invest in. Maria knew this. Nevertheless, she went on several dates with a recently divorced man because she thought just a few dates wouldn't hurt. After spending time with him, getting positive attention and affection from him, and seeing his many good qualities, she could not resist hoping she would be the exception to this rule. She played her role, put in a good-faith effort, and trusted. All of this is necessary and important in normal circumstances, but in a situation where the other person isn't psychologically and emotionally available, tragedy results. In

Maria's case, once a few challenges hit the relationship, he was gone. He wasn't ready for the commitment because he had not resolved his other issues.

Sadly, there are very few exceptions to this rule. Maria had fallen into the rebound trap despite all her investments and efforts. This was the risk she took when she decided to go on just those first few dates. From here forward, she needed to accept that certain unresolved issues—such as a recent death, divorce, or trauma, and a recent or ongoing drug, alcohol, pornography, or sexual addiction—would always cause significant problems. Until the person resolved the issue and was emotionally healthy over a decent period of time, he could not and would not be good for her long-term. If she were lucky enough to discover such issues before the first date, it would be better for her to state that she would love to go out with him once the problem was resolved, rather than accept even the first date. The temptation to think things would work out despite the problem was too great. She was ready to love and be loved, and putting in this protective measure was essential to increase her chances of dating only those men who were truly ready to love her back.

The good-for-now trap

Sharmaya was a strikingly beautiful woman who often dated men for a few weeks and then got dumped. These men seemed fascinated by her immediately, spent lots of time with her, and talked as if they could marry her, but would then disappear with no explanation. She couldn't understand how they could go from loving, affectionate, and adoring one week to neglectful, disengaged, and avoidant the next week. They seemed into her. How could their feelings change so quickly?

What Sharmaya din't see, but others did, is that she often read too much into her relationships. Most men liked her at first, but she took everything they said and did very seriously, even though they had just begun dating. If a man said she was the most beautiful woman he had dated, or he had never felt such strong chemistry before, she thought it meant he was ready to be serious with only her. If he called at 8:30 p.m. to invite her to come to his house (and pick up a video and pizza on the way), she thought he just really wanted to spend time with her right then. If he made out with her for hours or became sexual with her, she thought he was truly into her. She often waited by the phone in case a man wanted to make last-minute plans, tried to run into men she liked so they could hang out, and even began asking men hypothetical "If we were to get married" questions. These men didn't have to sacrifice much of anything to be with her, and before long, they got bored or felt too much of a threat of commitment. They weren't into her. She was into them. Their actions, not their words, said it all. She could change this pattern and find men who were into her, but only if she learned to follow the techniques for dating and keep it real.

The hanging-out and overanalyzing trap

Jeremy often spent time with women he liked, but would quickly find small, annoying flaws or issues he felt he couldn't deal with. He feared being strapped down (i.e., married) and having to accept and face these flaws (such as weird teeth, a strange laugh, lip hair, or any other annoying habit) day after day. He wanted a relationship, but couldn't commit when he believed there had to be women out there who had it all: good looks, a great personality, no annoying habits, etc. Everyone kept telling him, as he got older and older, that he had chronic commitment issues. He started to wonder if they were right. He questioned if he had what it took to be in a long-term committed relationship and be happy.

Jeremy's inability to get into relationships was not due to a lack of commitment, as everyone thought. He had a full-time job, a pet, and long-term friendships, which demonstrated his ability to commit. His problem was a lack of investment in the women he liked and in the dating process. He stayed safe by hanging out, being friends, and even having non-committal make-outs rather than sincerely dating and investing. He thought this would allow him to test a relationship out before he committed to dating a woman, but in the end, it just increased his annoyance, doubt, confusion, and disinterest in women. Without sacrifice and investment, he couldn't develop, grow, and love anyone deeply. To make the situation worse, he also tended to overanalyze the process early on, worrying too early—and with too little information—over whether he could marry the person; this increased the likelihood that he'd end contact sooner rather than later to avoid hurting her.

When I encouraged Jeremy to date women, it didn't mean he had to keep seeing a woman past the first six weeks. The goal of the first six weeks of dating should just be to make the other person feel great, practice, and have fun. After six weeks, he could then decide not to see a woman anymore, except in the case when she fit his Top-Ten List, and he discovered he really enjoyed her. Unless he invested at least this much time and effort into women, he would never develop love for anyone. If he kept overthinking the process and worrying about whether he could marry them, he would regularly and consistently avoid true dating and investment and find it to be a miserable experience.

Jeremy needed to relax, make a good-faith effort, date several women at a time, invest more deeply, and trust that if a relationship didn't last past the first six weeks (as most do not for a variety of reasons), he and she would both be okay and move on. He needed to simplify his expectations and focus on practicing and developing personal relationship skills through dating. Only then would he stop worrying, start enjoying the process, and begin making progress.

Why you can't afford to skip stages

You cannot create a secure attachment by skipping the early stages of dating and instead merely hanging out, making out, having sex, or acting like a friend. Doing these things is like putting the cart before the horse. You get the ease and convenience of being with someone without all the work, time, investment, and energy necessary on their part or yours to develop a secure and committed relationship. Instead of creating something lasting, you will most likely fall into one of the dating traps and never escape it. For example, once a woman falls into the just-friends trap, she usually eliminates herself as someone her "friend" could ever feel attracted to. She is a pal, not a gal, in his mind. He may or may not have been attracted to her from the start, but their friendship and her issues (which he easily discovered during the friendship) usually make him less attracted now (especially because he didn't make significant sacrifices before discovering her issues). Likewise, when a man falls into the too-nice trap, he sets himself up to be the friend a woman runs to when she needs help, but not the one she invests in and sacrifices for; this is because she no longer sees him as strong, confident, and physically attractive. Believing that these relationships might eventually change is a poor bet, and if you take it, you'll discover that you're always pushing the other person to give more rather than enjoying the benefits of mutual investment.

If you believe that being friends, hanging out, or acting like the good-for-now girl or boy (because you don't want to be alone and are willing to accept an inconsistent and uncommitted relationship) doesn't hurt you or the other person, think again. Not only are you wasting your time and theirs, but in male-female friendships and uncommitted relationships, someone always ends up caring more and gets hurt when the other person moves on with someone else. Don't believe you are the exception to this rule.

You need to recognize that you are holding the other person back from being with someone who could commit to them, or you have deeper feelings for this friend and more dependence on them than you'd like to admit. You might not want to let go, but you and they will never move on in your lives if you don't step forward and start dating or let go, so you have the emotional flexibility and availability necessary for someone else. If you want to love, be loved, and get married in the near future, you have to stop hoping that you will fall into a relationship in a convenient, effortless way. Start the process of moving forward now by really investing in the relationships you want.

Just as Peter, Maria, Sharmaya, and Jeremy learned, their dating and relationships followed specific patterns, whether they liked it or not. Such patterns and individual outcomes are predictable and avoidable. Once you understand these patterns, you can change or avoid them. Your lack of success is not innate. It is simply the result of bad techniques and a failure to understand and live by the techniques that would help you be safe, confident, and successful in the early stages of dating.

In this chapter, you'll explore techniques I've created through years of personal experience, professional study, and work with clients. They are meant to help protect you from common traps. They seem difficult and challenging, but they are also liberating. Those who are emotionally mature will respond well, whereas those who are abusive and manipulative will frequently respond badly, take offense, or be turned off by them. These techniques (and boundaries) require your active participation and investment, which increases your likelihood of success. They inspire you to act with confidence and faith that if a specific person doesn't respond as hoped, someone else will. They encourage you to play your role but protect you from acting over-responsible, which would only attract those who are irresponsible. They help you give the best of you, but only to those who invest in you.

These techniques matter. Review them regularly. You need them more than you know. Try to understand the concepts behind these techniques so that you can more fully apply them to your situation and circumstances. Remember, you want to love and be loved, not loved and then used, neglected, abused, cheated on, or abandoned.

The techniques in this chapter will help you secure more effective first dates, break or avoid common traps, and manage the first six weeks. Read both the male and female techniques to help you know how to recognize the efforts of others. You need to know more than how to play your role. Recognizing and appreciating people who play fair and sacrifice in meaningful ways will increase your odds of success.

You may say that the techniques won't work because others don't know them; however, they were created by observing naturally occurring patterns that confident, successful, and respectful daters tend to use. Thus, when you see someone using the techniques (such as not taking your calls immediately or not calling you every day), rather than feeling frustrated, as others might, recognize these people as having the self-respect and knowledge needed to play fair and do their part in a safe, confident, and successful way.

As you train yourself to look for, recognize, and appreciate people who play fair and do their part, you will discover emotionally healthier and happier people. Part of their emotional and relationship success is due to the boundaries they have learned to use and the confidence and results these boundaries have given them. You may have doubts, but there are many people who act according to these wise strategies all the time. Accepting this is simply a matter of awareness. Like buying a new car, you never notice how many people own that same car until after you have committed to investing in one yourself.

The techniques you need are outlined in great detail in this chapter. For video examples, refer to the Lasting Love Academy app or check out our courses at LastingLoveAcademy.com. Seeing these techniques in action as you practice them can greatly increase your confidence and skills.

Move texts to phone calls

- **When texting, move your contact to phone calls or face-to-face as soon as possible.** Texting, instead of calling, has become a staple of our modern culture. However, it leaves too much unsaid and undone. Without meaningful contact, people can become bored by, annoyed with, and critical of the other person. To avoid losing a woman's interest, send texts that encourage meaningful contact the way they want it. Ask them, "What do you prefer, texting or brief phone calls?" or "Some people get stressed out by phone calls, others get stressed out by texts. I prefer texts for little things and brief phone calls for catching up or planning dates. What's your preference?" Years ago, most women would have said that they preferred phone calls. Nowadays, it's hard to predict. Some women feel phone calls are uncomfortable and stressful, whereas others feel frequent texting is demanding and annoying, and too little texting is painful. By asking these questions, you can sort out their distaste for specific types of communication from their perception of you. So, *if in doubt, spell it out.* Remove the guessing, mind reading, and ghosting that is so pervasive in dating. Many singles worry that asking such questions will make them look needy when, in actuality, not speaking up makes them seem insecure or indifferent. By communicating with confidence, you will be viewed as a skilled dater who isn't afraid of what others think because you can handle it.

- **In general, make your first call one to seven days after you get her number.** To avoid looking too nice, overanxious, or less confident, do not call the same day you get her number. Many women can be flattered by an immediate phone call or date, but they can also quickly take you for granted because of it. You will look stronger and more confident if you wait a day or two to call instead. Just don't wait more than a week, or she will think she is on your B-list. Everyone on your A or B-list should be good quality people who fit your Top-Ten List. The difference between those on your A-list is that you're usually more excited about them than those on your B-list. Nevertheless, B-listers often become A-listers, so pursuing B-listers is a wise and important practice. No one wants to be a B-lister, but that is unrealistic. You are on someone's B-list, too. It's just life. As long as B-listers are treated with respect (because you call them in advance, take them on dates, and treat them well), there is no harm done, whereas those on the too-nice, just-friends, or good-for-now list don't get this level of engagement. Some friends are okay with getting called at the last minute, receiving little investment, and being taken for granted. However, maintain your self-respect and the respect of others by not treating anyone with less than B-list respect. When contacting A-listers, make sure you call or text within one to five days. When contacting B-listers, make sure you do this within two to seven days. The longer you wait to call or text, the less excited a woman will feel about you because it seems you're less excited about her. This can reduce the chance that she will act in a way that will encourage your efforts. Women on your B-list can easily move to your A-list after a great date, but this will only happen if you both treat each other great. Thus, it is better to start off by calling her sooner rather than later to increase the odds that something might develop. Do not feel guilty or worry about contacting a B-lister less aggressively than you pursue A-listers. Treating them differently is actually a kind practice because your less aggressive behavior with a B-lister helps her not to get as excited about you as she would if you were calling more frequently.

- **Do not call more than twice in one week.** A woman who is excited to hear from you will be sad if she misses your call; however, if you don't leave a message or send a text asking her to call, she probably won't. Seeing that she missed your call isn't enough. Many women don't want to appear over-anxious and can feel vulnerable or foolish about calling or texting you back unless you ask them to. So, don't call and then hang up when you get her voicemail. This leaves you to have to call back later, and calling too many times can make you seem creepy or obsessed. Instead, leave a message asking her to call you back and then wait for her to take action.

- **When she doesn't answer the phone, leave a message and then send her a text**. It has become common for people not to answer the phone. Even if you leave a message, which is recommended, people often delay listening to messages and prefer texting their reply rather than calling back. This practice has dramatically impacted relationships because it significantly reduces the availability, responsiveness, and emotional engagement that is needed for creating and maintaining secure attachments. Although this is now a common practice, do not contribute to this pattern. Instead, set a good example for others to follow, one that will actually create the secure attachment and connection you are seeking. When you call, and they don't answer, leave a voice message (rather than merely hanging up) so they can hear your strong and confident voice as you say, "Hey, Sally, give me a call. I'm planning some fun things for the weekend. I'd love you to join me. I look forward to hearing from you. Talk to you soon." After leaving this confident message, text her and say, "I just left you a message. Give me a call when you get a minute. I'm planning some fun things for the weekend. I'd love you to join me. I look forward to hearing from you. Talk to you soon." By calling, leaving a message, and texting her, you are showing her how confident and proactive you can be. And, if you schedule a time to call and she doesn't answer, leave a voice message saying, "Hi, this is John. I called at the time we discussed. Tag, you're it. Call me back. I look forward to talking with you soon." Now, the ball is clearly in her court. If she calls you back or texts you with a suggested time to call, she is giving you A-list attention (which is very encouraging).

- **When possible, avoid using texting to ask for a date. Ask what time would be good to call.** Most single women agree that when texting or messaging is the primary form of communication, it makes a woman feel less secure about your interest in her and consequently leaves her less attracted to and interested in you. Brief texts throughout the first week with few to no phone calls may be somewhat fun, but if done too frequently, they can quickly become tedious and even make you look too intense, too needy, or insecure. Texts in the second week with few to no phone calls may be tolerated, although they make a woman wonder if she is just on your B-list. But texts in the third and fourth week, with still few to no phone calls or dates, become deeply annoying and turn a woman off unless you're only on her good-for-now or just-friends list. Additionally, if you use texting to ask for a date, you will look passive or timid because it seems safe, or even lazy. A woman wants a connection, and texting feels like the bare minimum of effort needed to keep that connection. It also leaves too much room for misunderstanding and mind-reading, especially when emotions are being discussed. Men may see it as a simple and time-efficient way to keep in contact, but it requires too little time and makes a woman feel like she is not a priority. When you are calling and taking her on dates, a woman may see a brief text as a cherry on top, but it simply cannot be used as a replacement for real dating techniques. So, make yourself look like an A-list man and make her feel like an A-list woman by calling her at least twice a week and then sending a brief text to say hi or to let her know you are thinking about her in between phone calls or dates. A brief text to ask, "When would be a good time to call?" or to confirm the place and time of a date that has already been set is also nice. And, a quick text after your fourth date to state, "You looked beautiful tonight," is always great. There is one exception to this rule: if you both have been calling but missing each other, it's okay to simplify the process by texting your request for the date.

When she is slow to respond (or doesn't)

- **When a woman calls or texts you back, respond similarly.** When a woman calls or texts you back, respond similarly. When a woman responds and makes time for a phone call within twenty-four hours, she is giving you an A-list response. When a woman texts you back or responds days later, she is giving you a B-list (or worse) response, which is more difficult to interpret: *Is she brushing you off and doing the bare minimum, or is she sincerely interested but busy? Does she struggle with phone calls, or is she overthinking the process and feeling that phone calls are too much pressure?* Since you can't easily ask her, don't take it personally; instead, match her level of engagement by returning her same level of investment. If you haven't asked her already, text her: "What do you prefer, texting or brief phone calls? I'm good with either. What's your preference?"

- **If you don't get a return call, call back 24 hours to three days later and leave another message.** If she doesn't call back after that, wait one more week and try again. After the third unanswered call, be sure to state you will not be calling again out of respect for your time and hers. It is important that you show persistence and consistency, but also self-respect. Being persistent shows you have confidence, but to look secure and more desirable, you also need to state, "Oh, and by the way, I thought you should know I won't be calling again without a return call. I am definitely interested, but out of respect for both your time and mine, I intend to back off if I don't hear from you. I look forward to your call." She most likely will call back since it is possible she's just been busy or hasn't been able to access her phone, but if she doesn't return your call, you can take confidence in knowing you ended the encounter on your terms and with self-respect and strength.

Phone calls, better connections, and less pressure

- **To increase her engagement, take the pressure off and focus on having fun.** There are many triggers for loss of interest, the biggest of which is pressure. To reduce the risk of early rejection, express early on (whether face-to-face, on the phone, or by text), "Just so you know, dating can feel like way too much pressure. I don't have any expectations except to have fun and get to know you better. If we both treat each other with respect, neither of us will have any regret. If that sounds good, what kind of fun things do you like to do?"

- **When talking on the phone, state that you have about ten minutes to talk, but be prepared to talk longer if things are going well.** Don't feel pressure to schedule calls unless it is a phone date. This can increase pressure, expectations, and unnecessary commitment that can limit your and their other social options. Instead, call spontaneously when you have ten minutes and encourage her to return your call when she has a few minutes, too. Everyone can find a few minutes when driving, over lunch, or when at the grocery store. Casual opportunities like these can show you care enough to connect and are willing to include them in your day. Talking on the phone can be uncomfortable for both men and women. They can worry about what to say and how the other will perceive them. It can be less anxiety-producing for men and women alike if they both know that the conversation will be a shorter one. To take the pressure off, state early in the call, "My day is pretty busy, but I can always take ten minutes for what's most important, such as catching up with you and how you're doing." This technique works well because it shows you are a driven and hardworking guy who also values connecting with her. Be sure to ask her a few questions about her day or week and then share a few details about yours. When the conversation has lasted around ten minutes, hits a low, or becomes uncomfortable, state, "Wow, I've got to go. I'm sorry. I wish I had more time."

- **When on the phone, recognize words that are emotional and use them.** If you describe your day in a laundry-list fashion, "I got up late, went to work ten minutes late, had to deal with lots of problems today, and then came home ready for a nap," she will likely feel bored and disconnected from what you are saying. But if you describe your day with a few emotional words, "I felt so *frustrated* today. My alarm clock didn't go off. I had to rush to work without showering. My boss seemed *annoyed*. I felt *uncomfortable* and *nervous* about what he was thinking, but after lunch, everything got so much better. I feel so blessed to work with people who can make me laugh," she will most likely relate to your feelings, even if she can't relate to the situation. Emotion words are a great way to facilitate and keep a conversation going and are an essential part of female bonding. A woman needs to feel a connection to you through your emotions and through your response to her emotions. Review the list of emotion words in Appendix C. Read them often. Then, start practicing them when talking about yourself and when listening to others. For example, you could say to a woman who had a bad day like the one above, "I *hate* it when that happens to me. I bet you feel so *worn out* and in need of a *fun* escape. I'd *love* to take you out later this week and help you forget about all that for a few hours. When would be good for you?" As a man, it is best if you don't use too many emotional words when describing your day and life. Unfortunately, overusing emotional words will make you appear too sensitive or effeminate. However, you are sure to impress her when you use a lot of emotional words that show you truly understand how she feels.

Move from phone calls to dates (and how to end contact)

- **Avoid common traps and encourage date-like behavior.** It is important that you avoid falling into the just-friends, hanging-out, good-for-now, or other caretaking traps. To avoid this, encourage date-like behavior, not hanging out (especially after sharing several social interactions). For instance, if a woman seems to just want to talk like friends, say, "I can see this is important to you. I am so sorry that I can't talk for much longer, but I'd love to continue this over dinner or a fun activity." If she wants to hang out at the last minute, say, "I am not available tonight, but I'd love to plan something in advance or go on a date later this week." Or if she wants to complain about her problems, say, "That's really hard. I'm sorry you are having a hard time, and I am confident you will be inspired about what to do." Then follow up by stating, "I would really like to help you escape all of that for an evening by taking you on a date this weekend." If she accepts your offer, great. But if she makes excuses, acts too busy, or plays the victim, trust that you have prevented yourself from falling into a potential trap. She may not be ready to fully engage yet, but the good news is that she doesn't see you as an easy push-over either. Women need to see strength and confidence in men, or they won't respect them. Without boundaries, you will be taken for granted; but, with boundaries, you will get better behavior and investment from her. End the conversation by saying, "We can all be too busy, but it's also important to have fun. Let me know when you would like to take a break from it all. I'd love to take you on a date and get to know you better." Then back off and see what she does from there. The ball is in her court until she is ready to invest in date-like behavior. You are worth this level of engagement and she knows that you know it.

- **If during the conversation you decide you are NOT interested in going on a date, simply end the call.** Instead of making plans, say, "I need to go, but it was great talking with you. I hope you have a wonderful day." Don't allude to future calls or dates. If she asks or states that she wants to get together, say, "Let me get back to you on that." This is a gentle brush off that most people recognize as a very loose commitment or a polite way of saying no.

- **If you are interested in spending time with her, don't get off the phone without asking for a date.** After spending a few minutes asking her about herself and her day, don't hesitate to get to the point, even if (and especially if) she seems busy. Show her you have the strength and confidence to pursue what you want—and that what you want is a date with her. Women like to be pursued and to feel wanted, and are attracted to strength and confidence. Thus, pursuing her (rather than hedging or waiting for her to ask) makes you look more desirable. You do not need to be clever or witty or invest a lot of time in her before you ask her for a date. As a matter of fact, spending too much time before asking her out can make you look less confident. Just state, "I would love to do something fun with you this week. When would be good for you?"

Have fun (while decreasing pressure)

- **Don't let dating feel like a drag: take charge and make it fun.** Take the pressure off and increase interest by suggesting dates that are engaging, active, and creative. Doing this will help her to focus on the fun she'll have when with you rather than worrying about her feelings (or lack thereof); after all, the more she learns to relax and have fun, the more feelings she may develop. To do this, express that you have a variety of date ideas and would like to know her preference: "Do you prefer outdoor activities, indoor activities, entertainment, dinner, or something athletic?" Listen to her response and then add the option for additional mystery and intrigue by asking, "Would you like to pick from a couple of date options that fit your choice, or would you like to be surprised?"

- **Make dating more fun by creating and sharing your seasonal list of things you want to do.** Doing this will help you avoid the boredom and meaninglessness that you might otherwise feel when on dates. It keeps dates from being too stressful and you from feeling trapped into spending time with someone while doing something you don't appreciate. If you share some possibilities for low-pressure date activities, no matter how you feel about her, you will enjoy the date more.

- **Ask her to join you for short midweek or daytime dates that fit both of your interests.** Many of the activities in your seasonal list can be just a few hours long, such as trying a new bagel shop for breakfast, catching a game of racquetball after work, going on a bike ride on a Saturday morning, or having a picnic and flying a kite at the park on a Sunday afternoon. It may also be fun to encourage her to create and share her seasonal list with you.

Techniques for a stronger impression (using A-list dating skills)

- **If you can't tell whether she believes you're simply hanging out or going on a date, tell her it's a date.** Planning more casual, fun, low-pressure dates can become confusing for some women. They may think they are just hanging out, and as such, they may not value the date as much. Don't confuse her on this point. Instead, state clearly that you see this as a date by calling it such: "Great, it's a date," "I'm looking forward to our date," or "What time should I meet you or pick you up for our date?"

- **Ask for a date that is at least 24 hours from the time you call.** Do not ask for a date the same night that you call her. This makes you look too anxious, too available, and less confident. It can also make you look like either a player who is not invested enough to call her in advance or a lazy man who doesn't have a life full of plans, people, friends, work, and other interests. If you want her to feel like she is on your A-list, ask her for a Friday or Saturday date two to five days in advance. Weekends are often seen as prime time and something men prize.

Thus, asking her out for a Friday or Saturday makes her feel that you prize and value time with her, but only if you call in advance. Calling a woman at 6 p.m. on a Friday night to go to a movie at 7 p.m. makes her believe that your other A-list options fell through and that she is just a standby option. The only time a woman won't see this as an insult is when you get incredible last-minute tickets and state that you thought of her first. This will flatter her, and she may try to accommodate you, but if it becomes a pattern, she will see you as taking her for granted. Don't believe that you have to offer weekend nights, or she won't feel like she's on your A-list. Offering other, more casual, midweek date ideas can still send an A-list message, but with a lot less pressure than weekends can create. That being said, always offer a weekend date first to see how she reacts. If she goes for it, she is definitely giving you an A-list message in return. Singles treat their weekends as a high priority and save them for those they enjoy most.

- **If she is not available for a specific night, offer another.** If she can't go on a date for the day you suggest, pause and see if she offers another day and time, which is a good sign. If this is the case, set a date for that day. If she doesn't offer a different day, find out if this is intentional by offering a different, low-pressure option (such as a midweek, daytime, or shorter date). If she doesn't act ready to commit to this type of date, you are not on her A-list and probably not on her B-list. Increase the possibility that she will engage by taking the pressure off. Say, "Just so you know, I view dating as merely an opportunity to have fun and get to know each other. I don't want you to feel pressured. If you want to do something fun, we can look at a different day, or if you prefer, you can call or text me when you are ready, and I'll take it from there. Which do you prefer?"

- **After getting her feedback and suggestions for the date, state that you will call a day or two before the date to discuss the specifics.** It's always a good idea to follow up with her at least 24 hours before the date. This helps her feel more secure about your commitment to the date, solidifies the details, and gives you another opportunity to connect with her in a meaningful way.

Organize and remember important contacts

- **After getting off the phone, update your notes within her contact details.** Your phone provides a way to store and track important details about your contacts, such as their name, number, and email. Often, a contact also include a notes section. Use this feature to track important details you discover about her (such as the names of her family members, any struggles she is having, or fun things she enjoys). Before interacting with her again, refer to your notes so you can ask follow-up questions: "How did your test go?" or "Is your mother feeling better?" Remembering such details will make her trust your sincerity while also deepening your connection.

- **Make sure you organize your contacts to track and pursue women efficiently.** Some women may be frustrated by the fact that you're dating other women, but such an attitude is unrealistic and impractical. Until you both agree to be exclusive, you have the right to pursue other women, and so does anyone you're dating. Until this occurs, you need a system for tracking the women you're calling or dating. Trying to find one name among hundreds of business and personal contacts can make you forget or lose track of potential dates. Instead, put two initials before a woman's first name, such as *AA Kathy, AB Sariah, BA Jennifer, BB Casandra, NA Jessica,* and *RES Lisa.* The first initial refers to whether the person is on your A or B-list. The second initial refers to whether you're on her A or B-list. RES means she is on your reserve list (to follow up within a few months). NA stands for never again. Thus, Kathy is on your A-list and is giving you A-list attention back. Sariah is responding as if you're on her B-list. It seems you're on Jennifer's A-list, although she is on your B-list. And both you and Casandra seem to be on each other's B-list. You never want to go out with Jessica again, but you're keeping her in your contacts so you recognize her number if she calls (as a reminder not to answer). And Lisa is an option in a few months if you're both still available. These girls can quickly move from one status to another by changing their initials within your contacts. For example, you might change Kathy's contact to *NA Kathy* after a bad experience, while Jennifer becomes *AA Jennifer* after a fun date. Now, you can find, track, and follow up with each of them appropriately. Be careful not to store sensitive information within your contacts that you do not want others to see, since this may upset a future girlfriend. And, once you're in a relationship, be sure to change all contact details to a more appropriate designation or remove them entirely from your phone.

After the first phone call and before the date

- **Confirm your plans by calling 24 hours before the date.** If you already planned the date in a previous conversation, call 24 hours before the date to confirm it and finalize any specific details. Women often worry about whether or not they will be stood up and need more details in order to plan. This makes them feel they need to call and confirm so that they aren't left with doubts. By calling, confirming, and even telling her in advance that you'll be doing so, you make yourself look classy, you reduce her anxiety, and you help her feel safe and secure. Be sure to let her know what to wear (warm, cold, dressed up, or casual clothes), whether you will be eating during the date, and what time you will be picking her up (unless she wants to meet in town first because she doesn't know you well enough to give you her address).

- **When planning the first date, do not make it elaborate. Keep it short, simple, fun, and interactive rather than long, expensive, or passive.** Going all out on a first date is a bad idea. It creates too much pressure for both of you and can even make a woman uncomfortable. It can cost you too much money and time to prepare, and can set you up for gold diggers and the too-nice trap. It can also make women worry or overthink whether you are *too* into them *too* soon. Instead, plan a simple date. A lunch date is an acceptable first date, especially if you met online or have only briefly talked before. It is short and helps you know if there's enough connection to go out again. It also prevents you both from having to struggle through a few miserable hours if things don't go well. If you want to be a little creative, plan a daytime date, such as a short hike, a bike ride, rollerblading, or a walk through the park—complete with simple snacks, a packed lunch, and drinks. If you want to do dinner, go to a modest restaurant like Applebee's, Chili's, or TGI Fridays. If you choose an activity, miniature golfing, bowling, an amateur or professional sports event, a play, or a trip to the museum would be great. Try to avoid going to a movie or any activity that is passive and discourages interaction. Dating is about building a connection, and passive activities don't help you do that. They also don't give a woman an opportunity to invest in you by keeping the conversation going. For a first date, don't worry about doing dinner *and* an activity unless you are confident that there's enough connection that you both could enjoy a potentially longer date.

- **Solicit her opinion and suggestions for the date, but definitely show her you will take charge and plan the date.** Women hate it when a man says he doesn't care what they do on a date. It makes a woman feel that he is lazy, a pushover, or too passive to take charge, and therefore, she feels responsible for the date. Furthermore, women like men who take charge. Women don't want to be dismissed, dictated to, or dominated, but they also need to see that a man can make decisions and take action.

- **If it feels appropriate, ask her to plan a small part of the date.** In order to avoid the too-nice trap and to ensure that *you only give the best of you to those who invest in you*, ask her to participate in some part of the date. For instance, tell her, "I would be glad to bring the sandwiches, water, and snacks for the hike, but would you come up with a couple of places we could go for dessert after the hike? I will pay for it, but I would love it if you would plan that part of the date." If you are getting together for a brief lunch at the park, say, "I will bring the food and a blanket. Would you be willing to bring drinks?" If you are meeting for the first time at a restaurant for dinner, ask, "When you get to the restaurant, would you call me so I can meet you at the entrance?" Don't ask her to plan the date or do big things since this would make her feel less confident in your investment and interest in her, but do ask her for a few small things. If you don't feel comfortable having her do this for the first date, that's fine, but look to see if she voluntarily invests energy into you, and definitely start asking for small contributions before the third date. The purpose of asking her to plan a part of the date is twofold: (1) to see if she will invest in you and (2) to see if she will respond to your requests for help. Emotionally immature and toxic women will often be passive about investing in you or will invest only on their terms. When you ask for their help, they will act indifferent, seem offended, ignore your request, fail to follow through, or hold grudges. If you fail to ask for her help and only look at the things she does voluntarily, you will miss an important opportunity to discover the truth early on, before you get attached. If she resents your small requests now, she will resent them later, too.

Manage your excitement and potential disappointment

- **To avoid unnecessary heartbreak, keep it real. Limit thinking and talking about a woman you're dating.** Although it is common for women to analyze and worry about their relationships, men can also obsess about them, and it is equally painful for them. Those who suffer from an anxious attachment will worry about getting and keeping a relationship and doing something wrong. They can be caught in analysis paralysis and fear of making a mistake or taking action. They can stress about others' judgment and worry that they will appear foolish or needy. This can cause them to suffer in silence or seek repeated reassurance and validation. In all these cases, anxiety, common thinking errors, fears, and internal or external pressure can play a crucial role. If this describes you, then managing your relationship anxiety with the support of no more than three friends, redirecting your attention, and focusing on balanced and healthy beliefs is your best solution for staying engaged while stabilizing the highs and lows of dating. Without support, you will create faulty beliefs, experience more insecurity, and take your experiences personally. Thus, to help you keep things realistic, select the three people you will ask for ideas and support when you have a dating question. While waiting for a call or text, avoid checking your phone or reviewing your messages (for signs of your mistakes). Get busy doing things that grab your attention and physical senses (whether this includes TV, audiobooks, music, exercise, or getting together with friends and family). Avoid thoughts and phrases like, *she is the best, I don't want to blow it, I rarely meet someone I'm excited about, and I'd be lucky to be with her. Such statements show all-or-nothing thinking, a scarcity mentality, fears of missing out, and overgeneralization.* Instead, believe in your goodness and remind yourself that she isn't perfect, and you don't need to be either. You only want to be with someone who values you and will do their part with you. When others give you advice, ensure it reflects balanced and practical information, and then practice it before seeking more advice. This will help reduce any risk of rumination. It is also essential that you continue your other dating efforts so you feel less pressure for exclusivity or daily contact (which may push a woman away or cause you to become overly committed before you know her). Think about others, yourself, dating, and relationships in a balanced way, and you will feel more balanced, too.

- **Remember and use the truths and balanced beliefs you created in Chapter 2 to combat your fears and unhealthy beliefs.** Repeat to yourself: *If she is the kind of person I'm looking for, she will see my value, respond to my efforts, match them, and provide options that work for both of us. We don't need an immediate relationship. We both can manage our anxieties and fears individually while the relationship progresses appropriately. I am meant to love and be loved. I am lovable and desirable. I will do my part with several people and only choose to be with those who do their part, too. I'm a great catch and deserve their mutual investment.* The more you keep your expectations, emotions, and beliefs in check, the more realistic, challenging, happy, confident, and attractive you will be.

- **Recognize that drama, anxiety, and romantic notions are not an indication of love but of infatuation and an anxious attachment.** Drama and stress are often romanticized in our modern culture as necessary and unavoidable burdens of true love. *If you aren't thinking about them all the time, are in pain when not with them, or are only okay when you have their approval, they must not be the one, or you do not really love them.* Unfortunately, movies, music, and books build on such themes because they have to exploit strong emotions to sell their products. Don't be deceived by our modern culture's toxic misrepresentations of infatuation as love. Healthy relationships are far more balanced, secure, fun, and stable.

- **Don't let your anxiety and fears steal your attention by focusing on only those individuals who are rejecting or manipulating you.** It is common for people to long for resolution relative to their difficult, rejecting, and unresolved relationships and then seek individuals who are similarly toxic, rejecting, or manipulative. Believing that love is supposed to include painful longing and a compelling need for the other's affection will often lead you to illogical relationships with co-dependent and addictive elements. You can be in control of your emotions, expectations, and romantic experiences. The heart may want what it wants, but you are not a slave to your feelings. You can plant a seed and grow a tree anywhere you choose and enjoy how its strong and flexible branches flow in the wind (rather than living a life that is aimlessly being driven like a plastic bag in the wind of your fleeting emotions). Your feelings and attitudes will bend, deepen, and grow when you choose to direct and nourish them where the heart and mind recognize wisdom.

Guidelines when meeting from online, dating apps, or social media

- **When messaging, transition your conversations quickly to phone calls, FaceTime, and in-person meetings.** Switch from messaging to phone conversations, ideally within the first two weeks. Do this sooner rather than later. If you are still interested after your call, suggest grabbing a quick bite to eat or enjoying a fun public activity together.

- **Be safe and smart about how much information you share with someone online or through dating apps.**

  - » **Be supportive as a woman sets boundaries about meeting you for the first time.** Remember that a woman's number-one need is to feel safe and secure. Do not ask her for identifying information, such as where she lives or works, her address, the names of her children, or even her last name. Be content to just get her first name for now. You can ask her what general area she lives in, but do not ask her what city she lives in.

» **Expect to meet her in a crowded, public place for a first date rather than at her or your home.** And do not tease, joke, discourage, or make comments about any of this. Remember, you are a stranger, and she can't be assured that you really are who you say you are. Dating apps give predators a lot of room to misrepresent themselves. So, support, encourage, and even request that she do whatever it takes to make her feel comfortable.

» **If you meet a woman through a dating app or website and then recognize her on social media, don't send her a friend request unless she's actively engaging and encouraging more contact with you.** If she hasn't shared her last name with you and isn't responding to you frequently, or at all, she won't like knowing that you now have her last name and have access to her social media pages. Being too aggressive about finding a woman's information can make you seem creepy and like a stalker, so be cautious in this regard until you know her better.

» **Don't share personal information that makes you vulnerable to exploitation.** You may feel you need to give her your last name so she feels more comfortable meeting you, but do not feel pressured to tell her where you work or live. Just because she is a woman doesn't mean she isn't a threat. Women can stalk men, too. Some of this is normal (such as doing random internet searches or Facebook-stalking to see what she can learn about you); however, it's important that she can't learn where you live or work from these searches. Protect this information and make sure it is not public through any of your social media pages. It is always better to be safe than sorry, and she doesn't need this background information in order to meet you in a public place for a first date.

» **If you have achieved financial success or social status, being too public about your success can make you a target for money-diggers.** Give a general impression that you are successful, but let them discover the details from you over time. For example, you could state what type of profession you are in, such as the medical, legal, health services, or public services professions, while stating, "I'll tell you more once I know you better." Because it is important for women to know that the men they're dating have jobs and are stable in their careers, you could also say, "I work full-time and have a steady income. I make enough to meet my needs and many of my wants. But I prefer to wait until I know someone better before I share exactly what I do." If she asks why, say, "Everyone wants to be seen and appreciated for who they are, not what they do." Most women will respond well to this kind of answer. If she doesn't, move on. Her reaction may reveal that she does not have sincere intentions.

Strategies for successful long-distance dates and meaningful connections

- **When dating long distance, use WhatsApp, FaceTime, or Marco Polo before discussing travel arrangements.** Insisting on using video chat apps and features may seem tacky, but you will be glad you did. Seeing someone in real-time will give you a more accurate understanding of the other's appearance, social skills, and issues before you spend hundreds of dollars and valuable time traveling.

- **Show a woman you are serious about dating her, despite being long distance, by surprising her with fun activities during your video-chat dates.** Make her feel great by sending her packages (if she feels comfortable sharing her address) with games to play during your next Facetime date. You can offer to have her favorite food delivered to her door with Uber Eats or exchange recipes you both have to prepare. You can order food, games, and other essentials from a Walmart near her and have her pick it up before the date. The extra effort you put into planning these activities will go a long way in making her feel special. At the same time, you stand out as a man who can handle any dating situation with class.

- **Engage in various conversations and activities to stimulate real-world and deeper connections.** Talking on the phone may fill the void and ease loneliness, but until you meet face-to-face, you won't know if you are reading the situation correctly and are truly attracted and interested. However, engaging in fun activities can help while planning and waiting for that first live interaction. Ask both of you to write questions you want to learn about the other person and cut each into strips. While preparing dinner together (for a date activity), you can each draw random questions and take turns answering them. You could do a virtual museum tour together, engage in a photo contest while hiking, and share what you see on the trail. The one who snaps the most unique or stunning image could surprise the other with a game they want to play together during the next date. You could both go on a geocaching adventure in your city and share your screen while trying to locate the treasure (search for geocaches near you to learn more). You could share your video while binge-watching someone's favorite movie or TV series on Sunday afternoons. Reading a book, listening to podcasts, discovering a new hobby, engaging in an online yoga session, shipping an art set to paint something together, playing bingo, a card game, or classic games like Battleships can be fun. Sharing favorite recipes, cooking together, and talking about each other's day during a drive home or before bed are all examples of everyday activities that can be shared through video and phone calls. Be creative, and you will find long-distance dating isn't as impossible or unfulfilling as you may fear. Just make sure you are doing these things in between regular visits, and not as a replacement for them (or you may discover that the other person isn't who they appear to be, and you wasted your time, money, and attachment on someone who is catfishing you).

- **During video calls, avoid unintentionally communicating negative or personal habits that would be a turn-off.** During your video chat, make sure that the room you are in (as seen from the other person's vantage point) is free of offensive pictures, clutter, or noises that could give them a bad impression of you or the way you live.

- **Prepare as you would for a date. Wash your hair and style your beard.** Trim unsightly hairs (on your face, chin, neck, eyebrows, or nose. Wear flattering, clean, modern, and wrinkle-free clothes. Not doing these things for a date is not only a poor reflection on you but also sends a message about how much you care about and respect your date.

- **Set up the camera at eye level and use good lighting on your face.** Lights above your head (trigger harsh shadows). Cameras below eye level will exaggerate a double chin, and those above eye level will do this to your forehead. The further you are from the camera, the better. Buying a tripod for your phone is a cheap and effective option for creating ideal and stable camera angles. Purchasing a ring light can soften wrinkles and even out your skin tones.

- **Limit unnecessary distractions such as intruding pets, children, and other unnecessary calls or environmental problems or noises** (when possible). Set your phone to quiet mode (after you get on the video call).

When traveling to meet each other

- **Make sure you either offer to go to her town or help pay for her expenses to meet you. Plan to stay the night in separate locations.** The more a woman invests, the more vulnerable she feels. Be sure that you make her feel secure by making more of the financial or physical sacrifices. If you both meet halfway, it's appropriate to let her pay for her driving expenses, but be sure you pay for the date and activities. Make arrangements for her or you to stay at a friend's house when possible. If this is not available, be sure to get two different hotel rooms. Don't give in to the idea that sharing a hotel room won't cause problems. Not only can this make you look like you have a sexual agenda, but it can also make one or both of you feel more vulnerable, attached, or distant and sabotage what might have been a wonderful trip. If you can't create separate sleeping arrangements, plan the date early in the day to allow time for driving back home. This shouldn't be a problem if you are no more than 300 miles apart. If she drives to your town, realize that she will feel awkward, uncomfortable, and insecure if you don't make time for her, so clarify how much time you can spend before she finalizes her plans.

Avoid the hanging-out and just-friends traps

- **To avoid falling into any of the common traps, act confident, have boundaries, show self-respect, and ask her to sacrifice for you as well,**

or she will not respect you. Women are attracted to strength and confidence. If you do not act strong and confident by setting limits on how and when you are available and saying no sometimes, you will be more likely to fall into the just-friends, good-for-now, or too-nice trap (women are turned off by men who are too nice. Women like nice men, but they do not trust too-nice men because they seem weak, too eager to please, insincere, or easily manipulated and, as such, less desirable, which is why women who do not trust and respect their men fall out of love. If you give her unlimited time, attention, and help without expressing your feelings, needs, and opinions, she simply will not trust your intentions. In addition to expressing your opinions, you also need to ask her to invest in you sometimes, or she will never fall in love with you (because the more deeply a person sacrifices, the more deeply they love). Additionally, she needs to be aware that you are dating others occasionally. Although women fear competition from other women, they will feel no need to secure a commitment from you if you have already reduced or eliminated your possibilities. If you do all of these things while making her feel safe and secure, you will increase the odds that she will fall in love with you. Women thrive when they feel safe and secure. It is a man's ability to make a woman feel safe and secure, help her feel great, and show self-respect, all while pursuing her, that often causes a woman to fall in love with a friend.

- **To avoid or break the hanging-out pattern, directly state that you would enjoy going on a date.** If a woman frequently engages in casual activities with you, you can't know if she is doing so because she is hoping you are interested in her, or she merely sees you as a friend. If you prolong your hope that she will fall in love with you rather than make a move, you may discover that she is unable to shift her feelings for you later. You need to encourage chemistry sooner rather than later and discover if she will go on a date or not. She doesn't need to feel that each date is a high-pressure event or that she has to be ready to commit to being exclusive. Instead, encourage her to view your time together as a casual, fun, and thoughtful opportunity to see if a romantic connection grows. Accepting a date says a lot about her potential willingness to consider investing in you while exploring the possibility of more. She also shouldn't view you as being all-in, which is too much pressure when she isn't there yet. So, encourage her to just have fun while you both explore the possibilities and see how it feels. If she insists on defining your time together as merely hanging out or being friends, recognize this is a strong indication that things will probably never progress because you are not her type. Remember that without her increased investment and engagement in dating, simple affection, and meeting your mutual needs, nothing more will grow, especially after a month or two of hanging out. Her feelings and doubts about you will not change as long as she remains passive. Passiveness leads to passionless feelings; contrarily, sacrifice is deeply connected to love. If she is unwilling to let you pay, plan in advance, or call your time together a date, then she may have problems with trust or commitment. Unless she is unwilling to do her part (or empathize with your feelings), don't pursue her for too long. Instead, pull back so she sees that she can't take you for granted.

- **Make your intentions to date clear by prioritizing dates with her or others over time spent hanging out with her.** If you are to move this relationship from just friends or hanging out to dating, then you need to show your self-worth and self-respect by clearly communicating that you are looking to date or move on with others. To do this, when hanging out, occasionally leave early and on a high note, so she doesn't feel she has enough time with you and wants more. Be sure to cheerfully ask her the next time she suggests that you get together, "Is this a date or hanging out? I am fine with either, but I don't know what my role is if I don't ask. To be clear, I'd love to make it a date if you would enjoy that, too." Then, wait for her response. If she says, "It's a date," answer, "Great." If she says, "It's hanging out," say, "Thank you for being so clear. I'd enjoy hanging out, too, if we can do it on a weekday. I usually schedule dates on the weekend. Text me some of your ideas, and maybe we can hang out sometime next week." If you say this with warmth and use confident behavior, she will probably see you as an even more attractive friend. Since you aren't pushing to do something right away and leaving the ball somewhat in her court, it shows that she could be losing some of the time and investment she once enjoyed, since you are merely friends. She may be turned off or hurt by you pulling back, but this also shows that she has an attachment to you. By setting boundaries, you show her that you don't give the best of you to those who don't invest in you (or who take you for granted). If she misses you, gets upset, or asks for more time with you, then share with her, "I really would love to see you more often because I value you and our friendship, but I am in a place where I need to prioritize dates over hanging out. I hope you will understand, but let's definitely schedule or do something last minute on occasion since I hope we can stay friends." If you want her to know that the possibility of dating is still on the table, add, "And if you would like to try going on dates, I'm cool with that, too. Just know that unless you say something, I will keep assuming that we are just friends, and we are both cool with it." With a little time apart, she may invest in more meaningful and clear ways. Either way, spending too much time together will not help either of you to move on and find someone who enjoys chemistry and mutual commitment.

- **When you hang out with her and her friends, be sure to flirt with her friends, not her.** Don't linger too long when hanging out, and don't hang out very often. Leave each event on a high note. And if you find one of her friends interesting, don't hesitate to ask that friend to exchange numbers and do something fun to get to know each other better. If your original friend takes issue with this later, state, "I'm confused. I thought you were only interested in friendship. Did your feelings change?" Confronting the incongruency in her statements (while showing kindness and confusion) may reveal her feelings or expose a tendency for a friend to call dibs on a man and expect others to stay away. This isn't a reasonable expectation among friends when dates are usually casual experiences that don't go anywhere. Having respectful expectations in social groups is important, and it isn't a good sign when friends try to control others' lives and choices (especially when they only have an infatuation, were never in a relationship, or didn't have sexual contact).

- **When at all singles events, hang-out opportunities, or social activities, leave them curious, wanting more, and impressed that you are driven and busy.** While at the event, take the opportunity to relax, have fun, make others feel great, and fully enjoy the moment. You can attend several of these events and casually build a reliable and respectable reputation; however, once you scout a few people you are interested in, try to get a one-on-one conversation going. To do this, you can look for a time when they are sitting alone, offer to help them as they clean up, or suggest that you walk with them to their car. You can then state, "I'm not able to consistently attend these events and would love to keep chatting. Can I get your number so we can do something fun and keep chatting?"

- **Take the pressure off by stating (within the group) that you view dating as a fun, low-pressure way to get to know others.** As shared previously, when in mixed groups, singles often complain about the opposite sex and dating. By contrast, when you show that you have a positive view of the opposite sex, enjoy having fun, and don't over-analyze dates as being a serious activity (beyond mutual respect), thus gossiping or claiming dibs on a crush is unrealistic, others will be more likely to consider going on a fun date or activity with you. You have nothing to lose by acting sooner rather than later, which adds to your overall desirability in the eyes of everyone.

- **If a woman hesitates to accept a date, take the pressure off and state that you understand that she may prefer to hang out in a group first.** Some women hesitate to go on dates with near strangers and only trust men they meet socially or develop friendships with first. If you show women that you understand this reasonable need, they will relax and enjoy you more. However, it's also a good idea to encourage them to let you know if or when they would be open to a date. This requires that they invest and risk more when they feel ready. While hanging out or at events, make time to talk, ask questions, and engage, but don't linger past ten minutes or dominate her attention, or she will feel pressured. Instead, leave her curious and wanting more. You can also state, "It really is hard to have good conversations here, and it would be so much easier if we exchanged numbers so we can talk more later." If a woman seems too reluctant to engage or invest in these ways, she may have trust issues, avoidant tendencies, feel too much stress in her life to consider dating, or believe that you are not her type.

- **Always handle rejection well, acknowledge and engage casually, and act as if her reactions don't change the way you feel about yourself.** When in social situations with someone who rejects you, snubbing them will make you look like a jerk. Likewise, cornering them to engage in conversation when their social cues are showing discomfort (or they are intentionally avoiding eye contact) will make you seem like a stalker. Contrarily, casually smiling, saying hi, asking short questions for a few minutes (while assuming a leaned-back posture), and then walking away will make you seem confident and unaffected by your previous rejection.

When you're stuck in a just-friends, good-for-now, or too-nice trap

If you have already become stuck in the hanging-out, just-friends, good-for-now, or too-nice trap, you need to invest in her while also expressing your opinions, feelings, or needs and saying no sometimes. If you have fallen into any of these traps, chances are you have not acted strong and confident, have been excessively available and accommodating, have failed to occasionally say no, have neglected to express your feelings and needs, or have denied her the opportunity to sacrifice for you and the relationship. To break these traps at this point, you need to follow the steps below:

1. **Make her feel special by investing in her and the events or activities you do together.** If you are to be desirable to a woman, you need to show drive and determination in your efforts to pursue her and her attention. Women like to be pursued and to feel wanted. To set this process up for success, show her that you will take charge, pursue, and invest in the things you care about. Even if you think you are technically hanging out or acting like friends, insist on paying for at least one event a week. Open her door and treat her like a lady. If you feel comfortable, try referring to these events as dates; either way, you need to spend some money on her, or she will think you see her as only a friend.

2. **Be there for her, but not all of the time.** For the next four weeks, it is essential that you keep up some of the behaviors you've engaged in with her (such as calling her, spending time with her, going to the gym together, etc.) so she feels safe and secure in your interest and investment in her, but you also need to start becoming busier and say no to her 5 to 15 percent of the time. This means you are still investing in her and saying yes 85 to 95 percent of the time, but not making plans at the last minute very often, or jumping at her beck and call. Show her you will meet her needs in a timely manner, but on your time frame, not hers. Show her you will meet her needs in a timely manner, but on your time frame, not hers. Try saying, "I am sorry. That won't work for me right now, but I would be happy to do it on Monday," or "I would love to do that with you, but I already have plans that night," or "I am sorry. I normally try hard to say yes to you, but this time, I need to say no." If you do this, she will stop taking it for granted that you will always be there as a good-for-now man she can fall back on if her A-list options aren't available.

3. **Express your needs in a way that makes her feel safe and secure while making you look strong and confident.** Be clear and direct by simply saying, "Would you do _________ for me? I would really appreciate it." You need to discover whether or not she will sacrifice to meet your reasonable and nonsexual needs, just as you strive to meet hers. So start expressing them—both big and small. This is the only way you will know if you are not wasting your time

by investing in the relationship. So ask her to come to your house sometimes, express a desire for her help with a project, or ask her to just drop by and see you for a few minutes. Do this in a way that makes her feel safe and secure by being direct and to the point rather than passive, inconsistent, indirect, or sarcastic: for example, "Would you do _______________ for me? I would really appreciate it" (clear and direct) instead of "I was kind of hoping you would _________, but it isn't really important" (passive and inconsistent), "I had a girlfriend once who never met my needs" (indirect), or "I must be the most important person in your life because you never think about me and my needs. Ha Ha" (sarcastic and confusing). Communicating in these passive ways will make you look less strong and confident and as though you have no conviction regarding the importance of your needs; it will also make her feel manipulated. Additionally, using moping, brooding, or the silent treatment to express your needs makes women feel punished or ignored and makes you look weak and retaliating. You may see this as a powerful way to get a woman's attention and show your anger without acting aggressively, but these behaviors will dramatically reduce her attraction to you and even turn her off entirely, especially if you consistently act this way. She will also feel less safe and secure and lose respect and trust for you (especially when there is poor communication). Likewise, you will also want to avoid acting angry, aggressive, demanding, intimidating, and rejecting to express your needs, or she will see you as the too-nice guy who finally showed his true colors and was a phony all along. If you use demands and intimidation, you will make her feel threatened and controlled, the opposite of feeling safe and secure. She might give in, and you'll get what you want for a short time, but she will probably resent you for how you treated her, as will her friends and family. This may seem like you have to avoid a lot of landmines, but simply asking her to meet your needs and then commenting when she doesn't is powerfully effective with emotionally mature women who have empathy. Resorting to more drastic and manipulative tools is a sign that either she doesn't have empathy (and that is why you feel desperate enough to try these techniques) or you don't have empathy (and therefore don't realize the significance of how these behaviors affect women). If you feel that just asking for her to meet your needs is not enough to get her attention, remember to also square your shoulders, look her in the eyes, stand on your back foot, and keep your chin forward so you look more attractive and self-assured. Unless you are several feet away, do not lean forward when expressing your needs. Stay on the back foot or lean back in a chair. This avoids the possibility that you will look too intense, vulnerable, or intimidating while increasing the possibility that you will look broad, strong, and confident. It also helps you feel less stressed because it improves your circulation and breathing.

4. **Be prepared to hear no sometimes, but express that you trust she will meet your needs.** Women need to feel that they can say no sometimes (at least 5 to 15 percent of the time) in order to truly feel free to say yes (85 to 95 percent of the time). Your ability to handle rejection well makes you appear stronger, more confident, and worthy of her respect while also making her feel safe and

secure. When she says no, be sure to keep your chin forward and state, "I like it when you express your feelings and needs. I can handle hearing no. I need to say no sometimes, too. I trust you will say yes to me most of the time. No worries. I will find another way to meet this need for now." By expressing your trust that she will meet most of your needs, you increase her desire to do so. You also show her less fear and weakness.

5. **Once you have expressed your needs and she agrees to meet them, watch to see how she responds, and comment if she doesn't.** Do this by simply stating, "I couldn't help but notice that after you said you would help me, you didn't follow through. Help me to understand. What is the feeling you want me to have when you don't meet my needs?" or "Are you aware that you either say no or ignore my requests frequently? Do you realize that this makes me feel unimportant to you? Are you okay with me feeling this way?" This helps her know that you feel your needs are important, it makes her confront the reality that your needs should be met, and it shows her that her response to such requests communicates her intentions for the relationship. Pause and let her respond. Remain strong, confident, and self-controlled, thus worthy of her respect. Wait until later to react. This leaves her feeling a reasonable amount of anxiety. It is important that she feels some discomfort, or she will never rethink her behavior and change.

6. **Do not apologize for your needs or feelings.** Instead, if she fails to meet your needs upon request, ask her again to meet these needs. Do not minimize your needs or say they don't matter. Instead, be persistent and repeat your request that she meet them. If she is to fall in love with you, she needs to sacrifice for you.

7. **If these techniques do not make a difference in her hearing and meeting your needs, walk away.** If, after four weeks and multiple requests, she still does not respond well to hearing your needs, does not meet your needs, or does not have good answers when you point out that she failed to meet them, then know that she does not have empathy, self-control, and personal responsibility. She does not hear your needs now, so she will definitely not hear or care about them later. You are wasting your time and valuable emotional energy. Walk away so you can move on to someone who does care about your needs and feelings.

8. **If she meets your needs, treat her like she is on your A-list and pursue dates with her accordingly.** Most women like dates, simple gifts, surprises, reasonable spontaneity, and excitement, which can be fun and make you stand out (especially if you don't overdo these, or you could make her feel suspicious and pressured). You will make her feel special, important, and thought of if you follow the other rules for dating that are in this chapter, such as calling to confirm the date and time, making plans in advance, and letting her know what type of clothing to wear. Let her know you will be picking her up, which delineates that this is a date. Meeting in public is what friends and strangers do, and she is definitely more than that. If you are tempted to believe that you can skip from being friends to immediately being in a relationship, you are wrong. You need to

date first. Even married couples need to keep dating once a week. It is a huge part of developing love and keeping love alive. So clearly delineate the change in the relationship from friends to dating.

9. **If she says she is uncomfortable moving the relationship to another level, persist anyway.** If she consistently resists your efforts to pay for meals, events, or activities, or in any other way minimizes the time you spend together by emphasizing that you are not on a date, comment on it by saying, "I really enjoy being with you. I know what I want, and you have a lot of the qualities I am looking for. I am not asking to date you exclusively. I think we should both keep our options open for at least six weeks to see if this feels right for us, but I want to date you. I don't want to just be friends anymore." She will most likely agree, knowing that she has six weeks to explore the idea and that you aren't expecting immediate commitment.

10. **If she frequently changes her mind or resists your efforts to date her, be persistent up to three times, but then back off and move on.** In this case, state, "No worries. I understand that things happen sometimes. However, I don't keep calling after a woman cancels plans a couple of times. How about if you call me when you would like to get together next, and then I'll take it from there?" This clearly states that you respect yourself too much to be strung along and shows her that you know your worth, which makes you highly attractive as you end the friendship-only relationship. It can be hard to end a relationship after you have invested so much time and energy, but a woman who is unwilling to date you probably has issues with trust or commitment. It is better to move on sooner rather than later. She probably will never invest more in you. You have already invested months of your time in her, so move on, or you will just waste more time. The ball is in her court. She needs to make the next move. Don't wait around.

On dates, leave them wanting more

Most people don't go on dates because they want to eat an average overpriced meal, chit-chat about nothing, or participate in an activity with a stranger for whom they may have little in common. They go on dates because they hope it could lead to something more: a spark, connection, enjoyment, excitement, chemistry, or happiness that is only found in relationships. For this, they will endure an awkward hour or two with all the politeness and feigned interest they can muster, even when they have sized up their partner (within the first 30 seconds of meeting them) and are not optimistic. After another disappointing experience, they may resolve to give up and stop trying; nevertheless, they will eventually try again because they truly want the next date to be different. Their hope may be fragile, but their desire for love and companionship remains, nevertheless, compelling.

When considering the overall determination of single men and women (and the millions of dollars they willingly spend on dating apps and dates), it is surprising that so many men and women find dating and relationships to be elusive. Why do these encounters leave them feeling disinterested, bored, repelled, or friend-zoned? The answer is often in the subtle details: their tone of voice, body language, mannerisms, conversational topics, and inability to flirt or pursue with confidence. Fortunately, this also means that the power to influence and change the outcome is also in their control.

To help you make the most out of each of your dating experiences, this chapter condenses all the theories and strategies that you have learned so far and translates them into practical techniques for your application when on a first date or encouraging future dates.

To graduate from the dating game, focus on what's going right

To succeed at the dating game, you need to shift your paradigm from what others (or you) are doing wrong and focus instead on your efforts, progress, growth, and personal successes. When you focus on what's going right (and with whom), you will see that each interaction, date, and relationship experience adds to your overall ability to progress (from the minor leagues of dating) and succeed in (the major league) or relationships.

As in any game, a successful performance (or date) begins and ends with the right attitude and a resilient mindset. Whether a date progresses to follow-up dates or ends after just one encounter, you can feel empowered, confident, and likable. When you experience rejection, you can remember that it is not personal (since they do not know you). Their behavior has more to do with them and their situation, which could be explained by a dozen variables, all of which are impossible for you to determine and have little to do with you. Yes, your experience might be educational (through exposing a flaw in your approach to the date), but focusing on your shortcomings or failures is not liberating. To transcend your circumstances, you must focus on what is working (within your experiences or others') and do more of that.

When you choose to consistently focus on your efforts, personal success, and victories, through identifying any evidence and positive outcomes from your actions, healing and interpersonal development will flow more easily and consistently. Success requires time, an experimental attitude, and numerous mistakes, failures, or losses (all of which are unavoidable and essential to growth); thus, you need to anticipate them, rather than fear them. Because those who succeed fail more than those who refuse to risk and endure loss, your mistakes and ongoing redirection are the surest sign you're on the right track. If you aren't experiencing rejection, then you are not really trying (or being vulnerable enough) to win the prize. Progressing in the face of uncertainty and embracing imperfection as you progress is powerful. Meanwhile, those who insist on waiting for the most sure, risk-free path (which doesn't exist) often discover that their perfectionism and fear have stilted their progress. Passiveness only creates passionless experiences (stagnation and lost opportunities), and lasting love is found through connection, not perfection. So, embrace the moment, have fun, shake off your mistakes more quickly, and remember that your efforts say great things about you and your character.

With each new skill you practice, recognize your personal success or victories. Your achievement should not be measured by one person's actions (or inactions) but by focusing on your emerging skills of emotional awareness, empathy, connection, communication, playfulness, confidence, and ability to handle difficult situations with resiliency and class.

No matter how challenging or unfulfilling a specific date may be, you can walk away feeling confident and resolved about how you handled the situation. As you record your efforts and measure your success, you will feel greater hope both during the gaps between your dating highs and lows. With each skill you develop in your personal and relationship toolbox, you become more resilient, flexible, and capable of sustaining the lasting love you desire. As you discover those people who actively participate, you feel greater appreciation and respect for what they bring to the experience and how their efforts increase their ability to love you deeply, too.

Review your existing skills and progress (and reward your efforts)

Before jumping into the specific dating techniques that will help you make others feel great on a date (while looking great, too), let's first acknowledge all the skills you have practiced thus far. Doing this will boost your confidence and set you on the right path toward a resilient, growth-minded perspective. If you use the Lasting Love Academy Get the Date course, marking its lessons (which correlate with this book's chapters) as complete can trigger the reward center in your brain through providing a dopamine boost. Anytime you accomplish this, you reinforce your developing habits and your commitment to progressing along your lasting love journey.

In this chapter, you will learn how to make your dating experiences more fun, more connected, and more meaningful, but don't forget to reward your progress, too. If you are motivated by accomplishment, reviewing your progress may be enough to inspire more investment. However, you might also appreciate rewarding your efforts when you achieve specific goals, apply a particularly challenging technique, or bounce back quickly after rejection.

Your rewards might include making a purchase, enjoying your favorite meal at a restaurant, indulging in an activity or sporting event, investing in a new electronic device or outfit, planning and going on a vacation, or enjoying a simple guilty pleasure. Make sure that you either match your rewards to the value or effort you invest over a week or month, or commensurate with the difficulty of a specific skill. As long as you make it fun and meaningful, your sacrifices will help you to know your efforts are worthy of your attention and celebration!!! Just be sure to keep your commitment and fulfill your promise to the one person you should never neglect: you!

Pure and lasting change flows from your strengths

When faced with rejection (or recognizing the need to walk away from someone who isn't good for you), you must remember your internal value and all you have to offer. It is important that you don't focus on what is lacking, but on what is amazing, valuable, and inherently good about you. To assist you in identifying these traits both now (and regularly from here forward), answer the following questions about the many qualities and attributes that you offer and why they make you a great potential partner. Remember that manifesting these attributes imperfectly but consistently is the only proof you need. No one is perfect, but that isn't what defines their values. It is not how you act when things are easy that defines you, but by what you do when things are hard and how your consistent efforts over time prove your character and sincere intent.

My innate nature and personal strengths include:

On a separate piece of paper, answer the following questions.

1. Briefly describe your strengths, skills, talents, accomplishments, and the difficult goals you've achieved (or the challenges you've overcome). ________________

2. Relative to the question above, what would your friends or family suggest that you include in this list?____

3. What do these experiences reveal about your personality, character, or values? For example, "I strive to be...hard-working, driven, humble, loyal, honest, kind, thoughtful, teachable, educated, growth-minded, empathetic, responsible, patient, self-aware, controlled and discipline, improvement focused, teachable, spiritual, loving, forgiving, strong, independent, or a good person."__________

4. In what ways do these traits and strengths make you a great friend, dating companion, family member, and partner? ________________________________

Prepare for the beginning, middle, and END of your journey

Even though it often doesn't feel this way, every difficult experience you have has a beginning, middle, and end. You may fail to see the resolution of your past challenges because you fondly remember the good times, while frequently viewing the bad times as mysterious, unpredictable, and victimizing. This tendency is natural.

Fortunately, for those who acknowledge the end of a challenge as a transformative experience or a lesson learned, they are able to see the past as a hero's journey that had meaning, purpose, or healing. You may not yet recognize your personal victories and the hidden resilience they reveal, but it is important that you take the time to do so now. These experiences (both in your own and others' stories) will provide powerful insight and perspective when you are once again at the bottom of a new and overwhelmingly complex dating or relationship situation (and problem or trauma).

It is inherently human (and spiritually healing) when you are able to turn injury into strength, trauma into thriving (as opposed to merely surviving), failure into wisdom and empowerment, and loss into connection and rebirth. You and your value are greater than your experiences or what has been done to you (no matter who abused, exploited, or abandoned you). Not all people are inclined to feel so optimistic, especially when they are trapped within a perpetual circumstance that feels beyond their control. However, even when life includes ongoing or intermittent health, financial, social, employment, emotional, and interpersonal challenges, perpetual problems have solvable components and transforming developments that make a burden lighter along the way. To see these hidden gems of power, control, growth, and resilience within yourself, you must look closely at what is working, going right, or changing around you and as a direct result of your (and others') efforts (including those of a spiritual nature). You are meant to love and be loved, and you can have the knowledge, power, and skills you need to succeed if you persistently seek and act on the truths you discover.

To expose your pattern of success and resilience and learn from the wisdom of others during their trials and triumphs, answer the following questions.

Identify Your Pattern of Success

1. When you struggle, make mistakes, or experience failure, how have you risen above them? ____

2. What keeps you motivated, supported, encouraged, or empowered during the hard times, gets you back on your feet when you feel broken, and helps you to eventually succeed? *Consider your educational, professional, sporting, personal, and relationship struggles to discover the hidden secrets that could apply to your current situation.*____

3. Now that you have the benefit of 20/20 hindsight, what character traits, resilience, strength, or courage helped you during your darkest times to keep moving on? ____

4. Who has supported and encouraged (versus discouraged) your progress (and who can you rely upon currently)? _______________________________________

5. What daily routines, patterns, or habits were necessary to your past success, and which of them would be essential to a positive outcome now?_____________

Identify Others' Patterns of Success

6. Identify those you respect due to their successes in relationships, and outline the actions or daily habits that contribute to their past and present happiness in marriage. *When needed, list examples from within the Lasting Love Academy that inspire your hope or confidence.* _________________________________

7. What attitudes and actions do you appreciate and respect relative to how others interact with you (or their closest friends and family)? __________________

8. Among those who are happily married, who could you turn to for advice and perspective during your dating and relationship challenges?________________

9. What stories, past experiences, or spiritual practices and influences encourage you to succeed because they encourage the meaning, purpose, and resolution that help you to transcend your circumstances? ______________________

Create a Personalized Guide for your dating and relationship journey

10. What lessons, habits, people, and strengths will you rely upon during the next few months and years until you achieve a loving and committed relationship? ____

11. What challenges can you predict will sidetrack, overwhelm, or derail you from your relationship goals? ____

12. How can you plan for and manage these distractions, especially when you are in the difficult (and most challenging) part of your journey? _______________

13. What stories, past experiences, or spiritual practices and supportive influences can you rely on to expose the purpose and meaning inherent to your journey while supporting your faith and hope in its resolution? _______________

14. How will establishing and maintaining these patterns of success help you to maintain a lifetime of lasting love (rather than just fulfilling your immediate dating challenges and marriage goals)? _______________

The hidden signs you're pushing others away (versus bringing your A-Game)

Now that you have assessed your strengths and committed yourself to following a pattern of success through focusing on what works and following your pattern of success, it's time to discover if you are engaging effectively or missing the mark.

A good thermostat measures the temperature of the room and makes small adjustments to stay at an optimal temperature. Likewise, you need a realistic and ongoing measurement that your behaviors are on track for encouraging the dating or relationship stage you are in. You will continue engaging in this reality check throughout your journey, but for now, let's check how you are doing relative to encouraging your and others' dating behaviors.

To assess whether your behaviors and words are pushing others away or inviting them in, review the questions below.

The Hidden Signs You're Pushing Others Away (self-test)

Choose the answer that best describes your behavior.

1. When in social situations...

    a. I stay aloof, focus on my phone, or limit eye contact.

    b. I wait for others to approach me and engage only if they do.

    c. I say hi and smile warmly.

d. I approach several people and either use their name or introduce myself, and learn their names. I ask questions that show I'm interested in them.

e. I approach many people, show enthusiasm, touch them on occasion, give compliments, and tell them I would love to spend more time getting to know them.

2. **When reviewing others' dating app profiles...**

a. I am quickly repelled by others' mistakes, grammar, and pictures, or rarely swipe yes while complaining that there aren't any good singles on dating apps.

b. I occasionally swipe yes, but wait for others to send the first message. If they don't ask me a question, I don't respond, or I send only a simple, short response or an emoji.

c. I sometimes swipe yes and also send the first message to say hello. I keep it short and simple and don't ask questions because they need to start or keep the conversation going. I don't want to work harder than others do.

d. I frequently swipe yes and then send a message asking them a question about what they shared in their profile or what they have been doing for fun lately.

e. I frequently swipe yes, ask about something in their profile, share something about myself, and use positive or warm emotion words that seem enthusiastic (for example, instead of saying, "You seem nice or it would be good to chat sometimes," I might say, "You seriously made me laugh, and so I couldn't help but say hi. It would be awesome to get to know you.")

3. **When others send me a message...**

a. I often feel annoyed by their messages and believe they aren't really trying or didn't read my profile. I frequently ignore others' messages because I don't have the time and feel put off by the pressure. When I respond, it may be days or a week later, since I regularly avoid getting on the app.

b. I check my messages and respond within a few days, but I use a simple, short reply because I believe they should encourage the conversation or share more before I open up.

c. I respond within a few days and use emotion words or emojis that show I'm glad they texted. For example, "That sounds fun," followed by a smiley face emoji. Sometimes we will exchange several messages and replies, but if they don't suggest that we talk on the phone or go on a date, I don't either. When our messages die out, I often feel confused, disappointed, or annoyed that they wasted my time.

d. I respond within a day or two and ask them questions about their day. I also ask them questions or try to say something nice or funny. Once we have done this for a while, I might hint at things that I like to do or activities I enjoy, hoping that they follow up with a request to exchange numbers or plan a date.

e. I respond within a day or two. I show enthusiasm about the things they share, open up about similar topics, and ask questions. After a couple of messages (or sometimes sooner), I suggest that it would be exciting to talk about these things over the phone, by text, or while doing something together. I make some suggestions and share that I would love to exchange phone numbers to text or work out the details.

4. **When texting with others, and they suggest we talk on the phone or do something fun together...**

a. I ignore the comment, change the subject, or stop messaging them.

b. I say that would be fine or nice, but then I wait for them to work out the details. I don't want to look needy, desperate, or controlling. If they don't share more or follow up, I assume they've lost interest (or I hope that they assume I'm not interested). If they message again, I'll keep responding, but without any reference to planning a call or date. If I lose interest, I don't respond (rather than telling them).

c. I say that would be fine or nice, but I don't suggest a day, time, or activity. If our plans are vague or I'm not certain whether I am interested, I won't follow up on our plans by text. If they reach out to clarify our plans, I will either go ahead with the date or offer to reschedule. When they call, I will respond by text, but I often don't answer or call them back. I might reach out later (if I feel guilty), but I will not bring up the missed phone call or date. I will apologize or act confused if they mention it.

d. I express willingness to talk or go on a date and offer some days or times that might work for me. I follow up when they leave a message or send text responses. When they call me, I respond by answering or calling them back. I warmly ask questions when the details aren't clear.

e. I express excitement and say that I would love to get together. I suggest some things we could talk about on a call or do on a date. I offer some days or times that might work for me. I asked how I could help with planning the date to show gratitude for their efforts. I express that I'm excited to talk with or see them soon. I make an effort to plan ahead and treat our time together as a priority.

5. **When I am in need...**

a. I suffer in silence and feel lonely, sad, or unimportant.

b. I find a way to take care of the problem on my own rather than wait for others' help (so they can't disappoint or reject me).

c. When sharing about my life, I act as if I have everything taken care of and that I don't need help. Overall, I try not to need others.

d. I share what is happening in my life, but I wait for them to ask if they can help. When they offer, I accept and show appreciation.

e. I share ways others can help me and how much I would love their support. I encourage them to participate in my life and offer to do the same.

6. **When others or I feel sad, hurt, or offended...**

a. I withdraw, assume the worst, and emotionally distance myself or end the relationship.

b. I don't hold back. I tell them exactly how I feel, how they are wrong, and why I am right.

c. I ignore the problem and just act warm or respectful, hoping the issue will go away.

d. I speak up and express a desire to talk through the issue.

e. I show faith and trust in the goodness of our relationship and express interest in resolving the problem. We come up with a clear plan of how we can avoid the problem or handle the situation better next time.

Push Aways

*If you respond to **two or more** of the questions above with **"a" or "b"** answers, then your words and actions are stating that you want to keep your distance and aren't interested in them or spending time together. They may assume that you're too busy, you're happy on your own, or you simply don't like or trust them. Since they have little to go on besides your written words, your lackluster and limited responses have a significant bearing on their resulting enthusiasm and provide them little to work with. This can cause them to feel confused and brushed off. Thus, neither of you is likely to participate in a meaningful way (even if you both are interested) because the exchange is largely unfulfilling and hard to maintain.*

Stalemates

*If you responded to **two or more** of the questions above with **"c"** answers, then you're sending stalemate messages. You may be acting somewhat warm and engaging, but you are not taking any meaningful risks. You are leaving others with the responsibility for taking action, being vulnerable, and making things happen while you are acting lukewarm and merely friendly (rather than interested or excited by your communication). This may not seem clear to you because you feel you are doing your part, but singles need more than a polite exchange if they are to get excited about someone, maintain communication, or push for phone calls and dates. If you don't take a risk by showing more enthusiasm, using emotional words, or assisting with the details needed to share numbers, make phone calls, or plan dates, they won't either. You both need to share in the required vulnerability and effort if you are to develop any chemistry or excitement.*

Invitations

*If you responded to **one or more** of the questions above with **"d" answers**, then you are sending clear messages that you like yourself and value others, too. You are confident and willing to do your part, but others may not be able to tell if you are interested in them. Your exchange is warm and respectful, but if on the call or date you don't show more enthusiasm, they may perceive you as being friendly rather than exuding a flirtatious vibe that could develop chemistry. They may give a second or third date a try, but if you don't increase your expressions of excitement, flirty playfulness, or simple touch, their feelings will flatline because your engagement is too safe and uncertain.*

Many times, you are more responsible for the distance you feel in your relationships than you realize. Focus on sending clear invitations, and you will either create closer relationships or feel more confident when walking away.

*For those who are confident and willing to engage in **two or more "e" answers**, you probably have no problem getting dates or repeat dates. It is easy to move quickly to phone calls and make clear plans for time together because you are so clearly inviting and confident. You may get frustrated or confused at times, but because you are willing to ask simple questions to clarify your plans, spending time together is more straightforward and uncomplicated. Dating is fun and doesn't feel like too much pressure, especially since you pace your efforts based on their responses and engagement. You may get some negative or passive responses from others because they are not used to such enthusiasm or engagement. However, they won't feel pressured by you if they are participating, too. For example, "These are the times that I am available. I'd love to get to know you better. If that is something you would enjoy too, share your thoughts and details. It would be so fun to talk with or see you soon." If you include a winky face emoji, it will come across with a confident and flirty tone. If they respond and engage, you are both showing mutual investment.*

Bring your A-Game to dating

Like many singles, you may have been surprised that your a, b, and c interactions were far more neutral or rejecting than you realized because you thought you were being vulnerable and invested. It is easier to criticize others' actions as being confusing and a lackluster without recognizing your own hypocrisy (especially when you think being nice is the same as being flirty or appropriately pursuing).

In many ways, this dynamic (and its resulting lack of chemistry) is the standard pattern. When singles events and dating apps fail to yield relationships, they are conveniently blamed when, in fact, the participants are poorly prepared to do what it takes to make others feel great.

Fortunately, with a more accurate understanding of what truly inviting behaviors look like (which are illustrated by e behaviors, and to a lesser degree, d behaviors), and why they are necessary to creating excitement and chemistry, you can turn the tide in your favor.

     Single? It's Not You. It's Your Technique!

Some women may worry that providing options, details, and days or times is taking over and being too pushy or needy. However, as long as men and women match at a pace similar to those they are interacting with, then both will simply seem confident and happily engaged in life. If they interpret the other person's response (within two hours or two days) as a healthy and appropriate response (rather than getting frustrated), they will appear chill, relaxed, and appropriately busy. Either way, their lack of distress proves they are ok going on a date or moving on to those who do engage. Understanding these differences and choosing to follow the "e" model of sending clear invitations for meaningful contact reduces the unnecessary overanalysis, worry, and confusion that too many singles participate in.

Knowing how to anticipate and engage with an "e" level of confidence helps you to engage and respond in a secure way. These patterns of engagement are not gamey, but appropriately responsive and encouraging.

Knowing how to act in these ways, without depending on others' reactions to drive your confidence, is how you develop an A-game strategy for being your most confident and engaging self during dates. If others don't respond, this doesn't change or define your success or worth, because you aren't competing against them and losing. Instead, you are competing against your own personal demons and challenges and succeeding with every positive action you take on a date. If others have fun with you, awesome, you both win! Either way, you feel good about what you offered and its potential for a stronger connection or excitement.

When preparing for each date

- **Show that you care by planning time to make yourself look and smell great.** Nothing says, "I don't care about you or myself," like dressing sloppily, having oily hair, smelling bad, wearing wrinkled and dirty clothes, and not brushing your teeth or trimming unsightly hairs (such as lip, nose, eyebrow, or ear hairs—*this advice is for both men and women*). Always carry mints or gum with you and pop them in your mouth if you anticipate close contact. If you have yellowing teeth, consider using Crest Whitestrips, which are easy and inexpensive to use. A white smile goes a long way. Remember, *it's not you—it's your technique.* The way you dress and groom yourself is an important technique you cannot afford to ignore. Make investing in and taking good care of yourself a priority so that you will feel more confident and make other people feel great about being with you.

- **Anticipate offering a compliment early in the date; make it meaningful but short and to the point.** If the other person looks or smells great, say so immediately. First impressions and immediate compliments make a big difference. Don't overdo a compliment, though. Saying the same thing too many times looks desperate or needy and can set you up for the too-nice trap. Say it once, maybe twice, and then trust that they hear and believe you and let it go. If you want to make sure they feel the sincerity of your compliment, look them in the eyes and express the compliment a little slower and with more emphasis on specific words. For instance, "You look *really nice*" with "really nice" being stated with a lower tone of voice and slowly. If you do this, it will make a lasting impression.

- **Prepare to accept a compliment while not drawing attention to your flaws.** Men like women who like themselves, and women are attracted to strength and confidence. If someone gives you a compliment, accept it gracefully. Do not argue or minimize the compliment. It doesn't make you appear humble; it makes you appear insecure. Also, do not emphasize your fears or personal weaknesses. Often, the thing that you fear others will notice, they will only see (or focus on) when you point it out or make an issue of it. Your height, hair, weight, zits, or other personal flaws will not matter as much if you square your shoulders, keep your chin forward, act confident, and make others feel great. There are many bald men and overweight women who are perceived as desirable and attractive just because they have learned how to do this.

- **Remember that the goal is to have fun, make them feel great, and practice rather than act perfectly.** If you make dates a lot of work, if you feel a lot of anxiety about doing things perfectly, or if you analyze everything you or your date do or say, you will not have fun—and neither will they. Take the pressure off by intentionally being a little flawed and imperfect. Whether you like it or not, you will do or say at least one thing wrong on a date, no matter how hard you try. You might as well prepare for it, and consciously square your shoulders and make eye contact anyway. Once you do this, it will be easier to relax, laugh, and trust the process. When stressed, try repeating, *I might as well be myself, have fun, and practice. If I see them again, great. If not, I will at least have had fun. After all, relationships are created through connection, not perfection.* Sitting back and having fun might even turn a bad date into a great date.

- **Prepare to express your feelings, needs, and opinions, or say no (to observe their response) at least once on every date.** You will never know who someone really is if you try to act perfectly or be the kind of person you think they are looking for. Instead, you need to be yourself (i.e., flawed, imperfect, human, lovable, and confident). A person's character is not defined by how they act when everything is easy, but by how they act when things are imperfect, awkward, unexpected, or hard. If you appropriately and respectfully express your feelings, state your opinions, ask your date to meet a few small and appropriate needs, say no on occasion, request a different restaurant, activity, or movie, or respectfully comment if they do something that bothers you (e.g., arriving twenty minutes late, texting others during the date, talking during the movie, or accepting phone calls throughout the date), you will have a valuable opportunity to see how they handle the situation and you. For example, watch how they respond when you say, "I couldn't help but notice that you are taking a lot of calls. Is there some kind of emergency?" Then, if it is not an emergency, ask, "Would you mind letting the calls go to voicemail? It would really mean a lot to me." Doing these things shows that you have good communication skills, faith in them that they can handle your appropriate needs, and the confidence and self-respect necessary to negotiate for change. This is the single most important technique you can apply. It does more than reveal those individuals who are potentially abusive and manipulative; it also attracts emotionally mature people who appreciate and value straightforward communication. If you want to develop even greater confidence in your ability to recognize the emotionally immature from the emotionally mature, review the Lasting Love Academy's other books on this subject before or after a date and discuss your experiences with a trusted friend.

- **Encourage reasonable generosity that provides for the other person, rather than paying for half of the date or for just your expenses.** In most cases, the man should pay for at least one date or event a week; however, if a woman wants to pay for some of the activities or events, it is wise for a man to let her. If she is to love him and if he is to avoid the too-nice trap, it is essential that she invest in him, too. He needs to recognize her willingness to do this as a token of her appreciation for his sacrifices. The goal while dating and building a relationship should be to be generous with each other, according to each individual's means, which may differ dramatically. A woman's sacrifices do not need to be equal to his financially or physically sacrifices (at this stage), but she should occasionally offer, according to what she can afford, to buy snacks at the movie, to buy dessert after the date, or even to pay for a second meal during the week. If either of you refuses the other's sacrifice or suggests that you both just pay your own way or for half of the expenses, problems may follow. It is better that you both develop an attitude of treating each other great, rather than of taking care of yourselves or carefully measuring the equality of the other person's sacrifices; this shows either that you don't trust each other or that you are not really invested in the other's happiness. Life isn't fair; don't measure a relationship by fairness but by the mutual willingness to invest in each other.

- **Prepare to relieve anxiety, slow things down, or prevent pressure by expressing that you want to have fun without expectations.** If either of you gets too into each other too quickly, shares too much personal information too soon, fears hurting the other person's feelings, or stops having as much fun, don't give up, avoid them, or just hope that the relationship will correct itself (especially if they were on your A-List). Your date will most likely not know how to get your interactions back on track. So remember, if in doubt, spell it out. Take the pressure off by directly facing the situation at the end of the date. Warmly say, "Just so you know, my approach to dating is to focus on having fun without pressure or expectations beyond mutual respect. I'm not someone who overthinks the early stages of dating. I'm having a lot of fun, though. Thank you for a fun date. Let's do something again next week."

- **Avoid future problems, anger, or hurt feelings by committing to keep affection simple and uncomplicated.** Some people treat kissing very casually and don't have an issue with kissing someone who is dating and kissing others; however, many people (especially women) do not appreciate such an attitude. To prevent future problems or hurt feelings, casually discuss how singles can view common dating situations very differently. This can create great conversation and clarify expectations. To do this, casually state (while on the phone, enjoying a leisure activity, or driving together to an event), "Singles are so funny. We have so many different ideas about dating and affection. Some people think holding hands makes you exclusive. Others treat kissing like a recreational sport. Others think it means you like each other, but it doesn't mean commitment, as long as you are only kissing each other. How do you and your friends view it? Kissing means _______ to me." Such an approach is ideal, especially if it occurs before the first kiss. However, bringing it up after the first kiss can work equally as well. The important point is not to prove that others are wrong but to discover what it means to you and your date so you can match your expectations, thereby avoiding future problems, hurt feelings, or anger.

- **Protect children from unnecessary attachments to the people you are merely dating (and don't know well).** As stated earlier, most relationships do not make it past the first six weeks, so no matter how great someone appears, remember that you won't truly know them within just a few dates. Your children do not need any more abuse, hurt, or loss than they have already suffered. If a date suggests that your or their kids be included in your activity, explain to them your concerns by saying, "I don't feel comfortable meeting your kids (or vice versa) yet. Let's wait a bit and see where this goes before we take that step. If we see each other less often for a while, that's okay. I don't want the kids to get attached and hurt if things don't work out." If your date is emotionally mature, he/she will understand the importance of going slowly, using self-control, and making sure things are what they appear to be before getting the kids involved. They should be looking to build an adult relationship with you, not find a mother or father for their kids or a child to fulfill their needs. Adults who seem anxious to develop relationships with children more than with adults usually prove to be manipulative, abusive (emotionally, physically, or sexually), neglectful, or exploitative. By holding off on letting your date meet your children, you will discover his/her true intentions and feelings for you. Furthermore, meeting the children too soon often creates too much pressure for everyone. Get to know each other first. After six weeks or more, introduce your kids to those you date, but keep it casual and preferably in a group setting. Keep your interactions as a couple with the children to once or twice a month until you are ready to become exclusive and know each other well enough to believe such contact would be wise, safe, and appropriate.

Make women feel great during the date

- **Treat her like a lady.** Women like to be pursued and to feel wanted, and women long to feel adored, so don't hesitate to open her door, help her with her coat, or stand when she gets up to leave the table (if you are in a convenient and appropriate situation to do so). Treating her like a lady shows extra effort, makes her feel special, and makes you more desirable. To increase comfort, create more chemistry, and decrease defensiveness, take appropriate opportunities to initiate simple touch. To do this, offer your arm as she walks across the ice, touch her on the mid-section of her back as you guide her through a door, and playfully nudge her with your upper arm when either of you acts playful or tease the other. If she resists letting you do these things, do not take it personally. Some women struggle with touch or take a while to relax and get comfortable with a date. Just keep acting confident. Pull these behaviors back a little, but not entirely, or it could seem as if you are now nervous about touching her. When offering to get her door, if she refuses, express, "I love being a gentleman. If you're willing, I'd like to get your door for you. But if not, that's ok. I want you to be comfortable. What do you prefer?" If she refuses, she may have trust and vulnerability issues. Hang in there for a few weeks to see if she warms up. If not, it could be a warning sign that you'll have ongoing trust issues later, which is good to discover early on. Also, don't worry that being a gentleman will set you up for the too-nice trap. It won't if you apply the techniques outlined in Chapter 9

- **Make the evening fun, light, and comfortable.** It can often be easier to come up with light and comfortable conversation when doing something that provides entertainment or stimuli for conversation: for example, miniature golfing, hiking, walking, watching a local baseball game, or perusing bookstores, art galleries, and museums. So, plan your dates in a way that encourages active participation rather than passive interaction (such as watching a movie). Try to always have something planned for the evening, rather than just hanging out, watching movies, or playing video games at each other's homes. You need to show her that you're invested in getting to know her. If you don't make any plans, you will look passive, lazy, or insincere in your intentions, especially if hanging out leads to kissing, making out, or sex. Your dates do not need to be expensive. They just need to be active and thought out. A day at the park, throwing a Frisbee, listening to music, flying a kite, or playing card games with a picnic lunch can be a great and inexpensive date that still makes you look like you put thought and effort into it.

- **Include humor and touch, and avoid sarcasm or demeaning jokes.** Women often like men who can make them laugh. So, spice up the date with a healthy dose of humor. The best way to do this is by using observational humor (i.e., commenting on things or events around you). Avoid jokes that demean anyone, especially her. Don't comment on her or another's weight, breath, appearance, cultural differences, or clothes. This can make you look critical and even prejudiced, and make her feel less secure and comfortable with you. If she does something embarrassing, laugh with her about it and say, "I hate it when that happens to me." Then, share a similar experience in which you felt embarrassed, and try to get her to laugh about your experience with you. When laughing with her, lean toward her, touch her on the arm, or even hug her. Laughter and appropriate touch can dramatically increase a person's comfort and interest in others. If humor or joking is not your strong point, no worries. Remember, her primary need is to feel safe and secure. Focus on your natural strengths and your ability to treat her well instead.

- **As appropriate, be playful.** Men often like to tease and be playful, which can be a great way to introduce or create a little touch. If you do these things, do them for only brief moments. The safest and best place to tickle is not her stomach; try squeezing her leg just above the knee instead. When roughhousing or playing around, never pull anything over her head or intentionally mess up her hair. Most people, especially women, are very sensitive about having their head touched, and you might accidentally hurt them. If you attempt to pick her up or carry her, be sure you put her down if she complains or asks you to; women can easily feel vulnerable and overpowered by men. One out of three women has been sexually assaulted, so make sure you listen if she asks you to stop; doing this will help her develop more trust and confidence in you. When teasing about something funny that she does or says, mention it only once or twice. Anything repeated too often can become irritating or insulting. As long as she is dishing it out as much as she takes it, touching you too, and smiling or laughing, then you're probably striking the right balance.

- **Act strong and confident.** It is important that you act masculine, confident, capable, and controlled during the date. If you point your feet inward and slouch as you share details about your childhood, drop your chin and use a soft voice when she asks about your job, jiggle your foot as you wait for dinner, or use exaggerated gestures and a higher-pitched voice as you tell her about your day, you will seem less confident. She will see issues there even if there are none. Thus, if you want to get and keep the attention of a greater number of women, you need to maintain good posture. So remember to keep your chin forward, square your shoulders, plant your feet, talk with a lower voice, lean back or on an armrest, and find a position and stay in it for a while. Doing all these things will help you feel calm and will help her believe you are comfortable with yourself and her. They will also help you avoid the too-nice and just-friends traps.

- **When she is talking:**

  » **Make eye contact.** For a woman, eye contact calms anxiety and gives her some indication of what you are thinking. Constant eye contact is unnecessary—and staring is uncomfortable—but frequent eye contact is essential. Furthermore, a man who does not make and regularly keep eye contact when a woman is talking looks bored and irritated, judgmental and arrogant, or insecure and ashamed, any of which can lead to misunderstanding and rejection.

  » **Lean slightly toward her.** It is important that you show a little vulnerability and investment in her by leaning toward her on occasion, especially when she is speaking. If you don't, instead of looking confident and casual, you will look cool, aloof, arrogant, and even like a player. This is particularly the case when a man is very handsome or established in his career. When leaning forward, avoid rolling your shoulders by straightening your lower back and drawing your shoulder blades closer together. Good-looking and broad men can afford to slouch and may even need to on occasion in order to look more likable, but average men should prevent it when they can, especially for the first six weeks of dating. To lean forward in a way that keeps you looking confident and casual, shift from the back of your seat to an armrest or table. If these aren't available, put your elbows on your knees with your back straight and your shoulders square. Or assume a more upright and broad posture by placing your right ankle on your left knee and your right hand on your ankle.

» **Inject short statements that show you are listening.** While she is talking, be sure to nod on occasion and say something periodically, such as "Uh-huh," "Wow," "Sure," "No way," or "You have got to be kidding me." Use emotional words (as illustrated in Appendix C), make comments, and ask questions, but avoid sarcasm and don't change the topic very often. If you or someone else interrupts her, make sure you show her you were listening by coming back and saying, "I'm sorry. Please finish telling me what you were saying." Showing her your attention in this way can dramatically increase her interest in you because it makes her feel you are truly interested in what she has to say.

- **Be prepared for deeper and more personal conversations by using active listening skills and encouraging balanced conversations.** Women love to do activities, have fun, laugh, and be active, but they primarily bond through talking about people, problems, feelings, and ideas. Consequently, your conversations need to become somewhat personal by the fourth to sixth date, or she will doubt your interest in her and lose interest in you as well. To create a deeper connection, you need to:

  » **Ask her questions.**

  » **Show her that you are willing to answer her questions.**

  » **Demonstrate your trustworthiness and confidence by being honest and direct when she asks you about your past or problems (if her question is appropriate).** If her question is not appropriate, rather than dodging, avoiding, excusing, minimizing, or lying (she will have a hard time forgiving a deception or lie if she discovers it later), state, "I don't have anything to hide and as we get to know each other better, I'll share what you want to know, but for now, here's a quick and general response." Provide an honest but appropriately discreet statement that fits the depth of your current relationship.

  » **Help her feel understood and increase her interest in what you're saying by using more emotional words.** Emotional words are critical to creating stronger and more interesting connections for women. If you need suggestions for how to do this, refer to Appendix C.

- **Balance your time together with conversations and activities that keep the date fun and light.** Men bond more through talking about things and doing activities (especially when they are younger) than they do through talking about people, problems, feelings, or ideas. This is one of the primary differences between men and women, and why women often talk about their past relationships on first dates (because talking about people, problems, feelings, and ideas is how women feel close to other women). Although men like women who have opinions and assert their needs, talking about people and problems is frequently uncomfortable for men (which older women often find unpleasant, too). It feels like gossip, seems negative, appears critical, and can quickly become boring. A little bit of this is not a problem, but if it lasts for more than twenty minutes at a time, it can quickly overshadow the fun of the date and stress one or the other out. People simply don't know what to do with a date's unresolved emotions of anger, hurt, resentment, fear, depression, or anxiety, and they feel these emotions make others less attractive; this is the primary reason many relationships don't make it past the first three dates: the conversations were too heavy, lasted too long, and happened too soon. People like to help, but you both need to save your issues for friends, family, or a counselor, even if one of you is genuinely concerned and interested. Whereas sharing personal facts or emotions on a first date can make a person feel that the other is dumping on them, doing so in brief detail after three to six weeks of dating can make them feel that you are developing a deeper connection and trust in each other (which can be very rewarding). So, don't worry about avoiding personal issues altogether; just keep it short and to the point. When appropriate, share new ideas and discuss feelings, but keep the details about either of your past traumas to a minimum. In general, focus on having fun until you both are invested over a period of time. Then, sharing the details of your personal feelings and experiences will be mutually rewarding. After the first six weeks of dating, continue to carefully balance the time and conversations you have together to spend two-thirds of the time talking about things or doing activities and one-third of the time talking about feelings, ideas, people, and problems. A careful balance in this manner is necessary if you are to feel a secure and meaningful bond and connection that meets both of your individual needs. Although there are always exceptions to this general rule, and some men may genuinely enjoy deeper conversations, in most cases, a two-to-one ratio of light, everyday interactions to deeper conversations is usually necessary if you are to maintain balance and avoid making the relationship too heavy and burdensome for one person or the other. Maintaining the joy, fun, and humor of a dating interaction is critical if a relationship is to eventually mature enough to handle the weightier issues.

- **Show her you care about her safety and comfort, both during and after the date.** Pay attention to her needs and show you care by offering your jacket when she is cold, using your coat or an umbrella to shield her from rain, cleaning off her windshield (if there is snow), keeping a blanket in the car (in case she gets cold); and asking her to text you (if she has to drive home after the date), so you know she got home safely. Chivalry and thoughtful concern go a long way in making a woman feel you genuinely care.

- **Before ending the date, be sure to keep the pressure and expectations low.** The danger of being warm and engaging during a date is that one or both of you may feel too much pressure or have increased hope and expectation. Mitigate this risk by warmly saying, "Just so you know, I don't have any expectations in dating except to have fun and to treat each other well. I had a wonderful time getting to know you better. Thank you for the great date." If you've stated this before, saying it now will still be appropriate. However, from here forward, be careful not to overstate it, or it will seem odd and off-putting instead of anxiety-reducing.

- **When saying goodbye, make your interest known in one of the following ways:**

  » **If she is on your N/A (never again) list**, say, "Thanks for the fun evening," without suggesting another date. Offer her either a handshake, side hug, or brief hug (with your arms staggered, one higher and the other lower, as is commonly offered to friends). Include brief pats on the back to keep the hug more casual. Say goodnight and end the evening without looking back.

  » **If she is on your B List**, say, "It would be wonderful to do this again sometime. I'll be in touch, probably within the next few weeks." If she offers a handshake, use the double-handed handshake (as taught in Chapter 5) or offer a hug instead, since this is a warmer way to end the evening. When going for the hug, extend your arms from a relaxed lower position rather than staggered (like friends, with one arm up and the other lower) or in a higher position (as is more common for women). Your arms should cross around her lower or mid back (which encourages her to grasp around your shoulders or neck). Give a firm hug, but do not linger for very long or squeeze tightly, as this might indicate a stronger interest in her than you currently feel. If she expresses a desire to hear from you soon, reduce her expectations by saying, "Things are crazy for me right now, but I'll probably be in contact within the next few weeks." This gives a noncommittal response that leaves the door open while limiting her expectations. Say goodnight and walk away.

  » **If she is on your A-list**, say, "I'd love to do this again. You're amazing, and I had a wonderful time. Thank you." Offer a hug that includes a warm squeeze and gentle but connected embrace. When coming in for the hug, extend your arms with palms up from the height of your waist rather than providing one arm up and the other down (as is common among friends). Include a relaxing, full breath to show you are enjoying the hug. If you sense that you both feel a strong connection as you linger in the hug, build the chemistry a little by slowly pulling out of your hug, looking at her eyes, then her lips, and back to her eyes with a smile and a fun, confident wink or raised eyebrow.

  » **If you are unsure of her interest in you**, ask, "When would be a good time to call?" Her response to this question should be telling. For example, if she states that you can call anytime or encourages a call within the next few days, you are on her A-list. If she says she's pretty busy for the next week but would love to work something out in a couple of weeks, you are on her B-list. If she says, "Life is pretty crazy, so I'll reach out when I'm free," she's probably not interested in going out again (you're on her Never Again List).

- **If you kiss, keep it simple and sweet (leaving her wanting more).** It is usually best not to kiss on the first date, but if this occurs, make it short and memorable (rather than making out or engaging in sexual contact, which could leave her feeling insecure about your true interest in her). Instead, end a night out within the first three hours, and before midnight. Avoid late-night conversations, which can make either of you feel bored or worried about the time and how you are going to get away without hurting the other's feelings. You do not want either of you to feel anxious. Assertively, look at your watch (or phone) and say, "I hate to end the night, but I need to go home soon." Doing this when you truly don't want to say goodbye is often the perfect time to say goodbye because it ensures that you both feel you didn't get enough time together and are excited to see each other soon.

- **Do not confirm a specific day and time when you will call or go on another date until later.** Rushing a commitment to see each other could make either of you feel too much pressure or look overanxious. Women experience great frustration and loss of interest when a man commits to calling at a specific time or suggests a date and then fails to follow through. You may have good intentions, but unless you're willing to schedule a reminder on your phone's calendar so you don't forget to call, it would be better to reassure her that you will be in touch soon (or say nothing). In this way, you can call when it feels best for you.

Resilient practices (for avoiding burnout and unnecessary heartache)

- **Keep your emotions in check by basing them on the facts you know rather than on what you believe or hope.** No matter how excited you are about someone, how good-looking, successful, or kind they seem, or even how much they appear to fit your Top-Ten List, you need to remember that you do not really know this person. It takes time—six months at least—to see people for who they really are. You cannot afford to fall in love with the idea of someone or fill in the gaps between what you do not know and what you want to believe. This creates too much pressure and excitement, and can cause you a lot of anxiety or despair if they do not call. You need to keep your eyes open and focused on the facts so you will stay grounded and balanced and clearly see their issues, past, and behaviors, both good and bad. Everyone has issues. So instead of saying, "I have finally met the one," or "He/She is simply perfect," or "I am so lucky to have found him/her," say, "So far, it seems that he/she has many of the qualities I am looking for. We will see." This may not seem very romantic, but it is realistic and less likely to cause you extreme despair if things don't work out.

- **Fill your life with activities, hobbies, friends, family, and goals.** No matter how good things are going on in the first six weeks, do not change your plans with friends and family or drop everything you have going in your life to be with someone you just met. Doing so will only make you more disappointed, depressed, and lonely if the relationship doesn't last past six weeks, as most don't. Rushing a relationship does not increase the probability of success. In fact, it actually makes you more vulnerable to abuse and manipulation because the more you sacrifice friendships, family relationships, hobbies, money, and work to be with a person, the more dependent you feel upon him/her, making it harder to recognize and act on the warning signs if you see them. Furthermore, you need lots of relationships and distractions in the first six weeks of dating if you are to avoid thinking about, worrying over, or analyzing one relationship too much. Telling yourself not to think about someone won't work. You have to redirect your attention to something else if you are to manage your thoughts, feelings, and emotions, and decrease the likelihood that you will feel miserable and thus push the relationship or abandon it (to end the pressure and uncertainty). If you already have a full and happy life with lots of friends and activities, this will not be hard to do. So, fill out your calendar and be sure to look for other singles while you are doing these activities. Leave one or two nights a week available for dates, but fill these with alternate activities at least 24 to 48 hours in advance if no one calls or returns your calls for a date.

- **Do your part without expecting anything more than to be treated with respect in return.** It can be hard to give without expectation, but to do otherwise will make you appear insincere, self-serving, and manipulative. Let go of the future for now. Make a good-faith effort today and trust that if a specific person doesn't respond well, someone else will. Take it one week at a time and one date at a time. Set goals and focus on practicing your skills. Look for signs of success and improvement. Once you have dated one person for six weeks, then you can analyze whether or not they're compatible enough with your Top-Ten List to continue dating.

- **Keep pursuing, flirting, and dating others for at least the first six weeks.** If you immediately stop dating others, you will quickly appear needy and vulnerable or be prone to the just-friends, too-nice, or good-for-now trap. Men want women that other men want, and women want men that other women admire. Dating others helps you feel confident and make better decisions. It makes you appear more desirable and challenging. It protects you from being taken for granted, abused, or manipulated. And it helps you handle rejection better. As you keep your dating options open, be sure to be respectful to those you are dating: do not act overly flirtatious with others in front of them, and don't talk in detail about other dates when you are with them.

- **Work on your appearance and image.** It is critical that you remember: *your situation does not define your value; it is not your perfections that make you lovable, but your imperfections; and the kind of person you are looking for is looking for someone like you, will see you for what you have to offer, and will invest in you.* Nonetheless, you also cannot ignore the fact that image matters in the singles world. If you are going to manage the highs and lows of dating, you need to date several people at a time until you get past the first six weeks of dating someone you are ready to be exclusive with. To date this many people, you need to increase your ability to attract the attention of more singles. Improving your appearance and image is a great way to get this attention, and it increases your confidence, too. Don't focus on perfection (through losing twenty pounds or undergoing plastic surgery—although if you are more than forty pounds overweight, you will struggle to get as much attention). Just focus on maximizing your strengths and minimizing your weaknesses. To do this, review Chapter 5 for tips on how to improve your appearance and image.

- **Date people on your B-list and accept that you are on others' B-lists.** To determine who is on your A or B-list versus your N/A (Never Again) list, always refer back to your Top-Ten List. A person who fits your Top-Ten List and with whom you also feel a strong connection ***would be on your A-list***. A person who fits your Top-Ten List but you don't feel as excited about ***would be on your B-list***. Someone who makes you uncomfortable, is an ex, treats you badly, isn't in a good place right now, or is very attractive but does not fit your Top-Ten List ***would be on your N/A (or never again) list***. Most people expect that they should only date people who are on their A-list. However, it is okay, necessary, and appropriate to keep dating people who are on your B-list. After all, you are on someone's B-list, too. All you owe them, and all they owe you, is a good time. So, play fair, act nice, and have fun with those on your B-list for up to six dates (but no more). They can use the practice, too, and you never know, someone on your B-list may rise to being on your A-list after a few dates.

- **Only share your dating experiences with three friends.** Because most relationships will not last six weeks, you will handle the lows and letdowns of dating better if friends and family members aren't constantly asking you for an update. Only talk with three friends about the people you date, and with everyone else, use a memorized response, such as "I'm dating several people right now. There is one I like more than the others, but I don't want to talk about it much until I've dated him/her for at least six weeks."

- **Choose to be steady, stable, consistent, patient, and emotionally balanced.** To have a good relationship, you need to be in a good place in your life. If you move frequently, lose jobs often, ignore your mail, pay your bills late, abuse substances, act compulsively, quickly jump into or abandon relationships, rack up credit card debt, fail to discipline your children, or ignore important problems in your life, you will want to be rescued from your life and will feel dependence and attachment too early in relationships. This will make you more vulnerable to the abusive and manipulative and less attractive to the emotionally mature. Emotionally mature people have friends, family relationships, work, school, activities, and hobbies that are important to them and will not appreciate the added pressure of your feelings and needs too early in a relationship. So, prepare now for a relationship by getting in the habit of being consistent, stable, patient, and emotionally balanced in all areas of your life, from work to household responsibilities, family, friends, money, spirituality, and leisure time. Create balance and set boundaries with others so they don't cause chaos in your life. Prioritize work and recreation, alone time and time with friends, and personal and family needs.

- **Protect yourself from shame or regret by not sharing deeply personal feelings, needs, or problems, and discourage others from sharing these things, too** (unless they reveal warning signs you can't afford to dismiss). Talking about your past childhood abuse, your resentment toward others, your emotional, physical, financial, or health problems, or your fear of rejection can turn people off, make them feel too much pressure, or give them opportunities to exploit you. Avoid the regret, shame, abuse, neglect, or abandonment that may follow by not giving the most private parts of you to those who have not invested enough to appreciate and value you. Once someone sacrifices for you over a period of time, then you will know whether you can trust them. If someone asks something that is deeply private, say, "I don't have anything to hide. I just don't know you well enough yet to go into something that personal. If we are still interested in seeing each other after a month or so, or we get serious, I'd be glad to come back to this topic." Similarly, if they start to share too much information (such as sharing issues from their childhood, struggles with an ex, or their deeply complicated emotions), save them from feeling regret later—and yourself from losing interest or feeling pressure to take care of them—by saying, "That seems really hard. I'm sorry you went through such a difficult experience. I'd love to help you escape that for an evening." If they resist your efforts to change the subject and keep coming back to their problems, recognize this as a warning sign. Such behavior either proves that they are in a bad place to begin a relationship right now, or they lack empathy (because they failed to recognize and respect your feelings and needs). Don't overlook the significance of what this means. At this point, don't shut them down from sharing details about their inappropriate, abusive, or addictive behaviors. Instead, let them continue long enough to solidify your confidence in their lack of empathy, self-control, and personal responsibility (E.S.P.). The information you gain can be invaluable in convincing yourself that, no matter how good-looking they are, they belong on your N/A (Never Again) list. If you divert the conversation from their problems and you both relax and start to have fun, it will be easy to forget or justify the strange things they did or said in the middle of the date. To avoid this, end the date sooner rather than later, if possible. Make sure to restrict or end contact with them from here forward. Be kind, but don't rethink your decision when you see obvious issues with a lack of E.S.P.

- **If a relationship doesn't progress, honor and respect your emotions for a time, and then redirect your attention to what is going right.** Too many people minimize their vulnerable emotions and then over-focus on their fears and self-judgments. This is unfortunate because the truth is, *your emotions will never hurt you, but your judgments can.* For example, if you spend a few days validating and respecting your feelings by saying, "I feel sad, disappointed, and hurt," you will begin the healing process. But if you say, "This always happens to me. I will never get married. What is wrong with me?" you will only become more depressed, afraid, angry, and resentful. So respect, honor, validate, and give voice to your emotions while avoiding your judgments. To do this, say, "I feel __________ (one or two words: let down, angry, afraid, etc.)," and leave it there so you don't create an elaborate negative myth full of judgments and assumptions about yourself or your future. Let these emotions be felt and expressed for a time, and then, when you are ready, redirect your attention to what went right or felt right, what you learned, how you are getting better, and what skills you were able to practice. Doing this will help you find wisdom and endure the highs and lows of dating while maintaining and encouraging your faith.

- **When you go through slumps, pace your efforts so you don't burn out.** No matter how skilled you become at dating, you will go through slumps in which you aren't dating anyone and don't have any attractive prospects. During these times, as in all times, you need to continue to invest in the dating process even though you are not getting results. It is easier to continue working at something when you see results and much harder when you don't. If you feel depressed, stressed, or frustrated, reduce your efforts to match what you can emotionally give for a while. For instance, instead of actively practicing five techniques each week, practice one or two. Instead of going to three singles events in a month, go to three family events and look to see who might be single at the location of your event. Practice your techniques for a few minutes, and then resume focusing on your family. Don't give up; just slow down. When you feel more motivated again, resume giving more time and attention to the dating process. As long as you don't stop trying, you can trust that, at some point, things will click and change. If you quit trying, however, you will just get older and more cynical, angry, and convinced that the things you feared all along are true. It takes action to maintain faith and to create change. Without action, you will be left alone with your fears and just keep repeating your past.

Manage the first six weeks of dating

How you manage the first six weeks of dating can set you on a path to disconnection, premature attachment, or a progressively fun and balanced connection. There is much that singles must know and do during this time to both encourage the possibility of a deeper connection and establish a solid foundation that could lead to a secure attachment (if the relationship continues).

To help you time and pace your dating experiences so they are less stressful, confusing, or unpredictable, Section Three provides techniques and guidelines that will encourage a personally secure response that is attractive and inviting (rather than anxious, clingy, or too distant).

Too many singles attempt to read others' minds. Some singles analyze every text and stress about the best way to respond, while others shut down, feel indifferent, and withdraw. Whether you struggle with feeling anxiously attached or avoidantly indifferent, focusing on secure behaviors and forms of engagement will balance the scales in the right direction for both you and those you date. As you learn to casually and effectively minimize the predictable challenges that frequently plague singles during this early stage of dating, you will inspire others to do the same because secure behaviors are both attractive and inviting.

Many of the strategies offered throughout this section require self-control. They encourage you to consider the bigger picture and the needs of others while also promoting opportunities to relax and have fun. Self-control and empathy are the foundation of all sacrifice. Likewise, sacrifice is deeply connected to love. As you offer empathy and self-control to others, these not only increase the possibility of connection but also deepen your self-respect.

The techniques you learn in Section Three about timing and pacing dating (for optimal engagement that is not too vulnerable to the wrong people and too distant for the right ones) can also seem boring or too sterile if they are followed too precisely. Thus, finding a balance between reasonable emotional engagement and spontaneity while avoiding excessive risk or regret is essential.

With this in mind, review the chapters to consider the benefits, pros, and cons of the guidelines and techniques outlined. Understand the underlying principles, and then experiment and modify them to fit you and your situation. Most importantly, invite a date's input and allow for some spontaneity, too.

Feelings of attachment are dependent on being present and connected to the experience. If you are stuck in your head, this disconnects you from the moment and robs you of the emotions and experiences you are sharing.

Implementing a few techniques on a date (for practice and personal growth) is essential, but each should be short in nature and not provide a distraction from the overall experience. Remembering this should allow you to relax, let go, and have fun.

Some techniques will make sense and provide you with a feeling of relief since the structure offered is simple and minimizes the risk of being too engaged too quickly or too confusing and distant. Other times, you will need to stretch uncomfortably as you communicate, set boundaries, or increase your vulnerability and affection (or reign it in). As long as you strive to find the right balance for yourself and don't disregard the wisdom behind these suggestions, you will find that many singles respond well to the way you approach dating.

You won't get immediate results (since dating will take time before you find the right match), but you will increase your fun, the number of repeat dates you get, and your efficiency at connecting meaningfully with others.

Occasionally, you will get negative responses to these techniques; however, that will be a blessing since negative reactions to healthy communication and interactions are more common among those who are toxic and lacking in empathy, self-control, and personal responsibility (or E.S.P.) because they hate boundaries and asserting your needs will turn them off. The sooner you discover this, the better. You can't afford to face this truth after you are already attached.

As you and your partner exercise self-control early on, you will be more likely to develop a secure foundation and confidence in each other's commitment and loyalty. In contrast, if you rush relationships and ignore warning signs, you may discover that the relationship is plagued with lingering issues, doubts, insecurity, anger, fear, or selfishness due to its unstable foundation.

The recommended techniques offered in this section may seem calculated and even unnecessary at times. As you read them, you may argue that there is an exception to every one of them. However, success with any endeavor, skill, or talent often depends upon practicing the tried-and-tested rules or drills that increase speed and efficiency before breaking them, improvising, or ignoring them. If you don't learn proper techniques, bad habits will be hard to change later, or you may get hurt. Furthermore, the right skills are often necessary for mastering more complicated techniques later.

Thus, practice and apply each of the recommended techniques. They will help you be safe, confident, and successful. Once you have done this, you will understand the right time and place to break or change them.

You can do this! Hang in there. Apply a few concepts in short spurts. Trust that this is enough. Allow for imperfection (because perfection makes everyone uncomfortable anyway), and most importantly, focus on what's going right. You and your efforts are enough for those who are looking for someone like you and are prepared to invest, too.

Confidently manage and pace dates

Anxious and avoidant attachments are common problems in relationships and marriages, but they are also pervasive in dating. You can learn more about how to recognize anxious and avoidant behaviors and create secure attachments in the Lasting Love Academy's other books and courses. However, it is important to know and apply secure behaviors well before entering a relationship. Your (and others') propensity to act in anxious or avoidant ways can create problems as early as the first few interactions. Often, these manifest as anxiety, premature attachment, neediness, criticism, feelings of indifference, or rejection. Yet, what singles need is not more awareness of what is going wrong in themselves, their partners, and their relationships (especially if a toxic or abusive relationship is not a concern). Instead, they need a confident and hopeful redirection to what works in creating and supporting secure attachment behaviors so they can build their dating upon this foundation.

You have learned many concepts so far (and the techniques for putting them into action should have resulted in more dates if you are applying them). Unfortunately, you are now entering the longest and hardest part of your journey because, like a merry-go-round, you can't be sure when you will get off the ride and advance to the more action-packed thrills. For this reason, you need to be prepared with numerous options for engaging differently (not to create perfection on each date, but to allow for your ongoing growth and potential for a healthy relationship).

Each of these techniques is designed to encourage secure behaviors both in yourself and those you date (for the ultimate goal of achieving a meaningful connection or relationship). Until that day comes, the actions and investments you make also need to support your growth, resiliency, emotional connections, and long-term attachment skills (which you will need throughout all of the later stages). As you repeatedly practice these techniques, they will keep you actively engaged, hopeful, encouraged, and productive. By contrast, when you become passive, it will lead to regression, loss of strength, and hopelessness. You need action and consistent effort because it is essential to the confidence and energy that will sustain you (especially when you choose to measure the growth and small achievements you are making).

Yes, you will inevitably need to take brief breaks because of the highs and lows that dating can trigger, but being prepared for these struggles and maintaining your resilience will see you through to better days and keep you in a positive mindset.

In many ways, the cycling reality of the dates and micro relationships you will experience during the revolving door of the first six weeks is best conceptualized as the working stage. Like planting a garden in the spring (for which you will not obtain sustenance for many months), building a house (that may take a year to complete), starting your higher education (that takes four or more years to finish), or embarking on a new career and business venture (in which you will be engaged for decades), it is the little day-to-day choices you make that will add up to the life-changing benefits and stability you desire.

The results you dream of now will only come after consistent effort, in which you endure the boring and monotonous repetition of the same important actions and habits. However, this is the pattern of life and all progress. Innovation requires dreaming and creativity, followed by monotonous action, time, and interpretation of results, followed by learning, changing, monotonous action, repetition, endurance, finding joy along the way, more monotonous action, and eventually the rewards or conclusion of your quest (which is often interrupted by yet another challenge).

Since this monotony is an unavoidable part of success, the greatest lesson in life is often that of living with your challenges and working on them while embracing the moment. This is as important as any other skills you learn because if you can't enjoy the journey, you will eventually burn out or despair. Thus, expect to work, learn, laugh, love, grow, and enjoy every stage so that the next one isn't so frustrating or despairing.

Don't spoil the ride. Enjoy the journey!

Like it or not, the monotonous engagement required to maintain all good things in our life during the beginning, middle, or end of one challenge will unwillingly transition to the next challenge. This is the unavoidable pattern of life. The secret is to find joy in the journey and to fear the future less because you know that you are resilient and powerful enough to face what comes.

When you spoil the ride by worrying about the future or obsessing about the past, you rob yourself of the joy you can have in the present (by seeing everything that is good around you and embracing it). Although you need to be strategic about avoiding the toxic and abusive and knowing when to stay or leave a dating or relationship situation, you can still be more present, learn to relax, and have fun, too. Additionally, anticipating worst-case scenarios ensures your suffering because your fear and anxiety now are painful, and then if you unavoidably face the thing you fear, that will be doubly painful. Potential problems rarely play out the way you think they will, in spite of all your worrying. Instead, your planning and preparation could be redirected to your resilience and strength. When you are willing to be open and teachable, you can have the knowledge, power, skills, and strength you need as you need it. This power will not be provided relative to the problems you might have, but will be available for the challenges you do have (and when it is immediately relevant). So enjoy the moment, trust yourself and the future, and don't spoil the ride.

When you choose to be resilient enough today while adding joy and creativity, you will be powerful enough tomorrow to do the same. So, do what it takes to breathe, smile, smell, laugh, feel, listen, touch, taste, and see the world more fully each day (if only for a relaxing 20-minute mindfulness exercise). You need to enjoy the journey rather than endure your challenges. The latter is inevitable, but the former is entirely up to you. During today's or tomorrow's challenges, you can choose to act peacefully, be progressive and growth-minded, love and laugh, and dream of a better world while changing the one you are in (because you see the good around you as worth the effort of resisting the bad).

If you can embrace this common-sense truth, you will be okay. And, when you feel your vision is obscured and your resilience is depleting, we will be here to support you as a knowledgeable and calming guide to move you through the dark of one night to the light of the next day. This is the purpose of the Lasting Love Academy and the many features and encouragement we offer. Please don't believe that you need to do this working stage of the first six weeks (or any stage thereafter) alone. Reach out to us and our supportive community in the Lasting Love Academy app or on our website at LastingLoveAcademy.com. For now, keep moving forward one day (and one reasonable technique) at a time. You will get there, and we are excited to celebrate every step in your lasting love journey.

This chapter on timing and pacing dates and the many techniques surrounding each encounter may seem overwhelming, but if you apply a few techniques a little at a time, before long, the strategies will make more sense and have a lasting impact. These strategies are meant to balance the anxious and avoidant space between singles and offer a secure invitation to engage with mutual and calming confidence. They may feel strange and uncomfortable, but as you understand the underlying principles, you will find more courage to try them. With more exposure to these ideas, they will come to your conscious awareness when you need them most, like a dating coach in the back of your mind. In many ways, when the student is ready, the teacher appears; thus, allow the repetition of the merry-go-round of your dating experiences to continue your knowledge and skill base until they become habits and muscle memories that take over when you need them most.

If you mess up one dating situation, trust that you handled it the best you were able at the time and that all of your experiences are meaningful and will add to your eventual success. If it's a challenge you need to manage differently, you will have another chance to experience it, but this time you will be ready.

Don't sweat it! You are doing better than you think you are. Additionally, your worth and value are most obvious to others when you focus on your successes and intrinsic worth rather than on your mistakes or lost opportunities. So smile, laugh at your missteps through life's journey, and trust that they don't really matter because when you step back and see the bigger picture, you are truly doing great things in spite of the messiness of life.

Increase your investment or the relationship will lose momentum

Jannica liked Marius from the start. They had much in common, and he was attractive and kind. He was consistent about calling and asking her out, and he always treated her well on the date; however, he never held her hand or attempted to kiss her, and they seemed to talk only about superficial things. At first, she hoped he was holding back because he was interested in her and didn't want to rush things or ruin the relationship, but now that they'd been on five dates, she'd started to worry that he just wasn't that attracted to her. She wanted to feel something more, and their contact seemed too safe and impersonal. She needed touch or at least a more intimate conversation. She was losing interest fast.

Touch and personal conversations are critical to increasing familiarity, closeness, and comfort. Jannica believed that men should make the first move, but she could have done much more to encourage the process. This could have included giving him a warm smile and hug when he arrived, occasionally touching him on the arm as they talked, putting her arm through his as they walked across the road, and asking him about his life while including emotional words to keep him sharing ("That must have been so hard. What did you do next?"). Increasing her proximity by standing or sitting closer to him or leaning on the armrest in the car could also send an encouraging and inviting message. All of this could be combined with instances in which she bit her lip, looked at him, smiled, or slowly said something like, "You are so sweet. I really enjoy spending time with you."

Doing these things would not have been too forward, especially because he was obviously taking the lead by calling and asking her out. Increasing her efforts (in these ways) with each date would show investment on her part and a willingness to match his efforts, which would encourage him to continue pursuing her. Without these sacrifices, Jannica appeared too reserved, casual, or even indifferent. If Marius had to judge her interest in him based on her behavior, he would logically conclude that he was only on her B-list. As it was, Marius was at risk of losing interest as well if Jannica didn't start emotionally investing in the dates in a way that would meet his needs and encourage him to take more risks.

Someone had to help move the relationship forward, and these kinds of emotional sacrifices on her part were the perfect complement to his physical sacrifices of calling, asking her out, treating her great, getting to know her, and paying for the dates.

She implemented these techniques, and within a few weeks, Jannica and Marius were having more fun than ever. Not only had they kissed, but their conversations had become more meaningful, and they were now seeing each other twice a week and talking nearly every day.

Avoid sexual contact by being emotionally honest and clear

Sam dreaded seeing Sophia at church. She was a great girl, but he wasn't as interested in her as he'd once been. He also feared what she and her friends would think if he stopped seeing her. They'd only dated for a few weeks, but he was confident Sophia had shared information about their dates with others at church. He'd known better than to date women in his church group; there was always the threat that someone would get their feelings hurt, friends would take sides, and the person who'd initiated the breakup would be seen as a jerk. To make matters worse, they'd fooled around last night, and now he felt sure he would be viewed as a player if he stopped seeing her.

Sam did not feel right about engaging sexually with Sophia. It had been late, and his emotions had gotten the better of him. The problem was that kissing had become boring after a while. His mind had started to wander, and the temptation to spice things up a little had created a thrill. He wondered, "If I kiss her neck or touch her sides and belly, will she stop me? That's more exciting. She didn't say no. How far will she let me go? Well, what if I move my hands to touch . . . ?"

He didn't worry until after the fact that Sophia might act funny, like so many other women do after sexual contact, expecting to become exclusive, wanting more commitment, or feeling led on and manipulated if he did not call her again. He liked her, but everything felt complicated and heavy now, and he just wasn't interested enough to work through difficult emotions like these, especially because the relationship was so new and could be easily abandoned.

Sam explained that when he saw Sophia from across the room, he wanted to bolt and find a different church meeting to attend. Instead, he smiled, nodded his head in acknowledgment, and looked away without looking back again. He hoped that if he stopped calling, she would get the hint that he wasn't interested anymore. He wanted to believe that perhaps she hadn't told many of her friends after all, but he realized when he looked at her face, it was hopeless. He was going to be seen as a jerk.

The pressure and decreased interest Sam felt after sexual contact is common. It wasn't that he had dated a woman from his church group that made the situation uncomfortable (although it often can), but that he had acted sexually with her. There are many things that complicate and burden new relationships, and sexual contact is the greatest offender. Women might give sex (or engage in sexual contact) for love and in an effort to facilitate a relationship (because they don't understand what really maintains a man's interest and investment). Men might give expressions of love to get sex (because in the moment of lust, they feel really into her). Still, in the end, neither feels more secure, bonded, committed, or invested. Often, one or the other even feels repulsed or offended (particularly if either of them isn't clear about their intentions or expectations after being intimate).

Lust is not love. In fact, early and non-commital sex does not rush or ensure love, but rather, it predicts an insecure attachment pattern. Dating that is based on sex rarely results in secure and long-lasting relationships. Those with an anxious attachment style who engage in sexual contact often feel less overall satisfaction or confidence about it. Those with avoidant attachments often experience very few bonding outcomes.[6]

Thus, when a relationship is based on sexual contact, men (or the avoidantly attached partner) can quickly become bored by the emptiness and self-centeredness that remain, especially after the challenge is gone. Since non-commital sex requires no significant sacrifices or investment in the person, the relationship seems largely meaningless and disposable.

Similarly, without commitment, sexual contact does nothing to make a woman (or the anxiously attached partner) feel safe and secure in the relationship. It also does nothing to increase her trust and respect for him.

Consequently, when the added pressure of being incompatible, having to deal with the real emotions, problems, and needs of the other person, unplanned pregnancies, and sexually transmitted diseases surface, the lack of real commitment or interest in developing a real relationship becomes obvious, and abandonment usually follows.

Since most dating relationships won't last beyond the first six weeks, those who rush to engage in sexual acts are often left with dissatisfaction, regret, or increased self-centeredness.

Early sexual contact is a vulnerable gift that can result in numerous consequences, from STDs, pregnancy, abortion, child support, and co-parenting responsibilities that endure for decades. Rather than a secure attachment, it can bring out the worst in both individuals, including selfishness, insecurity, fear, shame, clingy behaviors, anger, and a tendency to avoid or escape the demands of life and real relationships. The goal of sacrificing, investing, and making each other feel great in a lasting way is replaced with the short-sided goal of making oneself feel great in the moment, and in the end, no one feels great.

Only sincere investment and commitment create a lasting, positive outcome for all involved.

Avoid things that complicate and burden new relationships

Sexual behavior is a major contributor to early loss of interest and rejection, but it's not the only one. Spending a lot of time together right away, overthinking the process, sharing deeply personal issues and insecurities, meeting a date's family or their children too soon, treating a date like a job interview, trying too hard, being too available, worrying about commitment, and discussing the relationship within the first six weeks are common offenders as well and can quickly suck the joy out of dating.

---

6 Nunez Segovia, A., Maxwell, J. A., DiLorenzo, M. G., & MacDonald, G. (2019). No strings attached? How attachment orientation relates to the varieties of casual sexual relationships. Personality and Individual Differences, 153, 109644. https://doi.org/10.1016/j.paid.2019.109644

Sam was struggling with several of these, and all of them made him feel too much pressure. He just wanted to relax, have fun, and not worry about whether or not he was going to hurt the girls he dated. Sam contacted me after he heard me speak at a singles conference, hoping I could help him overcome the barriers that caused him to stop dating within the first six weeks.

I suggested a simple way for him to confront the most difficult situations head-on. When feeling pressure, he should touch his date on the arm and say, "Just so you know, I believe dating is about having fun and getting to know each other without any pressure or expectations, especially at first. As long as we treat each other with respect, we'll have no regrets. I'm sure you are dating others, and I am too, but I'd love to keep having fun and get to know you." I encouraged him to keep the comment casual, short, and to the point. Doing this within his first few interactions with women who are on both his A and B lists would remove most of the pressure and anxiety he was experiencing. This should help him relax and just enjoy dating again.

Sam returned two months later and stated that the strategy had worked great. One of the women freaked out and demanded that if he kept seeing her, he would have to stop seeing other women, which he thought was strange after just two dates, but overall, the women to whom he said it responded well. He was in his fifth week of dating a woman on his A-list and was enjoying himself. He knew he wasn't ready to be exclusive with her, but he was ready to see her a couple of times a week, kiss her, and pace his other B-list dates farther apart, which is exactly the pace I would have recommended.

We reviewed the techniques for avoiding sexual contact to ensure his affection remained simple and clean and to prevent too much pressure, and he was on his way.

Sam was having fun again.

The techniques that follow will help you prepare for situations like the ones David, Jannica, and Sam experienced, as well as many others, so you can navigate the first six weeks of dating with greater success.

Refer to the videos available at LastingLoveAcademy.com or in the Lasting Love Academy app courses for examples of how to apply these techniques. Seeing them in action can greatly increase your confidence and skills.

Prepare for the highs and lows of dating

David had not dated much and had never been in a relationship, although he was attractive and fit. Therefore, he was pleased that within a few months of coaching, a woman responded with warmth and excitement when he asked for her number. He called and discovered, to his enjoyment, that talking with her was comfortable, light, easy, and rewarding. He asked her out and had a great experience on the date. He kept pursuing her, and during the dates, she leaned toward him often, smiled at him frequently, said wonderful things about him, showed appreciation for their dates, and laughed easily. On occasion, she even reached down and briefly held his hand. So, he was quite confused when, after six weeks, she stated that she just wanted to be friends. This is what he'd heard all his life, and hearing it again played on his fears that a woman would never love him.

David needed to understand and accept that most relationships would not last beyond six weeks. Her loss of interest was not necessarily personal—it just happened. Everyone is dealing with unique circumstances in their life and is not always able to invest in and commit to every relationship they explore. Nonetheless, this woman's reactions during the dates proved that David's techniques worked. She leaned toward him because he made her feel safe and secure, and she grabbed his hand because she liked how he treated her—she clearly felt attracted to him in those moments. She smiled at him and laughed because he made her feel comfortable and made the date fun and enjoyable. His techniques worked and would work again with someone else, perhaps someone in a better position to commit and invest than she was. The experience was a success, not a failure, even though it did not end in a more serious relationship. David needed to stay focused on practicing his techniques and playing his role while increasing his resilience to the highs and lows of dating.

Know your physical and sexual limits (and the connections you want to invite)

Affection can sometimes develop quickly. This can lead to one or both parties feeling unattended pressure for more touch, kissing, making out, or sexual contact than they would feel good about later. There is a delicate balance between being too distant and too physically affectionate early on. Some people engage more quickly or naturally with simple touch, whereas others can have very little experience or comfort with affection, be leery of abuse or exploitation, or struggle to express their discomfort and boundaries.

Since intimacy can occur as early as the first contact and without commitment or sincere intentions, the following descriptions highlight the many types of affection from those that can be mutually desirable or socially appropriate, up to and including sexual intercourse and possibly unwanted sexual practices. These descriptions make it easier for you to recognize what would be enjoyable and mutually beneficial, so you can communicate effectively and avoid potential complications arising from unexpressed limits or premature affection.

Please consider the reality that those with secure attachment patterns typically engage in simple affection (because they are not as anxious, afraid, or manipulative) and wait until commitment or marriage for sexual contact. These individuals experience a higher satisfaction and connection with their partner after sexual contact (as opposed to the insecurity and detachment of those with anxious and avoidant patterns). You may have a pattern in which you either engage in sexual intimacy before you are ready (to avoid losing someone's interest), withhold due to fear (of being vulnerable and abused), or participate noncommittally (with no intention for attachment);

nevertheless, you can fake it til you make it, by acting in similar ways to those who have a pattern of success. It is far more valuable to know what it looks and feels like when things are going in the right direction than knowing when they are going in the wrong direction. Thus, a warm, clear, and direct invitation to get back on track by following a wiser path of simple affection and self-control will usually be met with positive results.

Thus, be careful not to focus exclusively on what you don't want. Make sure you consider what you would enjoy and why it would be mutually positive and connecting for both of you. It is not enough to avoid unwanted sexual contact; you also need to consider the benefits of simple affection, how it builds potential chemistry, adds value to your life and the happiness of others, or increases your mutual potential for a secure attachment.

Relative to affection in the first six weeks of dating

When reviewing the following list, respect your values and standards while considering the many possibilities that could increase your chemistry and connection in mutually beneficial ways.

Circle the actions you would enjoy offering or receiving, **cross out those activities in which you do not want** to participate until commitment or marriage, and **black out those in which you would never feel comfortable** participating.

- handshakes

- double-handed handshakes

- grasping (or touching) the wrist or upper arm (above the elbow)

- hugs (both as friends with one arm up and the other lower or prolonged and grasping hugs)

- playfully nudging, pushing, or using body bumps that could include the knee, upper arm, hand, or hips

- guiding (or being guided) through a door with a brief but warm touch on the small of the back or arm

- holding hands or resting a hand on a knee for a few minutes or longer

- leaning next to someone with the head on their shoulders, chest, or lap

- cuddling in a light or full embrace (without kissing or sexual stimulation)

- sharing passionate, fun, playful, or simple kisses that are short in nature and don't involve the tongue

- sitting or standing next to each other while kissing

- one person straddling the other, whether sitting, lying down, or on top of the other, while kissing

- engaging in occasional or consistent open-mouthed kisses that could include the tongue and are prolonged and emotionally arousing (often known as making out) without sexual touch of breasts or genitals

- entering a car, home, or bedroom to engage in kissing

- kissing or caressing the neck, arm, stomach, back, or legs without genital or breast contact

- caressing breasts, buttocks, genitals, or rubbing these areas against the other's body (with clothes on)

- caressing each other's bodies with or without clothing on

- engaging in sexual contact without intercourse or oral sex until the point of orgasm or ejaculation

- engaging in (or receiving) oral sex

- engaging in protected intercourse

- engaging in intercourse without a condom (when a woman is on birth control)

- engaging in unprotected intercourse (without other birth control measures)

- participating in unconventional practices (such as anal sex, roleplaying, fetishes, watching or recording pornography, participating in threesomes, engaging in master and servant activities)

- engaging in drug or alcohol use (with established consent and boundaries)

- engaging in drug or alcohol use without prior consent about whether sexual contact can occur

1. Describe when or how you would be open to more contact (and the positive or negative consequences you or they may feel afterward). ______________________________

2. How would not participating in any of the actions from the list above (during the first date or up to the first six weeks) impact your connection? ____

3. If you wouldn't enjoy any of these actions, why do they seem undesirable or repulsive (and what actions could you take to become more comfortable with sharing some of these actions with a date or potential partner)? ____

4. How can you clearly, confidently, and firmly express your boundaries while showing respect and positive assumptions about your date's intentions? *(For example, I could state, "I thought you would appreciate knowing that I'm a slow mover when it comes to affection and enjoy keeping things simple and uncomplicated" followed by a firm "I'm not comfortable with this. Can we go back to ______" if they pursue something I'm not comfortable with.)*______________________________

5. If your date doesn't react respectfully to your boundaries, what might that say about their potential issues with empathy, self-control, and personal responsibility (or the sincerity of their interest in you)?______________________________

Encourage a first kiss

- **If you really want her to know that you like her, you need to get close to her occasionally and touch her when you can.** Women like to be pursued and to feel wanted. Thus, increasing physical contact is necessary if she is to see you as a strong and confident man who isn't afraid to pursue her and if she is to feel attractive and desired by you. Getting a little closer and touching her more also gives you a chance to see if she likes you and wants you to kiss her. If you get closer to her and she doesn't pull back, step back, or look uncomfortably away, then she likes the closer contact. To get closer to her, you can:

  1. **Take a step closer to her for a few minutes.**

  2. **Lean toward her and whisper, which invites her to get closer as well.**

  3. **Gently bump into or tap her as you joke and tease.**

  4. **Tickle her by squeezing her leg just above the knee.**

  5. **Sit close enough to her that your arms, hands, knees, or feet touch occasionally.** If she doesn't move her arm, hand, knee, or foot but lets it linger next to yours, it's a good sign she is interested in more.

- **Hold her hand.** When you reach for her hand, grab it with confidence and even give it a gentle squeeze rather than timidly reaching for it and just resting your hand on hers.

- **Put your arm around the back of her chair.** You will feel more confident about doing this if you have already included some touch throughout the date.

- **Notice if she puts gum or a mint in her mouth, leans closer, smiles, looks from your eyes to your lips, or gently bites her lip.** If she does these things, she is probably trying to encourage a kiss. If she does none of these things, and especially if she consistently leans away, looks away, or keeps a distance between you, she is not interested in a kiss.

- **Get even closer—within six inches—linger for a moment, and then lean in for a kiss.** If you get within six inches of her face and she doesn't move away, go for the kiss. Make it sweet, tender, passionate, or simple, but don't make out or act sexually. Leave her wanting more. Women want men who hold off sexually. It makes them feel respected and wanted rather than feeling like an object.

- **As an alternate and more advanced technique, get close, gently brush her hair away from her eyes, and then slide your hand to the back of her head to hold it as you move in for the kiss.** This is a highly effective technique that most (but not all) women find to be a very sexy, confident, and passionate way to kiss a woman. Those men who know how to do it are seen as more exciting, passionate, and skilled.

- **When kissing, do not immediately attempt to French kiss (i.e., the tongue-in-mouth approach).** Some women do not like French kissing, especially when it comes to a first kiss. It can be too wet or intimate too soon. If you do like French kissing and want to test the waters, start first by slowly moving your tongue across your own lips while you kiss. She will most likely feel the tip of your tongue across her lips as you do this. If she likes it, she will respond similarly or initiate French kissing. If in doubt about whether you want to take a risk with a French kiss, it never hurts to just avoid it until you have kissed a few more times. All your kisses, but especially your first kiss, should be short and sweet anyway. If you want, you can even casually bring up the topic of French kissing before you attempt it so you can be sure she's okay with it first.

- **Leave her feeling confident about your interest in her (especially since you just kissed her) by saying, "I'd really like to see you next week. When would be a good time to call so we can make plans?"** A woman's number-one need is to feel safe and secure. By kissing you, she now feels a little vulnerable. If you say you will call soon, she will feel more confident and secure in your interest in her, which, if she is on your A-list, you should want her to feel. If she is on your B-list, you shouldn't be kissing her anyway (unless no one is on your A-list and you want to see if more chemistry could develop so she could move to your A-list).

- **If she's on your B-list and you want to see if you feel more chemistry after a kiss, do so, but with a personal commitment to call her if you don't feel a connection** so you can explain rather than just disappear. There is no harm in giving simple affection and kisses to see if you feel more of a connection. In some ways, this can be better than just avoiding the investment necessary to really develop a relationship or stalling the kiss (which may mean she is forever a pal and not a gal in your eyes). So, if she is on your B-list (and no one is on your A-list), go in for a kiss. What do you have to lose? However, if you don't feel more of a connection, you need to not just disappear (as so many men do). Instead, show her a minimal amount of respect by calling a few days after the kiss and saying, "I respect you too much to stop calling without an explanation of why. I do not feel enough of a romantic connection to keep going on dates. You have been great, and it has been a pleasure dating you. Thank you for treating me so well, and I hope you feel I've done the same."

Techniques for Avoiding sexual contact

- **Insist on only dating people who show sexual self-control and respect for others.** Everyone knows it is completely inappropriate for someone to pressure, expect, or demand sexual contact from others. Such expectations do not usually surface in early conversations, however. They begin subtly, with little comments that the other person does not stop or express discomfort over. From there, manipulators will carefully progress their efforts, reducing the other person's boundaries, increasing familiarity, creating pressure, and playing on the individual's emotions and fears of rejection. Within a few days or less, sexual contact often occurs, whether the other person feels ready or not. Sexual manipulators, players, or predators are not always men. Some women use seduction and sexuality to get and maintain a man's interest and attention and to get what they want—be it a relationship or anything else. Truth be known, these women see sex as power (to reward, withhold, and punish) and will continue to treat it as such even after marriage. Thus, you need to remember not to give up what you want most—a loving, long-term marriage with a sexually available and invested partner—for what you want in the moment (attention, validation, and pleasure). Though temporarily exciting, immediate sexual relationships often leave both partners alone again and sexually unfulfilled, typically within weeks. Such experiences have no meaning or value, especially when sexually transmitted diseases, deception, infidelity, abuse, or lies surface. The best predictor for a good, long-term, and sexually available relationship in marriage is not sexual contact while dating, but the skills of empathy, self-control, and personal responsibility. The first six weeks of dating are the most critical time to discover whether someone has these skills. One way to assess these skills is through the process of talking about difficult issues (which may include discussing your or their sexual history, issues, boundaries, needs, and fears of becoming pregnant or getting sexually transmitted diseases) and then observing how others react.

- **State that you are uncomfortable with sexually inappropriate conversations.** If you are with someone who has empathy, you will probably never need to use this technique because they will not start or maintain sexually inappropriate conversations; however, in the event that a sexually explicit topic comes up, state, "I feel comfortable talking about sex, but in a respectful way and not in explicit detail." Then, observe what they say and do. If their intentions are innocent and they are emotionally mature, they will quickly and happily change the subject. If they are not emotionally mature, they will act critical, sarcastic, angry, or rejecting. Stop seeing them immediately.

- **Dress thoughtfully and respectfully on each date.** Carefully scrutinize the posts you make, the pictures you add, the things you share, and the people or groups you follow on social media. Consider the message your posters, decals, or T-shirts communicate. Do they marginalize women or glorify drug and alcohol use? Women may be offended by Playboy symbols, sexy screensavers on your computer and phone, or foul or coarse language. What assumptions might a woman make about you, your values, and your attitude toward women based on these things? Would you seem like a man she could trust or a player? If you want a woman's respect, you need to show her respect, too, by removing anything that potentially demeans or shows contempt for women. When interacting with a woman, don't talk, joke, or tease in a way that would make her feel uncomfortable. Treat her like a lady, not like one of the guys (thus, bodily noises and insensitive comments about others are definitely out). Just as a woman needs to think like a man, you need to think like a woman. There are many ways people express their personality, so make sure that the things you do, wear, and say express the best in you, not the worst. A woman needs to feel that you have empathy and self-control if she is to respect you and feel emotionally safe and secure in a relationship with you. As she develops more trust in you and your goodness, your human side may humor her, but save that for later.

- **Hopefully, within the first few dates, but definitely before or immediately after kissing, state, "I like to go slow, especially physically."** Amazingly, you can casually and naturally set boundaries relative to affection and kissing, and the sooner you do it, the more confident and easier it will be. When doing this, be sure to positively reinforce the interactions you are enjoying and want more of. For example, "I'm really enjoying our cuddles and short kisses and would love to continue those." When you delay saying something until after things have gone further than you desire, you will have a harder time speaking up for fear that the other will feel bad or get upset. It's harder to step back from physical contact than to set your limits early on. Additionally, this gives you a chance to observe their reactions and what it says about their empathy and self-control.

- **Remember that women find men who hold off sexually while still pursuing appropriate touch and affection to be very desirable.** Such behaviors make a man appear strong, confident, and attractive. When a man shows that he's not afraid to engage fully while still setting healthy limits relative to what he is willing to do, he seems more trustworthy and desirable. His efforts to be close to her, but with self-control, dramatically increase her feelings of safety and security. So, as your dates progress, be sure to increase your affection. Guide her through a door, hold her hand, get close, cuddle, be playful, and hug her spontaneously when it seems appropriate (based on how well she is responding to your simple gesture and affection. Consent is incredibly important. This can be provided both verbally and nonverbally, but if in doubt, always ask if she is feeling comfortable or encourage her to let you know her preferences. Asking to kiss someone before you kiss them may kill the mood, but you can have a preemptive conversation to feel out her preferences and then act accordingly in the moment. Either way, be sure to state, "Just so you know, I believe in keeping kissing very respectful. So, once we kiss, I will keep it to a few minutes or less. I find this to be the best way to keep dating and relationships on track" (which is true because too often sexual contact decreases a man's interest afterward). In most cases, you will find this technique literally makes a woman more assertive because it takes the pressure off, and she trusts that you are interested in her, not just her body. When you set sexual limits, she can relax and enjoy herself rather than being on guard for wandering hands. Your ability to maintain control helps her enjoy being close and affectionate with you, which means she may push the limits. If you give in, she will trust and respect you less because you didn't stand by your expressed values. If you maintain your limits, she may feel a little frustrated (in the moment), but if you are kind, she will respect and trust you more, too. Show your determination to keep your affection from getting too intense by limiting your kisses to five minutes or less and ending the night early so you aren't unduly tempted. Fortunately, if you use this technique with a woman who depends on sexual power to get and maintain control in a relationship, you will discover that it elicits very dysfunctional behavior out of her. She will attempt to seduce you, become rejecting or critical, act insecure and self-deprecating, or lose interest in you altogether. Count her reactions as a huge discovery of her lack of empathy or manipulative intent. This is a blessing; she would have been emotionally draining and sexually destructive in a marriage. Thus, using this technique not only helps you be valued and appreciated by good women while exposing manipulators, but it also protects you from the too-nice and just-friends traps because you are acting more confident and assertive about sharing appropriate affection and building chemistry with her.

- **Have a plan for how you will enjoy affection while avoiding unnecessary temptation.** Provided below is a list of dating boundaries that you should discuss with someone you are kissing. It is best that you involve them in your efforts to keep your boundaries. If the other person cares about meeting your needs and respecting your sexual boundaries, then they will be glad to give their input and suggestions on how they can help avoid sexual contact. By soliciting their participation, you will appear consistent and determined but also trusting and interested in their contributions and ideas, which will make them feel included rather than controlled and distrusted. Additionally, they may offer great suggestions, and the more invested they become in the process, the harder they will work to avoid triggering their or your temptations.

  » **Focus on enjoying touch and affection that is simple and clean, rather than focusing exclusively on controlling lust, temptation, and sexual contact.** In a world of disconnection, simple affection helps bridge an important gap that can't be ignored. Those who experience little to no affection are more likely to be vulnerable to sexual impulses. If you both focus on enjoying cuddles, hugs, holding hands, soft touch, or playful and affectionate teasing, you will feel more connected and at ease with the other. Resting a leg on the other, tickling a back,   and stroking hair are great signs that you are comfortable being affectionate. So, keep your affection simple and clean rather than focusing on all the things you can't do. Being connected in these ways also makes it easier to control your thoughts and temptations.

  » **Agree to keep your kisses short (five minutes or less).** This is enough time to show and feel affection while not triggering and feeding lust.

  » **Give passionate kisses only when you are standing or sitting next to each other.** When standing or sitting next to each other, it is simply too uncomfortable to kiss for more than a few minutes. The head and neck feel too kinked. You know that it is time to stop passionately kissing when you want to get comfortable by leaning back, lying down, or sitting on someone's lap.

  » **Avoid making out.** The longer you kiss, the more comfortable you make yourself while kissing (e.g., lying down, leaning back, or straddling the other's lap), and the more you press yourselves against each other or roll around—which always increases sexual arousal—the more difficult it will be to control your passions and avoid sexual contact, especially if you kiss late at night. Making out will only increase your risk of sexual contact and decrease your desire to avoid it. If this relationship is to have the time it needs to develop a secure foundation, you cannot minimize the importance of avoiding making out.

» **Plan activities for when you are together.** Do not just hang out or watch movies. Idle time and boredom dramatically increase the risk of making out. Doing activities is one of the best ways to build relationships and control the mind. It also reduces anxiety and pressure and creates common goals and interests. If you fear that a date will turn into hanging out, ask before the date begins, "So what are we going to do?" You can then give suggestions or even say, "I am flexible. All I ask is that we do an activity that doesn't include us hanging out at either of our homes alone."

» **Spend time together doing things with friends and family when you can.** This is a great way to keep the pace of dating slow and steady and to give your friends and family a chance to weigh in with their thoughts before you get too attached.

» **Avoid sexually stimulating movies or conversations** (especially together), which can increase your feelings of lust, weaken your boundaries, and dramatically increase your likelihood of engaging in sexual contact within the next few hours or days. This may mean you need to carefully select what PG–13 or R–rated movies you choose.

» **Stay out of each other's bedroom.** There is only one place to sit comfortably in a bedroom together, and that is on a bed. It is just too easy to then start kissing, lie down, make out, and touch each other, especially when you know no one else will be coming into the room.

» **Avoid drinking, drug use, and any powerful emotions that could impair your reasoning and weaken your boundaries.** It is impossible to reason with someone who is drunk. Similarly, those who are Horny, Angry, Lonely, and Tired (i.e., H.A.L.T.) can be equally impaired. As an illustration of this point, it has been repeatedly documented that tired and angry drivers can cause accidents as deadly as those caused by drunk drivers. Thus, when you know you are in a horny mood, have had a bad day, are excessively angry, feel terribly lonely or sad, or anticipate you will be getting together late at night, HALT and change your plans. The relationship and your self-respect (as well as respect for each other) are worth a little inconvenience. Having sexual contact will be more devastating to your new relationship than rescheduling a date. Emotions can be powerful triggers for sexual contact, as can drugs, alcohol, and prescription use. Avoid all of these influences, especially when you can see the risk, and do something to alter it in advance.

» **Say goodnight by midnight at the latest. Preferably, say goodnight by 11 p.m. and before you become too tired.** It can be hard to leave when you are having a good time, but lingering too long can decrease your or their interest. Making out (which is common late at night) can lead to sexual contact, and being tired the next day can cause issues at work. Trust the relationship enough to know that if you end the date on a high note, they will just keep coming back for more.

» **Never stay the night at each other's homes.** Spending the night in each other's arms means you are not only too comfortable but also in close contact past midnight and throughout the night. You can't play with the fire of temptation and not eventually get burned. Plus, this kind of closeness and familiarity tend to just propel early relationships into premature commitments that quickly add too much pressure and lead to rejection. You don't need the attachment and then the loss. You need to protect yourself from the highs and lows of dating by not spending the night. You may long for and desire this companionship at night, but will it do you any good if you have it for a night or two here and there instead of for a lifetime? Remember to repeat to yourself: I won't give up what I want most for what I want at the moment.

» **Do not remove or move clothing to touch or massage your date.** It can seem so innocent to massage someone's aching back, but simply removing or moving their shirt can increase familiarity and lead to sexual contact. Play it safe by avoiding it. There are so many meaningful ways to make a connection, and a back massage on top of clothing can still feel good.

» **If you desire and need motivation or support to keep your boundaries, ask a trustworthy friend and make a $20 commitment that you will express and keep your boundaries** (especially the one about not kissing while lying down). If you aren't accountable to someone (besides your date) for avoiding sexual contact, you will quickly abandon your boundaries. If you need the added incentive, getting support from others will motivate and inspire you to stay on track or encourage you to get back on track if you falter. In spite of your best efforts, at some point, you will probably stay out past midnight, kiss lying down, go into someone's bedroom for a few minutes, make out for half an hour, or fall asleep in someone's arms. Sometimes, breaking these boundaries will not end in sexual contact, but this, in many ways, makes the temptation to push your limits that much stronger. It is so easy to be lulled into a false sense of security. But with each boundary that you break and keep breaking, you will get closer and closer to the edge where your commitment and resolve will lessen, and your sexual weaknesses and vulnerabilities will take hold. If you avoid passionate kissing while lying down, you can avoid the edge, which is making out. Once you start making out and stimulating your passions, it is so easy to go over the edge and begin the rapid downhill slide of sexual contact. Stopping sexual contact can be as difficult as stopping a snowball rolling down a hill. The longer it rolls, the more mass and momentum it builds until it is nearly impossible to stop and leaves a path of destruction in its wake. So find a friend or family member who will follow up with you, who will remind you of why you don't want to get involved sexually, and who will insist that you pay the $20 you have committed if you don't respect these limitations. Write a check for the $20 to a charity of your choice rather than to this person, so they don't have a financial interest in your failure. If you find that $20 isn't motivating enough, make it $50 or $100. If that doesn't work, commit to involving more friends, family, or spiritual leaders in your efforts each time you bend and break your sexual limits (or feel pressure to do so, which could be a red flag). Choose those people who will empower, not shame you.

Pacing the first six weeks of dating

The following pages outline strategies for appropriately pacing each new relationship so it progresses for optimal health. These strategies are broken down by what is best for each of the first six weeks—whether you see each other only once a week or more. When deciding which week's advice applies to your situation, focus on how many weeks you have been on dates with a person rather than on how many dates you have had. For example, if you have seen each other seven times in the first three weeks, you should still follow the techniques for the third week of dating, whereas if you have only seen each other two times in the first four weeks, you would still be in the second week of dating because you only saw each other during two of those four weeks.

I do not recommend that you see each other more or less frequently than is outlined week by week if you can help it. Seeing each other too frequently early on can make you vulnerable to early loss of interest and boredom, abuse and manipulation, excessive excitement and attachment, or the too-nice trap. Similarly, seeing each other too infrequently can cause a loss of momentum or connection and trigger early rejection.

Appropriate pacing is the primary way other people can gauge your interest in them. You cannot verbally tell someone they are on your A or B list, which would be weird. Instead, you have to show them. The challenge is to make sure your behaviors send the right message. If they are on your A-list, but you treat them like they are on your B or N/A-list, then you need to step up, risk, and invest more, or you will lose their interest. The more deeply you sacrifice, the more deeply you love.

The strategies you learn for the First Six Weeks of Dating are meant for at least six weeks until you and the other person agree to be exclusive. It will probably take you three to four months of active dating before you will discover one relationship that makes it past the first six weeks. Then, it may take a few more months before the other person will feel ready to date you exclusively. So be patient and use this time just to practice and refine your skills as you have fun, make others feel great, and do your part to deepen and progress your connection.

Lastly, if you struggle to find someone who qualifies for your A-list, at least get in the habit of treating one of the people you date as if they are on your A-list. If you don't, you will never develop the personal characteristics and qualities necessary to sustain a long-term relationship. People need to be a priority in your life now, or they may never be. Because you will not date anyone for more than six weeks if the relationship doesn't feel right, don't put unnecessary pressure on yourself. Just have fun, make them feel great, and practice your techniques. If you are worried about giving A-list attention to someone who you doubt will ever be anything more than on your B-list, then only give them A-list attention for up to two weeks. After that, give it to someone else. The point is that you give it to someone every week.

Remember, if you treat someone great and they don't respond, someone else will—and it might just be their cute friend. Thus, treating people like they are on your A-list might just pay off in unexpected ways.

Techniques for the 1st week or date

- **Whether *she* is on *your* A or B-list, at a minimum, treat her well.** This includes calling and setting the first date at least 48 hours in advance, following up before the date to confirm your plans (as explained for the techniques before the date from pages 242 to 243), arriving on time (or calling if you are running behind), planning a moderately priced date (to reduce your risk of exploitation and to avoid giving the best of you too soon), paying for the date, and treating her like a lady.

- **If *she* is on *your* B-list, follow many, but not all, of the techniques for making a woman feel great during a date** (from pages 246-253). Offer a shorter date to eliminate pressure and provide a fun or positive experience. Weekday evenings and experiences that are around an hour are good options for casually encouraging contact. A weekend and longer date increases pressure, so keep it simple. Don't touch her as much as you would someone on your A-list. This may include guiding her through a door, but no more than three simple forms of touch (if that much). Be sure to end the first date by saying, "I'd like to do this again. I'll reach out, and we can discuss options in the next week or so," which indicates you will not be calling right away.

- **If *she* is on *your* A-list, apply most, if not all, of the techniques for making a woman feel great during a date** (from pages 246-253). In case you are on her B-list, keep the pressure low by offering a short date in a public place while also offering at least a two to three-hour date if she would prefer (in case you are actually on her A-List). You should be able to determine her A or B list enthusiasm based on her level of engagement and interaction so far, but this is not always obvious or accurately determined (since women can appear more passive or enthusiastic when they actually feel differently). Thus, offering two options will help to reveal her interest and allow you to modify the pressure and expectations she feels. Get her in by midnight, avoid making out if you kiss, and end the date by stating you would love to take her out next week. Don't lock her into planning a date or when you will call. Instead, express that you will be in contact soon to discuss options. This keeps her feeling curious, wanting more, and experiencing less pressure.

- **If *she* moves to *your* N/A (or Never Again) list during the date, be polite and help her have a good time, but end the date by simply saying goodbye.** You can't afford to give the best of you to someone who will not invest in you, cannot invest in you, or would invest in you but is completely wrong for you (as outlined in the reasons for not accepting a date from pages 173 to 177). It is appropriate to say goodbye and not suggest you will be calling, texting, or going out again. It would also seem weird to tell someone after a few short interactions and one date that you aren't interested in seeing them again. No response or engagement is perfectly acceptable. However, if she calls or texts you, rather than ignoring her message, it is kinder to be upfront and say, "I think you are a great woman. It was fun getting to know you, but I just didn't feel a romantic connection. I truly wish you the best." Men hate spelling out the truth, but women appreciate it just as much as men do. Do not resort to politely leading her on, hoping she will figure it out, or making out with her in a moment of convenience, which would treat her like a good-for-now girl. Treat her as you would want to be treated either by disengaging or being honest if she reaches out. Furthermore, women talk, and they and their friends will definitely share what they know about you with others.

Techniques for the 2nd week or date

- **If you haven't done so yet, be sure to discover her preferred forms of communication and match them.** As shared in Chapter 7 relative to the techniques for moving texts to phone calls (pages 209 to 214) you need to communicate in the most comfortable and meaningful ways for both of you. To discover these preferences, you need to casually ask, "What do you prefer, texting or brief phone calls?" or state, "Some people get stressed out by phone calls, others get stressed out by texts. I prefer texts for little things and brief phone calls for catching up or planning dates. What's your preference?" Once you know their preference, it is important to act accordingly until the relationship progresses. This prevents unnecessary pressure and helps you to interpret her responses more accurately (or lack thereof) as not being about you but about her discomfort with texting or phone calls (which is common these days). It doesn't hurt to mention these preferences when needed by saying, "I know you prefer texting and aren't available during the day, so respond when you have time later. Also, if you want me to call instead, let me know. I'm happy to accommodate either preference."

- **If *she* is on *your* A-list, call within two to four days after the first date (or text a few times during the week) and try to set a second date for that week.** Texting is treated as more casual, so a couple of texts will show more enthusiasm and interest. If she prefers phone calls, this will seem more meaningful; thus, until you are sure what her preference is, attempt a phone call to see how she responds (in case this makes a better impression than texting alone). Optionally, you can reach out the day after the date, which will show enthusiasm but could also make you seem overanxious or needy. Be sure to note her response time to make sure you are not accidentally creating pressure by reaching out so soon. Always text or call to confirm details of an upcoming date a day prior, so she doesn't feel anxious. This also eliminates confusion and reduces the chance you will be stood up. When you call, don't feel pressured to talk for more than fifteen minutes.

- **When planning the second date, keep it simple and not too elaborate.** This protects you from coming on too strong or falling into the too-nice trap. Get her to invest in you as well by asking her to plan or help you with a small part of the date. But make sure you pay for all the activities on the date (asking for her help is just to see if she will hear your requests and invest in you as well). During the date, focus on making her feel great and treating her like a lady. Include touch, such as guiding her through a door. Be sure to tell her you would like to see her again. Assume that if you had a good time, she would like to keep seeing you. If you sense, however, that either of you is feeling too much pressure or might feel it after the date, then be sure to state that you are looking forward to just getting to know her and having fun to keep the pressure and expectations low (provided there is mutual respect). These strategies help both of you to relax and have more fun (as explained on pages 214-215).

- **If *she* is on *your* B-list, don't feel pressured to call or text right after your first date.** If you call or text within two to four days, she may think you are more interested than you are. Waiting five to ten days to reach out will show her you are reasonably interested, but she isn't on your A-list. Additionally, this shows you have a full life but are also willing to invest in continuing to get to know her. The goal is to have a date within two weeks. The longer you span out your dates, the greater the risk that you will lose her interest completely. It is a reasonable level of engagement, but not an anxious one that could get her too excited or make her feel too much pressure. In this way, your behavior will be consistent with your B-list level of interest. Continue treating her with respect by planning all dates in advance. Don't ask for a last-minute date unless you have an unusual event or situation that doesn't allow for advanced planning. Calling at the last minute or to make out is what guys do when they see someone as a good-for-now girl.

- **When on the date, make her feel great while offering appropriate words and affection to match your interest.** Treating others well might create a connection that changes everything, so use many but not all of the techniques taught here (more techniques for those on your A-list and fewer for those on the B-list) until you feel differently. Avoid touching a woman very often or kissing her so she doesn't mistakenly assume you are looking for a hookup or like her more than you do. Be especially careful when touching and kissing if you are kissing someone else. And if you say you will call, don't say it will be next week. Instead, say, "I will call you in the next week or so. I know next week is a bit crazy." This helps her know not to expect you to call right away.

- **If *you* are on *her* A-list, you will know it** because, in most cases, she will return your calls and texts within twenty minutes to twenty-four hours. She will make time to fit in a date within the next week if she can (but definitely within the next two weeks), and she will be glad to help plan a small part of the date. Looking for these behaviors is an effective way to gauge a woman's interest because most women who like someone are very responsive; however, occasionally, you may date someone who is really interested but excessively busy, out of town, or unaware of how to date effectively. In this case, she may take longer to get back to you. However, she should still act excited about seeing you again and will try to fit a date in as soon as she reasonably can.

- **If *you* are on *her* B-list, you will know it** because she won't call or text you back as quickly (between twenty-four hours to three days), she won't fit you in for that week, she will seem only politely interested in getting together, and she will not suggest options for seeing you soon. As long as she treats you well on the date and you have fun, keep her on your B-list. Keep pursuing to see if things change for both of you, but don't go on more than six dates unless your feelings and her engagement change. Limiting B-list options to six dates is when no one is on your A-list, proving that you are willing to discover and explore all your good options. However, if your feelings are not growing romantically, you need to acknowledge this.

- **If *you're* on *her* good-for-now, just-friends, or too-nice list, you will know it** because she will rarely make plans with you in advance, will break plans if something better comes up, will arrive late for dates, will come around when she is in need and then forget about you for long stretches of time. She will also act inconsistently (hot and then cold) depending on her mood or need, will not call you back when she says she will, and will ask you to help her with her bills, save her from her problems, or take care of her in other ways. Thus, do not continue interacting with anyone who engages in these ways with you. Such disrespect should not be tolerated, no matter how excited you are about them.

Techniques for the 3rd week or date

- **If *she* is on *your* A-list, continue your previous techniques; however, this week, call or text her no later than three days after the date and attempt short calls once or twice a week in between your weekly dates.** Ask her for another date that is no more than five to seven days away to see if she will fit you in. Increase your efforts to deepen a connection by using the techniques for chemistry and simple affection, which can include playfully nudging her, holding hands, or short kisses, depending on what feels mutually desirable (if you haven't already been doing so). At the end of the third date, express an interest in taking her out for a short midweek date (as a way of offering more spontaneous or casual encounters). Her responses to these efforts will either clarify that you are on her A-list (and as such, she is eager to spend more time with you) or that you are on her B-list (because she responds more passively or minimally to some of these efforts, without discouraging them altogether). If she gets excited about the possibility of seeing you for a short midweek date, participates in simple affection, or spontaneously suggests other activities or time together, then you are definitely on her A-list and are pacing things well. If she seems busy or reserved about the idea, or you find her interactions are difficult to read or could indicate disinterest, you may be on her B-list, and as such, you need to pull back some of your efforts to match her level of engagement. Any woman who accepts dates but is acting passively or confusingly (after the third date) needs to be encouraged to engage more. Without mutual investment, she will not develop stronger feelings.

- **To encourage more investment, be warm, clear, and direct about it.** To do this, lean back and casually say, "I really like spending time with you and would love to keep going out. I'm a no-pressure guy, and I just want to have fun and get to know you. That being said, I can't tell if a woman wants me to keep pursuing unless she also calls me, sends me a text, or does something nice for me on occasion. Such things really encourage me to keep investing." Saying this nonchalantly and then changing the subject shows that you're confident and know what you're worth, and it leaves her with a clear understanding of what she needs to do if she wants you to keep investing in her. A man who isn't afraid to walk away and expect a woman's engagement (without pressuring her to commit) seems more attractive and desirable. This also prevents you from getting caught in the too-nice or just-friends trap because it shows her that her engagement is necessary for getting more of your attention. If you suspect that she just has a reserved personality and doesn't know how to show her interest, you could try a different technique. Simply ask her, "When you like a guy, how do you show him?" If she responds to this with a detailed description, then you can use her words as a measure of her interest. If she treats you in the ways she described, you are probably on her A-list. If she avoids the question, changes the subject, or doesn't act in the ways she describes, she is probably not interested. After using either technique, hug her and say goodbye, this time without saying you will call. Wait a week or two to see what she does. If she doesn't do anything and you still enjoy going out with her on occasion, call a week later to see if she wants to do something, but understand that you are definitely on her B-list, and make sure she is on your B-list, too. Don't take her on more than six dates, however. Only those who have evolved to your A-list and provide A-list engagement in return should continue past the first six weeks or six dates. You will be wasting your time if you are not mutually investing on an A-list level with each other beyond this.

- **If _she_ is on _your_ B-list, do not call her every week or text her more than a couple of times a week, since she may mistakenly assume she is on your A-list.** And when you end a date, be sure to say you will call sometime in the next few weeks to do something fun again. If you want to be clear about your intentions, take the pressure off to see if it helps you both connect and enjoy each other more. To do this, tell her at the end of the third date, "In fairness, I thought you would want to know that my feelings often develop slowly, and I'm not ready to become serious. If you are cool with that and want to keep having fun on occasion, I would like to call you every once in a while. If that sounds okay to you, let me know. If not, I totally understand, and I appreciate the fun we have had so far." If she agrees, continue treating her with respect and making her feel great on each date, but pace your dates and don't go on more than six dates without making a decision to increase your contact with her to A-list interaction. Unless you believe you might develop more A-list feelings, more than six dates would be impractical. Rather than prolong things, you need a reasonable endpoint.

- **If *you* are on *her* A-list, you will know** by the third date because she will act excited when you call and text and will follow through when you ask her for help with planning the date. She will lean forward often, follow up with questions about your life, touch you occasionally, and encourage you to keep calling. She will be excited when she sees that you call more frequently and will be glad to schedule dates closer together when she can. When dating someone who is excessively busy, travels a lot, or is unaware of how to make men feel great, she may take longer to get back to you; nonetheless, she will encourage your efforts and be excited to see you.

- **If *you* are on *her* B-list, you will know** by the third date because she will be inconsistent about planning a small part of the date, touching you during the date, making time within seven days for another date, or following through with the things you said would encourage your calls.

- **If you are feeling frustrated and confused by her reactions,** either review the things she shared about her preferred forms of communication (as encouraged previously) or make sure to ask her now while sharing your preferences, too. If she acts inconsistently with what she has expressed and isn't stretching to match your preferences, then take comfort in knowing that you have done what you can. If you aren't enjoying her interactions, either walk away or express your confusion about the inconsistencies to see if this helps her to engage more meaningfully.

- **If *she* ghosts *you*** (i.e., doesn't return your calls or texts), either follow up or end contact on your terms. To do this, call or text again 72 hours after she ignored your message and state, "I'm not sure if you got my last message. I look forward to hearing from you." If you don't get a response, don't obsess about why she isn't calling or why she lost interest. This is all just part of the first six weeks of dating and simply cannot be taken personally. She does not really know you. Do not torture yourself with endless questions, worry about what you did wrong, or waste your time on what-ifs. When you think about her, just repeat to yourself, It is what it is, and start pursuing others. She is not your only chance for happiness. She did not respond, but someone else will. If you apply the the techniques for resilient practices when managing the highs and lows of dating (from pages 253-257), you will be less emotionally impacted by one person's actions or inactions. As you handle rejection well, you will look and feel more confident and self-respecting. That being said, if you want to show her that you are walking away on your terms, text her one last time (about a week later), and state, "I didn't hear back. I hope everything is going well for you. I won't be reaching out again unless I hear from you, but I will be assuming that good things are happening for you. I truly wish you the best, and it was fun getting to know you."

Alternatively, you could say, "I'm not sure how we lost touch. I hope everything is okay for you. I won't be reaching out unless I hear back. If you lost interest, no worries. I don't take those things personally. If you are still interested in doing more fun things together, let me know. Either way, I truly wish you the best." Showing that you can handle rejection on your terms, without fear of walking away, demonstrates self-respect and makes it easier for you both to acknowledge each other when you are at social events.

Techniques for the 4th week or date

- **If *she* is on *your* A-list, call more often and plan something a little more fun, creative, expensive, or unusual for your next date.** Try to also squeeze in a short midweek date or spontaneous activity, such as taking her to lunch at the last minute or offering to drop by with a treat (such as ice cream, bananas, and chocolate to make sundaes for her and her coworkers). Women like surprises, gifts, reasonable spontaneity, and excitement. The extra effort makes them feel special. Note how she reacts. If she gets excited, is quick to respond, acts impressed, or expresses sincere regret if she isn't available, then you are definitely pacing your efforts appropriately. Throughout the week, look for opportunities to build a deeper emotional connection by being prepared for longer phone calls in case she wants to share something personal, planning a longer date, asking her more questions, and sharing more about yourself. To encourage more time together while not adding pressure or excessive expenses, consider date ideas and opportunities that are free, outdoors, or more casual. This can include cooking together, going to a park, riding bikes, or being creative. She needs to feel she is getting to know you, and you are getting to know her, or she will start to lose interest. If you haven't attempted to hold hands, cuddle, show playful and affectionate teasing, or kiss her yet (as explained on pages 270 to 273), you definitely need to engage in simple affection soon—if not now, then no later than the sixth week. If you are holding back due to her behaviors that suggest she doesn't want to be affectionate, you need to confidently ask her about this. For example, "It seems that you are very cautious or a slow mover relative to physical touch. Is there something I can do that would help you to feel safe and comfortable with simple affection?" If you are the one holding affection back, you need to address why this is the case. Simple affection is essential to developing chemistry and connection. If you are afraid of feeling too much pressure for commitment, how can you communicate this to her, and what simple touch would you both enjoy? If you are uncomfortable with touch, consider options for increasing your confidence and comfort with it. If you are afraid it will mean more commitment from you than you are ready to provide, consider how you can discuss and prevent this. You can't delay physical affection for very long before it will cause problems like the just-friends trap. Additionally, women will start to make negative assumptions about you or themselves. These may include doubts about whether a woman is on your A-list, suspicions that you are not actually confident, worries that you may be too passive to take charge and pursue what you want (whether this is a relationship or other professional and personal issues), or fears that you may lack attraction to her or could be gay. Once you kiss a woman, don't leave her wondering if you are going to disappear like so many other guys do. Instead, leave her feeling safe and secure by stating you will call. If she or you are not ready to kiss before the sixth date, but you are engaging in other affection like holding hands, cuddling, and playful touch, no worries. You are going in the right direction. Give each other more time.

- **If *she* is on *your* B-list, but she treats you well and invests in you, and no one is on your A-list, treat her as if she is on your A-list (as described in the section above).** You should have told her by now that you are dating others, so she shouldn't be expecting too much, especially if you keep your affection simple and appropriate. Investing more this week will help you to discover if deeper feelings may develop. Continue taking the opportunity to treat her like she is on your A-list for a few more weeks (especially if she is giving you A-list attention). If you don't feel more chemistry after the increased effort this week, consider not going on more dates. If you feel the same and want to continue going on up to six dates (and you sense that you are only on her B-list), then pace the next two and last dates farther apart and just have fun while you continue to practice your techniques. No one is hurt by fun dates with reasonable expectations and investment. Saying you don't feel a romantic connection after six dates is a respectable time frame. Hopefully, offering six dates in this manner helps you to comfortably walk away without regret or feeling you wasted your or their time.

- **If *she* is on *your* B-list (and you don't want to continue pursuing her), stop reaching out or let her know.** If you haven't kissed a woman and you aren't worried that she will be hurt to not hear from you again, then ending contact is normal and appropriate. This is what most singles do. However, for your peace of mind and hers, you can end your interactions on a high note by calling her (if you have kissed) or sending a text. Express, "I respect you too much not to share where my thoughts are. I have really enjoyed how kind and fun you are (or thoughtful and outgoing, generous and creative, good-natured and intelligent), but I'm not feeling enough of a romantic connection to continue going on dates. You are a great person, and I sincerely wish you the best. Thank you so much for treating me great, and I hope you feel I've done the same." This is a great way to wrap up a positive and respectful experience, and it proves you are a class act. Few people show this level of confidence, maturity, and empathy.

- **If *you* are on *her* A-list, you will know it** because she matches your efforts, invests in you, responds to your calls more quickly, and makes you a higher priority as the weeks progress. She will also call, text, or send you messages, do things she thinks you might like, mention an activity you could try together, or offer to pay for dessert or plan a date for you sometime. If you have communicated a feeling, need, or preference, you will notice her efforts in these regards.

- **If *you* are on *her* B-list or worse, you will know it** because she won't invest much in you and won't consistently make time for you. She may make a lot of excuses for why she isn't available (such as being busy, having family issues, or going out of town), but she won't express a desire to talk or get together in between these events. She will also act increasingly cool and casual regarding your dates (i.e., not preparing for and looking good on dates or canceling and rescheduling them). Some women don't know how to reject a man. Some women like a man and don't know how to show it. The problem is that you don't know which of these scenarios reflects her motivation for acting this way. In either case, such interaction is unfulfilling. So, stop calling her for a few weeks to a month (especially if you have communicated the types of behaviors that help you to feel confident that a woman wants you to keep pursuing). See how she reacts. If she calls or goes out of her way to contact you, you will know that she is interested. If not, and you still feel doubt, a month later, send her a text or message saying, "I hope you are well. I just wanted to touch base and explain why I stopped calling. I couldn't tell whether you were interested. If I misread that and you are interested, give me a call. Either way, I hope you have been doing well." This technique is not essential, but it has proven to be effective in those cases when the person was busy or had to reschedule several times, but was interested.

Techniques for the 5th and 6th week or date

- **If *she* is on *your* A-list, keep up the same pace and efforts** as described for the fourth week, **but start calling more often or daily** (if you both seem to enjoy it). Include occasional casual activities and last-minute plans. Consider hanging out occasionally, but definitely continue planning dates each week. Weekly date nights mean a lot to women and are essential to creating and keeping a romantic connection. Even married couples need them to keep their love alive. You need to view dates as a must-have forevermore—after all, they are infinitely cheaper than marriage counseling or divorce. With the added contact, pull back from dating women on your B-list. You will just waste your time and money, both of which you will have less of because you're giving more to this woman on your A-list. However, continue being open to meeting and pursuing new women sporadically until you are exclusive. You do not want to rush the commitment and pressure that exclusivity can prematurely cause. Even if you both think you are ready for it. You both may want an immediate relationship, but you will trust and value a slowly progressing relationship more. This is why people who are consistent and steady but take their time seem more confident and desirable (provided they are warm and engaging, too). So, keep going on at least one date a month with other women. If this relationship suddenly ends and you are still going on occasional dates with others, you will handle the rejection and disappointment better. If you have not kissed her by the sixth week because she expressed a need for the relationship to go slowly, express again that you will keep your kisses and affection simple. Say it directly or show it by keeping your kisses to five minutes or less. Do not wait to have simple affection beyond the sixth date. If you are not cuddling, holding hands, or (hopefully) kissing by now, you will potentially waste your time and set yourself up for the too-nice, just-friends, or good-for-now trap. You need to see if she will invest in you, trust you, and show some affection for you. If she refuses to become minimally affectionate (i.e., holding hands, affectionately teasing, or cuddling) by the sixth week, she is not being honest with you about her feelings and intentions. This may be due to excessive anxiety and a lack of dating experience (which could warrant a few more weeks of flexibility); however, when this is not the case, her resistance could be due to a lack of empathy regarding your feelings and needs as valid. If she has trauma issues but isn't taking responsibility for addressing and resolving them, this is also concerning. Move on once you've discussed your needs for further trust and engagement, and she won't see the importance and benefits of engaging in physical affection for both of you.

- **If *she* is on *your* B-list with growing potential for your A-list,** and no one else is on your A-list, **for two more weeks, show her A-list attention** as clarified above, especially when you believe she has A-list feelings for you.

- **If *she* is on *your* B-list, and it seems you both are good with only occasional dates, enjoy your time together.** However, have only one or two more dates. If you still don't feel a connection, stop dating, or you will confuse her. Instead, encourage friendship or wish each other the best, and move on.

- **If you know *you aren't interested*, share that you appreciate her but won't be pursuing further dates.** It would be better to refocus your energy on meeting new women. If you have kissed her, make sure you do not kiss her anymore, which treats her as a good-for-now girl.

- **If *you* are on *her* A-list, you will know it** because she will engage fully and respond well to your efforts.

- **If *you* are on *her* B-list, you will know it** because she will not invest in or act interested in increased attention or affection. Either stop seeing her at this point or (if she is on your A-list) state, "I don't sense that you are interested in deepening a connection in a way that I need. I would like to continue to see you. Let me know if or when you would enjoy engaging more fully. I would love to reconsider seeing you then." You need to give the best of you to those who invest in you. Do not transition into becoming friends. You are not looking for a friendship or a good-for-now experience. You are looking for and can have a mutually invested and joyful relationship.

Techniques for determining if you have sufficient chemistry

When determining if you have sufficient chemistry to continue dating, redefine your definition of chemistry to *a feeling or desire that compels you, when in the presence of a particular person, to want to please them, touch them, and make them happy.* That's it! Too many singles associate chemistry with the desperate feelings, longing, and compulsive thoughts that are actually a common sign of insecure attachments or addictive, abusive, or manipulative relationships. If you think that chemistry is something you should feel all the time, that the person should always be on your mind, that your desire to be with them should be intense and constant, and that your fear of living without them should compel you to tears, you will only find yourself in dramatic, intense, and unstable relationships that are prone to extreme emotional upheaval.

The emotional highs, and intense moments of love and affection, that are characteristic of these relationships are actually no higher than those in normal relationships, but when they come after another episode of neglect, verbal abuse, or threat of abandonment, the attention and affection seem more dramatic and fulfilling (i.e., addictive). Thus, the highs in these relationships are usually only in contrast to the extreme lows (especially as the relationship progresses). Additionally, one or both of the partners in these relationships are often consumed with fears of losing their intense connection (and for a good reason, since the highs only get lower, as do the lows); thus, they become consumed with thoughts of the relationship, feel increased insecurity, and struggle to focus on the demands of life or be effective in work, school, or other relationships.

By contrast, when you are in a healthy relationship, you will notice that the chemistry you feel, though strong when you are in the person's presence, is not compulsive or consuming when you are away from them. You feel intense spikes of desire to touch or kiss them, but usually only when with them. When away from them, you feel a desire to see them again soon, but (after the first few weeks of initial excitement about the new relationship) you feel content to see them every few days rather than feeling a desperate need to see them every day. You find it easy to continue your work, school, relationships, and other obligations. You feel okay without them and understand that they are not your only chance for happiness. This is not to say you don't want to be with them. You enjoy the relationship and feel no desire to end it, but you do not feel a compulsive need for them to validate you and your worth all the time. They make you feel safe and secure with yourself, with them, and with your relationship (due to their investment and efforts in the relationship) so that you can easily live your life and enjoy it. They make your life better rather than making your life revolve around them. Thus, it can be easy to question your chemistry with them from time to time, because it is not as compulsive or consuming as singles often think chemistry should be. However, even when you have doubts about your connection or chemistry, you will notice that when you see them again, BAM! the desire to get close, touch, or kiss them returns.

To say these feelings should be constant is wrong, especially as the relationship progresses. There will be many times when you will be with them and will feel just common or mundane feelings, but consistently and predictably, the feelings will stir again later and continue to do so throughout the duration of the relationship.

Thus, a healthy chemistry is one you experience when in the presence of the other person. It's not compulsive, addictive, or consuming. It enhances the relationship and makes physical contact desirable. It's not the stupid or compelling examples that so many TV shows, books, and movies portray of two lovers throwing away everything they have worked hard for in their lives (their families, careers, values, children, and money) to be together. Only those who lack empathy, self-control, and personal responsibility would be okay with such reckless and destructive forms of love. It's important that you understand the difference.

Chemistry is critical to a successful relationship and something I recommend everyone look for, but you need to be able to tell the difference between healthy chemistry and compulsive, addictive relationships, or you could end up in a world of pain later.

Discover if you have a healthy chemistry

- **Ask yourself**

    1. Do I want to get close to them, touch them, or kiss them?

    2. Do I like it when they get close to me, touch me, or kiss me?

    3. Do I consistently enjoy being with them and experience stirring emotions when near them?

- **When away from them, ask yourself**

    1. Do I feel a desire to see them, while still attending to the needs of my life?

    2. Do I feel they are not my only chance for happiness, while also feeling no desire to end the relationship?

    3. Do I feel capable, confident, and of worth both when I am with them and when I am away from them?

    4. Do I feel good about the relationship, the things I know about them, and the way they treat me (versus feeling increased anxiety, fear, shame, or discomfort about myself, them, or the relationship when I'm away from them)?

- **Ask others**

    1. Do you see this relationship as enhancing my life and other relationships (versus increasing my fears, insecurities, and compulsive behaviors or restricting my other relationships)?

    2. Do you see me as confident in this relationship (versus consumed and compulsive about this relationship?

- **When, or if, you feel a need to take a break or step back from the relationship, ask yourself**

    1. Do I feel free to step back (versus feeling anxious and afraid of what might happen or what they might do)?

    2. And when I take a break, do I feel a loss and deepening connection to them (versus feeling extreme panic or relief)?

If you can answer positively to most, if not all, of these questions, you probably have a healthy chemistry.

Repeat, enjoy, learn and progress

Since most of your dating experiences will not make it past the first six weeks of dating, you need to maintain a resilient, growth-minded, fun, and positive attitude that doesn't personalize this natural reality. In many ways, you may get frustrated with the revolving-door reality of dating, but in time, this, too, shall pass.

Choose to believe that you are meant to succeed and that the kind of partner you are looking for is looking for someone like you. You will reach the end of this trial and achieve a long-term relationship and marriage.

When that day arrives—or until that day arrives—the Lasting Love Academy offers many books and courses for deepening connections, creating secure attachments, recognizing early red flags and toxic people, building faith in yourself, others, and relationships, and addressing anxious and avoidant attachment patterns in yourself and others.

And when your journey isn't progressing as desired, our community and coaching resources can help you to transform your situation in mutually effective ways that will empower both you and your partner.

You have already achieved so much, but being at the end of one trial means you are beginning another. Don't let this discourage you. We will help you continue to find joy, meaning, confidence, and relational growth throughout every stage of your journey.

No matter what the next few months or year look like for you (whether that includes a loving relationship or a short-term but valuable experience), always remember that your situation (and others' reactions) do not define your value or your progress. There is a beginning, middle, and end to every trial (and this relates to your experiences, too). Keep doing your part. Hang in there. Lasting love is worth it!

The courage to love without fear

As shared in the Preface chapter of this book, my journey, like yours, has been full of many highs and lows. The growth I found, only because of my suffering (during the beginning, middle, and end) of my trials, added to the quality of my relationships and made them more meaningful.

However, my rebirth (which was attached to my grief and loss) came at a time when my daughter's grief was just beginning.

When you are ready to progress to an exclusive relationship, remember they and their children (or yours) will have stories at the beginning, middle, or end of the healing process, too. Learning to be open to their journey and join them with patience was a lesson Eric and I had to learn with our daughter, Leia.

Learning to hold space during an extended period, even when it complicates our relationship, can be hard, but that's what lasting love requires.

Love without fear

In 2010 (a year before our daughter was born), Eric and I began our foster care classes. We wanted to adopt a baby, but were shocked and saddened to learn that 60% of the children that came to our home (whether for months or years) would return to their birth families. Understanding this reality, along with the extensive needs of foster children due to their trauma, further shredded our illusions that foster care or adoption would solve our problems (and for a good reason).

While struggling to accept this possibility, the words of a previous adoption worker became ever clearer:

> "Adoption isn't about your losses, dreams, or hopes for a child. Adoption is about the child. When a child is placed in your home, they are not the solution to your infertility problems. They should not be molded into a shadow of your limited dreams. They will have separate needs, attachment challenges, and identity struggles that you must provide space for. No matter how much you love them,

you must join their journey and allow it to unfold in the way that is right for them. Your painful journey may feel like it has come to an end, but you can not forget that their struggles are just beginning."

With this in mind, I began to look at foster care as not a resolution of my losses, but a meaningful opportunity to be a part of another child's life, come what may. My goal was to love another child, and foster care might be more difficult than I ever imagined, but there were many children who could benefit from what I had to offer, and my desire to love was greater than my fears.

Surprisingly, while we were in the final weeks of the foster care process, as we began preparing a baby's room, a birth mother (with three children) chose us to adopt her unborn child. This good news didn't feel like a guarantee, so I couldn't quite allow myself to accept it fully. Just as there was no certainty how long a foster child would remain in our home, I couldn't let myself embrace the idea that this child would be ours until the paperwork was signed and she came home with us.

My goal was to love another child, but the fear of losing the baby would prevent me from enjoying the moment (and cause me to hold something back). Thus, I knew that the only path to truly loving a child was to not control the outcome but embrace the now with my whole heart and trust that if loss came, I would be able to handle it one day at a time until the pain healed. Thus, the only true way to love is to do it one day at a time, today!

With this in mind, I decided to focus on the beautiful experience right before me. I was having the rare opportunity to share in the journey of a birth mother. With each email we exchanged, I learned about her life, the tragedies she had experienced in childhood, the reason she needed to place her child, and her concerns for the three children she was raising. She was a mature, responsible single parent and was concerned about all of the needs of her family and unborn child. She wanted the best for each of them. As I got to know her, I became even more determined to make sure she did only what was right for her and the baby. If that was us, wonderful, and if not, we would be ok. We would have other options through foster care.

In time, the birth mom invited us to ultrasounds and doctor appointments, and she asked us to be in the delivery room. When the baby was born, we interacted freely with the birth family. We transported her kids to visit their mom and baby sister in the hospital. Since we had to remain in the state for a couple of weeks, the time we spent together helped us all develop an easy, natural connection.

In the end, we didn't just adopt our daughter, Leia, we embraced an ongoing, open relationship with our birth family. Leia's siblings struggled with the adoption, and this open relationship allowed them to come to terms with the confusion and pain of losing a sibling. Our birth mother was a respectful and mature woman who supported our role as Leia's parents. Having open contact with us allowed her space to find peace with her choice. And we were all blessed to enjoy a larger family experience.

As we brought our daughter home, I looked back on my grief and loss and couldn't help but acknowledge the miracle that had unfolded. I never imagined that my dream of having another child would not occur until I was 40 or that our birth family would be the answer to our suffering (and prayers) just as we were to theirs. In so many ways, God's plan for all of us proved to be so much better and healing than we could have imagined!

For a few years, it seemed all of our losses were restored, but in reality, our adoption worker's words were prophetic. Leia's struggles were just beginning.

Leia's journey

During Leia's early years, we had an easy and carefree experience. She was a happy, delightful baby and toddler who brought us joy every day.

However, when Leia was three, she started to show signs of attachment issues that were hard to ignore. She experienced prolonged temper tantrums and couldn't calm herself down or accept our efforts to comfort her. I thought all of these issues would pass with time, but instead, she became aggressive toward me and even struggled in kindergarten with bullying behavior.

We didn't know how to reach her or what was wrong, so we began counseling to work on her attachment issues with me and better understand her behavioral challenges. As Leia learned to express her emotions, her behavior toward others improved. She began making friends and doing well in school, especially after identifying her ADHD diagnosis. This was encouraging. However, her attitude toward me remained consistently aggressive and rejecting. It was coming from pain, but we seemed unable to reach her effectively.

Perhaps Leia's attachment challenges stemmed from her strong affinity for her birth family. She looked so much like them and would talk about our family's differences in appearance. She longed to see them and would cry when they left. She would let me comfort her at these times, but she rarely allowed it at other times. She had a strong attachment to her dad, but with me, it seemed distant and dismissive.

I didn't regret my decision to involve her birth family in our lives, as it truly felt right and healthy at the time, but this might have hastened Leia's awareness of her adoption issues and attachment challenges. Such issues are common for girls and their adoptive mothers.

However, I wish I could say that I didn't play a significant role in her frustrations with me. It would be convenient to blame Leia's attachment issues, ADHD, and difficulties with emotion regulation on her adoption or genetics, but in truth, I brought the wrong parenting techniques as well. What worked for my son only made things worse for her.

As I learned and implemented new, more effective strategies, these gave me hope and improved Leia's behavior in many areas of her life. Nevertheless, real change in our relationship didn't happen for many years.

Fortunately, as Leia matured, she became more accepting of me as her mom and began to relax and engage playfully with me. This didn't occur until she was in her mid-teens. I had begun to accept that, perhaps, for us it would not change, but fortunately, it did!

Grief and loss often take years for kids to resolve. Like adults (who have a greater ability to understand their experiences and have more choice in them), a child's life can also deviate from what they want. Whether this comes from trauma, divorce, death, or other challenges (like being displaced from a family they've lost), children won't have the mental and emotional maturity to process these experiences for many years to come.

Throughout these years, it did help to remind myself, "There is a beginning, middle, and end to all trials, and this one will end, too." Although at times I wasn't confident that a miracle would happen for Leia and me, it did!

There was no easy answer for her grief and loss. For this, she needed patience from her family and the time required for her emotions, understanding, and experiences to evolve and mature. Adoption issues aren't resolved by closed adoptions or open adoptions. They are resolved over time, with love and a desire to support the child's needs.

Because our story is not that different from the experiences of many blended families, I can now relate more empathetically to the needs of step (or bonus) parents and the feelings of rejection and dislike they can sometimes feel from their bonus children. One fact remains, however, these children and families, like us, are meant to succeed!

Your lasting love journey

At times, you and your partner will struggle with various aspects of your past, as will your mutual children. You will wonder whether there really is a beginning, middle, and end to each of your trials. But take heart. When love is the goal, you'll be amazed at how many happy endings you will discover.

The most important lesson I've learned is not to lose faith when you are in the middle of any challenge.

Your journey has taken you this far. When you see more obstacles ahead, don't lose hope. You may need to change your techniques or refocus your attention on the options available to you (rather than the closed doors you've been trying to force open or the dreams you've been trying to resurrect).

Don't let comparison be a thief of joy. Whether comparing a current partner to others (or your past dreams), remember that you alone get to discover what is right for you. No one is perfect, and neither are you. No family is free of problems, and neither will yours be, but you can enjoy the privilege of learning how to live a real life with real people, while offering real love!

You can't love freely if you stay focused on your fears of loss or missing out. Yes, you need to be smart about who you marry, and you shouldn't neglect the red flags or your significant areas of incompatibility, but you are meant to love and be loved. And, you can learn to solve problems effectively, together.

As you acknowledge and grieve the journey behind you, you'll find freedom in the new adventures and opportunities ahead of you (including the children you can love).

When love is your goal, you can and will experience it. "For God hath not given us a spirit of fear, but of power and of love and of a sound mind" (2 Timothy 1:7, King James Bible).

I hope you choose the courage to love and be loved without fear. You truly can experience lasting love!

With sincere confidence in your future,

Alisa Goodwin Snell

AFTERWORD

Single? It's Not You. It's Your Technique!

Appendices

The 17 Secrets to the Male Psychology

1. Men seek out relationships that make them feel trusted and respected.

2. Men develop love through sacrifice.

3. Men are largely logical about their relationships and commitments; thus they do not commit easily to things they have not invested in over a period of time.

4. Men are driven to succeed, face challenges, and compete.

5. Men like women who like themselves.

6. Men love to be heroes.

7. Men like being appreciated.

8. Men like femininity.

9. Men like women who have opinions and assert their needs.

10. Men pursue women who are approachable and appear to be available.

11. Men who have empathy want sex with a woman who feels good about having sex with them and will wait until commitment or marriage (especially if they both share similar values).

12. Men need to be needed.

13. Men are repelled by criticism, nagging, and whining.

14. A man experiences anxiety in every conversation a woman initiates until she tells him what she wants him to do.

15. Men bond more through talking about *things* and doing *activities* than they do through talking about *people, problems, feelings, or ideas.*

16. Men adore women who give them love, attention, and affection.

17. Men are often willing to talk openly and honestly when they feel it will help them or another person to do so.

Alisa Goodwin Snell, M.A.

Please note that not all of the 17 Secrets to the Male Psychology presented above were discussed within the chapters of this book. Other courses in the Lasting Love Academy illuminate the importance of those secrets that were not addressed in this volume.

The 17 Secrets to the Female Psychology

1. Women thrive when they feel safe and secure.

2. Women develop love through sacrifice, but need men to communicate their needs if that sacrifice is to be helpful rather than hurtful or over-responsible.

3. Women often take a man's words very seriously, get excited, assume commitment, and then get hurt when he pulls away due to the added pressure.

4. Women are insecure about their bodies and fear competition from other women.

5. Women are attracted to strength and confidence.

6. Women are turned off by men who are too nice.

7. Women often fall in love with friends.

8. Women like to be pursued and to feel wanted.

9. Women enjoy touch, kissing, and affection, but feel vulnerable and prone to shame after sexual contact (especially when a man withdraws afterward).

10. Women want men who hold off sexually—it makes them feel respected and wanted rather than like an object.

11. Women want immediate relationships, but trust and value slowly progressing relationships.

12. Women long to feel adored.

13. Women are repelled by moping, brooding, and the silent treatment.

14. Women worry—they need to know they are not alone in dealing with the problems of the relationship.

15. Women who don't trust and respect their men fall out of love, especially if there is no communication.

16. Women like gifts, surprises, reasonable spontaneity, and excitement—the extra effort makes them feel special.

Alisa Goodwin Snell, M.A.

17. Women would rather have open and honest communication about misdeeds than be protected from the truth.

Please note that not all of the 17 Secrets to the Male Psychology presented above were discussed within the chapters of this book. Other courses in the Lasting Love Academy illuminate the importance of those secrets that were not addressed in this volume.

Using Emotion Words

A primary desire of every individual is to be truly and deeply understood; therefore, you need to have the tools and skills necessary to communicate in a way that deepens your understanding of others and vice versa. To help you deepen your emotional expression and create meaningful connections, follow the steps below.

1. **Familiarize yourself with emotion words and use them in relating your experiences.** Each night, review your thoughts and experiences from the day. Then scan the emotion words that have been provided (or others) and fit them into a sentence, like, "I felt _______________ when ____________." For example, "I felt angry, frustrated, and embarrassed when my boss corrected me in front of my coworkers," or "I felt revved up and delighted when my project at work finally began operating as I had hoped." Connecting with your own emotions will help you connect with others' emotions.

2. **Start incorporating emotion words into descriptions of your day so others will feel more connected and interested.** It is difficult to listen to a laundry list of activities, such as "I went to the store, bought milk, came home, watched TV, and then went to bed." It is much easier to relate to emotions. For example, "By the time I got to the store, I was *drained* and *exhausted*. And can you believe my luck? They were completely out of the milk I *like,* so I had to grab skim milk. *Yuck!* I came home ready to collapse and watch TV. Thankfully, my *favorite* show was on. By the time I got to bed, I felt tons *better.*"

3. **When listening to others, respond with emotion words and interject with such words to show you are trying to understand and connect with their experiences.** Interrupting others is not rude if you aren't changing the subject or taking over a conversation. Inserting brief, empathetic comments can make others feel you are truly listening; you understand them. For example, if a date is talking about a vacation they just took to Europe, you could interject with, "*Wow,* that is so cool! How *thrilling* to get a chance to stand under the Eiffel Tower." When a person is *happy* or *excited,* your recognition of these emotions can make them feel connected to you and want to keep sharing. Likewise,

Alisa Goodwin Snell, M.A.

recognizing their *hurt* or *disappointment* can be equally effective in developing a bond, especially if you do so in the moment that they are upset (or shortly thereafter, which can be preferred by men). For example, if they accidentally tripped and broke a project they had worked on for a month, you could say, "Man, you worked so *hard* and were so *excited* about how it turned out! I bet you feel *sick* about it. I am so sorry." In these situations, using emotion words like *flattened, deflated, empty, or let down* could also be appropriate in helping them know you understand. Just consider how you would feel in the situation and choose your words accordingly.

4. **Don't tell people that you know *exactly* how they feel.** Most people hate to hear others say, "I know how you feel," because it often minimizes their feelings rather than building understanding. Instead, experience the emotions with them by saying, "I bet (or I imagine) you feel ______________," "That would totally make me feel ______________. Is that how you feel?" or "It would be natural if you felt ______________. Does that fit?"

5. **When replying, repeat the emotion words they are already using.** It is always safe and effective to use the same or similar emotion words to what others are already using as they try to express themselves. So, if your efforts to improvise with various emotion words don't seem to fit or make a connection, just repeat their words. For example, if you said, "Do you feel angry?" and they respond by saying, "No. I feel more disappointed and hurt." Then you could follow up with, "Well, that makes sense. I'd probably feel disappointed, too. It's got to hurt to go through this." If they don't express many emotion words, say, "Please, tell me more," "I'm listening," or "I want to understand—please explain." This will at least keep them talking while giving you time to get in their shoes and perhaps find the underlying emotions they're struggling to express.

Use the following emotion-word tables to help you experiment with and practice the emotion words in each category and how they could be worked into a sentence. The emotion words listed are by no means a comprehensive list, but they should give you an idea of the variety of emotion words you could use. The more emotion words you learn and use, the better your chances for finding the right word when the need arises, thus enhancing your connection with others.

Relative to the early dating phases, it is best for both men and women to stay away from heavy or deep conversations since such conversations could tax the other person or create an intense and immediate connection too early in the relationship, increasing the likelihood that the relationship will fall flat.

If your date attempts to talk about a difficult situation, validate their emotions and then move on to a lighter topic. However, by the fourth to sixth week of dating, you need to be sure to have more emotionally meaningful conversations, or the other person may begin to lose interest. This is particularly true when trying to maintain the interest of women.

Men, unfortunately, should use caution in the first few weeks of dating relative to using complex emotion words. A man who discusses his personal life while using a wide repertoire of emotion words, especially in a dramatic, flamboyant, or vulnerable way, may appear less strong and confident and inadvertently either turn women off or fall into the too-nice trap. It is not that a man shouldn't share his more intimate emotions—it's just how and when and with whom. Again, it's about *only giving the best of you to those who invest in you.* So, until the fourth to sixth week, a man should keep his emotional expressions about his *personal* experiences to a minimum while simultaneously using a greater repertoire of emotion words (which will impress her) when connecting to *her* experiences. Then he can begin to test the waters to see if she will value and appreciate his emotions. Once he has established his confidence, he can begin to reveal how deep or complex he really is, which will only make her feel more intrigued and curious about what else there is to discover.

Words related to:

excited				
energized	revved up	happy	anticipating	delighted
hopeful	passionate	thrilled	enthralled	empowered
hopeful	invigorated	strengthened	motivated	stimulated
anxious	keyed up	restless	jumpy	jazzed up

"You seem very energized *and* hopeful *today. Good things must be happening. What's going on?"*

happy				
ecstatic	joyful	light	jolly	merry
pleased	peaceful	cheerful	relieved	overjoyed
sunny	thrilled	tickled pink	upbeat	light-hearted

"It's fun to see you so peaceful *and* light-hearted. *You must feel* good *about something. Do tell."*

helpful				
caring	compassionate	supportive	agreeable	kind
gentle	loving	neighborly	friendly	giving

"You are so kind. *I can always count on you to be* supportive *and* caring. *Thanks."*

love				
cherish	adore	admire	crazy about	enchanted by
fond of	in love with	concerned about	care for	fall for
fancy	prefer	treasure	wild about	appreciate
affection for	attentive to	concerned for	friendly	generous
passionate for	reverent	kind	liking	romantic
tender	thoughtful	warm	warm-hearted	zealous about

"You are so easy to like. *I* appreciate *how* kind *and* warm-hearted *you are. I really* admire *you."*

confident				
assured	bold	fearless	brave	outgoing
determined	eager	firm	strong	peppy
tough	hardy	inspiring	secure	fearless
hopeful	positive	upbeat	courageous	sure
certain	driven	ambitious	competent	capable

"I am often inspired by how determined *and* assured *you are as you* bravely *pursue the things you want in life. I* admire *your* courage.*"*

surprised				
confused	baffled	taken a back	jarred	bewildered
mystified	startled	shaken	shocked	flustered
puzzled	jolted	stunned	astounded	dumbfounded

"I am really stunned *by what happened. I imagine you feel* shaken *and* confused. *This is so* strange *and* shocking. *What are you going to do?"*

Single? It's Not You. It's Your Technique!

sad				
down	depressed	blue	low	hurt
melancholy	weary	despairing	in the dumps	powerless
gloomy	heartbroken	despondent	dismal	pessimistic
distressed	troubled	bitter	dejected	dark
discouraged	miserable	oppressed	serious	unhappy
unsatisfied	upset	wretched	dreary	stricken
sorry	sorrowful	grieved	grief-stricken	heavyhearted

"If I were experiencing what you're going through, I would feel pretty bitter, wretched, *and* depressed. *I don't know how you're coping. It would be easy to* despair *when you feel so* heavy-hearted."

tired				
exhausted	sleepy	annoyed	beat	bored
broken-down	burned out	consumed	drained	droopy
drowsy	empty	exasperated	faint	fatigued
fed up	finished	irritated	overtaxed	irked
pooped	run-down	sick of	spent	wasted
worn out	flat	humdrum	worn	jaded

"I imagine you feel pretty run-down *after everything that's been going on. It's only natural that you're* burned out, tired, *and* exhausted. *How can I help?"*

despair				
disappointed	empty	numb	dejected	miserable
drained	desperate	deflated	disheartened	gloomy
melancholy	sorrow	discouraged	defeated	dropped
flattened	hopeless	helpless	distrustful	alone

"Sometimes when I feel defeated *and* alone, *I just become* numb *and* empty. *It's easier to not care than to keep trying, only to* fail. *Do you feel any of these things? If so, I want you to know I am here and ready to understand."*

fear				
terrified	anxious	jittery	upset	paranoid
scared	alarmed	cornered	nervous	threatened
troubled	uneasy	trapped	desperate	despairing

"It's only natural to feel alarmed *and even* paranoid *about what could happen. I hate it when I feel* threatened *and* desperate*. What are your options?"*

lonely				
isolated	abandoned	kept apart	forsaken	rejected
slighted	lost	scorned	snubbed	deserted
alone	ignored	jilted	left out	forlorn

"I hate it when I am left out, ignored, *or* snubbed*. I feel* sad *that you are going through this."*

anger				
cranky	annoyed	bitter	furious	irritated
frustrated	outraged	resentful	pissed	steamed
hostile	cruel	retaliating	disgusted	hurt

"I would feel so steamed *if I were you. I bet you feel* outraged *about what happened at work."*

belittled				
putdown	insulted	injured	ignored	intimidated
dejected	persecuted	minimized	defeated	dismissed
unimportant	insignificant	unworthy	shamed	scorned

"I hate feeling ignored*. It makes me feel so* unimportant *and* insignificant*."*

Alisa Goodwin Snell, M.A.

Having spent over 30 years as a marriage counselor and dating and relationship coach, Alisa Goodwin Snell has helped thousands of singles date more, find love, and get married.

Alisa is the author of eight books and numerous audio and video resources. She's been on over 100 TV and radio programs nationwide and is a popular public speaker. She created the Lasting Love Academy dating system and courses, available at LastingLoveAcademy.com.

After a brief marriage in her 20s, which included the birth of her son, Todd, she was single for over three years. This experience solidified her passion for singles' issues. Eric and Alisa married when she was 32, and he was 35. Having struggled with avoidant attachment issues, this was Eric's first marriage. They were later blessed to adopt their daughter, Leia, who is now 14.

During the final decade of Alisa's career, the family is determined to continue her mission of lasting love by reaching a new generation. Todd's degree, experience, and dedication has lead to the creation of the Lasting Love Academy app, podcast series, and social media campaign.

Thus, your love life is truly their family's passion!

www.ingramcontent.com/pod-product-compliance
Lightning Source LLC
Chambersburg PA
CBHW071730150726
47998CB00005B/1580